THE PROBLEMS
OF PHILOSOPHERS

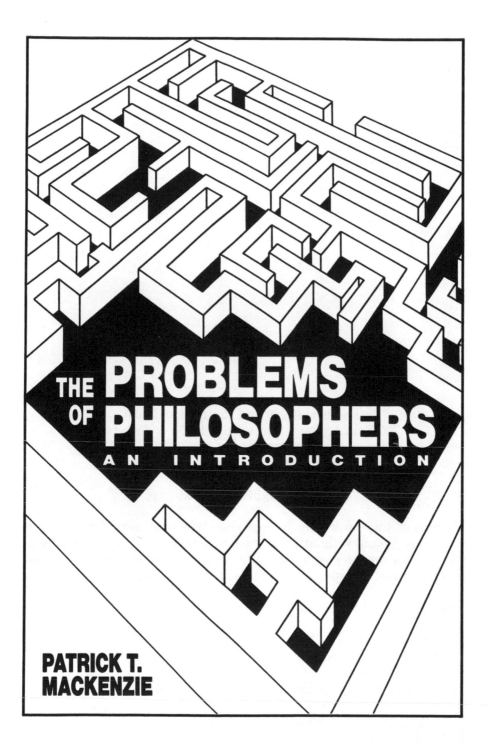

THE PROBLEMS OF PHILOSOPHERS

AN INTRODUCTION

PATRICK T. MACKENZIE

PROMETHEUS BOOKS
BUFFALO, NEW YORK

Published 1989 by Prometheus Books
700 East Amherst Street, Buffalo, New York 14215

Copyright © 1989 by Patrick T. Mackenzie

Library of Congress Cataloging-in-Publication Data

Mackenzie, Patrick T.
    The problems of philosophers / Patrick T. Mackenzie.
        p.   cm.
    Includes bibliographical references and index.
    ISBN 0-87975-486-9
    1. Philosophy—Introductions. I. Title
BD21.M22   1989
100—dc19   88-17724
                                                               CIP

Preface

While on a sabbatical several years ago, I decided to write an introductory book in philosophy that would approach the subject in a way that was different. I wanted to deal with the main problems of philosophy but approach them through the writings of a number of influential thinkers. In this way, the reader could be taken to the heart of philosophy via a gentler, less austere route.

In order to get the most out of this journey, the reader would do well to have some important classics on hand: Lucretius' *On the Nature of the Universe* (it has been translated by R. Latham in the Penguin series), Plato's *Republic* (translated by F. M. Cornford and published by the Oxford University Press), and *Descartes' Philosophical Writings* (translated by E. Anscombe and P. Geach). There are many other excellent translations of these classics on the market, but these are, I think, the easiest to understand.

I should like to thank the members of the University of Saskatchewan Philosophy Department for their constructive comments, and my wife, Eileen, for her moral support.

Contents

6   Contents

Introduction

One would expect to be told here what philosophy is, and there is no doubt that many introductory texts begin by attempting to do just that. However, it is my experience that most of them say either something absolutely banal or something the beginner could not possibly understand. The reason for this is not hard to find. Suppose that someone who had no mathematics at all, who was so removed from mathematics that he did not know how to add two and three, were to ask you what mathematics is. I am sure that you would have the greatest difficulty in answering his question and would ultimately attempt to answer it by teaching him some mathematics. You might begin with such lessons as: Don't you see that if you have two matches in the box and you add three more to the box, then you have five matches in the box?

The situation is just the same with philosophy. It is very difficult to tell someone who has not had any philosophy what philosophy is. The best way to begin to explain to him what philosophy is, is to do some philosophy. And that is just what we shall do here. We will begin by discussing some ancient philosophers and what they said, move on to some more recent philosophers; and only then will we raise the question of what philosophy is. Not that the question will then be easy: Think of the difficulty you would have in trying to explain to someone who was at home with mathematics what mathematics is.

1

Some Pre-Socratics

THALES

It is commonplace for philosophers today to claim that Thales—who lived in Miletus, a small Greek city on the coast of Asia Minor, during the sixth century B.C.—was the first Western philosopher. Now that immediately raises the question of why people think that he was the first Western philosopher? Surely there must have been other thinkers before him. Why begin with him and not someone else? Well, the reason, I suspect, is that he was the first to ask an interesting philosophical question. But, unfortunately, he did not give a very exciting answer. At that time it was believed that the world was formed out of four elements. At the top of the scale was fire, followed by air, water, and then earth. Earth could change into water, water could change into air, air into fire, and fire could change back into air, and so on. As a result, people were inclined to think that there was something common to all four. Now the interesting question that Thales asked (at least for philosophers) is, what is common to all the elements? Thales was the first to realize that if fire can change into air (and is not *replaced* by air) there must be something that fire and air have in common that is neither air nor fire. If fire is replaced by air then they need not have anything in common. But, if fire changes into air, then there must be something that they both share.

Thales concluded that water is common to all things. This is not a particularly good answer because, if air can change into water, it is difficult to see how water can be what the two of them have in common. If water and air share water in common, then what is it that distinguishes water from air? Perhaps what Thales wanted to say is not that the four elements had water in common, but that there really was only one element and that was water, and the other "elements" were water in disguise.

13

As well as being interested in philosophy, Thales was also curious about astronomy. He managed to predict correctly that there would be an eclipse of the sun on May 28, 585 B.C. He was also interested in other branches of natural science. It is owing to this interest that he picked water as the common substance. Thales believed, with some justification, that the nourishment of all things is moisture, and that the seeds of all things have a moist nature. He felt that since moisture is the basis of all life, water is most likely what is common to all things.

An amusing but somewhat apocryphal story concerning Thales has come down to us: In order to make his astronomical predictions, Thales had to spend a great deal of time gazing at the stars. One night he was so carried away in this endeavor that he fell down a well. The local Milesians thought that this was a great joke and made fun of him. Thales decided to prove to the locals in a way they would understand that his star gazing was not a waste of time. He realized through star gazing, so the story goes, that there would be a bumper crop of olives during the following summer. He secretly went around the country and leased all the olive presses. As a result when the bumper crop came, if a press was to be obtained for making olive oil, it had to be leased from Thales, no doubt at an exorbitant fee. In this way, by cornering the olive press market, Thales made a great deal of money and suitably impressed the local populace. It is only fair to warn the reader, however, that, although Thales was the first philosopher to make a lot of money, he was, as far as I know, the last.

ANAXIMANDER

Although Thales did not give an interesting answer to the question concerning what underlies all change, he had a disciple by the name of Anaximander (born circa 612 B.C.) who did. Anaximander realized that that which was common to fire, air, and so on had to be different from them. But what could it be? If all that we could see was either the elements or composed of the elements, what could be this stuff of which the elements were composed? Anaximander realized that it had to be something that could not be seen, heard, or felt. He called it *apeiron*, which means roughly "indefinite, infinite, and unknown." The elements of this world come into and go out of existence, but the unknown out of which they come is immutable and eternal. The idea that there is something indefinite and eternal had an enormous influence upon Western philosophy, as we shall see.

PARMENIDES

One of the ancient philosophers whose views were most influenced by this idea was Parmenides, a native of Elea, a Greek city in southern Italy. He was born around 515 B.C. In a dark fragment that has come down to us, he says that there are only two ways that one can pursue knowledge:

(a) One way—that it is and cannot not be. This is the path to truth.

(b) The other way—that it is not and must not be. This way, I tell you, is altogether unthinkable, for you could not know that which is not, that is impossible, nor utter it.

No doubt these pronouncements are very obscure, but what Parmenides has in mind is this: you can only think about what exists; you cannot think about what does not exist. If you try to think about something that does not exist you are either thinking about something else or thinking about nothing—that is, not thinking. For example, suppose that you owned a female dog and you thought your dog was going to give birth to a puppy. In fact, so sure were you that you gave the puppy a name, say "Mirenbad." But the pregnancy turned out to be a pseudopregnancy and your dog had no puppy. Now what are you thinking about when you think about Mirenbad? Obviously, you are not thinking about anything. Not even a fetus. But, if you are not thinking about anything, you are not thinking!

Not only can you not think about Mirenbad; you cannot make any statements about Mirenbad. For "Mirenbad" to act as a name, it has got to name something. If there is nothing for "Mirenbad" to name, such statements as "Mirenbad does not exist" are quite meaningless. Of course, you can talk about the word "Mirenbad" and say such things as " 'Mirenbad' does not name any puppy," but you cannot talk about Mirenbad.

From these dark premises Parmenides derived some strange and surprising conclusions. The first is that the universe has no beginning and no end. If it had a beginning, there must have been a time when it did not exist. But we cannot think of the universe as not existing. What would we be thinking about?

Now someone might object that we have made the groundless assumption that that which is unthinkable cannot exist, for surely some unthinkable things—for example, atomic wars—could exist. However, this is not the sort of thing Parmenides had in mind when he talked about unthinkable things. He had in mind things that cannot be thought of and cannot exist: an object that is both spherical and cubical at the same time, or the occurrence of an irresistible force meeting an immovable object.

The second and much more surprising conclusion that Parmenides wanted to draw is that there is no motion in the universe—things simply do not move. Of course, he was aware that things *appeared* to move, but he felt that if reason led to a particular conclusion and the senses led to a different conclusion, then it was wiser to put one's trust in reason than in the senses. After all, the senses often mislead us with hallucinations, and with illusions.

Parmenides' reason for saying that things did not move is that in order for things to move they need empty space. But to conceive of space as empty or unoccupied is unthinkable and it must not exist. What is there to think about? Suppose I put my hands together. Here it would be quite proper to say that there is nothing between them. But if I move them apart (in a vacuum) can I still say that there is nothing between them? I can say there is *space* between them, but if I do say this, then I must mean something *different* from when I said there was *nothing* between them. But if I mean something different, there must be *something* between them (a plenum). But if there is something between them, then they cannot move.[1]

Not only can things not move, they also cannot change their properties. Suppose, for example, that you have a pair of blue jeans that you think have become faded over the years. That could not happen. In order for the blue jeans to fade either (a) the particles that carry the darker blue would have to move (away) or (b) the dark blue would have to cease to be. But the particles cannot move and the dark blue cannot cease to be. Therefore, the blue jeans cannot fade. Finally, if nothing can move and there cannot be empty space between any two objects, then there cannot really be two objects. In other words, the universe is one.

Surprisingly, Parmenides went on to argue that the universe is limited. This conclusion was based on the claim that if the universe were without a limit, then it would stand in need of one. He then concluded that the universe, being motionless, is "like the body of a well-rounded sphere." This conclusion is surprising, for if what *is* is limited, then empty space must lie beyond it. But empty space is, according to Parmenides, impossible; therefore what *is* cannot be limited. This error was corrected by Melissus, a disciple to Parmenides, who presumably realized the force of this argument and declared that what *is* is infinite. That is to say, there is no empty space.

There is an amusing, if not Monty-Pythonesque, story concerning another of Parmenides' disciples. This person (whose name is unknown), while haranguing a large mob in a market square and trying to convince them of the truth of Parmenides' teachings, became carried away and was waving his arms with such abandon that he dislocated his shoulder. He fell to the ground in great pain. Fortunately, there was a doctor in the audience who came to the budding philosopher's rescue. Unfortunately for the disciple, the doctor said, "In order for me to repair your shoulder, I shall have to put the ball back into the socket. That means I shall have to move the ball from one location to another. But as you have pointed out, motion is impossible and so I cannot repair your arm." As a result, the poor disciple was forced to recant and admit that motion was, after all, possible. Once he had done this, the doctor fixed the ball back in the socket.

ZENO

Parmenides had other disciples who, presumably, did not meet with the same fate. One such student, named Zeno, constructed a number of paradoxes that were designed to show, among other things, that motion is impossible. As you can imagine, people were inclined to laugh at Parmenides and to dismiss as preposterous his conclusion that motion was impossible. What Zeno wanted to do was to show, by means of these paradoxes, that to assume the existence of motion is also preposterous. For our purposes, it will be sufficient to discuss only three of these puzzles: "The Racer," "Achilles and the Tortoise," and "The Arrow." The first two are similar and so they shall be discussed together.

A runner wants to run from point A to point B;

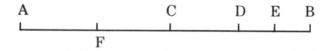

however, before he can get to B, he has to cover the distance from A to C. Suppose he has completed this distance and is about to run from C to B. However, before he can complete this distance, he will have to complete the distance from C to D. Suppose again that he has completed this distance and is about to run from D to B. Again, before he can complete this distance, he will have to complete the distance from D to E, and so on. The racer will get closer and closer to the end of the race course but will never finish, because in order to finish, he will have to cover an infinite number of distances in a finite amount of time, and this is something no mortal runner can do. Not only will the runner never arrive at B, but he will never get started, for to get to C, he will have to cover the distance to F, and so on. Therefore, contrary to all appearances, the runner cannot even get started.

The second paradox concerns a race between the fleet-of-foot Achilles and the traditionally lethargic tortoise. Being a sporting fellow, Achilles gives the tortoise a head start, let us say 50 feet. And let us also assume that Achilles runs twice as fast as the tortoise. Achilles begins at point A in the diagram below, and the tortoise begins at point B.

0		50'	75'	87.5'	100'
A		B	C	D	

Now, in the time that Achilles has run as far as B, the tortoise will have run another 25 feet to C, and by the time Achilles has finally reached C, the tortoise will have moved on another 12.5 feet to D. Achilles is always getting closer but he never quite catches up, because by the time he has reached the place where the tortoise was, the tortoise has moved on. But this conclusion strikes us as absurd, since it flies in the face of common sense. Therefore, the assumption that motion is possible is also absurd.

The Arrow

Consider an archer who has just fired an arrow into the air, and suppose that the arrow is now (T^1) at place P^1.

Zeno says of this arrow that either it moves in the place where it is (P^1) or is in the place where it is not. But, it cannot move in the place where it is (no room) and it cannot move in the place where it is not. Therefore, the arrow cannot move. The main point in the argument is that place P^1, where the arrow is at T^1, is exactly the same shape and size as the arrow. It fits the arrow like a tight-fitting glove, thus the arrow cannot move at P^1. But, since it obviously cannot move where it is not, it follows that, contrary to all appearances, the arrow does not move.

We are now faced with the task of showing that Zeno's paradoxes are fallacious and that motion really is possible. If we fail with the demonstration, then we will have to accept Parmenides' conclusion that either the motion we experience is illusory or that reason is not reliable. There will still be the problem concerning empty space, but I think our discussion would be better served by shelving it until we have moved on to Lucretius.

We may begin our attempt to solve the first two paradoxes by taking note of the following: both suggest that the runner comes to a halt at the end of each distance. Now it is certainly true that if the runner (and Achilles) came to a halt at the end of each distance, the runner could never complete the course and Achilles would not catch up to the tortoise. But the runner does *not come* to a halt at the end of each distance. He does not, in this sense, have to run an infinite number of distances. What he does is to *cover* (without stopping) an infinite number of distances, and this does not seem to be quite as difficult a feat.

But this solution is not altogether satisfactory for it might be objected that even if the runner does not stop, he still has to cover an infinite number of distances, each with a finite length, in a finite amount of time, and this is something no mortal runner can do.

It will be easier to solve this deeper problem if we take a look at another paradox that was popular at the time: Take any physical object, say a piece of chalk. This object is, at least in thought, infinitely divisible. What I mean by "in thought" is that even if we divide it down to a piece (call it "A") that is uncuttable, we can still draw a line across A and consider X and Y (the two halves) as pieces that make up A. They are there but we just cannot divide them.

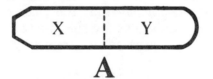

Now, since any physical object is in this sense infinitely divisible, we must ask ourselves whether each part has *some* size or *no* size. If each part has some size, then since we have an infinite number of parts, each with finite size, the object must be infinitely large. Whereas, if each part has no size, the object as a whole can have no size either; a conglomeration composed of an infinite number of sizeless parts would also be sizeless.

The same paradox could be presented using lines. Consider the following line. Let us call it Z.

———————————————————————————

(Z)

Now Z can be cut into segments, and those segments can, at least in thought, be cut into smaller segments, and so on. It would seem that we will have to say either that Z is infinitely long or that it has no length. The reason this is so is that if Z is "in thought" infinitely divisible, then either each segment has some length or it has no length. If each segment has some length, then, since we have an infinite number of them, Z will be infinitely long. If each has no length, then since $\infty \times 0 = 0$, Z will have no length.

The way out of these paradoxes is to be found by asking ourselves what it means to say that our piece of chalk is, in thought, infinitely divisible? What it means is not that the chalk consists of an infinite number of pieces, but rather, if we were to say of the piece of chalk itself—or any subpiece—that it could be divided, even though we might be saying something false, we would not be saying anything self-contradictory. A self-contradictory statement is a statement that consists of at least two parts wherein what is said in one part is contradicted by what is said in the other. For example, the statement "John is a husband but he is not married" would be self-contradictory. To say that John is a husband is to say that John is a married male, and to say that someone is a married male but is not married, is to say something that contradicts itself. In other words, it is to say something that is self-contradictory.

Let us return to the piece of chalk. If I were to say of subpiece "A" that it is divisible, I would be saying something false, since it cannot be divided. But I would not be saying something that was self-contradictory. Thus, when I say that the piece of chalk is infinitely divisible, all I am saying is that for the piece of chalk as a whole or any subpiece thereof, it is never self-contradictory to say that it can be divided.[2]

It does not mean, and so does not truly say, of this piece of chalk or any other physical object, that it consists of an infinite number of pieces. And if this is not what is being said (indeed that claim would be false) the question of whether each piece has some size or no size does not arise.

We can now apply this point to the racetrack paradoxes. The racetrack may be said to be infinitely divisible but this only means that of any distance we take, it is never self-contradictory to say that it can be divided in half. It does not mean, and indeed it would be false to say, that it now consists of an infinite number of distances. And this explains how the runner can get to the end of the race course. He does not have to cover an infinite number of finite distances, in a finite amount of time. He only has to cover a finite number of divisible distances in a finite time, and this is something some mortal runners can do. Similarly, Achilles does not have to cover an infinite number of distances in a finite amount of time. He only has to cover a finite number of divisible distances in a finite amount of time.

Let us now move on to the paradox concerning Zeno's arrow. Zeno claimed that since the arrow cannot move where it is not, and cannot move where it is, the arrow cannot move. Even though motion has vexed thinkers at least down to the time of Leibniz (Descartes was inclined to think that the things of the world moved in jumps, or more precisely that physical objects were created anew at each instant), the solution to Zeno's paradox is fairly simple. As a rule, when it is said that a physical object is at a given place, this suggests that the object is there for a duration. Now, if an object is at a given place for a duration, then for that duration the object does not move. Thus, when we say that the arrow is at place P^1 at T^1, we suggest that the arrow is there for a duration and so does not move. But since the arrow is not there for any duration but only for an instant, the arrow can be at place P^1 at T^1 and still be moving. However, this does not quite get rid of the paradox, for we are inclined to think of instances as very small durations and so, if the arrow is at P^1 for an instant, it looks as if it must have been at rest. What we have to do is discover a way of thinking about instances without thinking of them as small durations. Consider the following line:

There are two aspects of this line that have no length: the ends. The end of a line is not *part* of a line but rather its *limit*. In the same manner, we can also think of an instant, not as a part of a duration, not even an infinitely small part of a duration, but as the limit of a duration. T^1 is the limit of a duration that began when the arrow was shot. We can therefore say that even though the arrow was at place P^1 at T^1, the arrow was moving. The reason we can say this is that even though the arrow was at P^1, it was not there for any time. It is only there for T^1, and T^1 was the limit of a duration and not part of a duration.

What then is the answer to our original question—does the arrow move in the place where it is or in the place where it is not? The answer to this paradoxical question is the following paradoxical statement: the arrow neither moves in the place where it is nor in the place where it is not; rather, it moves through the place where it is (for an instant).

HERACLITUS

Not all Greek philosophers thought that what was real did not change and that change and motion were only illusions. Indeed, there was one, Heraclitus, who claimed that change is the only reality.

Heraclitus was an aristocrat, with aristocratic ideas, who lived around 500 B.C. (slightly before the time of Parmenides) in Ephesus, a city about fifty miles north of Miletus. One of the main threads in Heraclitus' thought is that things exist as a balance of conflicting opposites. For example, he says of a drink called a "posset," made of ground barley, grated cheese and wine, that "Even the posset separates if not stirred," and presumably ceases to exist. Realizing the importance of the conflict of opposites for the existence of many things, it is not surprising that he picked "fire" as the basic element. For fire, more than any other, seems to exist though conflict.

Even though it is true that some things cannot exist without there being a tension between opposites—for example, a violin cannot exist without there being a harmonized tension between the strings and the body of the violin—it is a mistake to think that most things are of this nature. After all, in order to have the tension, the strings and the box must exist, and these do not owe their existence to a tension between opposites. Or, to take a different example, although there cannot be a waterfall or a river without the flow of the water, that is, without change, the water presumably is formed out of minute particles that do not change. Perhaps we cannot step into the same water of a river twice, as Heraclitus would have us believe (though we can step into the same river twice), but we can, with the help of special instruments, pick up the same molecule of H_2O twice.

LUCRETIUS (*ON THE NATURE OF THE UNIVERSE*)

Although we have taken care of Zeno's paradoxes, we cannot, as yet, escape Parmenides' point that what is real cannot change. At the same time, we cannot help but accept that what we experience does change. One way to deal with this puzzle is to find a way by which we can say that even though what is real does not change, change is not an illusion. Lucretius was one person who thought he had found a way.

We know very little about the life of Lucretius. He was a Roman poet *cum* philosopher who was born soon after 100 B.C. His life was short; he died about 55 B.C. It has been said that he died by leaping into the crater of Mt. Etna after being driven insane by an aphrodisiac. But there seems to be little truth in this tale, although there may be some reason to believe in Lucretius' bouts of insanity. Even though Lucretius' famous work, *On the Nature of the Universe*, is a model of logical coherence, it does contain passages which suggest that the rationality of the author was slipping. As far as we know, this was his only work.

Although *On the Nature of the Universe* was written almost 500 years after the time of Parmenides, it must not be thought to be divorced from the problems that concerned philosophers at the time of Parmenides. *On the Nature of the Universe* is the clearest expression of a philosophical tradition called *atomism*, which began around the time of Parmenides. The first atomist was Leucippus, who is known primarily through his disciple Democritus (born about 460 B.C. and a native of

Abdera in Thrace). The atomic theory was used later on by the Athenian philosopher Epicurus as a prop for his moral theory, which was based on the premise that pleasure was the ultimate good. Many people have regarded Epicurus as an advocate of a life of wine, women, and song, but in reality he felt that the highest pleasure was to be found in a life of tranquility. He primarily enjoyed cultivating friendships in his garden while eating bread and drinking water.

Lucretius was a faithful disciple of Epicurus and is responsible for presenting the Epicurean philosophy of life, along with its atomistic underpinnings, in its clearest and most detailed form.

The atomistic tradition did not die with Lucretius. Although it was ignored for the most part by Christian philosophers who thought it too materialistic, it was revived in the seventeenth century by the French philosopher Gassendi and formed the philosophical basis of physics and chemistry until the beginning of the twentieth century. The splitting of the atom and the development of the atomic bomb changed all that—or so it appears.

Along with the other atomists, Lucretius was prepared to accept that without empty space, motion was impossible. However, since all our senses force upon us the belief that objects move, we simply have to accept that empty space exists—in spite of the intellectual difficulties that empty space presents. If we were not prepared to accept the testimony of the senses at such a basic level, life would be impossible.

Before taking a look at Lucretius' *On the Nature of the Universe*,[3] it might be worthwhile to see if we can find some way of showing how empty space is possible. Parmenides' pointed out that if space could be thought of, then it must be something, and so it would prevent objects from moving. This point was backed up by the argument that if I truly have nothing between my hands then my hands must be together. If my hands are not together, then there is something between them. But, if there is something between them, that something cannot be empty space.

How then do we come to have an idea of empty space if there is nothing there to have an idea of? Consider some object that I have in front of me, say a book, and imagine it moving completely out of the place it now occupies. Perhaps it cannot really move but at least I can *imagine* it moving. If it *did* move, the place it occupied would now, of course, be occupied by air. But suppose that nothing is allowed to take its place. Perhaps something will always take its place, perhaps ether. Still, we can conceive of nothing taking its place. That is to say, we can conceive of not anything taking its place. In this way then, we can arrive at the idea of empty space.

The same sort of point can be made about the argument concerning my hands. I can start with my hands together and move them apart (or so it seems to me) and I can imagine that nothing, that is, not anything comes between them. Perhaps I should not say that nothing or not anything comes between them, because this suggests that they are together, but at least I can say that there is only *distance* between them.

Our idea of empty space is oblique, but at least we can in the above manner form an idea of empty space. But, if empty space is thinkable, then we have lost our Parmenidian reason for saying that it does not exist. And, if we have lost our reason for saying it does not exist, then we have also lost our reason for saying that objects do not move.

With this difficulty out of the way, let us turn our attention to *On the Nature of the Universe*. After paying homage to an influential Roman politician by the name of Gaius Memmius, Lucretius begins to unfold his theory.[4]

Book I

1. His first main claim is that all physical objects are composed of microscopic, unsplittable particles called atoms. Although physical objects can cease to exist through being broken down into their component atoms, the atoms out of which these physical objects are composed, being unsplittable, can neither be created nor destroyed. His main reasons for saying that these atoms exist are as follows: First, we have all sorts of experiential evidence for the existence of atoms. When the wind blows against a tree, we see the branches move but we do not see the particles that *en masse* bend the branches. Gold rings wear smooth with the passing of time and yet we never see those particles. When a shirt is left to dry in the hot sun, the water leaves but we never see it go. It must therefore be composed of small particles that leave separately.

Second, if these unbreakable particles do not exist, then, given an infinite amount of time, everything would be ground down to such an extent that the future regeneration of living creatures would be impossible.

Finally, Lucretius alludes to the argument presented on page 19 above and says that if objects do not consist of atomic parts, then every object would consist of an infinite number of parts and so every object would be infinitely large. Unfortunately, the postulate of unbreakable parts will not save him from this paradox. If we take any atom we can always imagine a line drawn across it and talk about the left part and the right part. In other words, atoms may in fact not be divisible but they are in thought divisible and so infinitely divisible.

Lucretius claims, as we have seen, that atoms can neither be created nor destroyed. Given that objects can only be destroyed by being dismantled, and created by being assembled, it seems to follow that atoms, being unbreakable, can be neither created nor destroyed. But this conclusion does not follow. Why could not an atom simply pop into existence or cease to exist? Lucretius does not offer reasons to suggest that neither of these events could occur, but I would suspect that if pressed he would have offered the sort of reason given above by Parmenides (p. 15). However, it is not surprising that Lucretius accepts this conclusion; after all, it was not questioned until the time of David Hume (1711–1776), and does seem to square with common sense.

2. Lucretius' second major claim is that in addition to atoms there is also empty space. The main reason for this claim is the belief that without empty space the atoms (or anything else) cannot move. Lucretius offers an interesting argument in support of this conclusion. He invites us to consider whether a fish can move in (full) water. Someone might think that if the fish pushed ahead, it would leave enough empty space behind for the water in front of it to flow into; but as Lucretius points out, the fish cannot push ahead until the water moves away and the water cannot move away until the fish moves. Therefore the fish cannot move.

Is Lucretius correct in saying that there cannot be movement in a full world? I think that he is right in saying that the fish cannot *begin* to move in a full world. But this is not the same as saying that there could not be motion in a full world. What about motion that has no beginning? In fact, Lucretius will want to argue that atoms always have been in motion.

Let us begin our examination of this problem by considering the following toy train.

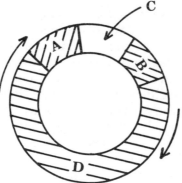

Space A is occupied by the engine, B by the caboose, and D by the rest of the train. Let us assume that the train is perfectly rigid. It would seem that this train would have no trouble in starting because there is plenty of space between the engine and the caboose for the engine to occupy. But suppose we place in area C an extra caboose that exactly fills the space. Can the train start? We might be tempted, along with Lucretius, to say no, but this would be a mistake. After all, the engine and the rest of the train could be fitted on the bottom of a perfectly rigid hula hoop and cause the hula hoop to begin to rotate.

However, it does not follow from the fact that a perfectly rigid circular object can begin to rotate in *our* world that one can in a *full* world. After all, one needs space around the hula hoop to get it rotating. Similarly, there would have to be space around the pistons and other parts of the train, which completely fills the circle, for it to get going. So perhaps Lucretius is right: in a full world there can be no initial motion. This does not, as we have seen, rule out the possibility of eternal motion. Imagine that the world is as Parmenides suggests: one giant, solid, adamantine-like sphere. But imagine also that encased in this sphere is a hula hoop—something like a ring encased in an ice cube. Needless to say, the hula hoop cannot *begin* to rotate, but can't it have been always rotating? I grant that there would be a problem about friction, but putting this to one side, is it not possible that the hula hoop has always been rotating?

This raises the problem of how there could be motion without a beginning. If we are prepared to accept that the atoms have no beginning, there is no reason not to accept that they have always been in motion.

We may conclude then that Lucretius is mistaken in his claim that space is necessary for motion. It may be necessary for linear motion but it is not necessary for eternal circular motion. However, this point does not really affect Lucretius' argument, because he will want to claim that we know through experience that atoms move for the most part in straight lines in every direction and that circular motion is the exception rather than the rule.

The second reason Lucretius uses to support his claim that empty space exists is that some substances are heavier than others. For example, a cubic foot of lead weighs more than a cubic foot of iron. The explanation he offers is that there are more holes between the iron atoms than between the lead atoms. Thus, vacuity (empty space) has to be postulated to explain the differences in density. But this is not the only possible explanation. Perhaps the iron atoms are simply made of lighter stuff than the lead atoms. By this I mean that a cubic centimeter of the stuff in an iron atom weighs less than a cubic centimeter of the stuff in a lead atom. Or perhaps there are no atoms and the stuff in the cubic foot of iron just simply is lighter than the stuff in the cubic foot of lead.

3. Lucretius' next claim is that nothing else exists besides atoms and empty space. Atoms are what is and empty space is what is not. Between these two there cannot be anything else, for either something is or it is not. What this is going to mean later on is that all mental and spiritual phenomena, such as thoughts and desires, will have to be explained by means of atoms.

4. The following picture of Lucretius' universe is beginning to emerge. It is composed of atoms and empty space. The atoms were never created and will never be destroyed. They move through the void; always have and presumably always will. A given atom is caused to move by being hit by another atom and so on back through time for all eternity. In a word, the universe is one large, eternal, and perpetual three-dimensional game of billiards. But how large is the universe? Lucretius' answer is, as you might have guessed, that it is infinite. His argument goes roughly as follows: Suppose it is claimed that there is a boundary to the universe. Then imagine going to that putative boundary and throwing a dart. Either the dart will stop or it will keep going. If it stops, then something is out there. This something is either finitely thick or infinitely thick. If it is finitely thick, then what lies on the other side? It must be space. If the something is infinitely thick, then the universe must also be infinite, for that something would have to fill an infinity of space. If, on the other hand, the dart keeps going forever, the universe must be infinite.

I used to find this argument convincing but I no longer do. Let's suppose I go to the putative boundary. In front of me there is what looks like a black wall. I push my arm against what appears to be the wall but it offers no opposition. As my arm goes into the darkness, it disappears. When I pull it back, I no longer have an arm. Now, if this were to happen, would we not say that we had reached the limit of empty space? Physical objects can occupy empty space but no physical object can exist beyond this limit. Of course, there, could be something there that causes my arms and other objects to disappear. (Sharks?) But there need not be. It is conceivable that there could be a limit to the space where objects can exist.

Book II

5. Given that we have uncreated atoms moving ceaselessly in space, the next question is how many atoms are there? Lucretius answers, as one would expect, that there is an infinite number of atoms. If there were only a finite number, they would long ago have become lost in space. Furthermore, physical objects are nothing more than clusters of atoms. Unless there were vast numbers of atoms to form these clusters, there would not be any physical objects. But there are physical objects; therefore, there is an infinite number of atoms.

We find in this world a tremendous variety of substances. Some, like lead, are soft and heavy while others, like diamonds, are hard and brittle. Some are liquid, and of these liquids some are thick and viscous (e.g., molasses), while others are thin (e.g., water or alcohol).[5] Since atoms are the basic building blocks of the universe, it is not surprising to find that these differences can be traced back to differences in the atoms. Water is composed of round, smooth atoms while a diamond is composed of hooked atoms that interlock exceedingly well. Not only is the shape of the atom responsible for the essential properties of substances, it is also responsible for the more peripheral properties. For example, honey tastes pleasant because it is composed of relatively smooth atoms, but briney water tastes bitter because it is formed partly out of sharp barbed atoms. Lucretius offers an interesting proof of this. Filter some brine through some layers of earth. The water that comes out has a pleasant taste. But since what was left behind in the filter would have been the hooked and barbed atoms, it must be these atoms that are responsible for the astringent taste of the brine.

Although there is a great variety in the number of types of atoms, Lucretius tells us that the number of types is finite.[6] He offers two arguments in support of this. First, the atoms are responsible for the sensations we experience, "For touch and nothing but touch . . . is the essence of all bodily sensations . . ."[7]; but there is a limit to the sensations that we can experience, so there must be a limit to the number of types of atoms. This argument, it should be noticed, is fallacious. There could be an infinite number of types of atoms with only a limited number of them being responsible for the sensations we experience.

The second argument is very obscure. According to Lucretius, each atom is composed of parts and there is only a small number of these parts. The claim that atoms have parts comes as a bit of a surprise. Are not atoms supposed to be unsplittable; in other words, indivisible? I suspect that what Lucretius has in mind, and so wants to say, is that there are a limited number of geometrical shapes that can and must go into the construction of an atom. Perhaps, but this is only a conjecture.[8] No atom can be broken down into those shapes. But they are in a sense in the atoms all the same. Now, given that there are a limited number of geometrical shapes that can go into the construction of an atom, then unless we duplicate those shapes, we will soon run out of ways that they can be combined. The only way that we could have an infinite number of atomic types would be through having some that were infinitely large, but since no atom is large enough to ever be seen, we know that there is a finite number of atomic types.

Perhaps the argument should be expressed more formally. As well as atomic types, we have atomic part-types. Two parts of an atom are of the same part-type if and only if they are the same shape and size. Now, given that we have a limited number of part types that can go into the construction of an atomic type—say a cube, a tetrahedron, and a dodecahedron—and each is of a given size, then it will follow that unless we have duplication we will have a finite number of atomic types. If we allow unlimited duplication, we can have an infinite number of atomic types; but then some atomic types, and so some atoms, would be infinitely large.

Given that we have, for these obscure reasons, a finite number of types of atoms, how many atoms of each type are there? Lucretius answers that there is an infinite number of atoms of each type on the ground that, if there were a finite number of each type and a finite number of types, then the total number of atoms would be finite. But, since it has already been shown that there is an infinite number of atoms, Lucretius claims that there must be an infinite number of each type. This argument is not valid. An infinite number of atoms of one type is sufficient to give us an infinite number of atoms. However, if the number of atoms of one type is infinite, it seems likely that the number of each type will also be infinite.

6. We have seen that most of the atoms are perpetually in motion and that as a rule they move in straight lines. It must not be thought, according to Lucretius, that atoms always move in straight lines and that their trajectories are rigidly determined by what went before since "at quite indeterminate times and places they swerve ever so little from their course" (*NU*, p. 66). Lucretius gives us two arguments in support of this theory, the first of which can be dismissed very quickly.

At some time in the past, before the existence of physical objects, the atoms fell in parallel lines through the void. Not only did they fall in parallel lines, they also all fell at the same speed. The reason they all fell at the same speed is that empty space, unlike air or water, offers no resistance. Now, if they all fell in parallel lines at the same rate of speed, it follows that no atom would come in contact with any other atom. But, if no atom comes in contact with any other atom, from whence come the log jams we call physical objects? Therefore, atoms must swerve at indeterminate times and places from their courses.

The weaknesses of this argument are (a) that since at the time referred to, there were no physical objects such as the planet Earth, then given an infinity of space, the atoms could hardly be said to have been falling; and (b) since the atoms have always been in motion there is no reason to postulate that there was a time when they moved in parallel lines. We must give credit to Lucretius for anticipating Galileo. But do not forget that according to Galileo, objects do not fall at a constant rate, they *accelerate* at a constant rate when they fall.

The second argument is much more interesting because it raises a philosophical problem that has taxed thinkers throughout the history of philosophy. It is a problem that we shall discuss on a number of occasions during the course of this book. According to Lucretius, if everything that happens in the universe can be analyzed into events concerning atoms, and if what happens to the atoms is rigidly determined by what went before, then everything that happens in the universe is rigidly determined by what went before. Yet we know that some of the things that happen in the world are free acts. For example, if

I take a sip from the coffee cup in front of me, my act of bringing the cup to my lips is, we think, a free act. But how could it be a free act if all the movements of my limbs are ultimately determined by the movements of atoms? Of course, if I have been hypnotized or drugged or if I am outrageously addicted to coffee, then my act is not free. But in the normal course of events, it seems that my taking a sip of coffee is a free act. I could have done otherwise.

Lucretius realized that if an act is rigidly determined by the prior movements of the atoms, it cannot be a free act. But since acts of the sort just mentioned are free, it cannot be the case that the movements of the atoms are always determined. There must be an element of indeterminacy at work in the universe, and that is why he says that at indeterminate times and places the atoms swerve slightly from their courses. Unfortunately, however, postulating indeterminacy will not save the day. If the movement of my arm when I reach out for the cup of coffee is partly the result of indeterminate movements of atoms, then the movement of my arm is only a sporadic random event. My reaching for the cup could not be said to be a free act.

When, in this century, Werner Heisenberg presented us with his Indeterminacy Principle, some philosophers thought that it would explain how human freedom is possible. However, it was soon understood that this was not the case. If the movements of my limbs are a consequence of the random movement of atoms, I have no more reason to say that they are free than if they are the result of the entirely determined movements of atoms. This ought to make us realize how puzzling the problem of human freedom really is. Whether we postulate complete determinism, complete indeterminism or a mixture of the two, we still have a problem. We shall come back to this point in chapter 6.

7. We mentioned before that, according to Lucretius, in order to experience any sensation, it is necessary to be touched by atoms; the sensation experienced is determined by the shape of the atoms. Honey has an agreeable taste because it is composed of smooth, round atoms while, presumably, burning tires have a foul, unpleasant smell because they give off hooked and barbed atoms that then come in contact with the sniffer's nose. If the shape or size of the atoms are what determine the sort of sensations we experience, the question arises: What properties can these atoms have? If the explanation of why roses have the odor they do is that the rose-sniffer's nose is bombarded with atoms of a certain shape and size, it seems clear that atoms themselves can have no odor. In order for an atom to have an odor, it would have to give off atoms of a particular shape and size, and this of course is something no atom can do.

Not only are the atoms devoid of odor, they are also colorless. The same argument applies. In order for me to experience a red apple, my eyes must be bombarded by a certain type of atom, and so, in order for an atom to be red, it would have to be capable of giving off the same type of atoms, and of course this they cannot do. As well as being odorless and colorless, the atoms are, for the same reason, devoid of temperature. Although atoms lack the above experiential properties, they still have some properties. As we have seen, they possess shape, size, weight, and density.

It has been common for philosophers and scientists to distinguish between *primary qualities* and *secondary qualities*. The former are represented by size, shape, weight, and so on, while the latter consist of color, sound, odor, and the like. Primary qualities are said to inhere in the single atoms as well as in their various combinations. The cup in front of me has shape as do the atoms that compose it. In and of itself, the cup, like the atoms that compose it, has no color. When the cup gives off atoms of a certain type, or light waves of a certain length, then I experience a certain color (say green). But, the color I experience is not *in* the the cup; it is a mental phenomenon caused by the atoms in the cup. The theory that secondary qualities are not in the object but are mind-dependent has been held not only by some of the ancient atomists, but by Galileo (1564-1642), Robert Boyle (1627-1692), John Locke (1632-1704), and Bertrand Russell (1872-1970). It was believed to have been refuted by George Berkeley (1685-1753), David Hume (1711-1776) and A. J. Ayer (1910-   ). Today, surprisingly enough, it seems to be undergoing a revival. At the heart of the theory is the following point: If the color I experience is caused by rays of light of a certain wavelength affecting my eyes, then the cup, which I normally believe to be green, is not only *not* green, it could not be any color. It must be colorless.

To what extent Lucretius held this theory is not clear. No doubt, for him atoms are devoid of secondary properties, but it is not clear that he wanted to hold that complexes of atoms are also devoid of such properties. Did he just want to say that the atoms that compose the cup are devoid of color, or did he also want to say that the cup is devoid of color? The reason an atom cannot be green is because in order to be green, it would have to give off atoms of a certain type. This may be something that atoms cannot do but it is certainly something that the cup in front of me could do. I suspect, however, that Lucretius would want to say that since the simple atoms that go into the complexes (physical objects) are colorless, the complexes must be colorless as well.

Book III

1. It is natural to believe that there is more to a person than simply a number of atoms arranged in a certain way. We may hesitate to say

that a person has a soul or a mind but we want to say that a person is at least (sometimes) conscious of what is going on around him. He sees and hears certain things and remembers others, knows some truths and believes others, doubts some things, fears some, and wants others. But, if a man is nothing but an assemblage of atoms, all of these abilities have to be explained somehow in terms of the coming and going of the atoms. And this is something that is difficult to do.

If we look at the history of that branch of philosophy known as metaphysics, we find that most philosophers can be classified as Materialists, Idealists or Dualists. Lucretius, along with the other atomists, was a materialist, for he believed that all of reality consisted of atoms and the void, and that everything, including all mental phenomena, could be explained in terms of the atoms. The ancient atomists were not the only materialists. The British philosopher Thomas Hobbes (1588–1679) was also a materialist and so were the twentieth-century behaviorists. The behaviorists believed that all apparent mental phenomena could be accounted for in terms of behavior. For example, suppose that you are on your way to catch a train and you believe that the train will be leaving very shortly. Your belief might be expressed in terms of your hurrying to catch a train. Most people would say that you hurry *because* you believe that the train will be leaving shortly, whereas the behaviorists would say that the belief *is* the behavior. Hurrying is not a mental but a physical, or, in other words, a material happening. One difficulty with this theory is that, if you did not really want to catch the train, you would not hurry even though you believed the train would be leaving shortly. It is difficult to see how both wanting to catch the train and believing the train will be leaving shortly can be identified with behavior.

Today, the philosophical arena abounds with a different kind of materialist. He does not want to identify beliefs and desires with patterns of behavior but with happenings in the brain. No doubt when I believe the train will be leaving shortly, this thought can be correlated with something going on in my brain. After all, I could hardly have this thought, at least this side of the grave, without a brain. But it is difficult to see how this going-on-in-my-brain could *be* the thought that the train will be leaving shortly.

The idealist stands at the other metaphysical extreme. He believes that all that exists are minds and the mental phenomena that they experience. This theory might seem rather bizarre, but there is this much to be said for it. We can be certain that we exist as centers of consciousness and that we experience all sorts of thoughts, emotions, desires, and sensations (of color, sound, and smell). What we cannot be certain of is whether anything exists beyond the mental phenomena that we experience. The image of a cup exists and is in my visual (mental) field but can I be certain that there is a physical cup beyond this image?

The most famous idealist was George Berkeley, who lived in the eighteenth century. Later, in the early part of twentieth century there was an influential group of idealistically inclined philosophers called phenomenalists. The main difference between their theory and Berkeley's was that Berkeley believed that there were minds as well as phenomena, whereas the phenomenalists believed that there were only phenomena. The reason they denied the existence of mind is that they had no direct experience of it, and the reason that both parties denied the existence of the physical world is that neither believed that they had any experience of it.

Between materialism and idealism lies dualism, which contends that, in addition to physical substance, we have mental substance. Put another way, along with the physical world, which is composed of material objects (perhaps ultimately atoms), we have the mental world, which is composed of minds and their ideas. Most people are inclined to be dualists for it seems almost self-evident that consciousness is a very different sort of stuff than matter, and that the idea of a piece of cheese is a very different thing than a piece of cheese. The most famous dualist was René Descartes. We shall take a closer look at his theory later on.

Although dualism is perhaps the most attractive of the three positions, it has its difficulties. The main difficulty, which we will discuss at length, is how there can be any interaction between physical things and the ideas we have of them. For example, suppose I desire to scratch my left ear. I decide to raise my left arm and then go ahead and do so. Now, how does my desire to scratch my ear and my decision to lift my arm, which are purely mental goings on, cause my arm to go up? Suppose there is a piece of chalk on the table in front of me and I want to raise it. I could say, "Please rise, piece of chalk" and urge the piece of chalk to rise. But no amount of mental effort of this sort can cause the piece of chalk to rise. How then can I cause my arm to rise through willing it to rise? Or, take a different example: When I look at a green cup in front of me, light of a particular wavelength moves from this cup and enters my eyes. Here it is converted into a series of electro-chemical impulses that are carried to the brain. Now the puzzle is, how does, and indeed how can, this physiological process give rise to the greenness that I perceive? It seems to be such a different sort of thing.

So, as illustrated here, the existence of mental life raises all sorts of difficulties. It seems that we must adopt either the stance of the materialist, the idealist, or the dualist; there are no others. Each takes care of some of the problems encountered by the other two but each raises apparently insuperable problems of its own. There may be difficulties in Lucretius' position, but then there are difficulties in every other possible position, too.

Lucretius, as we have seen, believed that the world and the people in it ultimately consisted of nothing but atoms and empty space. How then did he account for the existence of consciousness? His account, to the extent that he had one, was that even though no atom on its own can be conscious (just as no atom on its own can be colored), when enough of them are organized in a sufficiently complex way, then the emergence of consciousness—or, in other words, sentience—can take place. The pieces that belong to a computer are not capable of thought, but we are tempted to say that the computer they belong to, if it is complex enough, is capable of thought.

The seat of consciousness (according to Lucretius) is not located in the head, as we might expect. Instead, he locates it in the chest. One reason for doing so is that feelings of emotion, which would have to be classified as mental, seem to him to be located in the chest. Perhaps the Greeks and Romans were more emotional than we are. The seat of consciousness, which Lucretius calls the mind, is composed of at least three different types of atoms: wind, warmth, and air. It almost seems contradictory to our ears to say that the mind is composed of atoms. We can say (and rightly) that the brain is composed of atoms. But we usually reserve "mind" to refer to that which is not composed of atoms. In other words, that which is immaterial. This is why most materialists would want to say that the mind does not exist. When talking about Lucretius, we should take the word "mind" to mean no more than "center of consciousness."

Why did Lucretius think that the mind was composed of wind, warmth, and air? Well, at that time, people were tempted to identify life, and thus sentience, with breath. Indeed, the original meaning of "spirit" is "breath." Now, when a person exhales, there is the movement (wind) of moist air from the chest. (This gives us another reason for Lucretius to locate the mind in the chest.) Lucretius felt, as we would, that the coming together of wind, warmth, and air is not sufficient to account for the existence of sentience, so he added a fourth ingredient. He says, "We must add to these a fourth component which is quite nameless. Of this there is nothing more mobile or more tenuous—nothing whose component atoms are smaller or smoother" (*NU*, p. 103). However, it is difficult to see how the adding of any other kind of atom, no matter how small or mobile, could account for the existence of sentience. Finally, it is necessary that the mind-atoms be seated in a body in order for sentience to occur—"it is by the interacting motions of the two combined that the flame of sentience is kindled in our heart" (*NU*, p. 106).

The character that a person has is a consequence of the proportions in the mix of the different types of atoms, not just in people but in animals as well. The ferocity of lions is attributable to the predominance of heat atoms, the flightiness of deer to the predominance of wind atoms, and the calmness of cattle to the predominance of air atoms.

2. The most important conclusion to follow from the claim that the mind is composed of atoms is that man is mortal. When a person dies, his mind atoms leave the body by the mouth and are dispersed by the winds. This view is not too far removed from the view held by many people until the time of Descartes. There are many medieval paintings that portray someone dying in which the act of giving up the ghost is pictured by means of a cloud of what looks like smoke coming out of a person's mouth. It is natural for an atomist to view the cloud as composed of atoms that will be dispersed once it enters the surrounding air. Sentience is brought about through the certain number of mind atoms existing together in an ordered way in a body. Once those atoms have been dispersed, the center of consciousness ceases to exist. The atoms continue to exist but the center of consciousness, and so the person, does not. This theory, although similar, is different from its medieval counterpart. According to the latter view, what is "given up" is eternal.

Lucretius realized that since there is an infinity of future time, it is highly probable that the atoms that form a person will come together once again, but he also says that it would not be the same person, for the "chain of identity" would have been snapped. The atoms that form me must have come together many times in the past, but since I have no recollection of these previous existences I cannot be identified with them. If I have no reason to identify these past persons with myself, I have no reason to identify any future persons with myself.

Lucretius is aware that his rejection of life after death is important. As a result, he assembles a number of arguments to support it. First of all we notice that there is a fairly strong correlation between the state of the body and the state of the mind as a person proceeds through life.

> With the weak and delicate frame of wavering childhood goes a like infirmity of judgment. The robust vigor of later years is accompanied by a . . . maturer strength of mind. Later, when the body is palsied by the potent forces of age . . . the understanding limps . . . and the mind totters. (*NU*, pp. 109–110)

So, is it not likely that the mind collapses when the body does? Consider the following graph. The solid line represents the state of the body, while the dotted line represents the state of the mind.

State of Body and Mind

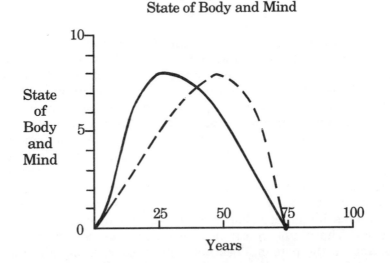

Now, if we project the state of the mind beyond the age of seventy-five (when the person represented dies), should we not use the past as a guide? Since the lines have risen and fallen together and since after seventy-five the body line proceeds at 0, should not the mind line also proceed at 0? The person who believes in an after life of the mind claims that the dotted line re-emerges at 8 or some lower figure and carried on at that value. But all evidence is contrary to this prediction.

Second, our day-to-day observations confirm that there is a close correlation between the state of the body and the state of the mind. When a man is besotted with wine, his mind is also affected. When a man is racked with disease and fever, his mind wanders. And finally, when the body is seriously wounded in battle the mind ceases to function properly.

3. It is tempting to think that Lucretius would view the mortality of men with melancholy, but this is not so. Indeed, it is Lucretius' belief that most of the social ills can be attributed to the common belief that man is immortal.

Most Greeks and Romans were afraid to die because they thought terrible things could happen to them. Part of this can be explained as fear of the unknown—something like a child's fear of the dark—and partly as fear of what they believed might happen to them in Hades. At that time, people believed that they would most likely go to Hades; there was not much chance that they would go to some sort of heaven. Once they were convinced of the teachings of Lucretius and Epicurus, they had nothing to fear (given, of course, that the teachings were true), for now the darkness had been swept away and they knew what was going to happen to them. They knew that they would simply cease to exist.

Lucretius, in a splendid outburst of rhetoric, lists some of the social ills he believes to be attributable to the fear of death. He claims that people associate poverty with death, for as he puts it, they see being poor as loitering at the gateway to death. They try to escape as far as they can from this poverty. And "so in their greed of gain, they amass a fortune out of civil bloodshed: piling wealth on wealth they heap carnage on carnage" (*NU,* p. 98). Furthermore, some people are so troubled with this fear of death that they commit suicide in order to get life over with as quickly as possible.

Not only does the fear of death bring about these excesses; it also colors more ordinary lives. People are often restless; never happy with where they are or with what they have. In rushing about, the individual is really attempting to run away from himself. "Since he remains reluctantly wedded to the self whom he cannot of course escape, he grows to hate him, because he is a sick man ignorant of the cause of his malady" (*NU,* p. 129).

According to Lucretius, Hell is not something that exists after death. It exists right here on earth. Sisyphus, the Corinthian king who was condemned in Hades, as myth has it, to push a heavy stone to the top of a hill and begin again when it rolled to the bottom, does not exist in an afterlife; he exists right here on earth. He is the man who struggles and strains to gain wealth and social status only to find that he is not happy when he has got them. The fear of death is what, unbeknown to him, motivates his endeavors. But his achievements do not make that fear go away. Only a firm grasp of his mortality will do the trick.

We must now ask ourselves whether, given that there is no life after death and that we do not believe there is life after death, we have no reason to fear or to be unhappy at the prospect of death. First of all, we should distinguish the act of dying from the state of being dead, for we may have reason to fear one but not the other. Let us begin with the state. One has no reason to fear the nothingness of being dead—as if it were a sort of darkness. In *Through the Looking Glass* by Lewis Carroll there is a wonderful line where the king asks Alice if she sees somebody coming and Alice replies that she sees nobody coming. Then the king says "I only wish I had such eyes. To be able to see nobody! . . . It is as much as I can do to see real people by this light." The philosophical joke (Lewis Carroll was a logician and a bit of a philosopher) is that nobody is not a special sort of somebody. To say that I saw nobody is a misleading way of saying that I did not see anybody. Similarly, nothing is not a special sort of something. To say that there will be nothing after one is dead is just to say that there will not be anything after one is dead. (I am not certain if Lucretius wanted to make this point but I suspect that he did. It seems embedded in many of the things that he does say.)[9]

Second, Lucretius wants to claim that a person should not be distressed at the prospect of being dead, even when it involves living a short life, because (a) lengthening his life will not reduce the time that he is dead and (b) even if his life is snuffed out in the flower of youth he will not exist to regret it. No doubt Lucretius is right on both these points, but he ignores the further point that since (in his theory) pleasure is the ultimate good, a person ought to want to extend his own life, given that it is a happy one, in order to maximize his pleasure. The person ought then to feel distressed at, for example, the knowledge that he is going to face the firing squad in the morning. The reduction in life will reduce the amount of pleasure that he can experience. Perhaps he does not have as much reason to feel distressed at the thought of being dead as he thought he did, given that there is no afterlife, but he still has some reason.

Let us now move on to the act of dying. Ludwig Wittgenstein, one of the greatest philosophers of this century, points out in section 6.4317 of his *Tractatus Logico-Philosophicus* that just as an instant is not a duration of time but the limit of a duration, so dying is not an event of life but the limit of life. But, if it is not an event that lasts for some duration, no matter how short, then we have nothing to fear. No doubt this is true, but as a rule when we talk about dying we refer to the events that lead up to the limit of life and not the limit *per se*. For example, people will say things like "It took British Admiral Nelson a long time to die." We do have something to fear here. We may well fear the pain and suffering that precedes the limit. Epicurus may, strictly speaking, have been correct when he succinctly said that death is nothing to us for when we are it is not, and when it is we are not, but he was misleading. We still have the event of dying to fear, that is, the events immediately preceding the limit, and we also should be distressed by the fact that dying and then being dead will always reduce the time that we could be happily alive.

4. Once we are freed from our fear of death, what sort of a life does Lucretius think that we should lead here on earth? First of all, there is no point in preparing for an afterlife; we must instead focus our attention solely on this life and no other.

We saw before that the source of all perception is touch. The sound we hear and the color we see are dependent upon the type of atom that touches our sense organs. Furthermore, whether we find a sensation pleasurable or painful depends on the type of atom. Smooth atoms as a rule give rise to pleasurable sensations, while hooked and barbed ones give rise to unpleasantness since they disturb the tranquility and harmony of the soul atoms. The ancient atomists were inclined to identify mental health and happiness with the harmony of the soul atoms. We have seen that the soul consisted of four kinds of atoms. Presumably that harmony would exist when they were in a state of equilibrium. If we do something that causes this equilibrium to be disturbed—such as eating foul-tasting food or (at a higher level) subject ourselves to great emotional stress—we will upset this harmony and experience pain and suffering as a consequence.

The way that we should live is now clear. Since there is no point in setting our sights on anything higher than our own mortal existence and since we know that leading a tranquil existence with nothing in excess will bring us the happiest life that we are capable of enjoying, this is obviously the sort of life we should lead. For this reason Epicurus recommended sitting in a garden and cultivating friendships.

Perhaps it might be wise to pause for a moment to appraise the atomists' moral theory. They may be right in saying that we should concern ourselves only with human interests, but they did not distinguish between concern for oneself and concern for the interests of others. As a rule, there will be, on the atomist's account, a harmony between personal interests and the interests of others. No one of us will deprive others of the necessities of life by living in a large mansion, driving expensive cars and eating lavish meals, because we know that they do not bring the tranquility that is necessary for our well-being, nor will any one of us refrain from giving grain from our granary to a starving mob because we would find their commotion distressing. But, if any of us did not find their uproar distressing and did not find the pleasures of sumptuous meals to be short-lived, then the atomists can offer us no reason for refraining. In short, the atomists' Hedonism may in some situations lead to the doing of what would normally be called immoral acts and should therefore be treated as suspect. Perhaps this theory can be patched up. We shall look at some attempts to do so in chapter 7. But, as it stands, it does have these dark implications.

There is one more thing that needs to be said about the Hedonism of atomists. As was pointed out earlier, given that we are mortal, the most we can look forward to is a life of tranquility. However, this is not quite correct. Suppose we were mortal but did not know it. Futhermore, suppose we believed that we could look forward to a wonderful afterlife. Then, perhaps we might find a much greater and deeper happiness in preparing for this afterlife. In short, the claim that the best that man can do is lead a life of (simple) pleasure does not follow solely from the statement that man is mortal. It follows from this claim in conjunction with a belief in human mortality.

Book IV

We have pretty well completed our sketch of Lucretius' theory, but perhaps a few more features should be noted in order to round it off.

(a) Theory of Perception

In Book II, Lucretius mentions that interaction between atoms is at the bottom of all sensation. In Book IV he offers us a theory of how this is supposed to work in the case of visual perception. The cup that is in front of me is constantly giving off films of atoms (presumably each film is one atom thick), which retain the shape of the cup. When I look in the direction of the cup, these films of atoms impinge upon the retina, and as a result, I see the cup.

We are inclined to smile at this primitive attempt to explain the mechanics of visual perception but it is not really all that far removed from our own theory. We would say that it is light waves that come from the cup that cause perception; but since light waves can be thought to be particles of light (photons), we do not find here any serious difference between his theory and ours.

The main difficulty with Lucretius' theory is that, if the films of atoms retain the size of the object, they will be too large to impinge upon the retina. However, we can take care of this difficulty in the following way. Let us assume that when the photons coming from the light source fall on any point of the cup (object), they bounce off in every direction. Since the photons fall on every point of the object that is exposed to the light source, we have a veritable sea of photons. Now, introduce into this sea the modern eye and we have all that is needed for perception to occur. The photons come from every illuminated point on the object (see the following diagram). Some enter through the lens at the front of the eye and form a perfect, though reversed, image on the retina.

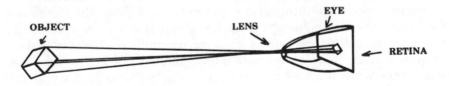

Lucretius thought that visual perception could not be explained unless the cluster of particles retained the shape of the object, but had he or any of the other atomists taken a look at the inside of an eye they would have seen that this postulate is not necessary. Nature was, as is usually the case, more clever than the philosophers!

(b) Dreaming and Imagining

The film theory is also used to explain dreaming and imagining. The films that emanate from objects have a long life. Although they become distorted with time and mixed with other films, their remnants are highly durable. When I am asleep and my guard is, so to speak, down, these films impinge upon my mind. Suppose for example that the film of a man becomes mixed in the right way with the film of a horse and impinges upon my mind during sleep: I will dream of a centaur.

The explanation of imagining follows much the same course. An atom is entirely passive in its movements. It will not move until it is acted upon by another atom. The mind is composed of minute atoms and so cannot actively imagine things. When I imagine a centaur, what happens is that a film of a centaur floating through space impinges upon my mind atoms. The same is true of all thought. I cannot form an idea of anything of my own free will. Any idea I have is the mechanical response to atomic stimulation. Of course, as we have seen, there is an element of indeterminism at work but this does not make it possible for me to work out ideas of my own free will. All that it does is introduce an amount of randomness into my thinking.

(c) Acts of Will

Lucretius then uses the film theory to explain acts of will. Suppose I now decide to walk across the room. I cannot decide to walk across the room until an image of walking impinges upon the mind, for as he puts it, "no one ever initiates any action without the mind first see-ing what it wills. What it forsees is the substance of the image" (*NU*, p. 158). Once an image of walking has impinged upon my mind—atoms, that is to say, jogged them into motion—I find myself deciding and then as a consequence, beginning to walk. Thus, if I want to walk, I must bring it about that an image of walking impinges upon my mind. But, given that my mind is entirely passive, how can I do that? Lucre-tius constructs a fanciful explanation. At any instant there are liter-ally millions of images on the threshold of the mind, waiting to be per-ceived. Included in this group will be the image of walking. So, all that I have to do is make an effort to perceive the image. If I make this effort all the others will pass without effect leaving only this one.

The trouble with this explanation, like so many philosophical ex-planations, is that even if the factual aspects were true, it takes for granted what it sets out to explain. It wants to explain how I come to have an idea of walking. The explanation is that this idea (or, in other words, image), along with many others, is waiting in the wings; I come to have this image by making an effort to perceive it. But, and this is the important point, how can I make an effort to perceive this image unless I already possess an image of what I want to have an image of? And how could I ever come to possess that image?

Furthermore, if I already have an image of the image of walking, then I do not need the image of walking, for in a sense I already have it. So, either Lucretius' explanation takes for granted what it sets out to explain—how I came to have the idea of walking—or it offers no explanation at all. Finally, since in order to walk I must bring it about that an image of walking impinges upon my mind, and since Lucretius offers no acceptable explanation of how I managed to do this, it follows that he offers no acceptable explanation of how I bring myself to walk.

We must not be too hard on Lucretius, for it is very difficult for any philosophical perspective to give an adequate account of free thought. The problem is this: I like to believe that, of my own free will, I decide what I am going to think about. But it would seem that before I could think of, say, a Big Mac hamburger, I would have to have the idea of a Big Mac. And, before I could have idea of a Big Mac, I would have to have an idea of that idea. Thus, it seems I have no control over what I am going to think about, and that thoughts simply occur—determined by some unknown process. Furthermore, if all my actions are determined by my thoughts, and if I have no control over my thoughts, then it follows that I have no real control over my actions. My actions are determined by my thoughts and my thoughts simply occur, determined perhaps by some unknown physiological process in my brain.

(d) Gods

There are two diametrically opposed views of the universe. The first, which might be called the teleological view, is that the universe was created by one or more deities with some goal in mind. Not only is the universe here for a reason but everything in it is here for some purpose or set of purposes. Man, some will argue, exists to serve God, and all the animals and things of this world exist to serve man. Sheep provide wool to make warm clothes, and deposits of iron exist to furnish weapons to kill animals for food. Not only are various objects and animals of the world directed toward this goal but the various organs of man and the animals are indirectly focused toward the same goal. Man and animals have legs so that they can move about, and both have eyes so they can see. This view was propounded by Plato and Aristotle and accepted by most Western thinkers until the rise of modern science in the seventeenth century.

The other world view, which might be called the mechanistic view, is that the universe has always existed; it exists for no purpose, and anything that happens takes place simply as a consequence of what happened before.

There is no doubt that Lucretius held the latter view. As we have seen, for Lucretius the universe is an uncreated, eternal three-dimensional billiard table. On it—or, rather, through it—the billiard balls (atoms) move ceaselessly. They have always been in motion and always will be in motion. If we ask why a particular atom is now moving in a certain direction at a certain velocity, the explanation has to do with what happened in the past. We explain the motion of atom *A* in terms of the motion of atom *B* and so on for ever and ever. There is no rhyme or reason to their motions, nor is there any purpose to the universe and the things in it. Our eyes do not exist so that we may see; we only see because we happen to have eyes.

The puzzle here—and this is why so many people until recently were reluctant to accept such a world view—is that if the furniture of the world just came about almost by blind chance, why are the things of the world as highly organized and structured as they are? For example, how does it come to pass that the eye is structured so that it will let in just the right amount of light and focus on the desired object? Lucretius offers two answers. The first is, given an infinite amount of time, an infinite amount of space, and an infinite number of atoms, it is bound to happen sooner or later that a world just like ours would come into existence. This argument seems unconvincing somehow. If experiments were carried out with monkeys to discover whether given an unlimited amount of time and an unlimited amount of paper and a battery of typewriters, lines of Shakespeare's sonnets might by chance be written, I dare say that the results would be very discouraging. Not only would the monkeys type no lines, but nary a word would be produced!

The second answer offered by Lucretius is much more acceptable. All sorts of beasts emerge from Nature at random. But only those species survive whose members live long enough to reproduce their own kind. What Lucretius is offering here is a primitive natural selection theory. We have eyes mainly because the species that did not have vision fell by the wayside. What is lacking is a detailed account of how natural selection could bring about highly structured species like ourselves. This account had to wait until the arrival of Charles Darwin.

Although Lucretius believed the universe to be something like an uncreated eternal machine, he still claimed that there were gods. Lucretius might just have been paying lip service to the established religion, but even so, he does offer a reason in support of his claim. To have an idea is to have an image (film) impinge upon one's mind. An image must not only have a source but be similar to its source. Since so many diverse cultures have had ideas of gods, deities must exist to be the source of these ideas.

Whether gods exist or not, Lucretius realized that they are not needed to assist in the running of the universe. However, for those who are not impressed with his world view, Lucretius offers independent reasons for saying that the gods play no part in the running of the universe. First of all, no being is capable of ruling, as he puts it, the measureless and the fathomless. Second, we have clear evidence that no divine being controls the universe, for the universe, or at least our corner of it, is filled with so many imperfections. Finally, it is quite certain that we were not created to serve some purpose—such as worshipping the gods—for what pleasure could perfect beings derive from its fulfillment?

Lucretius has touched upon a number of serious problems with which any believer in a monistic or personal God has to deal. We shall examine them more closely in chapter 5, on the existence of God. The main concern focuses on what is sometimes called the problem of evil, which can be stated fairly simply. If the universe was created and is controlled by a being who is all good, all powerful, and all knowing, then how does it come to pass that there is so much pain and suffering, the source of which is such natural phenomena as earthquakes, droughts, and volcanos? A second problem is this: if we were created for some purpose, what could that purpose possibly be? Surely a perfect being does not stand in need of the reassurance that worship and adulation provide. Such a being would be above all that.

NOTES

1. Some people have argued that there could be motion in a full universe, but let us wait until we get to Lucretius before we discuss that problem.

2. We can express this more formally. Given that we may only substitute proper names of pieces of matter for the variable X, what we mean when we say that "Matter is infinitely divisible" is "Any proposition obtained by substituting a proper name for 'X' in 'X is divisible,' is always synthetic and never self-contradictory." The reader might find it easier to understand this point after he has read chapter 3 on logic (see especially p. 138).

3. The reader might find it useful to obtain a copy of R. E. Latham's translation of *On the Nature of the Universe* (Baltimore, Md.: Penguin Classics Series, 1951). All of my references are to this work.

4. *On the Nature of the Universe* was written in verse. I have chosen a prose translation because I think people today find it easier to follow. At that time it was common to dedicate one's poem to a patron, or at least to a would-be patron. We have no reason to believe, however, that Memmius ever acknowledged Lucretius' dedication.

5. Lucretius does not consider frozen water.

6. I shall assume that two atoms are of the same type if they are of the same shape and size.

7. When you think about it you have to agree that Lucretius is on the right track here. How could you sense something unless something came from that object and "touched" one of your organs of perception? The main difference between then and now is that we believe that usually what comes from the object is not a particle but a wave. Sound is transmitted by sound waves and color by light waves.

8. A perfect solid is any three-dimensional enclosed figure where (a) each edge is straight and of the same length; (b) every surface angle is equal to

every other surface angle; and (c) every surface is equal in size and shape to every other surface. The five perfect solids were discovered by Pythagoras—another ancient philosopher! They are: (1) the tetrahedron (pyramid) bounded by four equilateral triangles, (2) the cube, (3) the octahedron, bounded by eight equilateral triangles, (4) the dodecahedron, bounded by twelve pentagons, and (5) the icosahedron, bounded by twenty equilateral triangles. Recently, it has been mathematically proven that there cannot be more than five.

9. The point is also discussed on p. 138, Ch. III.

2

Plato and Socrates

We have seen that Lucretius offered one solution to Parmenides' problem concerning change. If what is real cannot change and the world around us is alive with change, it appears that the world around us is not real. The solution offered by Lucretius is that the real does not change, for the real is constituted by the uncreated atoms that never change. Physical objects change, but they are nothing more than piles, mixtures, or combinations of atoms. On this view, the pen in my hand has no more reality than the pile of gravel in the driveway.

Although atoms do not change their size and shape, they do change their location; and this is a source of difficulty for Lucretius. In order for them to change their location there has to be empty space, and it's difficult to see how there could be such a thing.

Plato (428–348 B.C.) offers a different solution. He was prepared to admit that the things of the world perceived through the senses are, as Heraclitus had pointed out, in constant flux and are not real. However, he did not accept the view that there were unchanging atoms underlying the flux. Plato was not prepared to accept the view that nothing is real. According to Plato and the advocates of this world view, there is a world of unchanging objects that are apprehended, not by the senses, but by the intellect. This world he called the world of Forms. Consider, for example, the claim that $2 + 3 = 5$. What does this equation make a claim about? Well, for one thing, it claims that if two marbles are put in a cup and three more are added, then five marbles will have been put in the cup. No doubt this follows from '$2 + 3 = 5$' but this isn't what it says— or what it's about. Even if there were no physical objects in the world, and so no marbles, this claim would still be true. It seems we have to say that the claim is not about things but about numbers. But what are numbers? We aren't very clear on what numbers are, but we can at least say that they are unchanging and apprehended by the intellect, and not by the senses. They would count as members of Plato's world of Forms.

Take, for example, a circle that someone has drawn on the black-board. One thing that could be said of this circle is that its circumference is equal to two times pi times the radius ($C = 2\pi r$). But this claim wouldn't be accurate. One wouldn't find that the circumference of *this* circle stood in that relationship to its radius. Some microscopic error is bound to have occurred in the drawing of the circle. Well, if '$C = 2\pi r$' does not make an absolutely true statement about this circle, and would not, for the very same reason, make a true statement about any other physical circle, what does it make a true statement about? One is tempted to say that it makes a true statement about the idea of a circle, about something that exists in our minds. Although this answer is attractive it cannot be the correct answer, for '$C = 2\pi r$' would be true even if no one had ever thought of circles; even if there were no people to think of circles. Thus, it looks as though there must be an ideal or perfect circle, and that this statement is about such a circle. The perfect circle and other geometrical shapes count as members of Plato's world of Forms. This world is unchanging, apprehended through the intellect, something about which we make statements such as '$C = 2\pi r$', but we cannot perceive it through our senses. Naturally, our senses can perceive the circle drawn on the board, but this is only a rough approximation of the perfect circle. Our poor illustrations exist, according to Plato, only to remind us of the perfect circle. This is a theme that runs through a great deal of what he says—the things of this world exist in part to remind us of the things of the other world—the world of Forms.

The Forms, however, are not the only things that are real. Plato adopted the view of the Pythagoreans[1] that the soul, or at least its intellectual part, is eternal, unchanging, and therefore real. The soul that occupies a particular human body has occupied many bodies in the past and may occupy many in the future. Those who lead a piggish life will be reincarnated as pigs, but if they live an intellectual life they might slough off this mortal coil and rise to the world of Forms. (The Pythagoreans considered the body to be a sort of prison house from which the soul yearned to be liberated.) One facet of this doctrine was the belief that students already know everything there is to know and that all teachers could do is jog the memory so that students would be reminded of that which they already know.[2]

We shall talk more about the Forms in our discussion of *The Republic*, but for now it might be wise to take a look at Plato himself and the world that surrounded him. Plato was born into an aristocratic family in the city-state of Athens in 428 B.C. At that time Athens was a democracy under the wise and benevolent leadership of Pericles. However, the devastating Peloponnesian Wars broke out in 431 and Pericles died in 429 (the year before Plato's birth). The wars ended with the defeat of Athens at the hands of Sparta and her allies in 404. Plato would have been twenty-four at that time. The Athenians were driven out of their city and forced to tear down its walls. Democracy withered and, under pressure from the Spartans, was replaced by what came to be called the rule of the thirty tyrants in 404. There was counter-revolution in 403 and democracy was soon restored. However, by this time the spark had gone out of Athenian democracy and the people of Athens proved incapable of ruling themselves effectively.

Plato had in his youth planned to enter politics but, owing to the unsettled times, he decided against it. Then in 399 B.C., Socrates, the man who Plato most revered, was tried on the trumped up charge of worshipping false gods and corrupting the young. Socrates pleaded innocence before the Athenians but was found guilty and sentenced to death by drinking hemlock. Plato was so appalled by everything surrounding the trial, especially the death of his dearest friend, that he decided to devote the rest of his life to recording for posterity the discussions that Socrates had had in and around Athens. Plato embarked on a career that led him to write, as far as we know, thirty-six dialogues. The ones he wrote as a young man, for example—the *Apology* and the *Crito*—are believed to be fairly accurate recordings of some of the conversations that Socrates had had. The dialogues that Plato wrote in middle age—for example, most of the *Republic* and the *Symposium*—were expressions of his own thought. Socrates appears in them as the major character, but is only a mouthpiece. The dialogues that belong to Plato's later period—for example, the *Sophist* and the *Timaeus*—are also all Plato's work. Here we find not only that Socrates drops out as the main character but that the conversational or dialectical technique has less and less importance.

In addition to writing many dialogues, Plato also founded the school known as the Academy, which might be considered the world's first university. Aristotle was one of Plato's leading students and he stayed at the Academy for about fifteen years until Plato's death. Aristotle had expected to be made head of the Academy, but the position was given to Plato's nephew Speusippus. In a pique Aristotle went off and founded his own school, the Lyceum. The Academy—amazingly enough—lasted for 900 years (Oxford and the Sorbonne have only lasted for 700 years), while the Lyceum lasted for about 600 years. The Academy was finally closed by the Roman Emperor Justinian in 529 A.D.

SOCRATES

Socrates was an extraordinary person. Born in 470 B.C., the son of a sculptor and a midwife, his first interest was natural science, which paralleled the interests of philosophers like Democritus. After a while, however, Socrates turned to matters of human interest. He wanted to know how to lead a good life and realized that one prerequisite was possessing a knowledge of the various virtues such as justice, courage, and piety. How can we behave justly if we don't know what justice is? He realized that we cannot find out what justice is in the same way that we find out, say, what feldspar is. To find out what feldspar is, we subject it to some sort of chemical analysis. But we obviously can't pick up a piece of justice and examine it! The best way to discover what justice is, Socrates felt, is to enter into a discussion with some friends who might know. First, somebody would say what he thought justice was, then others would criticize his claims; these would then be modified, criticized, and so on. Through this ancient think-tank-process, or dialogue, a picture would emerge of what justice is. This may not seem like a very satisfactory way to proceed but who can suggest a better one?

At his trial, Socrates tells us that a friend of his once asked the Oracle at Delphi to identify the wisest man in the world? (Delphi was the religious center of Greece and the Oracle, as the name implies, was supposedly the spokesperson for the Gods, though in reality the Oracle spoke for the priests.) The Oracle replied that Socrates was the wisest. When the friend informed Socrates of this, Socrates was very puzzled because he didn't think that he was wise at all. He interviewed all sorts of reputedly learned people with the view of showing that the Oracle was mistaken. However, he could not find one who seemed to be at all wise. As a result, he concluded that the reason he was claimed to be the wisest must have been that while all the others thought that they knew something but knew nothing, he knew that he knew nothing. In other words, he knew something they did not know. As a result of all this he began to feel that he had a divine obligation to be a social gadfly, to point out to people that they were operating on the basis of false beliefs.

One of the disappointments about Socrates, it is felt, is that he never came to any conclusion concerning the true nature of concepts like courage and piety. This accusation is, however, a bit harsh. Socrates does leave us in a better conceptual position than when we started. Perhaps he didn't know what bravery was, but he did leave us in a better position to discover it for ourselves. He would have liked to discover what bravery, justice, and so on were, but he was incapable of doing so.

THE SOPHISTS

At the time that Socrates was wandering the streets and marketplaces of Athens and enticing people into philosophical discussion, there emerged a group of people known as the Sophists, who appeared to be doing much the same sort of thing. When living in a city-state that practiced direct democracy, it was useful to be a good speaker. It was then possible to sway the crowds to vote for particular motions and in so doing place friends in high office. Rhetorical powers also helped to win court cases and keep enemies at bay. The people who taught the art of verbal eloquence were the Sophists, an itinerant bunch, going (independently) from town to town and charging, according to Socrates, high fees for their services.

Socrates was disturbed by the Sophists, partly because they charged fees for their lessons and he did not, but more importantly because he felt that they were undermining the moral standards of Athens. In the early days of Athens it was believed that certain things were truly right and certain other things were truly wrong. But the Sophists taught that this was not so: they claimed that morality was based solely on convention and that people were told that specific things were right or wrong in order to get them to behave in certain ways. (We shall see that Thrasymachus, a Sophist who appears in the *Republic*, argues in just this way.) Socrates wanted to show that the Sophists were mistaken. He felt that if a concept—say, justice—could be defined and immediately apprehended as true, then the Sophists would be refuted. Once it was known what justice was, then it would be known that certain acts were truly just. Once it was known that certain acts were truly just, the Sophists could not claim that people only said, or could only say, that these acts were just in order to trick others into doing them. Of course it would still be possible to tell people that these acts were just in order to influence their behavior, but this would no longer be the only possible use for such a claim. It would be possible to tell people that these acts were just because they really were just.

Protagoras

The most famous Sophist was Protagoras (born in 481 B.C.) and his fame, at least today, rests largely on the following statement:

> Of all things man is the measure. Of things that are, that they are, and of things that are not, that they are not.

There are two (obvious) questions to ask about this quotation: What does it mean, and is it true? Presumably "measure" means "arbiter." The meter bar in Paris is the arbiter of the metric length of an object. If the object is fifty centimeters long according to the bar, then it really is fifty centimeters long. Similarly, according to Protagoras, if men believe that snow is white then snow is white, and if men believe that incest is wrong then incest is wrong.

A related problem is, what does Protagoras mean by "men"? Does he mean that incest is wrong, if and only if *all* men (persons) believe that incest is wrong, or does he mean that it is wrong if the *majority* of men believe it is wrong? Or does he mean that if I (alone) believe that incest is wrong, then it is wrong (for me)? We might accept the view that snow is white if everyone sees snow as white, but few would accept the view that to say that snow is white or that incest is wrong is to say no more than "I see snow as white" and "I believe that incest is wrong." And yet, there is fairly good reason to believe that that is what Protagoras means.

Let us move on to the second question. Is it *true* that each person is the final arbiter of "what is and what is not"? Part of the answer depends upon what is being talked about. If a man says that a wine tastes bitter, then no doubt he is making a subjective judgment; he is saying no more than that the wine tastes bitter to him. But if a man says that there is a pink elephant in front of him, then clearly whether there is or is not a pink elephant in front of him is independent of what he thinks is in front of him. He is saying much more than that it seems to him there is a pink elephant in front of him. Concerning such matters, it is hard to see how man, in any sense, could be the measure.

Antiphon

Although Protogoras was the most famous Sophist, Antiphon was perhaps the most interesting. According to Antiphon, there were two sets of laws competing for the obedience of men. On the one hand, there were the laws of the community, and, on the other hand, there were the natural laws. The laws of the community were man-made and arbitrary, while the natural laws were rooted in the nature of man. The most significant difference between them is that if a civil law is broken, a person might escape detection and hence punishment; whereas if a natural law is broken, that is, something is done contrary to human nature, then Mother Nature would always find out and punish the offender.

Very often there is a conflict between the two types of law. Suppose, for example, that a hungry, weak, and unemployed person is presented with the opportunity to steal some nourishing food from a store. If he breaks the civil law and steals from the store, he may be caught and punished, but then again he may not. On the other hand, if he breaks the natural law and doesn't give himself enough to eat, he can rest assured that Mother Nature will punish him through hunger pangs, a feeling of weakness, and perhaps disease.

What should be done in such a situation? The answer, according to Antiphon, is obvious: The rational man will always act so as to avoid punishment, and, as a rule, he will act on the natural law and not the civil law. Or as Antiphon puts it,

In the presence of witnesses, he (the rational man) holds the laws of the city in high esteem and in the absence of witnesses, when he is alone those of nature.

We shall talk more about Antiphon in chapter 7 on morality, but in the meantime the following points are offered. (a) Nature is not a person who lays down laws and punishes people who break them. The most that can be said is that we know that if we don't eat (for example) then we will suffer. We can't say that if we don't eat we shall be punished. (b) Even though it is rational (in a sense) to avoid pain and suffering, and even though the certainty of suffering is greater if we go against nature than if we break the civil law, it doesn't follow that when there is a conflict with the civil law, it is therefore, always rational (in this sense of rational) to act in accordance with nature. We have to take into account the probability of being caught and the severity of the suffering. If in our example the probability of being caught stealing, multiplied by the severity of the punishment, gives a higher value than the value given by the amount of suffering that not eating would bring in its wake, then it would be rational to refrain from stealing.

Socrates had a formidable job on his hands to show that the Sophists were mistaken and that such acts as stealing (even when it is to one's advantage), which conventional morality believed to be wrong, really were wrong. However, this is just the sort of thing that Socrates attempts to do in the *Republic*. In the first part, Socrates tries to show that the arch-Sophist Thrasymachus is mistaken to claim that morality is a put up job; Socrates wants to show that it really is rational to behave morally (e.g., refrain from stealing). Socrates is not very successful in his efforts. In the rest of the *Republic*, Plato takes up where Socrates left off and strives to show what justice is, and also to argue that it is rational to behave morally.

The first part is believed by many to be a fairly accurate record of the discussions that Socrates had had on justice. However, in the rest of the *Republic* Socrates is only a protagonist for Plato. When Socrates says something, we can be certain that it is Plato speaking. The first part of the dialogue was written when Plato was quite young. But the rest of the *Republic* belongs to Plato's middle period. One can't but suspect that Plato, through Socrates, attempted in the first part to show what justice is and that it is rational to be just, realized that he had failed on both accounts, put the manuscript away, and then at a later date, believing he had solved both problems, got the manuscript·out and carried on from where he had left off.

THE REPUBLIC

Introduction

One finds in the *Republic* that there are wheels within wheels; it's not
a bad idea to have a good blue print or map before beginning. The
main goals of the *Republic* are to show what justice is and that it is
in one's interest to be just. Justice is shown, to Plato's satisfaction, to
be a state of the soul (chapter XIV), but it's not until much later (chapter XXXIV) that Plato manages to "prove" that it is in one's interest
to be just.

In order to show that justice is a condition of the soul, Plato com-
pares the soul to the state. He feels that it will be easier to discover
the way in which justice exists in the soul if we can first locate it in
something analogous but much larger. The investigation of the place
of justice in the state leads to a discussion of what the perfect state
would be like, and this leads quite naturally to a discussion of the rulers
of the ideal state. Plato felt, and quite properly, that the education of
the rulers was very important. However, in order to rule properly it is
imperative that the rulers know what goodness and justice are. After
all, how can a ruler lay down a just law if he doesn't know what justice
is? Thus in the *Republic* we are presented with justice on two levels:
justice as it exists in the state and the soul, and the existence of justice
as an ultimate Form to be studied by actual and prospective rulers.
Presumably, justice as it exists in the state and in the soul is a reflection of the Form of Justice. Plato never tells us what Justice (the Form)
ultimately is. That is to say, he never tells us what is the real definition of justice.

One puzzle might be worth taking a look at before we begin. Plato
uses the dialectical technique in determining what justice (in the soul
and in the state) is. Socrates asks "What is justice?" Someone answers
"Justice is *x*." Someone then says that it can't be *x*, because there are
some acts which are *x* but not just. At this point, *x* is rejected, and
someone says that he thinks that justice is *y*. The procedure repeats
itself and they move on to some other definition.

Now the puzzle is this: How can people be in a position to reject
x, and so on, if they don't know what justice is? Rejection of *x* as the
definition of justice presupposes that one already knows what justice
is; but if one already knows what justice is, then one doesn't need a
definition.

The answer that Plato would give to this question is that we already do know what justice is. Our souls, according to Plato, are fully
immortal. They have always been in existence and always will be.[3] At
some time prior to our birth, we were acquainted with the Forms. As
a result we already know what justice is. But our memories are weak;

the reason for entering into a dialogue on justice is to jog our memories so we will recall what justice is.

Although this answer will do for Plato, it will hardly do for us. We don't accept that coming to know is just a matter of coming to remember what we once knew but have now forgotten. The puzzle still remains: How can we say that justice is not x if we don't know what justice is? Perhaps the answer is that we already know what justice is because we learned it when we learned how to speak. That is to say, we learned what justice is when we learned the language in which justice is discussed. However, even though we know how to employ the word 'justice', we have no clear idea of the concept. Our grasp of justice is good enough to say what justice is not, but not good enough to say precisely what justice is. Through a process of eliminating what justice is not we shall become clearer on what justice is.

For those who are interested, Plato's dialogue titled the *Meno* offers an intriguing "proof" that we already know all sorts of things of which we have no experience. Socrates wants to show that Meno's ignorant but intelligent slave boy already knows how to construct a square twice the size of a given square. Using a stick, Socrates draws on the sand with a stick a square similar to the following:

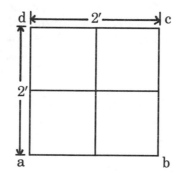

and asks the slave boy to draw one twice as large. The slave boy draws one like this:

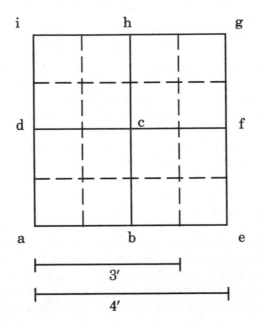

Socrates points out that this square is four times as large. (This is the first move in using the dialectic technique: show that the person's unreflective beliefs are mistaken.) The slave boy says "I know—construct it on a base that is three feet long." Socrates then points out that this answer also will not do, for this will give a square that is still too large. We want one that will contain eight squares, but this one contains nine. (This is the second stage in the dialectic technique. The subject must be in a state of bewilderment before he is capable of recalling the correct answer.) Socrates now invites the slave boy to consider the original square and at the same time he draws a line from d to b. He asks the slave boy how large is bcd of $abcd$ and the boy answers one-half. So Socrates asks how many times larger than bcd would be a figure twice as large as $abcd$? And the boy answers four times. "So," says Socrates "can you draw a figure four times as big as bcd?" "Yes!" says the slave boy, and draws $bfhd$.

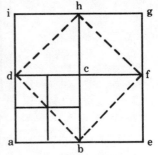

   The question that the reader must ask himself is this: If the boy didn't recall how to draw the required square, then how did he come to know how to draw the required square? Socrates didn't show him how, but he did drop hints (reminders).

Let us turn now to Part I of the *Republic*. In what follows I shall not attempt to give an outline, nor shall I attempt to clarify its more obscure parts. Instead I will concentrate on those aspects that are of philosophical and social interest. I shall also ignore Part VI.

Part I

The Republic[4] opens after a bit of theatrical stage setting with a discussion between Socrates; Cephalus, a retired wealthy merchant; his sons Polemarchus, Lysias, and Euthydemus; Plato's elder brothers Glaucon and Adeimantus; and Thrasymachus, the notorious Sophist. After a bit of banter about the virtues of age, Socrates asks Cephalus what he thinks justice is, whereupon Cephalus states that justice consists in telling the truth and returning objects that one has borrowed. Socrates objects that if this is what justice is then it would be just to return a weapon to a person who had become insane. At this point, Cephalus feels that the conversation has become too abstract for him and slips off on a pretext. Polemarchus takes over from his father and claims that what his father meant to say is that justice consists in giving each man his due, which means helping one's friends and harming one's enemies. Thus a borrowed weapon should not be returned to the friend who had become insane since this could hardly be helping him. The claim that it is just to harm one's enemies may strike the reader as rather unjust, but it must be remembered that this was an accepted view of justice in Athens at that time. Also it must be remembered that the attitude of people toward life in general has changed enormously since the fourth century B.C.— a change that is largely owing to people like Socrates. Perhaps, after all, there is moral progress.[5]

Socrates then asks Polemarchus if he meant to say that it was just to help only those friends who really are good or only those friends who are *believed* to be good, and vice versa.[6] Polemarchus answers that it must be only just to help those friends who are really good and harm those enemies who really are bad; otherwise one could be helping some people who are bad and harming some people who are good. But now Socrates asks a radical question for his time: Can it ever be just to harm anyone? He points out that it is never the job of a riding instructor to make a poor rider a poorer rider, so how can it ever be the job of a just man to harm an unjust man, and in so doing make him even less just? Polemarchus accepts the analogy, thereby agreeing that to define the just as helping those friends who are really good and harming those who are really bad has to be rejected.

There are two comments that should be made here. First of all, we have to be very careful about questions like "Should we do what is right or what appears to be right?" Obviously we can only do what appears to be right, because often we don't know what really is right. At the same time, we don't do what appears to be right because it's a good appearance. A confidence trickster may say to his confederates that they ought to do what appears (to others) to be right. But we (and most moral people) do what appears to be right because we take it to be right. The same point can be made about the question "Is it just to do what is good or what is believed to be good?" Again, if we are trying to be just, we are limited to what we believe to be good; but we don't do what we believe to be good because we believe it to be good. We do it for its goodness and not because of our beliefs.

The second comment is that even though people like the riding instructor or a school teacher have clear vocations, each has or can have pupils, and it's the job of each to make their pupils better at what they do. It's not at all clear that being a just man is a vocation in the same sense. What is the vocation of the just man, and who are his pupils? The analogy is very tenuous. More will be said about this later.

At this point Thrasymachus breaks into the conversation and says that he has had enough of this fooling around and that it's high time Socrates gave his definition of justice. However, the canny Socrates outmaneuvers Thrasymachus and talks him into giving his view of justice. Thrasymachus says that justice is whatever is in the interest of the stronger, and then goes on to say that by the stronger he means the rulers. Now it's not at all clear what Thrasymachus means here. One of the things that makes Plato's writing so interesting is that remarks like this are richly ambiguous. They can be taken in a number of different ways. Each gives us something to think about. I shall offer three different interpretations. No doubt there are more, but these will do for our purpose.

(a) Thrasymachus is offering a philosophical theory of politics that runs something like this: Before it makes sense to say of an act that it is just or unjust, right or wrong, there must be laws or rules. If the act is in accordance with one of the laws or rules, it will be just or right. If it's not then it will be unjust or wrong. Now although a tyrant will enact laws in his own interest, a democracy will enact laws that are in the interest of the people. Thus, in a democracy at least, stealing will be unjust because it will not be in accordance with the laws of the land, which have been enacted to maximize the welfare of the community. But in a state of nature such an act, if possible, will be neither just nor unjust. In order for it to be unjust there would have to be a rule or law forbidding it. When we interpret Thrasymachus in this way we get a theory that is fairly close to the moral theory of rule utilitarianism. More will be said about this theory later in the chapter on moral philosophy.

(b) Thrasymachus is not offering us a philosophical theory. Actually, he is only doing what he has been asked to do and that is, give us a definition of "justice." The word "just" simply means no more and certainly no less than "what is in the interest of the stronger party." Thrasymachus offers us some evidence that this is what we mean by "just." If we examine different sorts of states, we will find that all those acts that are called "just" turn out to be acts in accordance with rules that work to the advantage of the ruling class. So it must be the case that we all do agree that this is what "just" means.

(c) On a third interpretation, Thrasymachus is not offering us a theory or definition of justice at all. What he is doing is showing us that the word "justice" is really meaningless, that it's simply a trick word used by ruthless people to get others to behave in certain ways. If I tell a child that he ought to go to bed because it would be naughty not to go to bed, I use the word "naughty" to trick him into going to bed. Advertisements in magazines and on television use a lot of words of this type. On this view, according to Thrasymachus, the rulers pass certain laws that they know to be to their advantage. They call these statutes "just" and the acts in accordance with them "just" in order to trick people into obeying them. Ordinary people are tricked (brainwashed?) into believing that these laws are just, and out of their noble desire to do what is just they act in accordance with them.

Before we decide which interpretation, if any, is correct, let's take a look at Socrates' reply to Thrasymachus. Socrates asks him if it is just to obey a law that the rulers have laid down thinking it to be in their (the rulers') interest but in fact it is not? Thrasymachus replies that obeying such a law would still be the just thing to do. Socrates then points out that in this situation it would be just to do, contrary to the definition, what is not in the interest of the stronger, because it has been shown not to be in their interest.

An obvious way out of this difficulty is for Thrasymachus to redefine "justice" as whatever the stronger *believes* to be in his own interest. However, Thrasymachus does not offer such a counter argument. Instead, he says that a ruler *qua* ruler doesn't make mistakes. When a person who happens to be a ruler makes a mistake, he is not acting as a ruler. Socrates then points out that just as a shepherd *qua* shepherd works for the good of the flock, so a ruler *qua* ruler works for the good of his subjects and not in his own interest. Acting as a ruler in the true sense of that term, he will not create laws that are in his interest. Instead he will create laws that are in the interest of the people.

Thrasymachus quite rightly becomes annoyed with Socrates. He points out that a shepherd ultimately works only in his own interest. He takes care of sheep so that he can sell them at a good price. In the same way the ruler "fattens" up his subjects so he can fleece them through taxing more and more money out of them.

Having made this point, Thrasymachus goes on to say something that looks to be inconsistent with every one of our three interpretations.

He says that if a person is caught using force or fraud to plunder the goods of others on a small scale, he is punished and disgraced. But if he behaves unjustly on a large scale so that along with taking all the property of his countrymen he also enslaves them, people will call him the happiest of men and bless him.[7]

In other words, behaving unjustly on a grand scale will pay off. Now, when Thrasymachus previously said that justice was in the interest of the stronger, he had in mind acts that were in accordance with laws that were in the interest of the rulers. Such acts were just acts. But now when he says that injustice on a grand scale pays, what he has in mind is the laying down of those very laws—the laws that are in the interest of the rulers. He wants to say that the act of laying down such a law is an unjust act. But if the act of laying down such a law is unjust and the law itself is also unjust, it could hardly be argued that it is just to act in accordance with the law and unjust not to do so.

We can see from this that Thrasymachus held a very conventional view of the nature of justice. He really believed that to cheat or to be unfair to other people on any scale is to act unjustly. But if this is his real view of the nature of justice, what are we to say about his previous claim that just acts are those performed in the interest of the rulers? One thing we might do is argue that Thrasymachus didn't really mean to define just acts as acts in the interest of the stronger. All that he meant to do was to say that the rulers *call* laws that are in their interest, and acts that are in accordance with those laws, "just" in order to trick simple-minded people into obeying unjust laws. If this is correct then it looks as though we cannot accept any of the previous interpretations. We can, however, accept something similar to (c). Thrasymachus really does believe that the word "just" has meaning, and that it means roughly what the ordinary person thinks it means. However, and this is Thrasymachus' point, the word can (and is) misused. Unjust rulers, tyrants and the like *call* the laws that they enact "just" in order to trick people into acting in accordance with them. In other words, clever and unscrupulous rulers misuse words in order to trick people into acting in the interest of the stronger.

My own view is that although this is part of what Thrasymachus was doing, it is by no means all that he intended. I suspect that Thrasymachus also wanted to claim that "justice" really means what is in the interest of the stronger. But if this is what he wanted to claim, then we have to explain how Thrasymachus (and so Plato) could be guilty of such a glaring inconsistency. How could Plato have Thrasymachus saying both that tyrants acted unjustly in laying down laws that were in their interest, and that acting justly meant acting in accordance with these unjust laws? The explanation of how Plato could have made such an error will have to wait until chapter 3 when we take up the topic of logic.

To summarize: Thrasymachus appears to want to claim that acts in accordance with laws that are in the interest of the rulers are just acts. He also wants to claim that the rulers act unjustly in enacting such laws. But if the rulers act unjustly in enacting such laws, it's hard to see how such laws and acts that are in accordance with them could be just. A way out of this difficulty is to take Thrasymachus not as saying that these laws really are just and that it really is just to act in accordance with them, but rather that the rulers *call* them just in order to get the simple-minded citizens to obey them. Unfortunately, if we look at what Thrasymachus actually says, it's not clear that we can interpret him in this way.

It looks as though we are back where we started. Socrates still hasn't discovered what justice is or whether it pays. In the rest of Book I, Socrates attempts to show that justice rather than injustice pays, but his conclusion is unconvincing, partly because he hasn't discovered to his satisfaction what justice is and partly because his arguments are implausible. His most impressive argument runs something like this: one finds that a great number of things in this world have a function. The function of a thing is either whatever it does best or whatever it can do better than anything else. For example, the function of the eye is to see and the function of a knife is to cut. Now a virtue or excellence (according to Socrates) is a power that enables a thing to perform its function well. The virtue of the eye is the power of sight, and the virtue of the knife is its sharpness. The power of sight will enable the eye to see well; the sharpness of the knife will enable it to cut well. A thing can have more than one virtue.

Next it is argued that the function of the soul is to enable an organism to live. The Greeks considered what they called "the soul" to be a living principle—that which gave life to what had life. A virtue of the soul would be whatever enabled the soul to live well—that is, to be happy. Now since justice is a virtue, it follows that the just man will be happier than the unjust man. In other words, it is justice and not injustice that pays.

Where this argument goes wrong is that it hasn't been shown yet that justice *is* a virtue. In order to show that justice is a virtue it would have to be shown that justice helps the soul to live well—that it brings happiness. But this is the very point that Socrates is trying to prove.

There are a couple of other points that should be made about this argument. No doubt knives were created to cut. Their function was, in a sense, prior to their existence. But it's not certain that we were given eyes so that we could see. It could well be that eyes simply evolved. Perhaps we see, as Lucretius would put it, because we have eyes, rather than having sight given to us by some higher being. Still, it might be argued that, relative to the organism as a whole, eyes do have a function. We can only understand what an eye or an ear is by understanding its function relative to the organism. But then it couldn't be argued that the organism as a whole has a function, because if it had just evolved it could only have function relative to a larger organism. Each ant in the ant hill may have a function relative to the anthill, but it doesn't follow from this that the anthill has a function.

Still, it might be argued that in some obscure sense it is the function of the soul to enable the organism to live well and that living well involves happiness. But even so, it still doesn't follow, as we have seen, that justice is a virtue. In order to show that justice is a virtue it would have to first be shown that it enables the soul to cause the organism to live well, and this has not been done.

Part II

Neither Socrates nor Thrasymachus are happy with the conclusion reached at the end of Part I. Therefore, Part II begins with a recasting by Glaucon of Thrasymachus' argument. This is a step in the right direction. It's very difficult to deal with a thesis until it is made clear.

Glaucon begins by saying that there are three types of goods in this world: those we value for themselves, such as pleasant amusements; those we value for themselves and for their consequences, such as knowledge and health; and, finally, goods that are unpleasant in themselves and are valued only for their consequences, such as callisthenics. He says that he would like Socrates to show that justice belongs to the second class, and points out that most people believe it belongs to the third class—a thing practiced only grudgingly and for the sake of its consequences.

To elaborate this point, Glaucon goes on to mention some of the things that people say about justice. First of all, it is said that the best state for a person to be in is one in which he is able to do harm to others without them being able to do harm him. (Again we see a hint of the difference between their common morality and that of the just man.) The worst state to be in is for others to be able to harm him while he is unable to harm them. Now, because of the vulnerability of people, most desire to be in the first category than in the second. As a result, each man makes a compact with the others not to do harm to them on condition that they do no harm to him. In this way, each man removes the risk of landing in the second category, though he also deprives himself of the opportunity of being in the first category. Laws were enacted and adherence to them was called just. As a result of this, it is clear that justice (obedience to these laws) is practiced reluctantly and only for its consequences. It is also said, according to Glaucon, that if any person had the power to be in the first category, he would not enter into such a compact and would be considered a fool if he did.

Presumably, though this is not said, if a person who had entered the compact also had the ability, through stealth, to break the compact, then he would be a fool not to do so. In other words, it was felt that most people would agree with Antiphon when he said that a man "in the presence of witnesses will hold the laws of the city in high esteem, and in the absence of witnesses, when he is alone, those of nature."

To drive home the point that justice, like callisthenics, is practiced reluctantly and goes, so to speak, against the grain, Glaucon invites us to consider how a person would behave if he found himself invulnerable to others. He cites the fable of a person called Gyges who discovered a ring that could make himself invisible. What did Gyges do? He made full use of this new power by seducing the local queen, murdering the king, and declaring himself king. According to Glaucon, people say that anybody—just or unjust—would behave in just the same way if he gained the power of Gyges.

Finally, according to Glaucon, if we compare the paradigmatically unjust man—one who is unjust but appears to all to be just—with the paradigmatically just man—one who is believed to be unjust but is really just—there is no doubt who is the happier. The unjust man who appears just will hold high offices, marry into the best of families and take part in business dealings that are highly profitable. Under his cloak of respectability, he is an out and out crook. The just man who appears unjust, on the other hand, will be thrown in prison, tortured, and eventually murdered. Glaucon then points out to Socrates that if he is going to show that justice pays, he will have to show that the just man who is tortured in prison is really happier than the other man who is respected by all and makes significant sums of money hand over fist.

Adeimantus now takes up the case of Thrasymachus. He claims that the main thesis of the moral skeptic's argument has yet to be expounded. His first point is that when parents recommend to their children that a just life be led, they only recommend that their children lead a just life because of the reputation and other benefits that it brings in its wake. The parents are not really commending justice itself but only the benefits it brings. The second point is that when people praise others for being just, what they are praising is not justice itself but its outward manifestations. Thus it would appear that all people agree that the best sort of life is the life of a man who appears to be just while being truly unjust. That is to say, the life of the paradigmatically unjust man.

Adeimantus' argument contains a truth but that truth harbors a serious error that can also be found in Glaucon's presentation. Adeimantus is quite correct when he says that parents often encourage their children to be just in order to receive the consequences that such a life will bring—at least the consequences of keeping out of jail. But it is doubtful if most parents *only* recommend that their children lead just lives for that reason. Most parents, I suspect, also recommend that their offspring lead just lives because they think that justice in itself is of value. It is doubtful if many parents would commend the life of Glaucon's paradigmatically unjust man. Furthermore, when people praise others for leading what appear to be just lives, it's not the appearance of justice that is being praised. I may praise a scoundrel for leading a just life because I falsely conclude from his behavior that he is leading a just life; but it doesn't follow from this that what I am praising is the appearance of justice. I cease to praise him once I come to know that the man is a fraud. Indeed, I may condemn him for appearing to be leading a just life when he is not. Of course, it is possible to praise a person for appearing to lead a just life. One confidence trickster may praise another such trickster for putting on a skillful act. But ordinarily when people praise others for leading just lives, they are praising what they take to be justice and not the appearance of justice.

This point has a bearing on what both Adeimantus and Glaucon ask of Socrates. Adeimantus concludes by saying that Socrates must show that one is better off being just but appearing unjust than one who is being unjust but appears just. If Socrates fails in his attempts, then it shall be claimed that he is praising nothing more than the appearance of justice and recommending that we do wrong if we can do so without being found out. In the same vein, as we have seen, Glaucon claims that in order for Socrates to show that justice pays, he must show that the just man who appears unjust is happier than the unjust man who appears just. As he puts it, concerning the just man, "There must, indeed, be no such seeming: for if his character were apparent his reputation would bring him honors and rewards, and we would not know whether it was for their sake that he was being just or for justice's sake alone" (*Republic*, p. 361).

Again, no doubt each has a point. Socrates must be very careful to show that it is justice itself that brings happiness and not the rewards that are heaped upon the person who is believed to lead the just life. In order to achieve this it is not necessary for him to show that the just man who unfortunately appears to be unjust is in fact the happier. All he has to show is that the just man who appears to be neither just nor unjust is the happier (and this we find later on is all that Socrates does attempt to do). Furthermore, as we have seen, even if Socrates were to praise the just man who was believed to be just, it would not follow that Socrates could be taken as praising the appearance of justice or, again, recommending that we do wrong without being found out. If Socrates praises the man who is believed to be just, it is obvious that this man is praised for being just and not for appearing to be just.

Before we continue there are a couple of comments that should be made about the skeptical arguments of Glaucon and Adeimantus. It will be recalled that Glaucon called upon Socrates to show that justice belonged to the second category—goods valued for themselves as well as for their consequences. But it's difficult to see how Socrates could be expected to do this for he has already declared that one of his main intentions is to show that justice pays—that the just man is happier than the unjust man. But if justice is to be valued for the happiness it brings, then surely it is to be valued for at least one of its consequences and not for itself. Fortunately, this is not a very serious difficulty. When Socrates talks about consequences, what he has in mind are what might be called external consequences—such things as large houses and high public office. Therefore, when he is called upon to show that justice is to be valued for itself as well as for its consequences, he is being asked to show that it is to be valued for its intrinsic consequences—like the peace of mind it can provide.

The second comment is that Glaucon's social contract theory is not quite as scandalous as it first appears. He claims that, according to the contract theory, morality came into existence and is based solely on the contract—"they began to make laws and covenants with one another; and whatever the law prescribed they called lawful and right. That is what justice is and how it came into existence. . ." (*Republic*, p. 359). But he forgets that prior to the contract a person must be under a moral obligation to keep his promises. Thus it couldn't be that *all* of morality was based upon a contract. If the obligation to keep promises was not prior to the contract, then it would have been impossible for the contractors to place themselves under an obligation not to harm one another. So at least one moral rule must have existed prior to the contract.

Socrates now has his work cut out for him. In spite of the difficulties found in the skeptical arguments of Thrasymachus, Glaucon, and Adeimantus, their views point to the necessity for Socrates to show that there really is such a thing as justice (and also morality), what justice is, and that the just man—regardless of the rewards—is intrinsically happier than the unjust man.

Socrates begins with an attempt to demonstrate what justice is. After all, it's difficult to support the claim that justice brings happiness if justice is never defined. He decides that it would be wiser to attempt to locate justice in the state (Plato has in mind a city-state) before locating it in the person. He reasons that a state is very much like a person, only larger. Once justice has been located in the state, it will be a simple matter to go on and locate it in the person.

Socrates will want to argue that a state has different functional parts and that justice has something to do with the relation between them. In order to show what the parts of the state are, Socrates gives us a "likely account" of how states came into existence. Most states result from the benefits to be gained by a division of labor. Better that you make shoes and I grow grain than that each of us makes shoes and grows grain, especially if one of us is better at making shoes and one of us is better at growing grain. Also, when you and I take our produce to market, it's better that there be someone (shopkeepers) to take over the task of selling the produce than that each of us stand around all day while the fields and lasts lie unattended.

Owing to a division of labor, those who belong to a state will become wealthier than those who do not. As a result, a state and its citizens will attract assaults from those who are not members of any state. If any state becomes wealthier than its neighbors, the surrounding states will also be tempted to attack it. In order to keep the non-members of states and poorer states at bay, it will be necessary to have an army. However, one of the great fears about possessing an army, as the owners of vicious dogs (and also the citizens of Spain and Argentina) know only too well, is that the army may turn on the people and, so to speak, bite the hand that feeds it. In order to insure that this does not happen, it will be necessary, according to Plato, that the guards are not allowed to own any property. Plato felt that if the guards were allowed to have property they would be tempted to rob the citizens. Furthermore, since property seems to go hand in hand with wives and families, the guards will also not be permitted to marry and have children. At the same time, it would be unfortunate if members of the guardian class were not allowed to breed. As a result, they will live in barracks, mating from time to time with their common wives. The infants will be taken from the mothers at birth and raised in a common nursery. It will be impossible for either the mothers or the fathers to identify their offspring.

We are inclined to find Plato's measures to be rather harsh, but it is hard to think of a better way to deal with the problem of conflicting loyalties. Can a general be expected to always put his country before his family? If he has no family and no possessions, the problem does not arise. Or consider the Labour politician in Britain. He may well believe that the traditional public schools are partly responsible for the class system that exists, and that the class system is detrimental to the unity and prosperity of the country. As a result, he will most likely come to believe that they ought to be shut down. But he may also believe that they give his children a better chance of success. Since he wants only the best for his children, he will be inclined to enroll them. But if he is inclined to enroll them, he can hardly want the schools shut down.

In addition to military protection, it will be necessary to have rulers. Here, as in the case of soldiers, it's important that they have the welfare of the state and its citizens and not their personal welfare at heart. Rulers will set the policy and enact the laws required to effect the policy. The rulers, one would think, could come directly from the citizenship at large, but Plato decides that they should come from the military class. Thus, for the same reasons, they are not allowed to have property or families.

The education of soldiers and those who go on to be rulers is, according to Plato, very important. The soldiers must be brought up to be courageous and to obey their superiors. The rulers must be taught wisdom. How can they be expected to pass wise laws if they are not wise themselves?

So, according to Plato, any worthwhile state will consist of three classes: (a) the productive class, which will consist of laborers, farmers, craftsmen, merchants, and perhaps bankers; (b) the rulers; and (c) the soldiers and other guards, who, since they will be under direct control of the rulers, are to be called the auxiliaries.

We are now in a position to locate the traditional Greek virtues of wisdom, courage, temperance, and justice in the state. Wisdom, as one might expect, is to be found in the rulers. It is a virtue that would enable them to rule effectively. Courage resides in the auxiliaries. The productive class is not given a virtue. It's surprising that Plato did not give them the virtues of industry and thrift. The other two virtues of temperance and justice are to be found not in any class of the state but in the way the classes are related. Temperance consists largely in the acceptance by the members of the productive class of the ruling class's right to rule; justice, at least at a superficial level, will consist in doing what one does best. Cobblers, whose aptitude lies in making shoes, will stick to their craft and not try their hand at being warriors or rulers, and warriors will not try their hand at ruling or cobbling.

The reader may feel a bit cheated at this point. One expects justice to turn out to be more than minding one's own business—and of course it is. The rulers can hardly be expected to pass just laws if they don't know what justice is. So justice must mean more than the rulers' right to enact laws. Plato tells us that justice, as well as goodness, is something different. If we had time to take "the long way around," then he could let us know what justice really is. So we don't really know what justice is, but we do know, according to Plato, how it manifests itself in the state.

It should also be noted that the Greeks were fascinated by harmony in a way that we are not. There were opposites to be found in nature, in the state, and in the human personality. In nature there was night and day, chaos and reason; in the state there was the wisdom of the rulers and the passions of the mob; in the person there was reason and emotion. Just as for a violin to exist as a musical instrument there has to be (a) a conflict between the pull of the body of the violin and the pull of the strings and (b) a harmony in tension between them, so it was felt—and this is expressed in a great deal of Greek mythology— that in order for the natural world to exist there has to be a conflict and a harmony in tension between such things as night and day, chaos and reason. Similarly, in order for the state to exist as a state and not as a disorganized mass of people, there has to be conflict and harmony of tautness between its conflicting parts. Finally, as we shall see when we go on to talk about the personality, according to Plato, in order for there to be a structured personality or soul, there has to be a conflict and a harmony of tautness between conflicting parts.

Having located justice in the state, Socrates moves on to locate it in the person. He argues that the soul has three elements analogous to the three parts of the state, and that the four virtues manifest themselves in the elements of the soul in much the same way as they manifest themselves in the parts of the state. His first goal is to show that the soul consists of three parts or elements. Plato offers us a high-powered but rather superfluous argument, since, for his purposes, all he must show is that there are different dimensions to the human personality.

Plato's argument is based on the principle that the same unitary thing cannot be moved in two opposite ways at the same time. This can be called the principle of potential conflict. If something is moved or does move in two opposite ways at the same time, then it is not really one thing. It's not a unitary thing but a complex of parts. For example, the possibility of a man's torso remaining still while his arms move about is explained by his having parts. Plato wants to argue that this principle applies to the human personality as well as to physical objects. If a person really wants to drink and not to drink at the same time, this must be because the person consists of two parts, one that wants to drink and the other that does not.

Plato now attempts to show, on the basis of this principle, that the soul consists of three parts. We notice that sometimes a person will have a desire to drink but knowing that drinking will do him no good, will wish to refrain from wine. Thus the same person will want to drink and desire to refrain from it. But this is only possible if the soul consists of two parts. We know that the source of the wish to refrain from drinking is the reflective, rational part of the soul, and that the source of the urge to drink is the irrational, appetitive part of the soul. We come therefore to know what these parts are and that they are distinct.

As in the case of the state, Plato goes on to argue that there is a third distinct part of the soul. We notice that sometimes we have a desire to look at a gory car accident or the execution of a criminal, and at the same time we feel disgusted with ourselves for wanting to do so. In cases of this sort we have both a willingness to look and a willingness to not look; the source of each must be a different part of the soul. The source of our desire to look is the appetitive part; the source of the disgust—our willingness to not look—is the spirited part.

Having distinguished the rational part from the appetitive part and the appetitive part from the spirited part, it is now necessary for Plato to distinguish the rational part from the spirited part. If he doesn't do so, then we will have no reason to believe that the spirited part is not the rational part in disguise. This he now proceeds to do. We notice that infants are born with spirited feelings. They become furious when they are not given the bottle or the breast, but they are not rational. Therefore the spirited part is distinct from the rational part as well as from the appetitive part.

Besides being unnecessary, the main problem with Plato's argument is that, even if the principle of potential conflict applies by analogy to the human personality as well as to the physical, it's not at all clear that it applies to the physical world. If I have a block of steel and I place it between two magnets, can I not say that the very same object is being moved in the sense of being attracted in opposite directions at the same time? Is not the moon sometimes attracted in opposite directions by the Sun and the Earth? But even if we accept that the principle is valid for the physical world, it does not follow that it also applies to the human personality. First of all, conflicting desires are a pervasive and commonplace phenomenon. We often speak of people having conflicting desires. I would like to spend my Sunday afternoon skiing, but also watching a football game on television; I know that I cannot do both. I may have a desire to drink and also a desire to remain in good health, and I know that if I drink I will not remain in good health. Again, I have conflicting desires.

Furthermore, if we accepted that every time there was a potential conflict there was also another part of the soul, then since there is no limit to the number of conflicts that can break out, there is no limit to the number of sub-parts to the soul. This proliferation is not just confined to the appetitive part; it also breaks out in the spirited part. Suppose, for example, I become angry with someone I respect. Am I to say that my spirited part consists of two parts—the part responsible for anger and the part responsible for respect? I could also become disgusted with myself for becoming angry with someone I respect—and so on.

One of the sources of Plato's adoption of this inept principle may be a failure to distinguish opposites from contradictories. An object cannot have contradictory properties but it doesn't follow from this that it cannot have opposite properties. For example, a dish of food cannot taste sweet and not taste sweet at the same time, but it doesn't follow from this that a dish cannot taste sweet and sour at the same time, as those who frequent Chinese restaurants know only too well. Simply because it is logically impossible for an iron block to be magnetically attracted to the left and not magnetically attracted to the left at the same time, it doesn't follow that an object cannot be attracted to the left and to the right at the same time. For, as we have seen, an object can be attracted in opposite directions at the same time. Similarly, just because a person is unable simultaneously to desire to drink and not desire to drink, that the very same person can simultaneously desire to drink and desire to refrain from drinking.[8]

Even though Plato's argument is invalid, and we have no reason to think that each person is a number of different persons stitched up in the same skin, he seems to be right in saying that the human personality has different aspects that can be described as the rational, the spirited, and the emotional. We do notice in ourselves and in others a conflict between our baser desires or lusts, and our willingness to do what in the long run is in our best interest or what we believe to be right.

Although most people are inclined to distinguish between the emotional and the rational aspect, Plato also distinguishes between the emotional and the spirited. This does seem to be a distinction worth making. We are inclined to be amused by prudish people who spend a long time drooling over pornographic pictures and then go on to say that such pictures are disgusting and ought to be banned. Perhaps this phenomenon is a manifestation of the conflict between the spirited aspects of the personality and earthy desires. The person is sexually excited by the pictures, has a desire to continue viewing them, but at the same time is disgusted with himself for wanting to do so.

According to Plato, we have the three parts of the soul, which are roughly analogous to the three parts of the state. They shall, in the well-adjusted personality, stand to one another as the parts of the state stand to one another in the well-adjusted state. The intellect will rule with the aid of the spirited part, and the lower part will acquiesce to the guidance of reason. Plato noted that the spirited part was ordinarily the handmaiden of reason so that its acting in the aid of reason would not be unnatural.

Although there is some similarity between the parts of the soul and the parts of the state, the analogy should not be pressed too hard. The lower orders of the state consist of many classes of people: bankers, farmers, and saddle-makers, for instance. The members of some of these classes would have to be quite intelligent to carry out their tasks. But the lower part of the soul is composed of blind desires. Not the thirst for a hot toddy or the desire to eat caviar but simply the blind desires to drink and eat, for example. However, the analogy between the ruling class and the intellect is closer than might be thought. According to Plato, just as the rulers desire (as we shall see) to pursue their studies as well as to rule the state, so the intellect desires to acquire knowledge in addition to ruling the soul. It may come as a surprise to us to hear that the intellect has desires. Most thinkers, like David Hume, have thought of the intellect as being completely inert. On this view, the passions decide what goals shall be pursued and the intellect works out the best way to achieve those ends. Unless I desire to be healthy, reason is utterly helpless in getting me to be healthy. However, if I desire to be healthy, then reason can work out the steps that I must take in order to achieve my goal. But this view, as we have seen, is not Plato's view. According to Plato, the intellect has passions of its own—the desire to rule the soul and the desire to pursue knowledge. Who is right? To some extent, it's just a matter of classification. People like Hume do not mean by "intellect" what Plato means. But it's not altogether a matter of classification. Many people are curious; they have a desire to know and understand. Such desires seem to be very much the desires of the intellect or, as we would say, intellectual desires. On Hume's account, it seems almost inexplicable how one could have such desires. Hume can explain why a man would want to know how the controls of a car work if that man wants to use the car to drive around, but if the man desires to know how the controls of a car work for no reason other than to acquire the knowledge, then such a desire seems inexplicable.

Now that we have described the three parts of the soul, it's an easy matter to locate justice and the other virtues. Wisdom is of course the virtue of the intellect. It enables the intellect to reason well. Courage is the virtue of the spirited part. Temperance, as it turns out, is the ability of each part to respect the jobs of the other parts. Finally, justice in the soul consists in each part, so to speak, sticking to its own trade and working in harmony. Once again the reader may feel cheated. This doesn't seem to be what justice should be. Plato, however, felt that if anything is going to count as justice, it should satisfy two criteria: (a) it should be internal and (b) it should manifest itself in the doing of what we would normally call just acts. We have already seen that the first criterion is satisfied. What of the second? According to Plato, a person whose soul was in such a state would not embezzle funds, commit theft, neglect his parents or be unfaithful to his wife. Presumably, a person would only steal from another if his soul was in a state of disharmony and if his intellect was a slave to his lower desires and appetites. Furthermore (for those who feel cheated), Plato should not be taken as having shown what justice is. He has only shown how justice manifests itself in human affairs. To really know what justice is it would be necessary to undergo the long and arduous training that Plato mapped out for the prospective rulers of the ideal state, or at least spend a number of years at his Academy.

Finally, Socrates believes that he has done all that is required to show that justice pays. Just as health was thought to be the harmony of the body, so justice turns out to be the harmony of the soul. In other words, justice is the health of the soul. Now no one would deny that it pays to work toward having a healthy body, so no one should deny that it pays to work toward having a healthy, just soul (by doing just deeds and refraining from doing unjust deeds). Therefore, no one would deny that it pays to have a just soul. In Book IX, chapter 34, Socrates drives this home by painting in vivid detail the miserable life of the thoroughly unjust man.

Although Plato could always protect himself by pointing out that he hasn't actually said what justice really is, perhaps a few criticisms are in order. First of all, it's not certain that a person whose soul is in the state that Plato describes will always behave in a just way. Suppose that my soul is in such a state and that I live on an island with a few other people who are weaker than myself, a place where there is not enough food to go around. Since my intellect as guardian of myself will be concerned with my survival as a healthy person, it will be in favor of my taking more than my fair share. I shall remain strong and healthy while the others on the island become weak and puny. Such behavior (taking more than my fair share) might be called prudential but it could hardly be called just.

Second, since my intellect, as well as desiring to rule the body, also desires to know, couldn't this lead to unhappy results? If I had the power to do so, might I not set up a research station and force the others to work long hours toward its maintenance? Such actions on my part could hardly be called just.

Finally, it's not at all certain that justice should be located in the soul rather than in actions. One of Plato's arguments for not locating justice in actions goes something like this: When we praise the doing of what we take to be a just act performed by a confidence trickster, what we praise is only the semblance of a just act. What he does is not just, it only appears to be just. Now since there is no difference in what appears to us in the act of the confidence trickster and in the act of the genuinely just man, the act of the genuinely just man must also be a resemblance of justice. But if this is only the semblance of justice, then justice must reside somewhere else. The fault with this argument is to be found, as we have seen, in the first premise. When we praise the act of the confidence trickster, we may only be praising the semblance of justice, but we do not take it to be the semblance of justice. We have been taken in. And in believing that he has done a just act, we praise him for the doing of a just act. Both in the case of the confidence trickster and in the case of the genuinely just man, we praise the doing of just acts. Thus there is no reason, on this score, why justice cannot reside in the act. There are other reasons with which it is more difficult to deal. We shall leave them alone until the chapter on ethics.

Part III

Knowledge and Belief

Having shown to his satisfaction where justice resides and that it pays to be just, Socrates continues to fill in more of the details of his ideal state—the educational system, the equality of women, and how incest is to be avoided.[9] The question of how such a state could come into existence is then raised. Socrates replies that such a state could only come into existence when either philosophers become rulers or rulers become philosophers. This in turn raises the question of how one is to distinguish between philosophers and more ordinary mortals. The difference, as it turns out, is that the philosophers love the Forms (they are known later as the friends of the Forms), while the others love only particulars. This in its turn raises the question of the existence of the Forms. This topic is discussed and only discussed in the *Republic*, chapter 9. This is the only place where we get anything like an argument for the claim that there are Forms and that the things of this world (unlike the Forms) are not really real. The argument contains many false moves but we can, surprisingly enough, learn much through examining it.

First of all, it is claimed, following Parmenides, that only the real can be known. One cannot know that which is not. Second, it is claimed that one faculty (in other words, an ability) is distinguished from another by its object. For example, the ability to see and the ability to hear are distinguished by their objects. Colors and shapes, which are the objects of seeing, are different from sounds, which are the objects of hearing. It's on the basis of them that we can distinguish between seeing and hearing. Third, it is claimed that the ability to know is one faculty and that the ability to believe is another. Now, if the ability to believe is a different faculty, it must have a different object. But since the object of the ability to know is the real, the object of the ability to believe must be different. It can't be the unreal, because that, according to Plato, is the object of ignorance. The object of belief must then reside halfway between what is real and what is unreal, between being and not being. But what could that be?

Plato's next move is to argue that the objects of this world hover halfway between the real and the unreal, or, in other words, between being and not being. Take for example a statue considered to be beautiful. We can't say that it is beautiful, for if we look at it from a different angle it will manifest its opposite—ugliness. Similarly, take an act considered to be just. No act is absolutely just; examine it from a different perspective and it appears to be unjust. Thus both the statue and the act seem to hover between being and not being. The statue is and is not beautiful, and the act is and is not just. Presumably this sort of argument could be applied to any other object of the sensible world. Take, for example, the dog that I own; it's not a perfect dog—not even a perfect dog of its type. So it is and is not a dog. Or take the circle that might be drawn on the blackboard. Again it's not a perfect circle—it has some flaws. So it is and is not a circle.

Finally, since it has already been agreed that the object of belief must reside halfway between being and not being, and since the objects of this world do reside in this region, it follows that the objects of this world are the objects of belief and not of knowledge.

I shall now point out some of the difficulties with the argument, and then attempt to put it in a more convincing light. In the first place, most contemporary philosophers distinguish between knowledge in the sense of being acquainted with something or someone, and knowledge in the sense of knowing some *fact* about the world. For example, when Mr. Smith is asked if he knows Pierre Trudeau he is being asked if he is acquainted with Trudeau; but when he is asked if he knows *that* Trudeau has three sons, this has nothing to do with acquaintance. Smith may know this without being acquainted with (knowing) Trudeau. Now, in order to know, in the sense of being acquainted with, the object of knowledge must truly be. Smith cannot be acquainted with something that does not exist. Smith cannot be acquainted with Trudeau if the latter does not exist. But Smith can know all sorts of things ("thats") about illusions, holographs, shadows, and other things that do not really exist. For example, I can say such things as "I know *that* what I saw was not an oasis but only a mirage," "I know *that* what is in front of me is not a monster but only a pile of rocks that looks like a monster," and "I know *that* unicorns do not exist." So even if it's true that Smith can only know (be acquainted with) what is really real, he still can know all sorts of things (thats) about what is not really real.

Second, the difference between real and unreal is not quite what Plato suggests. As a rule, when we say that something is real, we mean to say that it is a real something or other. When we say that a belt is real, we mean that it is made of real leather; when we say that the man in a department store window is real, we mean that he is a real human being and not a mannequin or a robot. Notice further, when we say that the belt is not made of real leather we can go on to say that it's made of real artificial leather (as opposed to paper); and when we say that the figure in the window is not a real human being, we can go on to say that it is a real mannequin. We can even go so far as to say that what we see on the wall is a real shadow (as opposed to a painted one) or a real holograph, though I must admit I'm not certain what a fake holograph would be like. However, we must not push this point too far. If it turned out that we lived in a world of shadows and images—that is to say, real shadows and real images—then there is a sense in which we would have to say that the world we lived in was not real.

Third, the distinction that Plato draws between knowledge and belief is very different from the one that we draw. Plato says that knowledge and belief must have different objects, yet we feel that the objects can be the same. I can know of Trudeau that he has three sons, and I can believe that he owns an old Mercedes car. As a rule, I use "know" in the first person present when I feel certain, and "believe" in the first person present when I am not quite so certain. "I didn't say I knew that Trudeau owns an old Mercedes, I only said that I believed he owned one." However, the story is even more complex. When I say of someone else that *he* believes, I don't use "believe" in the same way as when I say that *I* believe. When I say "I believe," I use "believe" as an indication of caution. But when I say "He believes," I state a fact about that person. "He believes that the world is flat but he is mistaken." As a rule, I restrict "know" when talking about others to those cases where (a) I am prepared to claim that I also know, and (b) where I am prepared to claim that his belief is based on reason. For example, I might say of Smith that even though he truly believes there are Russian spies in the C.I.A., he doesn't really know this to be true, for he is not privy to the proper evidence.

Fourth, when Plato says that the statue is not really real, because it is in some ways beautiful and is in others ways ugly, he doesn't distinguish between the various uses of "is." Consider the following examples: "God is," "Tully is Cicero," "The cat is black." The first example contains the "is" of existence. To say that "God is" is to say that "God exists." The second contains the "is" of identity. To say that Tully is Cicero is to say that Tully and Cicero are identical. And the third contains the "is" of predication. To say that "The cat is black" is not to identify blackness with the cat, it is to ascribe the property of blackness to the cat. Now when we say that the statue is beautiful we are ascribing or attributing beauty to the statue. So the fact that the statue is in some respects beautiful and in some respects not has nothing to do with the existence of the statue. The statue must exist in order to be in some respects beautiful and in some respects not beautiful.

Even though we can find many faults with Plato's argument we must not dismiss it altogether. When we say that we know that something is the case, we express an absolute certainty. I cannot say that "I know x but I might be wrong." If this is true then it limits the number of things I can claim to know. Suppose that I measure the width of the desk that I am writing on and come to the conclusion that it is exactly 4 feet wide. Can I say that I know that the desk is 4 feet wide? It seems not, for it's always possible that I may be wrong. Perhaps the ruler is a bit bent or not properly made. Perhaps the ruler slipped a bit as I measured it. But the same sort of argument seems to hold for everything else in the sensible world. Can I be certain that the sweater in the store is yellow? Perhaps it's just the lighting or perhaps I don't see colors the way that they truly are. Or perhaps the sensible world is as Lucretius described it. Physical objects are really colorless even though they appear to be colored. If we can't know anything about the objects in the sensible world, is there anything about which we can know something? Well, it might be said that we can know that $2 + 3 = 5$, that the circumference of a circle is equal to $2\pi r$, and that the length of the hypotenuse of a right-angled triangle is equal to the square root of the square of the two sides ($h = \sqrt{a^2 + b^2}$). So there are things that we know something about. We can know things about numbers, the circle, and the right-angled triangle. We have already seen that these objects don't seem to belong to the sensible world; they look more at home in Plato's world of Forms. Perhaps Plato is right: the only objects that can be known are Forms. On this view, to say that a person knows (in the sense of being acquainted with), say, the ideal circle, would be to say that he knows all sorts of truths that follow logically from the concept of the circle.

This fits in well with a definition that is often given of knowledge. It is said that in order for someone to know statement S, S must be true, the person must believe S to be true, and he must be able to given reasons that prove absolutely that S is true; or, failing this, S must be self-evidently true. On this definition of knowledge, we can say that we know, concerning the right-angled triangle, that $h = \sqrt{a^2 + b^2}$ because we can prove, or at least some of us can, that $h = \sqrt{a^2 + b^2}$. But we cannot be said to know that the Empire State Building is x feet tall, because we cannot prove with anything like the same certainty that it is x feet tall.

But let us move on to talk about the things of this world. Granted, if we accept this strict definition of knowledge, then we cannot know anything about the things of this world. But does it follow from this that they are not really real, that they hover in a twilight zone between the real and the unreal? According to Plato, if we take any statue that is considered to be beautiful; there will always be some aspect in which it is ugly. It certainly follows from this that we cannot identify the statue with beauty. We may say, if we want, that beauty exists independently of the statue and manifests itself to some extent in this statue as well as elsewhere. But it still doesn't follow from this that the statue belongs to a nether-nether twilight zone and is not real. The "is" in "The statue is beautiful" is, as we have seen, the "is" of predication and not the "is" of identity. To say "The statue is beautiful" is to attribute beauty to the statue. But to attribute beauty to the statue does not preclude attributing other properties. One can say that this part of the statue is beautiful and that part is not, without in the least casting any suspicion on the reality of the statue. One can also say that the statue is beautiful in this respect and ugly in some other, again without doubting its reality.

Let us see if we can beef up Plato's argument. It has already been shown that we are inclined to consider the changing objects around us as complexes of smaller objects (atoms or smaller) that do not change, rather than unchanging objects that shift their location. In addition, we were inclined to believe that the changing objects gain their reality the way a sifting sand pile does—from smaller objects that do not change.

Now suppose that there were no smaller objects that do not change. This is the view of Plato. Plato did not accept the ancient atomic theory. It is also the view of many present-day physicists that ultimate particles are not particles at all but bursts or waves of energy. If this is so, can we say that the things of this world are really real? Perhaps they are not as real as we think.

The following picture might help to make clearer the way in which Plato viewed this world. Imagine a cinema where by means of colors, lights, and lenses, shaped colors dance on a screen in front of us. Over on the left is a blob of brown and to the right a circle of yellow. With the passing of time, the blob of brown becomes redder and then fades; the circle of yellow turns into a purple square that is eventually swallowed up by a blob growing above it. Can we say that the blob of brown and the circle of yellow exist? They have no mass or thickness. On the other hand, can we say that they don't exist? This is how I think Plato viewed the physical world, hovering like blobs of color on a screen halfway between existing and not existing.

Finally, there is one more thing that should be said in support of Plato. Perhaps we have been concentrating too much attention on the *objects* that we say we know (are acquainted with) and not enough on the *statements* that we say we know. Socrates says in the *Republic,* (p. 479), "It seems, then, we have discovered that the many conventional notions of the mass of mankind about what is beautiful or honorable or just and so on are adrift in a sort of twilight between pure reality and pure unreality." Now a notion is not an object, but a statement which is believed to be true. When we say of someone that his notion of a university is mistaken, we mean to say that his definition (statement) of or basic beliefs (statements) about what a university is are mistaken. Could it not be the case that Plato is saying something like this? Many of our conventional beliefs about what is just, right, wrong, and so on are correct but only at a superficial level. Suppose for the moment that the ultimate goal in this world is happiness and that the ultimate evil is unhappiness. Acts that promote happiness are right and those that promote unhappiness are wrong. Whether this is true or not need not concern us at this point, but it will later on. Suppose further that a great many babies are being born out of wedlock, and this is causing a great deal of unhappiness. In this situation the moral leaders of a society might try to bring the members of that society to believe that sex out of wedlock is wrong in itself. Let us suppose that they are successful. Most people in the group eventually come to believe that sex out of wedlock is in itself wrong. In this situation we might say that the notions of the ordinary members of the society were adrift in a sort of twilight. Their belief that sex out of wedlock is wrong is not mistaken, but their belief that it is wrong in itself is mistaken. They don't know what is really right or really wrong, what is really good or really bad. They do have correct beliefs about what follows from what is really good or really evil. Therefore we cannot really say that their beliefs are false but, on the other hand, we cannot say that they are true. Perhaps we should say that their moral beliefs are nothing more than the appearances of what really is (true). And this is precisely what Plato wants to do.

The Good, the Line, and the Cave

Having satisfied themselves that the rulers of the best of all possible states must be philosophers, which means they must have a love and knowledge of the Forms, the problem of how to insure that the future rulers have this knowledge is taken up. Socrates says that in order for rulers to have a knowledge of justice, courage, and other forms they must also have a knowledge of the ultimate form—the Good. This immediately raises the question of what the Good is. Socrates says to his audience that he cannot tell them what the Good is. In order for them to know what it is, they would have to go through the long educational process required of the future rulers. But he can tell them what the Good is not and, by means of an analogy, he can display for them how the Good stands in relation to the other Forms.

The Good, according to Socrates, is not knowledge (Socrates had at one time wanted to identify the Good with knowledge), because those who say that it is, when asked what it is knowledge of, answer that it is knowledge of the Good. But since it is absurd to say that the Good is the knowledge of the Good, the Good is not knowledge.

It might have struck the reader that this is a very weak argument. It doesn't follow from the fact that it is absurd to say that the Good is knowledge of the Good, that the Good is not knowledge. The Good, for example, might be knowledge of chemistry, physics, and so on. This is an excellent example of the *ad hominem* fallacy. (It will be discussed in chapter 3.)

The second thing the Good is not, according to Socrates, is pleasure. As we have seen, Lucretius and Epicurus identified the Good with pleasure. The reason we cannot identify the Good with pleasure is that some pleasures are intrinsically bad. But if some pleasures are bad, and the Good is identified with pleasure, the same thing can be completely good and completely bad. Since this conclusion is absurd, pleasure cannot be identified with the Good. Socrates doesn't give any examples of pleasures that are in themselves bad, but presumably the sadistic pleasure of torturing young children would be one.

If the Good is neither knowledge nor pleasure, then what is it? Socrates says that he cannot tell us what it is, but he can draw an analogy that will at least illuminate its relational aspects. In order to see the objects of this world it is necessary to have eyes, a light, and a source of light. One cannot see in the dark. The ultimate source of light, according to Socrates, is the sun. Not only does the sun make the objects of this world visible, it is also responsible (in the case of flowers and trees at least) for their existence and nourishment. Parallel to the way that the sun makes it possible for us to see by its light, so the Good by its light of truth, makes it possible for us to know the Forms. It radiates the other Forms with truth, and so in the same way that the sun makes the objects of this world visible, the Good makes the Forms intelligible. Furthermore, just as the sun is responsible for the existence of the things of the world, so the Good is responsible for the existence of the Forms.

It's hard to know what to make of all this. Presumably Plato wants to say that the Good is like the ultimate concept in a mathematical system. If we have a complex grasp of this concept, and this would mean being able to give a rigorous definition of it, then we can see how all the other concepts of the system follow from it. Once we have grasped the definition of the ultimate concept then the definitions of the other concepts can be deduced from it. So the ultimate concept is not only responsible for the existence of the other concepts, it also makes them intelligible. One difficulty here is that it's hard to see how both moral concepts and mathematical concepts could be derived from the same ultimate concept.

The members of the audience complain that they don't understand what Socrates is trying to say, so he tries once again. He invites them (and us) to consider a vertical line divided into two unequal sections, the upper section being larger. The upper section represents the intelligible world (the world radiated by the Good), and the lower section represents the visible world (the world radiated by the sun). Each section is then divided again in the same proportion. As a result we have a line that looks something like this:

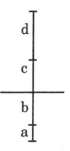

According to Socrates, "a" represents images, shadows, etc., while "b" represents the world around us: the world of physical objects. The objects of "a" are copies of the objects of "b."

The upper world is more difficult to describe. "C" represents the world of Forms as they are known independently of the Good, while "d" represents the Forms as they are known through the Good. The Good itself is also a member of "d." Just as the inhabitants of "a" are images of "b" so the inhabitants of "b" are images of "c."

The student, when introduced to geometry, has first to deal with diagrams of circles and triangles. Those belong to the section "b." Soon he realizes that his conjectures, thoughts, and proofs are not about the diagrams, but the ideal circle and triangle of which they are copies. And these ideals (the ideal circle and triangle) belong to the upper part of the line. One assumes that moral reasoning would follow the same Form. The student would begin talking about different moral situations, trying to decide which were just and which were not. He would then discover that what he was really talking about were not particular moral situations but the Form of justice. In ways like these the student is helped across the barrier between the visible world and the intelligible world. He moves from "b" to "c."

So far, however, the student has not achieved real knowledge, and he will not, until he sees how these Forms are derived from the Good. Mathematical reasoning in this section ("c") will take the form of starting with axioms of the Euclidian variety and then deriving theorems from them. Reasoning in section "d" will first take the form of seeing that what were taken as axioms are not really axioms but only hypotheses that also stand in need of proof. He will then, by means of a dialectical process (a la the opening section of the *Republic* where Plato wants to discover what justice is), move upward step by step until at last he is confronted with the Good. Again one can only conjecture, but I would assume that what Plato has in mind here is that at this point the student is confronted with a statement concerning a very special concept that strikes him as blinding and intuitively true. It would be a statement that he would not have been in a position to understand before, but now that he has moved up the dialectical ladder, he understands it; and in understanding it he cannot but accept it as the ultimate truth. Finally, once he has grasped this truth he can then derive all of the so-called axioms of geometry and principles of morality from it. It's difficult to think of what this principle could be like. One can imagine there being an ultimate principle of geometry from which all the axioms of geometry could be derived, and one can imagine there being an ultimate principle of morality from which all the moral principles could be derived. But it's difficult to imagine there being a principle from which both could be derived.

We have seen (p. 73) that Plato was inclined to postulate a different faculty, or at least state of mind, for each kind of object. The state of mind corresponding to the lower category ("a") can be thought of as the state of mind of an infant perceiving the world around him. He perceives colors and perhaps shapes but is unable to organize them into discrete physical objects. It can also be thought of (again Plato is ambiguous) as the state of mind of taking the popular moral beliefs at their face value. The state of mind of the members of our imaginary society who believed that sex out of wedlock was in itself wrong because they had been told it was so would be an example. Belief, according to Plato, is the state of mind corresponding to the second category, "b." Here Plato is thinking of the sort of awareness that ordinary people have of the sensible world. Such awareness gives rise to true belief but not to knowledge. In order to count as knowledge the beliefs would have to be derived from true statements about the Forms. Thinking, according to Plato, is the state of mind that involves the apprehension of the forms independently of the Good (section "c"). Knowledge, which corresponds to section "d," is the state of mind that involves a direct apprehension of good and the other Forms in their dependence on the Good. Strictly speaking, one can only know (in the sense of being acquainted with) the Good. If one knows the Good, then one can know the other Forms. But one only knows the other Forms in their dependence upon the Good. It's not clear what Plato meant by "thinking." He wanted a name for the state of mind that hovered halfway between knowing and believing, and "thinking" ("Dianoia") was as good as any.

This section on the distinction between the different states of mind is, in translation at least, an awkward one. The main reason for this awkwardness is that we have two uses of "know." We can talk of knowing in the sense of being acquainted with some object, and we can talk of knowing in the sense of knowing *that* something is the case. But we have in English no parallel uses for "believe." We can only believe *that* something is the case. Of course, we can believe *in* somebody but this only means that we have faith in him. Now in our translation of Plato we want to have a word that stands to "know" (in the acquainted sense) as "believe that" stands to "know that," but there is none to be found.

Socrates realizes that his audience is still very much in the dark. His illustrations have raised more puzzles than they dispelled. So he tries one more time. He invites us to consider the following parable. In an underground cave some prisoners are chained to a wall. Just above them is a parapet, and behind the parapet is a fire. Men carry cut-outs shaped like various types of animals and other objects along the top of the parapet. The fire casts the shadows of these objects onto the opposite wall. The shadows are all that the prisoners see. In fact, they are all that the prisoners have ever seen. As a result, the prisoners take the shadows to be real objects. Their life is fairly dreary, but they amuse themselves as best they can by trying to guess which shadow will come next and by various other games. They cheer those who are good at these games and laugh at those who are not.

One day one of the prisoners is unshackled by the guards and pulled up the stairs toward the mouth of the cave. First he is introduced to the cut-outs whose shadows are cast onto the wall. He is perplexed and is not at all certain which is real and which is not. However, it slowly dawns on him that the cut-outs are real and the shadows are not. Then he is introduced to the fire. The light dazzles him. Slowly, he is dragged up toward the mouth of the cave. Once outside, he is blinded by the light of the sun. At first he can only look at the shadows and reflections. But as his eyes become accustomed to the light, he can look at the objects around him and finally at the sun. Once the prisoner is accustomed to the upper world, he is loath to return to the dark cave. If, however, he were forced to return to tell the others of his experiences, they would not believe him; they might claim that all he got for his trouble was ruined eyesight. If he tried to force them to leave the cave, they would probably fall on him and kill him.

The prisoners in the parable are us. The shadows are the objects that we see. The fire represents the sun. It's not clear what the cut-outs represent. Perhaps they represent geometrical figures inhabiting a nether-nether land between material objects and pure forms. The upper world, is, of course, the world of intelligible objects. The objects are the Forms and the sun is the Good. The prisoner's reluctance to return to the cave is an allusion to the reluctance of enlightened people to take their part in governing. And the claim that the unenlightened might fall on the prisoner and kill him is of course an allusion to Socrates, who tried to enlighten the citizens of Athens through his dialectical technique. We have seen what happened to him.

The parable, like so many things in Plato's works, has a richness of ambiguity. It can be interpreted in at least three different ways. It may be telling us that the objects around us are not real in the way that the objects studied by the mathematician and the moralist are real. Somehow, this interpretation doesn't seem very exciting. Or it can be interpreted as telling us that after we die and our souls have been purged so that we can become members of the world of Forms, we shall realize that what we took to be real objects in our waking life were only shadows. Finally, it can be interpreted—and this is perhaps the most exciting way—to mean that we live in a world created by the newspapers, television, and other media where everything, as the hero in *Catcher in the Rye* would say, is phony.

I should like to say a couple of things about the second and third interpretations. First of all, is it conceivable that we could ever be in a position to say that the things of this world are only shadows of a more real world? Let us return for a moment to the men in the cave. They have always lived in the cave. Their language evolved as a result of the sort of beings they are and the sort of life that they have lived. Thus, even though they spoke a language that sounded like ours, it wouldn't be the same. The words in their language will not as a rule mean what they mean in our language. Because they are unable to turn their heads all they ever see are the shadows on the wall. The expression "real object" is used to refer only to these shadows. It has never been used to refer to anything else. Thus, what they mean by "real objects" is any shadow on the wall. Presumably an unreal or fake "object" would be something that looked like a shadow but wasn't— perhaps a spot where the wall happened to be a bit darker. If one of them were removed and shown that other objects cause what they call "real objects," this wouldn't lead the person to say that what he had called "real objects" were not real objects, but only that real objects do not have the independent existence they were thought to have. Thus even if we are in the position of the prisoners in the cave, we would never come to accept the objects of this world as not real.

It is of course possible that this argument is mistaken. Suppose that a group of people grows up in a cinema or glued to a television set (not a far-fetched supposition!). They never see anything except what appears on the screen. Their language evolves as a result of the sort of beings that they are and the sorts of experiences that they have, much like Peter Sellers in the motion picture *Being There*. There is a difference, however. Sellers's television world is filled with commercials and images disappearing and popping into existence. He can also make the images disappear with his remote control. Whereas in the television world I have envisioned, the people and objects behave exactly like the people and objects in our world. Now the interesting question is this (and one to which I shall return when we discuss Descartes): Can the audience take what they see on the screen, as other than what we would call real physical objects? That is to say, if, for example, they see the image of a chair on the screen, can they take it as different from what we would call a real chair? If the image is perfect—suppose that the image is three dimensional—then even though they only see images, they have to take it for what we call a real chair. Thus, even though their words refer only to images, these words could only mean what our words mean, given that the structure of their language is the same as ours. Even though they and we have different experiences, we would be speaking exactly the same language! This would make it possible for us to tell them that the objects they experienced were not really real. There is, however, a difference between the shadows in the cave and the 3-D images in the cinema. The shadows appear to be different from that which they represent, and so although the prisoners of the cinema would have to take the 3-D images to be what we call real objects, the prisoners of the cave would not and could not. Their language would have to be different from ours. Therefore, we couldn't tell them that what they call real objects were not real objects.

Let us move on to the third interpretation. Is there a sense in which it could turn out that the sorts of lives we lead are phony? We are inclined to say yes, for when we look at the past we come across all sorts of lives that strike us as fake. Take, for example, the lives of the people at the court of Versailles. We are inclined to say that their dreams, desires, and aspirations had nothing to do with the real world. Or consider great issues of the past: We are told that at one time in Russia thousands of lives were lost over whether the sign of the cross should be made with one finger or two. In the sixteenth and seventeenth centuries, hundreds of thousands of women were burned as witches for living the sorts of lives that one would expect elderly widows and spinsters to live. Whole books were devoted to the task of illustrating how to identify and prosecute witches and warlocks.

We don't have to look to the past to find unreal happenings. Hundreds of thousands of lives were lost and billions of dollars spent waging a war in the Southeast Asian nation of Vietnam, a military action that is now considered to have been utterly unnecessary. No doubt thousands of lives will be lost and millions of people made miserable in the political struggles of Latin America over what will someday be considered unreal issues. Finally, consider the life of someone who lives at the heart of the media world of New York or Toronto, perhaps a public relations man or a politician. His life seems not to be very different from the world of the actor Peter Sellers in *Being There*. Though the public relations man or the politician is concerned to manipulate other people, he becomes (or may become) so enmeshed in the language he uses that he manipulates and deceives himself in the process.

No doubt some of this is true, but we must be careful not to push this argument too hard. The public relations man may say that he is throwing another concentrate of combustible bio-mass into the caloric convertor, but he will not deny that he is throwing another log on the fire. The politician who looked upon South Vietnam as the last bulwark of freedom in Southeast Asia may have lived to some extent in a dream world, partly of his own making, but he is not in a dream world when he adds up the number of people who voted him into office.

As a rule, when we say that the Russians who fought over whether the sign of the cross should be made with one finger or two lived in a dream world, what we really mean to say is that they put too much value on something that was of little or no importance. We don't mean to say that they lived in a dream world like those who believe that they are surrounded by pixies and leprechauns. The Russians in question are not mistaken in their claim that some people make the sign of the cross with one finger and some make it with two. They are only mistaken about its importance.

Having dealt with some of the ways that the cave parable can be interpreted, I should like to turn briefly to some puzzles concerning the parable of the line and the sun. One puzzle concerning the cave has to do with the role the fire is supposed to play. We are not like the prisoners, for we can see the sun. Further, as was mentioned before, it's not clear what the cut-outs are supposed to represent, nor is it clear how we are to take the reflections in the upper world. Finally, Plato tells us that "every feature of this parable . . . is meant to fit our earlier analysis." (*Republic*, p. 517) But when we compare the parable of the cave with that of the line the fit is very poor. The most obvious difficulty is that the people in the cave are supposed to be equivalent to those who are in section "a" of the line. However, the people in the cave are supposed to stand for all people—those in section "a" represent only a few. Most people would be in section "b." An enormous amount of scholarly energy has been expended trying to show that the two accounts are parallel, but no one has yet succeeded. One wonders if Plato didn't make that remark with tongue in cheek. The main problem with the sun, the line, and the cave is that even though they are rich in suggestive metaphor, they do not express in a clear way what Plato means, and more important, they do not show that whatever he means is in fact true. Even if Plato could have expressed in a clear way what he meant by "the good," it still has to be shown that it does exist and that it stands in relation to the other Forms in the way that he says it stands. In other words, even if the sun, the line, and the cave do show us what Plato took to be the relation of the Good to the other Forms, they do not show that his theory is true.

Part IV

The Decline of the Ideal State, and the Life of the Despotic Man

If Plato's ideal state ever came into existence—which is doubtful—it couldn't, any more than anything else that belongs to the sensible world, be expected to last forever. Sooner or later the rot would set in. Perhaps the top rulers would make a mistake and children would be conceived out of season.

Plato outlines the fall of the ideal state, through Timocracy (rule by the military class), Oligarchy (rule by the few and the richer members of the lowest class), Democracy (rule by the many), and finally to Despotism, which is rule by a member of the lowest subclass of the lowest class. The fall is not supposed to be an account of the order in which the states would come into existence, rather it is an account of the order of goodness of the states. The Platonic state is the best, Timocracy is the second best, and so on.

Plato has already told us (*Republic*, p. 435) that the sort of state that evolves is a consequence of the sort of people who exist in it. Since there are four types of states, it is to be expected that there will be four types of people: Corresponding to the ideal state will be the just man;

his soul will be ruled by his intellect. The second state will be ruled by the timocratic man; he will be ruled by the spirited part of the soul. He is the sort of person who covets honor and glory in battle. Next comes the oligarchic man, who will be ruled by the upper subpart of the appetitive portion of the soul. He can be expected to devote his life to the accumulation of wealth. The democratic man is more difficult to describe. According to Plato, he is ruled in turn by each of the lower subparts of his soul. One day he desires wine, the next day women, the next day song, and so on. The despotically souled man is governed by unlawful desires that in most people only bestir themselves when they (the people) are asleep. He walks in a cloud of insanity, a slave to insatiable and base desires.

Socrates is now in a position to compare the perfectly unjust man (the despotically souled man) with the perfectly just man, and thereby show who is indisputably the happiest. To this end he offers three arguments. The first involves many of the ingredients that we have seen before. Socrates argues that the just man is happier for three reasons. (a) The despotically souled man is a slave of his passions while the just man is not; (b) the just man is wealthier in the sense that he can satisfy his desires while the despotically souled man cannot—his desires are insatiable; and (c) the just man is free from fear while the despotically souled man can never trust his cronies—since they are only attracted to him for reasons other than friendship, he never knows when they will turn on him.

Socrates goes on to point out that there is still one man who is worse off than he who is despotically souled, and that is the despotically souled despot. The private citizen at least has some protection through the state, but the despot has none. Dictators never know when their bodyguards are going to turn on them. And so it turns out that the man who Thrasymachus thought was the happiest of all is the least happy.

The second argument in support of viewing the just man as the happiest man begins with pointing out that each part of the soul has its own kind of pleasure and that this pleasure is experienced by anyone whose soul is dominated by that part. The businessman gains pleasure from making profitable deals, the soldier from winning battles and being honored for doing so, and the philosopher from learning more about reality.[8] Now which kind of pleasure is the best? One way of deciding is to find out which kind will be chosen by the man who has experienced all three. It turns out that only the philosopher has experienced all three, so the pleasure experienced by the philosopher must be the best. Furthermore, the philosopher's choice is backed up with the insight and reasoning that he uniquely possesses.

There are two difficulties with this argument. First, it's not certain that the philosopher really has experienced the other two kinds of pleasure. Second, isn't it possible that one of the men of the other types could have experienced the life of the philosopher and found it wanting? Plato's argument is loaded because he only considers those who remain philosophers. He does not consider lapsed philosophers. It must be admitted that some people find the intellectual life an awful bore.

The third argument begins by distinguishing spurious pleasures from real pleasures. Spurious pleasures are those that come from the relief of some discomfort: for example, the pleasure I get from eating when I am famished. Real pleasures do not involve relief from discomfort. They are pleasures like that of experiencing a meadowlark bursting into song or smelling an unexpected rose. This distinction can be made clearer by the following diagram.

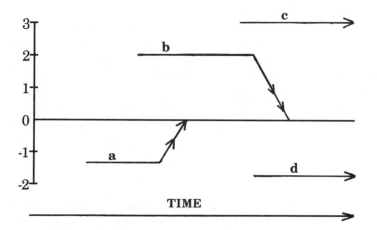

That part of the diagram marked "c" represents the experience of pleasure of an intensity of 3 over a period of time, while "d" represents the experience of pain of an intensity of 2 over a period of time. Line "c" is real pleasure and "d" is real pain. That sequence marked "a" represents a movement from pain to no pain; in other words, relief from pain. The segment marked "b" represents the loss of pleasure. Plato's point is that even if we experience "a" as pleasurable and "b" as painful, they can't really be so since "a" is clearly in the pain zone while "b" is clearly in the pleasure zone.

Plato is certainly on to something but it's not clear, at least to me, what it is. If someone is standing on my toes and then removes his foot, I might consider the relief pleasurable when clearly it is not. But if I go out for a long hike in order to work up a good appetite so that I will enjoy a T-bone steak, it seems mistaken to say that the pleasure I experience from eating the steak is spurious. Here we are inclined to agree with the old adage that hunger is the sauce. The pleasure is real, and the hike I took intensifies it.

The conclusion Plato wants to reach from all this is that intellectual pleasures are of the "c" kind while sensual pleasures are of the "a" kind, but this conclusion is mistaken. We have already seen that some sensual pleasures, such as smelling a rose, are of the "c" kind, and we know from our own experience that some intellectual pleasures are of the "a" kind. For example, I suffer a great disquiet through my inability to solve an intellectual problem. Finally, I hit upon the correct solution and this brings pleasure in the form of relief. On the basis of Plato's theory, it looks as though this pleasure, which is clearly intellectual, would have to be classified as pleasure of the "a" kind.

The argument continues in a strange manner. Pleasure is thought of as what comes from the experience of being filled up. Since the knowledge that fills the emptiness of ignorance is more real than the food that fills the emptiness of hunger, the pleasure derived from knowledge is more real than the pleasure derived from eating food. Apart from the fact that this second part of the argument appears to be inconsistent with the first (How can the pleasure that knowledge brings be real and positive if it comes from relieving ignorance?), there is the further point that just because the *source* of the pleasure is unreal the pleasure itself need not be unreal. The pleasure I may gain from dreams and fantasies can be *very* real.

General Criticism

We have reached the end of our journey through Plato's *Republic*. It is now time to make some general criticisms. I shall begin with Plato's argument for the conclusion that justice pays, after which I shall go on to say a few things about his ideal state. We have seen that Plato has identified justice, at least at the human level, with harmony of the soul. By a harmonious soul he means one in which, even though there has been a cultivation of some of the emotions and the spirited element, the rational part is in command. The best reason he can offer for identifying justice with harmony in the soul is that the harmoniously souled person will always act in what we would consider to be just ways. In other words, since the harmony of the soul is the source of just acts, it must be what justice really is. There are two interconnected difficulties here. First, it's not certain that the person whose rational part is in command can always be properly described as one whose soul is in a state of harmony. Consider, for example, the over-enthusiastic mathematician who ignores both his family and his health in order to get on with his research. We might say that the rational part of his soul is in command, but we could hardly say that his soul was in a harmonious state. Furthermore, it's not at all certain that this person will always behave in a just way. Suppose he is desperate to have a computer in order to carry on his projects. Isn't it possible that he would steal in order to acquire one?

Second, even if we restrict our attention to the harmoniously souled person, it's not at all certain, as we have seen, that he will always behave in a just way. He is a prudent person, one who is concerned with his own welfare in the long run. Thus if he were to find himself in a world in which there was not enough to go around, a world in which he could take what he needed from others with impunity, then he would do so. Such behavior could hardly be called just. If it's possible, and perhaps likely, for the harmoniously souled person to behave in an unjust way, justice cannot be identified with harmony in the soul.

We are driven, then, to the conclusion that Plato is mistaken on three counts. He wants to identify (a) justice with harmony, (b) harmony with the rule of reason, and consequently (c) justice with the rule of reason. But as we have seen, all these identifications break down. One can possess a harmonious soul and yet behave unjustly. The person whose soul is ruled by reason will not necessarily possess a harmonious soul. And the person who is ruled by reason will not always behave justly. In other words, we can't always count on philosophers!

The main trouble with Plato's account of justice—and this seems to be a failing of all ancient philosophers—is that he doesn't see that justice has to do with social relations, that to act justly is not always to act in one's own interest, even in the long run. This point will be pursued at greater length in chapter 7 on ethics, for it raises the question of how it could ever be rational to act justly.

Finally, we are led to consider Plato's conclusion that justice pays: that the just man is the happiest. There are two things that need to be said about this conclusion. First of all, we may be prepared to accept the view that harmoniously souled people are in the long run the happiest, but since we cannot identify justice with harmony, we cannot move from this to the conclusion that the just person is the happiest. Indeed, if acting justly is sometimes going to involve making sacrifices, it seems quite certain that he won't be the happiest. The second thing that needs to be said is this: When Glaucon and Adeimantus ask Socrates to show them that justice pays—in other words, that it is in one's interest to be just—and Socrates attempts to do so, what is being presupposed is that unless it can be shown that it is in one's interest to be just, then one has no reason—in other words, it's not rational—to be just. But this in turn assumes that it is only rational to do what is in one's interest. Again, in the chapter on ethics, I hope to show that this assumption is mistaken.

Plato's State

Just as Plato wanted to identify justice on the personal level with harmony in the soul, so he also wanted to identify justice on the state level with harmony in the state. Since his state was harmonious, he could go on to claim that it was a just state. This argument is based on two assumptions: that justice can be identified with harmony, and that a state is like a super person. We have already seen that the first assumption is mistaken and so, even if a state was a super person, it wouldn't follow that the harmonious state was a just state. We must now examine the assumption that a state is like a super person. There are, of course, analogies between the two. Just as some people are belligerent, others emotional, and still others rational, so, too, there are belligerent, emotional, and rational states. One finds in the state functional aspects that are analogous to the different parts of the personality. It is because of basic desires that we get enough to eat and drink. And so it is because of the workers in factories that there are, one hopes, enough cars and shoes to go around. It is largely because of our rationality that we humans are able to order our lives in an efficient way. Similarly, it is largely because of the civil service that a state can, but rarely does, plan its future in an orderly way.

While similarities do exist, there are enormous differences between states and persons. The main difference is that states are composed of persons, but persons are not composed of persons, even though Plato sometimes talks as though they are. The butcher, the baker, and the candlestick maker are all agents capable of free, rational, and moral action, but the desire for food and drink possesses none of these features. Thus, although acting justly may involve suppressing certain desires, it doesn't follow from this that acting justly at the state level involves suppressing certain groups of people. Or in other words, even if the just person was one who suppressed his desires, it wouldn't follow that the just state was one where there was suppression of persons. Such a state might conceivably be considered harmonious—though only by means of a very strange criterion—but it could hardly be called just. Persons are moral agents; they have rights. And any state that ignores these rights is not and cannot be just.

No doubt Plato's state has much to commend it. A division of labor based on aptitude is a salutary state of affairs. If I am better at making shoes than weaving cloth, it's better then that I make shoes. Even so, the choice should be up to me. If I am happier weaving cloth at a lower income than I could make in the cobbling trade, then it seems only fair that I should be allowed to do so. Plato's system of education must have seemed revolutionary at the time. Education that was open to all and run by the state was a new idea. The claim that a student's progress goes in the educational system should depend entirely on ability seems eminently fair. We might have certain reservations about the lack of special training for those who are to become workers, and about the emphasis put on physical and military education. Three years of physical education seems to be a bit too much. But even with these reservations, the educational system is difficult to fault.

There are, however, aspects of Plato's state that cannot be commended. In *The Republic,* page 488, Plato invites us to compare the ship of state with a ship at sea. The unenlightened crew argue with the master that navigation cannot be taught. With the help of opiates and strong drink they stupify him, take over control of the ship, and turn the voyage into a drunken carousal. The moral to be drawn from this, according to Plato, is that just as the ship at sea should be left in the hands of skilled navigators who have studied the seasons, the sky, and the stars, so, too, the ship of state should be left in the hands, not of politicians who only possess the art of stupifying the masses, but of highly skilled administrators who have studied the art of government. The analogy does not, however, lead to the conclusion Plato wants. Even though navigators may have the skill required to keep a sea ship on course, they don't have any privileged knowledge about where the ship should be going. Similarly, even though the able administrators may have the skill required to keep the ship of state on course, they don't have any privileged knowledge about its final destination. In the case of the ship at sea, it's generally the owners who decide where the ship should be going; if, therefore, we are going to take the analogy seriously, it should be the people (the master) who decide the goals of the state.

It might be objected that if the administrators have a real knowledge of goodness and justice, then they would know where the ship of state ought to be going. This is to say they would be in a position to decide what the general state policy ought to be. However, Plato does not tell us what the good is, or, in a clear way, how knowledge of it is to be acquired. So it doesn't look as though administrators could ever have the required knowledge. Furthermore, even if the administrators could have the required knowledge, it's not clear that they would thereby have the right to decide what the policy should be. The navigator may know where the cargo can be sold at the highest price, but the owners (citizens) have the right to decide not to go there.

Most people who critique Plato's state balk at his recommendations concerning marriage and the children of the ruling class. No doubt there is a risk that highly skilled administrators will put their interests and their families' interests before the interests of the state if they are allowed to own property, have spouses, and raise families. But Plato's cure seems to be worse than the disease. I pointed out earlier (see p. 66) the conflict that faced the British Labour politician who believed (a) that private schools were not in the public interest and (b) that they would give his children the best education. Because of *a* he would want to see them abolished and because of *b* he would want to see them not abolished. One way of avoiding difficulties of this sort would be to leave such questions in the citizen's hands. Issues of this sort could be decided by a direct vote. If the majority felt that the private schools should be bought with public funds and turned into state schools, then by means of direct vote it could be done. Thus one way of avoiding the difficulties that worry Plato is to leave the ultimate questions of policy directly in the hands of the citizens, though one would have to make sure here that individual rights were being respected.

NOTES

1. The Pythagoreans were a philosophical-religious sect who flourished at Kroton in southern Italy in the sixth century B.C. In addition to believing in reincarnation, they believed that numbers, which they viewed as very small physical objects, formed the basis of the universe. Pythagoras, of course, was their founder and leader. He is still remembered by the theorem that bears his name.

2. See pages 55-56 for an intriguing "proof" of this belief.

3. Notice that Christians only consider the soul to be immortal in one direction. Souls are created at conception but, being simple, do not cease to exist. Plato's view seems more reasonable. If souls cannot be destroyed, it would seem they cannot be created.

4. In what follows all references are to F. M. Cornford's translation of the *Republic* (Oxford University Press, 1972).

5. The view that it is just to give each man his due is not, however, in itself an altogether unenlightened view of justice. It is a view held by many people today. At the same time, as it stands it is a bit empty. We need to know what giving each man his due amounts to.

6. It is assumed by both that one would not befriend someone who was believed to be bad.

7. No doubt there is a great deal of truth in this. Charlie Chaplin made a film in the late 1940s called *Monsieur Verdoux*. Monsieur Verdoux married wealthy women and then murdered them. Finally, he was caught but argued convincingly in the court that when he committed crimes on a small scale he was vilified, but when someone (like Hitler) did so on a grand scale people thought he was a splendid fellow. However, we are not at present concerned with the truth of this statement but with whether it is consistent with Thrasymachus' prior claim that justice is in the interest of the stronger.

8. We must be careful here. Somtimes we use "he does not desire to drink" to mean "he desires to not drink" and this may lead us to think either that a person can desire to drink and not desire to drink at the same time, or that a person cannot desire to drink and desire to not drink at the same time. But as long as we keep in mind that these two expressions, when properly used, mean something quite different, then we should not be misled.

9. *The Education System*—The main purpose of Plato's educational system is to turn out a group of people who are capable of running the state efficiently and fairly. Since Plato only wants the best people to become rules, all children are to enter the education system. After they had been taught to read and write

and do a bit of arithmetic, they would also be subjected to a bit of physical training. The main purpose of all this is to bring the various parts of the soul into harmony. The function of physical training is not so much to strengthen the body but to stimulate the spirited part and bring it into tune with the intellectual part. Plato also wanted the children to grow up with a respect for law and for harmony. He thought that an exposure to carefully selected poems, epics, and pieces of music would do the trick. The training in literature, mathematics, and music, unlike physical training, would take the form of play, for according to Plato, "Enforced exercise does no harm to the body, but enforced learning will not stay with the mind" (*Republic*, p. 536) and "for the free man there should be no element of slavery in learning (*Republic*, p. 536). At the age of seventeen, after the basic education, the brighter lights would go on to an intensive course in physical and military training, lasting three or four years. Presumably the less bright would become craftsmen, farmers, bankers, and so on. Again, a group would be weeded out to become soldiers or, in other words, members of the auxiliaries. Those who were left, and that means those who were bright, brave, and strong (a rare combination indeed!), would go on to advanced mathematics. The purpose of this would be to boost them out of the world of sensible objects and into the world of objects apprehended by the intellect—the world of Forms. At thirty another selection would take place. Those who survived would then go on to study and make use of the dialectical technique. At thirty-five it would be time for each to do his bit by returning to the cave and lending a hand at the ruling of the state. From fifty on, each will divide his time between ruling and philosophy.

The Equality of Women—Plato is unique amongst ancient writers in arguing that women should have equal academic opportunities and equal access to all military and administrative positions. All girls, as well as all boys, would enter the educational system and be weeded out in exactly the same way. Plato doesn't tell us, though, what would become of those who were weeded out and joined the lower orders. Presumably a woman could become a cobbler, but if she married a cobbler she would be expected to behave in a way that the wives of Athenian cobblers were expected to behave—sit in the back room, do the cooking, raise the children, and that sort of thing. Plato's argument is interesting in that he takes the standard argument for inequality and shows that if it is properly interpreted it points toward the opposite conclusion. The standard argument is that since everyone should do the work for which nature has fitted him (or her) and since there is a great difference in nature between men and women, it follows that men and women should do different work. Plato's reply is that the only differences in nature that should count are those relevant to the occupations in question. Therefore, since there are no differences that are relevant— the only difference being that man begets and woman brings forth—it does not follow that men and women should do different work. What Plato is getting at here is that the various aptitudes are to be found scattered throughout the population. If there is need in the state for three mathematicians, and the three best unemployed mathematicians are women, then they should be hired. They have a nature that fits them for doing mathematics and so that should be their occupation. Plato is prepared to admit that the average woman is not as strong as the average man, and so women are not on the whole as suited for warfare as men. But it doesn't follow from the fact that the *average* woman is not as strong as the average man, that the particular woman is not as strong as the particular man. If we need to bring one more person into our army and it turns out that there is one woman who is stronger and braver than any of the remaining males, then she should be recruited. Plato wanted to have his state run by the best people. He realized that if you opened the top jobs to women you increased the chance of that happening.

Marriage and the Avoidance of Incest—In order that the rules and their auxiliaries could devote their time to their appointed tasks it was decided, as we have seen (pp. 66-67), (a) that they would not be allowed to have personal possessions and (b) that they (the male rulers at least) would have wives and children in common. (It follows from this that the female rulers would have husbands in common.) One problem that such a social arrangement raises is how to avoid incest. How does one know that the person one is about to mate with is not one's mother, father, son, or daughter? (Surprisingly, Plato does not seem to object to the mating of brothers and sisters.) Plato's solution is to have wedding festivals. Say that the festival lasts for one month and mating can occur only during that time, then all persons born around nine months after the time of the festival will be considered by those who took part in the festival to be sons and daughters. In this way one will know who to refrain from mating with at future festivals. The opportunities that the wedding festivals afforded for selective breeding were not lost on Plato. The selection of brides was supposed to be by a random draw. But Plato realized that it would be possible for the senior rulers to fix the draw so that the strongest and bravest bridegrooms would draw the best (most beautiful and intelligent?) brides. That Plato could have considered such a plan comes as a surprise. Since the rules had been taught all their lives to put the highest value on truth, it seems doubtful that they could be expected to stoop to such cunning acts of deception.

10. Notice that Plato has identified the Just Man with the philosopher.

3

Thinking Critically

Logic

1. Introduction

Before we enter the philosophy of René Descartes and examine a number of philosophical problems that he helped to bring into focus, it will be useful to arm ourselves with a bit of logic. We shall start with sentences and statements and then move on to arguments. Here I shall present a way of determining the validity of an argument. It works in some cases but not all. Finally, we shall take a look at some of the more famous, if not infamous, fallacies.

Once upon a time during the war in Vietnam, Richard Nixon and Henry Kissinger decided to start bombing Cambodia. Now it's very difficult to keep the bombing of a country secret. Word was leaking out, and newsmen in Washington wanted to know if the reports were true. For some time Ron Ziegler, the presidential press secretary, denied these reports, but soon the evidence was overwhelming and he was no longer able to deny them. He called a press conference and newsmen attended, looking forward to a confession from Ziegler that he had been lying all along. And what did he say? He said something like

> Everything that I have stated in the past concerning this topic (the bombing) is no longer operational.

Now we are inclined to laugh, nervously, at this without being quite sure why it strikes us as funny. I suspect it's because, although what Ziegler said in the past about Cambodia looks like the sort of thing that could no longer be operational, it is not. The sort of thing that might be said to no longer be operational is a set of barrack regu-

95

lations. If the commander of some barracks decided that the regulations in force were outmoded, he might replace them with a new set and say that the old ones are no longer operational. But why can one say that barrack regulations are no longer operational but not statements made in the past about bombing Cambodia? Well, one can say it used to be a rule that one had to turn out one's light at 10:00 P.M. but it no longer is. One cannot say it used to be the case that we didn't bomb Cambodia on March 15, 1972, but now it no longer is! The reason that a rule can cease to be operational is that a rule is in the imperative mood—lights out at ten. It makes no claim about the world. Whereas a statement does make a claim about the world. It can make a claim that is either true or false. It's one thing to tell a person that yesterday he was to have his lights out at ten, and it's something else to tell him that yesterday he had his lights out at ten. Only the latter can be either true or false.

It might be thought that certain statements can cease to hold (cease to be true), and so perhaps statements are not all that different from imperatives. For example, someone might say, "It used to be true that the income of Canadian farmers was rising, but it no longer is" or "It used to be the official position of the United States that the Russians are using chemical warfare in Laos, but it no longer is." However, neither of these examples supports this claim. Once we replace the first statement with one like 'The average income of Canadian farmers rose during the period from 1970–80 but has been declining ever since', we get a statement that is either true or false. It can't change its truth value.

The second example is more difficult to deal with. Roughly, what we mean when we make this claim is something like 'It used to be the official belief that the Russians were using chemical warfare, but it no longer is the official belief'. Although facts don't change—if the Russians dropped chemicals on Vietnam on June 15, 1982, then nothing can change that fact—beliefs about those facts *can* change. Ronald Reagan might once have really believed that the Russians dumped chemicals, but then ceased to believe it. If personal beliefs can change, so can official beliefs.

Thus we reach the conclusion that although statements look like linguistic entities that can be or cease to be operational, they are not. Why? Because they make claims about the world. Their truth is dependent upon what happens in the world.

In what follows we shall be entirely concerned with statements. Although commands can enter into arguments, we shall only be concerned with those arguments that feature statements.

2. Sentences and Statements

It's worth noting that there are different types of sentences: (a) commands and milder imperatives, (b) interrogatives, and (c) sentences in the indicative mood. The arguments that we shall be examining are formed out of statements. Only indicative sentences can be used to make statements. We are interested, then, in the distinction between indicative sentences and other kinds of sentences. Consider the following sentences:

1) Sam, smoke!

2) Does Sam smoke?

3) Sam smokes.

The important difference is that, as we have seen, only the last sentence can be true or false. Questions can be embarrassing, and commands can be out of place—such as when the buck private orders the general to stand at attention—but only indicative sentences, or at least the statements they express, can be true or false. I can check on the veracity of (3) but I cannot do so for (1) or (2).

Strictly speaking, we must not say that indicative sentences can be true or false. What can be true or false is not the sentence but the statement it expresses. In our example above, the statement it expresses depends upon the Sam to whom it refers. If I am referring to the Sam that is my horse, then clearly the statement is false; while if I am referring to the Sam who lives next door and who smokes two packages of cigarettes a day, then clearly my statement is true.

Sometimes the sentence will simply fail to express any statement at all: for example, when I write 'Sam smokes' on the board and then go on to say that it has two words, or when I start off a bedtime story with 'Once upon a time there was a mouse who was as big as this house'. Here I pretend to make a statement but do not. It would be out of place, but perhaps likely, for my child to say, "Daddy, that's false!"

Besides distinguishing between the sentence and the statement it is used to express, it is sometimes useful to distinguish between the sentence and the utterance of the sentence. If two people say of the Sam who lives next door that he smokes, then we have two utterances of one sentence. Both utterances express the same statement.

The same statement can also be expressed in another language. If Pierre says of the Sam who lives next door 'Sam fumé', then we have another assertion of the same statement by means of another sentence. Let us look at still another example. Suppose that Abel looks out the window of his Vancouver apartment and, seeing rain coming down, says (a) 'It's raining'. Claude, who lives on the floor below, looks out of his window and says (b) 'Il pleut'. Meanwhile, Baker, who lives in Saskatoon, looks out of his window. Just at that moment somebody who lives above throws out a bucket of water. Baker, thinking it's rain, says (c) 'It's raining'. Now the question is, how many utterances, indicative sentences, and statements do we have? Obviously there are three utterances and two sentences since Abel and Baker utter the same sentence, while Claude utters a different one. How many statements do we have? Since the same statement cannot be both true and false and since what Abel says is true and what Baker says is false, they cannot be expressing the same statement, even though they are uttering the same sentence. That they are expressing different statements is not surprising when it is considered that each is talking about a different weather system. So we have three utterances—a, b, c; two sentences—a/c and b; and two statements—a/b and c.

3. Analytic and Synthetic Statements

Consider the following lists of statements:

I	II
(a) All red roses are red.	All red roses are expensive.
(b) All husbands are married.	All husbands are over eighteen years of age.
(c) If Bill is a (blood) uncle, then he has a brother or a sister.	If Bill is an uncle, then he has kept it a secret.
(d) Either it is raining or it is not.	Either it is raining or it is snowing.

What are the differences between these statements? First, the truth of those in column II seems to be dependent upon the facts of the world. If it's raining then IId is true, but if it's clear then IId is false. On the other hand, it would seem that nothing could falsify Id. No matter what the weather is doing Id remains true. This suggests to us that although the truth value of those in column II (that is, whether they're true or false) is dependent upon the facts of the world, the truth value of those in column I is dependent upon something else.

If we look at Ib, for example, we notice that what makes it true is the way the words are defined. It says that all husbands are married. What is a husband but a married male? In other words, to say 'All husbands are married' is to say nothing more than that 'All married males are married'. We may take it then that a major difference between I and II is that the truth value of those in II is dependent upon the facts of the world, while the truth of those in I is dependent upon the way the key words have been defined. Those sentences in column II make statements about the world. Those in coumn I do not state anything about the world, though they sometimes appear to do so. If they made a statement about the world then we could envisage the situation under which each would be false. But this we cannot do.

Statements like those in column I are generally called *analytic,* and statements like those in column II are generally called *synthetic.* According to the famous German philosopher Immanuel Kant (1724-1804), the main difference between them is that in an analytic statement the predicate term is contained in the subject term, but not so in a synthetic statement. For example, in 'All husbands are married', the predicate term 'is married' is contained in the subject term 'husband', while in 'All husbands are over eighteen years of age', 'over eighteen years of age' is not contained in 'husband'. Although this criterion for distinguishing between the two has received a fair amount of support, it is too restrictive. 'Either it is raining or it is not' is clearly analytic, but its predicate term is not contained in its subject term for the simple reason that it's not a subject-predicate statement.

Kant, however, offered a second criterion, one that allows us to distinguish clearly between the statements in column I and those in column II. He pointed out that if those of the first type are denied, then a self-contradictory statement emerges, whereas if those of the second type are denied (negated) then no contradiction occurs. For example, the negation of

All husbands are married,

which is

It's not the case that all husbands are married,

or, in other words,

Some husbands are not married,

which is equivalent to

Some married men are not married,

is clearly self-contradictory. Similarly, the negation of

Either it is raining or it is not,

which is

It's not the case that it is raining or it is not raining,

which is equivalent to

It's not raining and it is raining,

is also clearly self-contradictory.

On the other hand, if a synthetic statement (for example, "All red roses are expensive") is denied, although a statement is obtained ("It's not the case that all red roses are expensive") that is the contradictory (of "All red roses are expensive"), no self-contradictory statement is obtained. One does not contradict oneself in saying "It's not the case that all red roses are expensive." Owing to its clarity, let us, adopt this as our criterion for determining whether a statement is analytic or synthetic. If a statement's negation is self-contradictory, it's analytic; if its negation is not self-contradictory, it's synthetic.

In order to make the criterion foolproof, however, we must add a clause. The negation of a self-contradictory statement is not self-contradictory (in fact it's analytic) and we don't want to find ourselves classifying self-contradictory statements as synthetic. Thus our criterion must run as follows:

An analytic statement is any statement whose negation is self-contradictory.

and

A synthetic statement is any statement whose negation is not self-contradictory and is not itself self-contradictory.

Consider now the statement 'All water boils at 212°F'. Presumably this was discovered to be true of water. Somebody at one time put some water in a pot, put a thermometer inside it, and discovered that the water boiled when the thermometer reached 212°F. Thus there seems no doubt that this statement is synthetic. Now suppose that scientists are looking for a better way of identifying water than as the stuff that comes out of taps, is found in lakes and rivers, and is good to drink. They decide that one of the conditions water-like liquid will have to satisfy before it can be called "water" is that it has to boil at 212°F. If this were to happen, then the sentence 'All water boils at 212°F' will no longer express a synthetic statement. It will now express an analytic statement.[1] You may wonder how this could happen. How can something that could have been falsified by a particular kind of experience become something that no longer can be falsified by an experience of that kind? The answer is that 'water' doesn't mean the same in the second statement. It's a different statement even though it looks the same. If we use 'water' in the first way and come upon some liquid that has all the features of water but doesn't boil at 212°F., then, after exhaustive tests had been carried out, we would have to say that our claim was false. If we use 'water' in the second way, and all this were to again happen, then we would say that this liquid we took to be water wasn't really water. If 'water' is partly defined as boiling at 212°F., and what we have in front of us does not boil at 212°F., then it is not water.

In what follows, we will find that an enormous amount of philosophical mischief has been caused by the failure to distinguish between these two uses of a sentence. For example, sometimes in a discussion on morality someone claims that all men are selfish. This looks at first like a profound truth about the nature of man, but we often find that when we press the speaker, he has defined 'selfish' in such a way that the sentence 'All men are selfish' expresses an analytic statement. Not only can others be deceived into thinking that a profound synthetic truth has been unearthed, but so can the speaker, since often he is not clear on how he is using his words.

4. Arguments

Having discussed the differences between indicative sentences and the other types of sentences, indicative sentences and statements, and analytic and synthetic statements, we are now in a position to distinguish between different types of arguments.

Logicians use the word 'argument' in a rather restricted sense. When we hear the pots and pans crashing against the wall next door, we are tempted to say that the Smiths, who live there, are having another argument. This is not what the logician has in mind. For the logician, an argument consists of a number of statements; some of them form the premises and usually one statement forms the conclusion. It is assumed that the conclusion in some way follows from the premises. An argument cannot be offered merely by stating a number of statements:

It's cold outside.

It's warm inside.

Jane is coming for tea.

is not an argument. I have to assert that one of them, the conclusion, follows from the other two. For example:

All men are mortal.

Socrates is a man.

Therefore, Socrates is mortal.

Notice that statements—not sentences per se—are featured in arguments. We assume that I am using 'Socrates is a man' to say something about something or someone—most likely the famous Greek philosopher. We can't assume that I am just practicing my elocution. Furthermore, I have to be using my words in a consistent manner in each of the statements. If I use 'Socrates' as it appears in the second premise (the statements above are all premises) to refer to the Greek philosopher and, 'Socrates' as it appears in the conclusion to refer to my cat, then clearly the conclusion does not follow from the premises.

Statements are not the only linguistic entities that can feature in arguments. Commands can also feature. For example:

Shop at the largest store in town.

Eaton's is the largest store in town.

Therefore, shop at Eaton's.

This is a perfectly respectable argument. We shall, however, restrict ourselves here to arguments that are formed out of statements.

5. Inductive and Deductive Arguments

Examine the following arguments. Can you notice any difference between them?

<table>
<tr><td align="center">I</td><td align="center">II</td></tr>
<tr><td>Lead melts at 327°C.[NAP].</td><td>Everytime we have melted a block of lead it has melted at 327°C.[NAP].</td></tr>
<tr><td>This is a block of lead.</td><td></td></tr>
<tr><td>―――――――――――――――</td><td>This is a block of lead.</td></tr>
<tr><td>Therefore, it will melt at 327°C.[NAP].</td><td>―――――――――――――――</td></tr>
<tr><td></td><td>Therefore, it will melt at 327°C.[NAP].</td></tr>
</table>

Both are respectable arguments. In both cases the conclusion could be said to follow from the premises, but there is a difference between them. It's tempting to express this difference by saying that in argument I, if the premises are true the conclusion must be true, while in argument II, if the premises are true, it's not the case that the conclusion must be true. But this way of expressing the difference is still very obscure.

It's not clear in what sense the conclusion in I must be true if the premises are true. Furthermore, this claim seems to be also true of II. After all, if we have tested lead many, many times and it has always melted at 327°C.NAP, then surely the next time we melt some lead it must melt at 327°C.NAP.

Perhaps a clearer way of expressing the difference is to say that in I, if the premises are true the conclusion logically must be true, while in II this is not the case. This is on the right track but it's not good enough, because it's not clear what is meant by the phrase 'logically must'.

Our reason for wanting to say of argument I that if the premises are true the conclusion logically must be true, is that if we were to assert the premises and deny the conclusion, we would get a contradiction, whereas in the case of argument II this is not so. We would not be contradicting ourselves if we were to assert the premises of argument II and yet deny the conclusion. We would be saying something idiotic but not contradictory. Now we know that a self-contradictory situation can never exist. The book that is in front of us cannot be in front of us and not in front of us at the same time. In order for a self-contradictory situation to obtain, the statement that describes it would have to be true. But self-contradictory (SC) statements can never be true. Therefore, self-contradictory situations can never obtain. Finally, given that an SC situation can never obtain, it follows that if the premises of argument I are true, the denial of the conclusion cannot be true. But if the denial of the conclusion cannot be true, then the conclusion itself must (logically must) be true.

Of course the conclusion doesn't follow in the sense that having asserted the premises we must go on and assert the conclusion. Having asserted the premises, we can stop talking or go on and say virtually anything else. But the conclusion does follow in the sense that if we were to go on and assert its denial, we would be contradicting ourselves.

Sometimes the difference between I and II is expressed by saying that in I the conclusion is contained within the premises, whereas in II the conclusion goes beyond the premises. This is not a bad way of marking the difference between the two, but it's not clear what we mean by "contained in." Furthermore, there are many deductive arguments for which this picture does not apply very well. For example, in

If it's snowing then it's cold.

It's not cold.

Therefore, it's not snowing.

the conclusion does not appear to be "contained in" the premises.

Having located the sense in which if the premises of a deductive argument are true, the conclusion must be true, we can go on to discuss the inductive arguments. There is an assumption underlying science that the future will be like the past—that like causes will have like effects. As a result, if every time we have melted lead in varying conditions we have found that it always melts at 327°C.[NAP] and never at some other temperature, then the more times this happens the more sure we can be that it will always do so. Or take a different example: Every time I drop an object, like a book or an eraser, I notice that it always falls toward the earth. As a result of this experience I come to be certain that next time I drop, say a pen, it will also fall to the floor.

It is this uniformity of nature—the future being like the past, then, that makes it possible to say of an inductive argument, if the premises are true and they point to a wide range of relevant data, the conclusion must also be true. It is for this reason that the premises of inductive arguments may be described as giving support to the conclusion. In a poor inductive argument they give little support; in a good inductive argument they give strong support; and in the best, overwhelming support.

The difference between a deductive argument and an inductive argument can now be expressed. In a deductive argument, if the premises are asserted and the conclusion denied, a contradiction will result. Let us use the word "entail" to express this relation. That is to say, a statement or set of statements is said to entail another statement if and only if to assert the first statement(s) and deny the second statement will result in a contradiction.[2] Thus a deductive argument is any argument where the premises entail the conclusion, while an inductive argument is one in which the premises do not entail the conclusion but instead give support to the conclusion.

6. Validity and Soundness

Sometimes we want to say of a deductive argument that it is valid, and sometimes we want to say (of another) that it is invalid. For example, we would want to say that

If it's snowing then it's cold.

It's snowing.

Therefore, it's cold.

is valid, while

If it's snowing then it's cold.

It's cold.

_____

Therefore, it is snowing.

is invalid. What then is the difference? The relevant difference is that in the first example it's impossible for the premises to be true and the conclusion false, while in the other case this is possible, for it may be cold and not snowing. The claim that if it's snowing it's cold does not preclude it being cold and not snowing. Or to put the matter differently, in the first example we cannot assert the premises and deny the conclusion without committing a contradiction, while in the second case we can. In the first case the premises entail the conclusion, in the second case the premises do not.

It's common to say that valid and invalid deductive arguments are two different kinds of deductive arguments in the way that mallards and canvasbacks are two different kinds of ducks. But since in an invalid deductive argument the premises do not entail the conclusion, it can hardly be said to be a different kind of deductive argument. It's not an argument at all. The difference between a valid and invalid deductive argument is more like the difference between a real duck and a decoy. A real duck is just a duck, while a decoy is not a duck at all but something that only looks like (has the same form as) a duck. Similarly, a valid deductive argument is just a deductive argument, while an invalid deductive argument is something that looks like a deductive argument but is not. If we look at matters in this light we can say that

If it's snowing then it's cold.

It's cold.

_____

Therefore, it's snowing.

is an invalid deductive argument because the premises appear to entail the conclusion but do not, while

It's cold outside.

It's warm inside.

_____

Therefore, Mt. Everest was first climbed in 1952.

is not. The trouble with the second example is that it doesn't even look like a deductive argument. In order for a set of statements to be classi-

fied as an invalid deductive argument it has to at least look like, but
not be, a deductive argument.

It's tempting to classify an inductive argument as an invalid deductive argument. But this is a mistake. Inductive arguments share with
invalid deductive arguments the feature that the premises do not entail the conclusion, but there is still a big difference between them. Invalid
deductive arguments look like deductive arguments, but inductive
arguments do not.

Logicians use the term "sound" in a rather restrictive manner. Most
people would say that if an argument is valid then it's sound, but
logicians; and we, too, from now on, restrict "sound" to those arguments
that are not only valid but have true premises as well. One useful feature of deductive arguments, as we have seen, is that if the premises
are true the conclusion is also true. So if the premises are known to
be true, we can rest assured that the conclusion is also true. Deductive
arguments are sometimes described as *truth preserving*.

If one or more of the premises of a valid deductive argument is
false, nothing follows concerning the truth value of the conclusion. Some
people are inclined to think that if the premises are false and the argument is valid then the conclusion must be false, but this is a mistake.
For example, in the valid argument

All Albertans are Texans.

All Texans are Canadians.

Therefore, all Albertans are Canadians.

both the premises are false, but the conclusion is true. Although an
argument can be valid with one or more false premises, such arguments
are obviously of little use. The same can also be said about inductive
arguments. When it's said that the premises support the conclusion it
is assumed that the premises are true. We wouldn't be interested in an
inductive argument with false premises.

As a rule the statements that form a deductive argument are synthetic, but there is no reason one couldn't form a deductive argument
out of analytic statements. For example, the following is a perfectly
valid argument.

All matrons are wives.

All wives are married.

Therefore, all matrons are married.

However, the premises are of little use since we already know from the meaning of 'matrons' that all matrons are married. The same point can be made about arguments where there is a mixture of synthetic and analytic statements.

All husbands are married.

Jones is a husband.

Therefore, Jones is married.

Here the first premise is superfluous. We can derive the conclusion directly from the second premise.

Finally, we cannot have an argument with analytic premises and a synthetic conclusion. The reason for this is that, as we have seen, analytic statements make no claim about the world. Their truth is independent of the way the world is. But synthetic statements make a claim about the world. Since the conclusion of an argument is in some sense contained in the premises, it follows that we cannot derive a synthetic statement from a set of analytic statements. We could only derive a statement that makes a claim about the world from a set of statements that also make claims about the world; in other words, from synthetic statements.

7. Contraries, Contradictions, and Inconsistency

We must be careful not to confuse contradictories with contraries. For instance, 'He is over 6 feet tall' and 'It is not the case that he is over 6 feet tall' are contradictories. (The symbol " $\sim$ " means 'it is not the case that', and is used to negate a statement.) If the first is true, the second must be false; and if the first is false, the second must be true. 'He is over 6 feet tall' and 'He is under 6 feet tall' are, on the other hand, contraries. Although they cannot both be true, they can both be false. They are both false when he is just 6 feet tall. Similarly, 'It is hot' and 'It is cold' are contraries, while 'It is hot' and ' $\sim$ it is hot' are contradictories. The statement ' $\sim$ it is hot' does not entail 'It is cold', for it may be lukewarm.

Although putting a "not" in front of a statement will give us the contradictory, sometimes putting "not" in front of one of the words will only give us the contrary. Take for example 'It was right of you to do x'. We might think that the contradictory of this is 'It was not right of you to do x'. But 'It was not right of you to do x' ordinarily means 'It was *wrong* of you to do x', and this is only the *contrary* of 'It was right of you to do x'. The contradictory of this last statement is ' $\sim$ it was right of you to do x', which means something like 'Either it was all right for you to do x or it was wrong of you to do x'.

It isn't necessary to assert two contradictory statements in order to be classified as having contradicted yourself or, in other words, to be classified as having said something self-contradictory. It is sufficient that the statements be contraries. If I say 'Jones is over 6 feet tall and Jones is under over 6 feet tall', my statement is self-contradictory and its denial '~ Jones is over 6 feet tall and Jones is under 6 feet tall' is analytic.[3]

Both contraries and contradictories can be classified as inconsistent. In the statements that follow, each pair is inconsistent:

(a) "Jones is over 6 feet tall" and "Jones is under 6 feet tall."
(b) "Jones is over 6 feet tall" and "~ Jones is over 6 feet tall."

In short, to say that p and q are inconsistent is to say that p and q are contraries or contradictories. From this it follows that if p and q are inconsistent, they cannot both be true.

8. Validity

Very often we know that the premises of our argument are true, but we don't know whether the argument is valid, and so we don't know if the conclusion is true. Consider the following argument:

If it's raining then it's cold.

If it's cold then I'll catch the flu.

Either I won't catch the flu or I won't be able to go on my holiday.

I shall go on my holiday.

Therefore, it's not raining.

It's not clear from looking at this argument whether it is valid. It would therefore be useful to have a technique that will enable us to test the validity of this argument. The following truth table technique will do the trick.[4]

Any synthetic statement, as we have seen, is either true or false. For example, 'It's raining' can be either true or false, and the same is the case for 'It's cold'. (From now on I shall often use "T" for "true" and "F" for "false.") What about 'It's raining and it's cold'? Well, it is a complex statement whose truth is dependent upon the truth of the simple statements. If both the simple statements are true then it is true. If at least one is false then it is false. We can express this in truth table form in the following way. ("R" = "It's raining," and "C" = "It's cold.")

R	C	R and C
T	T	T
T	F	F
F	T	F
F	F	F

Notice that this table gives us all the logically possible truth value combinations of R and C. One of the combinations must obtain.

We can generalize on this truth table. Letting p and q stand for any two statements (they may be called statement variables), we obtain a similar table.

p	q	p and q
T	T	T
T	F	F
F	T	F
F	F	F

Logicians make use of a number of connectives that, unlike English language connectives—such as "and" and "implies"—are defined by the truth table. The connectives are '~', '·', 'v', '⊃', and '≡'. As you can see from the following table that defines these connectives, '~' means something like 'it's not the case that', '·' means something like 'and', 'v' means something like 'or', '⊃' means something like 'if—then' and '≡' means something like 'is equivalent to'.

p	q	~p	(p · q)	(p v q)	(p⊃ q)	(p≡ q)
T	T	F	T	T	T	T
T	F	F	F	T	F	F
F	T	T	F	T	T	F
F	F	T	F	F	T	T

Although the symbols '~' and '·' are interpreted to allow a fairly close match with 'it's not the case that' and 'and', the 'v' symbol is only similar to the one use of 'or' and the '⊃' symbol is rather distant from 'if—then'.

We use 'or' in two different ways: inclusively and exclusively. If I say that you can apply for a particular job if you have either a B.A. or a B.S., I don't intend to stop you from applying if you have both. Here I use it in the inclusive way. But if it says on a menu that you can have apple pie or cherries for dessert, the menu is usually taken as saying that you can't have both. Here it is used in the exclusive way. Thus 'v' means the same as 'or' when 'or' is used in the inclusive way. When 'p' and 'q' are both true then 'p · q' is true.

Although '⊃' is somewhat distant from 'if—then', it does share one important feature. The logical relations 'p ⊃ q' and 'if p then q' are both false when the antecedent ('p') is true and the consequent ('q') is false. 'If it's raining then it's cold' is false when 'It's raining' is true and 'It's cold' is false, and 'p ⊃ q' is false when 'p' is true and 'q' is false. We can then, with certain reservations, use the truth table connectives as stand-ins for our ordinary language connectives.

Some statements when tested by our truth tables will turn out to be true under only certain conditions, some will be true under all conditions, and some will turn out to be false under all conditions. Those that are true under some conditions are synthetic, those that are true under all conditions are analytic, and those that are false under all conditions are self-contradictory. For example, 'Smith is 6 feet tall and Jones is 5 feet tall' is synthetic because its truth table would be:

S	J	S · J
T	T	T
T	F	F
F	T	F
F	F	F

It is true only where S and J are both true. But 'Either it's raining or it's not raining' is analytic because it's always true.

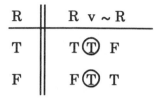

R		R v ~ R	
T		T Ⓣ F	
F		F Ⓣ T	

'It's raining and it's not raining' is self-contradictory because it's truth table gives us:

R		R · ~ R	
T		T Ⓕ F	
F		F Ⓕ T	

Notice that the negation of 'R · ~ R', which is ' ~(R · ~ R)', is always true. What this indicates is that the negation of any self-contradictory statement is analytic. It is also to be noted that the negation of an analytic statement is self-contradictory.

We can make use of truth tables not only to determine whether a given statement is self-contradictory but also to determine whether one statement is inconsistent with another, or in other words, whether one would be contradicting oneself if one were to assert both of them. For example, if one were to assert p and then assert ~ p one would be contradicting oneself. This fact is displayed by the following table:

p		~ p
T		F
F		T

We know that 'p' and '~ p' are inconsistent because there is no row where they are both true. On the other hand, 'p' and 'p v q' are consistent because in

p	q	p v q
T	T	T
T	F	T
F	T	T
F	F	F

row 1 and 2 both are true.

Now then, we have seen from our definitions of "deduction" (p. 104) and "entailment" (see the end of this section at p. 127, for a list) that a given deductive argument is valid if and only if the assertion of the premises and the denial of the conclusion will involve a contradiction. There will be no row where both are true. We have also seen that if a given argument is not valid, then the assertion of the premises is not inconsistent with the denial of the conclusion. That is to say, there will be a row where both the premises and the denial of the conclusion are true. Suppose we want to test the validity of the following argument:

(a) If there is klister on the skis the skis will stick.

The skis will not stick.

_____

Therefore, there is no klister on the skis.

First we put the argument into symbolic form:

(b) K ⊃ S

$\underline{\sim S}$

∴ ∼ K

then we see if we can, in the following manner, assert the premises and deny the conclusion without obtaining an inconsistency:

		Premises		Denial of the Conclusion
K	S	(K ⊃ S)	~S	~~K[5]
T	T	T	F	T
T	F	F	T	T
F	T	T	F	F
F	F	T	T	F

As we can see, there is no row where the premises and the denial of the conclusion are both true, therefore the premises entail the conclusion and so the argument is valid. If the argument had been invalid, then there would have been no inconsistency between the assertion of the premises and the denial of the conclusion; that is to say, there would have been a row where both the premises and the conclusion were true.

Consider for example the following argument:

> If he had smoked as a child his growth would have been stunted.
>
> He didn't smoke as a child.
> _____
> Therefore, his growth was not stunted.

It can be symbolized as:

S ⊃ G

~S
———
∴ ~G

which gives us

	S	G	(S ⊃ G)	~~S	~~G
1	T	T	T	F	T
2	T	F	F	F	F
3	F	T	T	T	T
4	F	F	T	T	F

and which we can see from row 3 to be invalid. It is possible to assert the premises and deny the conclusion without inconsistency, therefore it is invalid.

Let us now return to our original argument (p. 108). It can be symbolized as follows:

$$R \supset C$$
$$C \supset F$$
$$\sim F \text{ v } H$$
$$\underline{H}$$
$$\therefore \sim R$$

Unfortunately, our expansion of this will have 16 rows. However, we can simplify matters by only looking at the rows where all the premises are true. This is because the premises and the denial of the conclusion can only all be true in those cases where the premises are true. Fortunately there is only one such row. This is where we have $\boxed{RCFH}$ and so obtain $\boxed{FFFT}$

R C F H	(R $\supset$ C)	(C $\supset$ F)	($\sim$F v H)	H	$\sim\sim$R
F F F T	T	T	T	T	F

But in this row the denial of the conclusion is false. As a result, the assertion of the premises and the denial of the conclusion involves an inconsistency, and so the argument is valid.[6] The following argument forms are all valid, as may be discovered through application of the truth table technique. As a result, any argument of any of the following forms is valid. Each form has a name:

$$p \supset q$$
$$\underline{p}$$
$$\therefore q$$

Modus Ponens

$$p \supset q$$
$$\underline{\sim q}$$
$$\therefore \sim p$$

Modus Tollens[7]

$$p \supset q$$
$$\underline{q \supset r}$$
$$\therefore p \supset r$$

Hypothetical Syllogism

$$(p \supset q) \cdot (r \supset s)$$
$$\underline{p \text{ v } r}$$
$$\therefore q \text{ v } s$$

Constructive Dilemma (see page 141)

p v q   Disjunctive Syllogism
~p
∴ q

There are, of course, many, many more.

9. Logical Equivalence

If we discover by applying the truthtable technique to two statements that one is true when the other is true, and false when the other is false, then the two statements may be said to be logically equivalent. For example, 'p' and '~~up' are logically equivalent since

p	~~p
T	T
F	F

The statements 'p ⊃ q' and ' ~(p · q)' are also logically equivalent (LE) since in

p	q	p ⊃ q	~(p · ~ q)
T	T	T	T
T	F	F	F
F	T	T	T
F	F	T	T

where one is T the other is T and where one is F the other is F. As a result, we can interpret 'p ⊃ q' as 'It's not the case that p and not q' rather than as 'p implies q'. It is better to interpret it this way because "·" is closer to 'and' and '~' is closer to 'not' than '⊃' is to 'implies'. Some other equivalences are as follows:

1.   p · q   and   q · p

2.   p v q   and   q v p

3.   p ⊃ q   and   ~p v q

4. $\sim(p \cdot \sim q)$ and $\sim p \vee q$

5. $\sim p \cdot \sim q$ and $\sim(p \vee q)$

6. $\sim p \vee \sim q$ and $\sim(p \cdot q)$

7. $p \equiv q$ and $(p \supset q) \cdot (q \supset p)$

8. $p \supset q$ and $\sim q \supset \sim p$

10. Entailment and Implication

According to our definition of 'entails', to say that 'p' entails 'q' is to say that to assert 'p' and deny 'q' is to contradict oneself. In other words, 'p · ∼q' is inconsistent. The denial of any inconsistent statement is analytic. Therefore, if 'p' entails 'q' then '∼(p · ∼q)' is analytic. But if '∼(p · ∼q)' is analytic then 'p ⊃ q' is also analytic, since '∼(p · ∼q)' is equivalent to 'p ⊃ q'. Thus another way of saying that 'p' entails 'q' is to say that 'p ⊃ q' is analytic.

For example, we know from page 107 that "(K ⊃ S) · ∼ S" 'entails' "∼K." It follows, then, that [(K ⊃ S)˙ ∼S] ⊃ ∼K will be analytic. This gives us an alternative way to test an argument. Just put a horse-shoe (⊃) between the premises and the conclusion; and if the statement that has been formed is analytic, then the argument is valid. If, on the other hand, the statement turns out to be synthetic, then the argument is invalid.

The fact that valid arguments can be interpreted as analytic statements is apt to blur the distinction between the two. A deductive argument is composed of statements that may or may not be analytic. Most likely they will be synthetic. Corresponding to each argument is a statement that is analytic if and only if the argument is valid, and synthetic if and only if the argument is not valid. Even if an analytic statement corresponds to each valid argument, it doesn't follow that the argument is an analytic statement, or that it is composed of analytic statements. Some people are inclined to think that deductive arguments are composed of analytic statements but this, as we have seen, is mistaken.

Sometimes we want a word that is weaker than 'entails'. For example, someone might say, 'Those clouds in the sky imply that it is going to rain' or 'The fact that the iron ball is being heated implies that it is expanding'. What then is the difference between 'implies' as it is used in this context and 'entails'? The obvious difference is that we restrict 'entails' to those cases where it would be self-contradictory or, in other words, inconsistent to assert the premises and deny the conclusion. Let us now move on to clarify the sense in which the clouds imply rain, and the heating implies expansion.

We saw before that the premises of a good inductive argument give strong support to the conclusion. When we have an argument of this sort the premises may be said to imply the conclusion inductively. The claim that every time iron has been heated it has expanded implies that the next time it is heated it will also expand. When it is said that the fact that the iron ball is being heated implies that it is expanding, one points to this evidence. If iron balls usually didn't expand when heated, we couldn't say that the fact that an iron ball is being heated implies that it is expanding.

In the clouds-rain case, the implication is weaker. As a rule, it doesn't rain every time there are ominous clouds in the sky. But if it rains often enough, then we can say that the clouds imply rain—though perhaps it would be better to say that the clouds imply that it is likely to rain.

The horseshoe symbol '⊃' is sometimes called the sign of material implication. This is perhaps a misnomer since all we really mean when we say that 'p ⊃ q' is, 'it's not the case that p and not q'. There is nothing implicative about that. However, we are justified in using '⊃' as a substitute for 'implies' and for 'if—then', because every time we have a case of 'implies' or 'if p then q', we have a case of 'p ⊃ q'. In other words, 'p implies q' entails 'p ⊃ q', and so does 'if p then q'. The proof of this is quite simple. If 'p implies q' didn't entail 'p ⊃ q', then it would be possible to assert that p implies q, and deny that p ⊃ q without contradiction. This would mean that one could assert 'p implies q' and then go on and assert 'p · ~q'.[8] But having asserted, for example, that heating the ball implies that it's expanding, one could hardly go on and say that the ball is being heated but it is not expanding. In the same vein, having asserted that if the ball is heated it will expand, one could hardly go on and say that the ball will be heated but it won't expand.

There is one more pitfall that we must guard against. Because of the close relation between 'therefore' and 'entails', we are tempted to think that 'p therefore q' could be written as " 'p' entails 'q'," but there is a world of difference between the two. When I say 'Jim is married therefore he has a wife' I am saying that Jim is married. But when I say " 'Jim is married' entails 'Jim has a wife', " I am not saying that Jim is married. The point is even more obvious if we compare, 'The fuse has been lit, therefore the bomb will explode' with 'If the fuse has been lit the bomb will explode'. If someone makes the first claim, we have reason to run for our lives; but if someone makes the second claim, we have as yet no reason to run.

11. A Priori and A Posteriori

As well as being classified as analytic and synthetic, statements can also be classified as *a priori* and *a posteriori*. To say that a statement is a priori is to say that it can be known to be true independently of experience. To say that a statement is a posteriori is to say that it cannot be known to be true independently of experience. Any analytic statement can be known to be true independently of experience. We don't have to carry out a census to know that all husbands are married. Of course we do have to have enough experience to understand the statement, but we don't need any experience beyond that to know it to be true. Thus all analytic statements can be known to be true a priori. Most synthetic statements, on the other hand, can only be known to be true or false on the basis of experience. In order to know that all husbands in Canada are over fourteen years of age, we need more experience than what is required to understand the meaning of the terms. We need to go out into the country and take a look.

It looks as if all synthetic statements are going to turn out to be a posteriori. If a statement makes a substantial claim about the world then surely it can only be known to be true on the basis of experience. And yet the great German philosopher Immanuel Kant wanted to claim that some synthetic statements could be known to be true a priori. Consider, for example, the following: Suppose we have two fulcrums, A and B, which are some distance apart, and a number of cylindrical rigid rods that will just stretch from A to B. One of these rods is straight. And by "straight" is meant that if you look at it "end on" all that is seen is a circle. It neither bows to the left or right nor up or down. The other rods are bent in various ways. Kant would claim that the statement 'The straight rod is the shortest rod that stretches from A to B' is synthetic and can be known to be true a priori.[9] Obviously if this sentence is going to express a synthetic statement, "shortest" has to be defined in a different way from "straight." Perhaps the following way will do. Suppose we have an nonelastic measuring string. Let us call it 'α'. Now in order to measure the length of an object, we apply α successively along the length of the object. We cannot use a measuring ruler, because some of the rods are curved. The shortest rod will now be the rod that requires the fewest successive applications of the measuring string. And so the Kantian claim becomes: "The statement 'Of the rods that will just stretch from A to B, the straight rod is the rod that requires the fewest successive applications of α' is synthetic and can be known to be true a priori."

Is Kant right? Suppose, for example, that we find in a number of tests that rod II (a bent rod) in the following diagram requires fewer successive applications of the measuring string than rod I (the straight rod). Would this lead us to say that II was shorter than rod I?

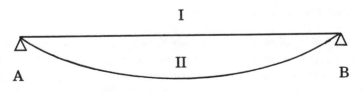

I think not. What we would say is that we must have made a mistake and mismeasured rod II. We would think that if rod II were straightened it would stretch past B as in the next diagram.

II

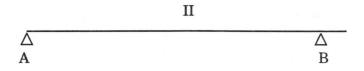

A   B

Suppose that we can straighten II and, much to our surprise, it doesn't stretch as far as B, as shown in the following diagram.

II

A   B

Would this lead us to say that II was shorter than I? Again, I think not. We would most likely say that II must have shrunk!—that II was longer than I, even though it is now shorter. In other words, nothing will move us from saying that we know, and know a priori, that I was the shortest. Thus I think we have to admit that at least one synthetic statement can be known to be true a priori. But if this statement is synthetic a priori then it is most likely that a great number of other statements of geometry are synthetic a priori as well.

Kant was greatly puzzled by all this. In fact, the moving force behind his *Critique of Pure Reason* (1781) was a desire to show how it was possible that some synthetic statements could be known to be true a priori. As well as many of the statements of plane and solid geometry, Kant also declared that many statements of mathematics were also synthetic a priori. Kant seems to be wrong on this later claim. No doubt many statements of mathematics are a priori, but this is only because they are analytic. For example, Kant wanted to claim that '7 + 5 = 12' was synthetic a priori. But if we accept that '1 = 1' is analytic, and that '2' is by definition equal to '1 + 1', '3' is by definition equal to '2 + 1' and so on, it will follow that '7 + 5 = 12' is analytic—at least in the sense that its denial will involve a contradiction.

It might be objected that Kant was also mistaken about 'A straight line is the shortest distance between two points' (see endnote 9 in this chapter). No doubt as this *sentence* is used in Euclidian geometry it expresses an a priori statement, but it also expresses an analytic one. Indeed there are other geometries in which this sentence expresses a self-contradictory statement. Furthermore, so the objection continues, if the sentence is used in the way that we have used it so that it expresses a synthetic statement, that statement, far from being one that can be known a priori to be true, is not only synthetic but actually false. The shortest distance between two points, when those points are stars at great distance from one another, is not a straight line. We may be obliged to think that a straight line is the shortest distance between two points, but this only tells us something about our psychological make up and nothing about the world.

I don't know what to make of this objection. One can imagine it being the case that we are psychologically incapable of thinking of a lion, say, as friendly. If someone claimed that he had a friendly lion, some psychological block would prevent us from accepting this. But this seems to be very different from our inability to think of a curved line as the shortest distance. (If bent rod II is straightened, it's just got to stretch past B.) Perhaps the point behind the objection is this: Light does not travel in a straight line. As a result, what appears to be a straight line is not a straight line. But if this is all that lies behind the objection, then we have not been shown that a straight line is not the shortest distance between two points. All that we have been shown is that what *appears* to be a straight line is not the shortest distance. However, I shall now leave this problem for the reader to tackle.

12. Necessary and Contingent

Finally, most statements can be classified as being either *necessary* or *contingent*. A necessary statement is claimed to be one that is true in all logically possible situations. No matter how the world is, it remains true. A contingent statement, on the other hand, is one that is not true in all logically possible situations. Its truth is contingent upon the way the world actually is.

All analytic statements would be classified as necessary statements since they are true in all possible situations. No matter what happens, all husbands will be married. It would even be true in a world devoid of people, for what it really says is that if any being is a husband, then that being is married. Thus it remains true no matter what. This, as we have seen, is only a result of how we have defined our words.

Synthetic statements that can be known to be true a priori will also, if they exist, be classified as necessary. Here the source of the necessity is different. It's not because of the way that we have defined our words that a straight line is the shortest distance between two points; given that what we have said above is correct, it's because of the way the world is. We might say that statements of this sort are necessary because they correspond to facts that are necessary, facts that would obtain in every logically possible situation. No matter how different the world was, a straight line would *still* be the shortest distance between two points.

It might be thought that any necessary statement, no matter what the source of its necessity, can be known a priori to be true. However, according to Saul Kripke, an influential philosopher and logician, this is not so. There are, according to Kripke, some necessary statements that can only be known to be true a posteriori. Let us look at some examples of where this might be thought to be the case.

First of all, we might discover the solution to a very long and complex mathematical problem by looking at the result printed out on a computer. No doubt if this is the solution, it is necessarily the solution, but it has been discovered by empirical means. Thus we can come to know that a necessary statement is true a posteriori.

I don't think that this argument supports the claim that some necessary truths are a posteriori. The fact that I can determine that $1,382 + 9,675$ is $11,057$ by means of my calculator doesn't mean that this statement is not a priori in the sense that we have been using the word. As we have been using the word, an a priori statement is one that is *capable* of being known to be true on the basis of reason and not on the basis of experience. It might be the case that the problem solved by the computer would take us a million years to solve. But still, we can imagine someone living a million years and solving it a priori in that time span.

Second, according to Kripke, being mammalian, for example, is a necessary property of tigers. As a result, the statement 'Tigers are mammals' is a necessary proposition. But since this is found out through empirical means, it is a posteriori. Kripke realizes that tigers might have turned out to not be mammals; his claim is that, given that tigers are mammals it's not the case that they might not have been mammals. No doubt Kripke has a point here. Being a mammal is essential to tigers in a way that having stripes is not. So we may agree that, given that tigers have yellow stripes, they might not have had yellow stripes; while given that they are mammals, it's not the case that they might not have been mammals.

Kripke is on to something here, but I think that all he is on to is a point about how we use language. Scientifically, we will want to identify objects by their more (physically) internal and stable features. Suppose, for example, a new disease develops; people turn purple and develop a high fever. As a result we call it Purple Fever. Now we know that one's color and one's temperature do not provide the best ways to identify a disease. The best way to identify it is by the bacteria or virus that causes it. Thus we might say (now) that if it turns out that a virus, call it Virus B, is the source of Purple Fever, then Virus B is necessarily present in anyone suffering from Purple Fever. Furthermore, we might say that one could suffer from Purple Fever and not be purple or have a fever! We keep the permanent identifying feature of Purple Fever in abeyance until its microscopic source is discovered. Once it is discovered it becomes the identifying feature, and once it (Virus B) becomes the identifying feature then sentences such as 'Virus B is the source of Purple Fever' will express analytic statements.

When we say that if Virus B is the source of Purple Fever, it is not the case that it might not have been the source of Purple Fever, what we are saying is that if Virus B turns out to be the source of Purple Fever, then we shall use it as the identifying feature. As a result, 'Virus B is the source to Purple Fever' will be used to express an analytic statement.

Similarly, if we have yet to approach tigers, owing to their dangerous dispositions, we might say that if tigers turn out to be mammals, they are necessarily mammals. But what we shall mean by this is that if the beasts we have formerly identified as tigers by their stripes turn out to be mammals, then we shall use 'being a mammal' as an identifying and thus logically necessary feature for being a tiger. As a result, the sentence 'Tigers are mammals' will be used to express a statement that is analytic.

13. Physically Possible—Logically Possible, Physically Impossible—Logically Impossible, and Physically Necessary—Logically Necessary

It is natural to think that logical impossibility is a super form of physical impossibility, and that the difference between them is just a matter of degree. We also assume that everything that is logically impossible is also physically impossible. For example, it's physically difficult for me to run the mile from point A to point B in 8 minutes; it's physically impossible for me to run it in 2 minutes; it's even more physically impossible (if one may say so) to run it in 2 seconds; and it's logically impossible for me to be at point A and point B at the same time. Thus it looks as though what is logically impossible is also physically impossible and that logical impossibility and physical ability form a kind of continuum.

This way of looking at matters is, I think, a mistake. When we say, for example, that it's logically impossible for a husband to be unmarried, all we mean is that the statement 'Someone is a husband and is not married' is self-contradictory. Similarly, given that we define a physical object as something that cannot be completely in two different places at once, it follows that the statement 'Physical object A is in two different places at once' is self-contradictory and that 'I am (my body is) in two completely different places at once' is also self-contradictory. Thus when I say that it's logically impossible for me to be at point A and at point B at the same time, all I'm saying is that the statement 'I am (my body is) at A and B at the same time' is self-contradictory. I appear to be making a statement about the world but actually I am only making a statement about a statement. On the other hand, when I say that it's physically impossible for me to run the mile from point A to point B in 3 seconds, I do make a statement about the world. I point to all sorts of evidence that rules out such a contingency. My statement is a synthetic one. Now if statements about physical impossibilities are synthetic statements about the world, and statements about logical impossibilities are really statements about statements, to the effect that those statements are self-contradictory, it follows that what is logically impossible cannot be said to be physically impossible.

The same sorts of remarks can be made about the other pairs. To say that it's logically necessary for husbands to be married is to say that the statement 'Husbands are married' is analytic. To say that it's physically necessary for iron to expand when heated is not to make a statement about a statement (or to offer an analytic statement); it is to point to the vast evidence that implies that iron will always expand when heated. It is to make a synthetic statement.

To say, for example, that it is physically possible for me to run the mile from point A to point B is to say that if I try hard enough I can do it. To say it's physically possible for a pair of dice to come up double sixes ten times in a row is to say that past experience does not rule out such an occurrence. When, however, we say that an event is logically possible we make a different sort of statement. To say, for example, that it's logically possible to walk on the ceiling is to say that statements of the form 'x is walking on the ceiling' are synthetic— that one does not contradict oneself in saying them. It follows from this that what is logically necessary is not also logically possible, for, as we have seen, to say that an event is logically necessary is to say that the statement expressing it is analytic, while to say that an event is logically possible is to say that the statement expressing it is synthetic. Since a statement cannot be both analytic and synthetic, it follows that an event cannot be both logically necessary and logically possible.

It also follows from this that since all statements that express physical necessity, physical possibility, and physical impossibility are synthetic, all three come under the heading of logical possibility. We might say, for example, that although walking on the ceiling is logically possible, it's not physically possible. In making such a claim, we would really be saying that although any statement of the form 'x is walking on the ceiling' is synthetic and not self-contradictory, it nevertheless always turns out to be false. (Assuming, of course, that only the names of people and not flies will be substituted for x.)[10] We can schematize what has been said about possibility in the following way:

Logically Necessary	Logically Possible Phys.N. Phys.Pos. Phys.Imp.			Logically Impossible
To say that a state of affairs is logically necessary is to say the statement expressing it is analytic.	To say that a state of affairs is logically possible is to say that the statement expressing it is synthetic.			To say that a state of affairs is logically impossible is to say that the statement expressing it is self-contradictory.

What about 'It's necessary that the shortest distance between two points is a straight line'? If Kant is correct, and this statement must be classified as synthetic a priori, then it will follow that this statement and others like it escape our classificatory net. We can't interpret the above statement as " 'The shortest distance between two points is a straight line' is analytic" because (given that Kant is right) it's not. We can't interpret as saying that it's physically necessary that the shortest distance between two points is a straight line, because if it were just a matter of physical necessity, we could imagine it being otherwise. And this we cannot do. All that we can do is interpret it as: "The statement 'The shortest distance between two points is a straight line' is true in all logically possible situations." But why it should be true in all logically possible situations remains a mystery.

14. Necessary and Sufficient Conditions

It is often important to distinguish between necessary and sufficient conditions.[11] For example, we might want to say that watering the garden was a necessary condition to getting a good crop but that it wasn't sufficient. In order to get a good crop one also had to add fertilizer. What, then, is the difference between the two? The difference might be presented in the following manner:

Necessary Condition (N)

To say that p is a necessary condition for q (for example, that gasoline in the tank is a necessary condition for the engine starting), is to say that q will not occur without p, or, in other words, '$\sim(q \cdot p)$'. This could also be expressed as '$\sim(\sim p \cdot q)$'. Or, to return to our example, it is not the case that there is no gasoline in the tank and the car will start. To say that gasoline is a necessary condition for the starting of the engine does not preclude there being other necessary conditions. For example, an electrical charge in the battery could also be a necessary condition.

Sufficient Condition (S)

To say that p is a sufficient condition for q (for example, that taking a teaspoon of arsenic is sufficient to bring on death), is to say that if p occurs q will occur, or, in other words, '$\sim(p \cdot \sim q)$'. Or, to return to our example, it is not the case that the victim took a teaspoon of arsenic and did not die.

To say that a teaspoon of arsenic is sufficient for death does not preclude there being other conditions that are (independently) sufficient for events of the same type, e.g., a push off a cliff. So, from the fact that the victim has died we cannot assume that the victim has been given arsenic. Notice that if something else is also sufficient, it follows that nothing is necessary. If arsenic and strychnine are independently sufficient to bring on death then nothing is necessary for death.

Necessary and Sufficient (N & S)

As well as talking about N conditions and S conditions, we can also talk about conditions that are both N and S. To say that p is N & S for q is to say that if p occurs q will occur and only if p occurs will q occur. For example, suppose that a doctor prescribes some medicine that makes a patient's spots go away, and that nothing else will make the spots go away. In this case we would say that the medicine was both sufficient and necessary to make the spots go away. In other words, if p is N & S for q, then '$\sim(p \cdot \sim q)$' and '$\sim(q \cdot \sim p)$'.

If p is N & S for q, then it follows that nothing else is N for q. For if there were, then p would not be S for q. Similarly, since p is N for q, it follows that nothing else is S. The medicine is necessary to make the spots go away and so nothing else is or can be sufficient.

We can apply this point to our first example. If gasoline is necessary but not sufficient to make the engine go, it follows that nothing else is independently sufficient. If there was something else that was sufficient, then the gasoline would not be necessary. It also follows that if the gasoline is necessary but not sufficient, then the gasoline forms part of a cluster of other conditions (charge in the battery and so on) that are jointly sufficient. Each is necessary, and together they are sufficient.

However, things are not always so straightforward in the real world. Suppose I have a car for which, although an electrical spark is necessary to make it go, it can run either on gasoline or on propane. How are we to classify gasoline? We can't say it is sufficient since an electrical spark is also necessary, and we can't say that it is necessary since the car can run without it! We might say that gasoline—

or—propane is necessary but this would be a bit awkward. Perhaps we should say that gasoline is contributory, and let it go at that.

Final Point

We say that p is N for q can be expressed by '$\sim(q \cdot \sim p)$'. And we say that p is S for q can be expressed by '$\sim(p \cdot \sim q)$'. From this we can extrapolate that where p is N for q, q is S for p, and where p is S for q, q is N for p. Finally, we can also see that if p is N & S for q, q is N & S for p.

15. 'If', 'Only If', and 'If and Only If'

Sometimes by 'only if' we mean that there is an 'if', but only one. For example, were a child to be told, "You may have your allowance only if you shovel the snow off the front steps," the child would have a right to feel upset if having shovelled the front steps he were told that he would also have to shovel off the back steps before his allowance was forthcoming. But as a rule, by 'only if' we mean that something is only a necessary condition for something else. For example, if we are told that the car will start only if there is gasoline in the tank, we are being told that gasoline is a necessary, but not necessarily a sufficient, condition. We cannot feel that we have been misled if we fill the tank with gasoline and the car fails to start.

By 'if' we mean that something is a sufficient condition but not necessarily a necessary condition for something else. For example, when we say that if he takes a spoonful of arsenic he will die, we mean that the spoonful of arsenic is sufficient to bring on death. But we do not rule out the possibility that something else may be also be sufficient.

From this we can see that when we say '. . . if and only if . . .' we mean that the latter is a necessary and sufficient condition for that former. For example, if we say that John will come to the party if and only if Mary comes, we mean that Mary's presence is both necessary (nothing else will do it) and sufficient to bring about the arrival of John.

I now want to mention a couple of other points that might be of interest. First of all, it follows from 'if p then q' that 'if not q then not p'. This can be shown in the following way. In 'if p then q', p is S for q and q is N for p. But if q is N for p, then if no q, no p. Therefore, if 'not q' then 'not p'. For example: If a spoonful of arsenic is sufficient to bring on death, then if no death, the victim to be cannot have taken a spoonful of arsenic.

This reflects what we have said about truthtables. The statement '$p \supset q$' is equivalent to '$\sim q \supset \sim p$', and '$q \supset p$' is equivalent to '$\sim p \supset \sim q$'. Second, the truthtable counterpart of 'q, if and only if p' is '(p ⊃ q) · (~p ⊃ q)'. But this equivalent to '(p ⊃ q) · (q ⊃ p)', which in turn is equivalent to 'p ≡ q'. This is reflected in the fact that 'q if and only if p' is often expressed as 'p is equivalent to q'.

It's sometimes useful to distinguish between logically *N & S* conditions and causally *N & S* conditions. And here it is to be noted that the distinction is very close to our distinction between "logically possible" (and so on) and "physically possible" (and so on).[12] We may begin by noticing that while gasoline in the tank is causally necessary for the car to start, being male is logically necessary for being a husband. As in the case of logical and causal necessity, it's tempting to think that if something is logically necessary for something else, it's also causally necessary. But this view is mistaken. What we mean when we say that gasoline is causally necessary for the starting of the car is that if there is no gasoline, the car won't start; but what we mean when we say that being male is logically necessary for being a husband is that the statement 'If a given person is not male then he is not a husband' is analytic. In other words, to say that one state of affairs is logically necessary (LN) for another state of affairs is really to make a statement about a statement, while to say that one state of affairs is causally necessary (CN) for another is to make a statement about the states of affairs. Thus if one state of affairs is LN for another, it is not CN for the other. That one state of affairs is CN for another must be expressed by a synthetic statement about the states of affairs, but that one state of affairs is LN for another is expressed by an analytic statement or at least a statement to the effect that another statement is analytic. And since an analytic statement cannot be a synthetic statement, what is logically necessary can't be also causally necessary.

The same sorts of remarks can be made about logically sufficient conditions, as well as logically necessary and sufficient conditions.

16. Definitions

The following definitions may be derived from what has gone before.

ANALYTIC STATEMENT: Any statement whose negation is self-contradictory.

SYNTHETIC STATEMENT: Any statement whose negation is not self-contradictory and is not itself self-contradictory.

ENTAIL: A statement *p* is said to entail another statement *q* if and only if to assert *p* and deny *q* would be to contradict oneself.

DEDUCTIVE ARGUMENT:	Any argument in which the premises entail the conclusion.
INDUCTIVE ARGUMENT:	Any argument where the premises do not entail but give support to the conclusion.
INVALID DEDUCTIVE ARGUMENT:	Any argument that appears to be deductive but in fact is not.
VALID DEDUCTIVE ARGUMENT:	Any deductive argument.
SOUND DEDUCTIVE ARGUMENT:	Any deductive argument that has true premises.
A PRIORI STATEMENT:	Any statement that can be known to be true independently of experience.
A POSTERIORI STATEMENT:	Any statement that cannot be known to be true independently of experience.
NECESSARY STATEMENT:	Any statement that remains true in all logically possible situations.
INCONSISTENT STATEMENTS:	Two statements are said to be inconsistent if it is logically impossible for them to both be true. They may be inconsistent either because they are contradictories or because they are contraries.

FALLACIES

Introduction

So far we have been dealing with ways that we can go right in reasoning; now we are going to look at a number of ways that we can go wrong. One common way of going wrong is through being seduced by an argument that looks valid but is not. An argument of the form,

$$\frac{\text{if p then q}}{\sim p} \\ \therefore \sim q$$

looks like an argument of the form,

$$\frac{\text{if p then q}}{\sim q} \\ \therefore \sim p$$

but as we have seen, not only is it not of that form, it is also invalid. However, it looks so much like the valid argument form that we are apt to be deceived by it. In fact it is so deceptive that it has been named the Fallacy of Denying the Antecedent. We shall see that there are lots of other forms that look valid but are not. These are all branded "fallacious argument forms." We may say then that a fallacious argument form is an especially deceptive invalid argument form.

Not only are what appear to be arguments branded as fallacies; any type of statement or trick that will lead one's train of thought astray may be branded a fallacy. Red Herrings are, as we shall see, a good example of this.

There are almost as many ways to classify fallacies as there are logicians. The reason for this is not hard to find. An author of a book on etiquette would have no trouble in classifying the various ways that a table may be set, but would have an impossible task in trying to classify the ways that one can *fail* to set a table. Similarly, logicians have an impossible task in trying to classify the number of ways that one can go wrong in thinking. So it must not be thought that my taxonomy of fallacies is in any way definitive.

Finally, we must be very careful in using the word 'fallacy'. If I say that Smith has just committed the crime of not declaring all his income, I am presupposing that it is a crime not to declare all your income. There are two questions to be asked here: Did Smith not declare all his income, and is it a crime not to do so? Similarly, if I say that Smith committed the fallacy of sweeping generalization, I presuppose that there is such a fallacy. Again there are two questions to be asked: Did he make a sweeping generalization, and is it fallacious to do so? Philosophers are altogether too quick to say that someone committed the so-and-so fallacy without showing that doing so-and-so really is fallacious. We might call this the fallacy fallacy!

Fallacies of Relevance

This class consists of those fallacies in which the premises, owing to peculiar circumstances—mostly having to do with the people surrounding the arguments—appear relevant to the conclusion but are not. We have already seen that premises may be relevant to the conclusion, either because they entail the conclusion or because they inductively support the conclusion. Fallacies of this sort are arguments where the premises either appear to entail the conclusion or appear to give inductive support to the conclusion, but in fact do neither.

1. Ad Hominem

The most famous fallacy of this sort is the ad hominem fallacy. What often happens here is that *A* says something and *B*, instead of questioning what *A* has said, questions *A*. For example, someone says that you don't want to adopt Smith's view that Indians are more susceptible to measles than whites, because Smith is a member of the KKK and you don't want to have anything to do with their ideas. The trouble here is that the truth or falsity of a view has got nothing whatever to do with who holds the view. It has only to do with the way things are. We should only adopt a view because it has been verified, and not because it is held or not held by somebody.

A second example is as follows: Dr. Blue says that the new Boeing 747 is structurally unsafe and should be grounded. Jones then says to Smith that there is no reason to believe the Boeing 747 is unsafe, because Dr. Blue, although a brilliant aircraft designer, owns many shares in Lockheed, Boeing's competitor, and so his judgment is not to be trusted. The fallacy here is grounded in the fact that what is true of Dr. Blue has nothing whatever to do with the structure of the Boeing 747. Strictly speaking, only claims about the plane itself are relevant to the question of whether it is structurally safe.

However, in ad hominem arguments the premises are not quite as irrelevant to the conclusion as one might think. Consider the following:

1. Whatever Jones says is false.

2. Jones said that the world is flat.

3. Therefore, Jones's claim 'The world is flat', is false.

4. Therefore, the world is not flat.

At first glance one might think that nothing could be more irrelevant to the shape of the earth than claims about Jones. What has Jones to do with the shape of the earth? But in spite of this it should be noticed that 1 and 2 entail 3, and 3 in turn entails 4, making claims about Jones relevant. How, then, are we to distinguish between acceptable and unacceptable ad hominem arguments? First of all, any ad hominem argument is suspect. When confronted with one, it is always a good idea to steer the discussion away from the person and back to the topic. Second, if what lies behind the argument is the suggestion that we shouldn't accept a certain claim, because it is held by so-and-so, and so-and-so is a person we don't want to associate with, then the argument must be rejected out of hand. Perhaps a good reason for not wearing, say, a certain kind of clothing is that we don't want to associate with the people who do. But that we don't want to associate with the people who hold a certain belief is never a reason for not accepting that belief.

2. The Genetic Fallacy

Instead of raising suspicions concerning the holder of a belief, we might raise suspicions concerning the source of a belief. To argue that we must not believe *x*, because its source is fraudulent is to commit the genetic fallacy. For example, to claim that we must reject chemistry because it grew out of alchemy would be to commit the fallacy. Similarly, if I were to point out that religion grew out of superstition, this would not be a good reason for rejecting religious claims.

3. *The Tu Quoque Fallacy*

Suppose you had been reading the works of Augustine and were impressed with his entreaties to lead the moral and religious life, but then you read that in his youth he had kept a mistress and had at one point prayed to God to take all these temptations from him and had gone on to say "But not quite yet!" You might not be so impressed with his entreaties to lead the moral life, and might think "Why should I lead a moral life when its main advocate only takes it up when he is too old to enjoy an immoral life?" Well, if you were to think in this way you would be guilty of committing the Tu Quoque Fallacy. The fact that someone doesn't practice what he preaches has got nothing whatever to do with the truth of what he preaches.

But let us examine a different example. Several years ago a group of people who were opposed to the hunting of seals in the Gulf of St. Lawrence confronted Canadian Prime Minister Pierre Trudeau on the steps of the Parliament buildings. After putting their case to the Prime Minister, he looked them up and down and said, "I see that some of you are wearing leather belts and others are wearing leather shoes. Where do you suppose the leather came from?" This question shut them up but it was quite irrelevant to the question of whether it is wrong to kill animals for human consumption, and in particular whether it was wrong to kill seals for their fur.

4. *Argumentum ad Verecundiam*

Here the fallacy is just the opposite. Instead of trying to get someone to question a belief through raising suspicions concerning the holders of the belief, we try to get someone to accept a certain belief through pointing to the splendid people who accept it. The reason it's called "ad verecundiam" is because it involves an appeal to modesty or sense of shame of the listener. For example, an inquisitor might have said to Galileo, "How dare you question whether the Sun goes around the Earth. Why that view has been held by Plato, Aristotle, and all the most learned members of the church down to the present day."

Because *ad verecundiam* is just the opposite of *ad hominem*, the same caution has to be taken. For example there is nothing wrong with:

> Jones has said that the nuclear reactor is unsafe.
>
> Jones is the world's leading authority on reactor design.
> _____
>
> Therefore, it's likely that the reactor is unsafe.

but there is with:

> You ought to eat Wheaties.
>
> After all, Wheaties is the breakfast of champions.

Wheaties may be the breakfast of champions, but most champions know very little about what is and what is not good for them. If an individual were to eat Wheaties because he unwittingly wanted to identify with the champions, then he would be guilty of committing this fallacy.

5. *Argumentum ad Baculum*

One has to distinguish between different sorts of reasons for believing. One reason for believing something is that, on the best evidence, it appears to be true. A second reason for believing something is that some awful consequence will happen if one doesn't. For example, in the early days of Ugandan independence, someone might have believed that Idi Amin was a great man. This person's belief might have been based on the best evidence available at the time. If, however, at a later date someone were to believe that Idi Amin was a great man because he thought he would be beaten up if he didn't, we would have a reason of a very different sort. In the first case the reasons are premises that give inductive support. In the second case the "reason," though it may be his reason, isn't really a reason at all. The only sort of statement that could count as a reason here is a premise that supports or entails, in conjunction with other premises, the statement that Idi Amin was a great man. Though at some time it must be admitted that the fact that one will be beaten up if one doesn't *appear* to believe that Idi Amin is a great man, might be a good reason for *pretending* to believe that Idi Amin is a great man.

To believe something because something awful will happen if the belief is not held, is to commit the fallacy of argumentum ad baculum or, in other words, the fallacy of arguing from force.

It may strike the reader that it's not likely that anyone will fall for this fallacy. Perhaps this is true, but fear can work in strange ways. If the president of a company says to his salesmen that they had better start believing that their company is a great one because if they don't the company will probably go bankrupt, then it's likely that a lot of salesmen will take that as a reason for believing and find themselves believing that their company is great.

Lurking in the background of this argument is a theory that might is right. That is, whatever those in power say is right is right. And so if someone in power tells you that you ought to do x, then it follows that you ought to do x. We discussed this theory at some length when we discussed Thrasymachus (chapter 2, pp. 57-62) and will discuss it at greater length in the section on morality. In the meantime, it's worth mentioning that it doesn't follow from the fact that A has power over B, and A says that B ought to do x, that B ought to do x. Suppose, for example, that tomorrow C comes to power and says that B ought not to do x. What ought B to do? It would appear that from our premises he both ought and ought not to do x. We can see from this that something is wrong with this theory.

6. Argumentum ad Misericordiam

This, like the other fallacies of relevance, gains its plausibility through having to do with the people who surround the argument. The best examples of argumentum ad misericordiam come from the courts of law. Sometimes in a jury trial the lawyer for the defense, instead of trying to show that the defendant didn't do what he is accused of doing, will talk at great length about the miserable upbringing of the defendant, how he was beaten by his father, ignored by his mother, and turned out to face the cruel world at an early age. What the lawyer is doing is appealing to the jury's sense of pity. He hopes that the members of the jury will find for the defendant, not because they think he didn't do the crime, but because they feel sorry for him! Such appeals are obviously irrelevant, though in the heat of the moment this irrelevance is often overlooked.

Part of the explanation for how this trick works is that appeals of this sort are relevant to how severe the punishment should be. It may be that the defendant really didn't have a chance or that he has suffered enough already, so the punishment should be reduced.

The most celebrated example of this fallacy appears in Clarence Darrow's defense of I. Thomas Kidd. Kidd was General Secretary of the Amalgamated Woodworkers International Union in the 1930s and was arrested on a charge of criminal conspiracy. Darrow said to the jury:

> I appeal to you not for Thomas Kidd, but I appeal to you for the long line—the long, long line reaching back through the ages and forward to the years to come—the long line of despoiled and down-trodden people of the earth. I appeal to you for those men who rise in the morning before daylight comes and go home at night when the light has faded from the

sky and give their life, their strength, their toil to make others rich and great. I appeal to you in the name of those women who are offering up their lives to this modern god of gold, and I appeal to you in the name of those little children, the living and the unborn.[13]

Inductive Fallacies

These are "arguments" where, owing to some oddity, the premises appear to give support to the conclusion but in fact do not.

1. Mistaken Cause

Sometimes where A is the cause of both B and C it is tempting to think that B is the cause of C. After all, in this sort of situation, wherever B occurs C occurs, and C never occurs without B occurring. For example, the ancient Egyptians believed that the flooding of the Nile was caused by the return of a bird called the Ibis. However, both the flooding of the Nile and the return of the Ibis were a result of the change of the seasons. Or, it might be inferred from the fact that alcoholic husbands are more aggressive toward their wives than non-alcoholic husbands, that the alcohol is the cause of the aggression. However, the conclusion doesn't follow. It may be that there is a common source of both the propensity to drink and the aggressive behavior.

Sometimes the effect is mistaken for the cause. For example, someone might notice that many successful businessmen drive Cadillacs and infer from this that if he were to buy a Cadillac he would also become a successful businessman. But, as it is all too plainly obvious, most successful businessmen buy Cadillacs because they are successful and can afford them. However, we mustn't be too hard on the person in our example. Some people become successful through buying Cadillacs. As a result of owning Cadillacs, other businessmen think that they are successful and so, competent, and for that reason want to do business with them. If this was his reason for buying a Cadillac, then his line of reasoning was not fallacious.

2. Confusing Necessary and Sufficient Causes

Just as one can talk about necessary conditions and sufficient conditions, so one can talk about necessary causes and sufficient causes. A great deal of confusion is perpetrated by failing to distinguish between the two. For example, suppose that someone were to say that reckless driving was the cause of car accidents, while someone offered that the cause was unsafe cars. Both could be right, and both could be mistaken in thinking that the other person was mistaken. The reason for this is that both reckless driving and unsafe cars may be necessary causes of most car accidents, and it may be the case that most car accidents only occur when unsafe cars are driven by reckless persons. The mistake that each person makes is in unwittingly thinking that his favorite is both necessary and sufficient. This is not surprising because, as a rule, what we mean by a cause is a something that is both necessary and sufficient.

It might also be mentioned that when we are concerned with stopping something from happening we focus on necessary causes, while when we are trying to make something happen we focus on sufficient causes. When talking about causes of car accidents, we talk about alcohol, while when talking about trying to get rid of insects, we talk about insecticide. Alcohol is a necessary but not a sufficient cause of some types of car accidents, while insecticide is a sufficient but not a necessary cause of the death of many types of insects.

3. Sweeping Generalization (Sometimes called "Accident")

Most people have a number of rules of thumb at hand, ready to be applied when required. For example: "Too many cooks spoil the broth," "If you look after the pence the pounds will look after themselves," and "Exercise is good for health." The simplicity of these maxims can sometimes be their undoing. Exercise may be good for the health of the normal person, but not for the person, say, who is suffering from kidney disease. Every maxim or generalization of this sort has its exception(s), and not to watch out for the exception(s) is to commit the fallacy of sweeping generalization. If I were to remove methodically and carefully the goods and chattels from my house, which was rapidly being consumed with flames, because I believed that haste breeds waste, then I would be guilty of this fallacy.

4. Hasty Generalization

The fallacy of hasty generalization is just the opposite. Here, instead of moving fallaciously from the general to the particular, one moves fallaciously from the particular to the general. Tourists are especially susceptible to this fallacy. They are inclined to visit a country for a few days and then trot off with all sorts of ill-founded generalizations about the dispositions of the natives. For example, if one were to pay a visit to Warsaw in the middle of the winter of 1983 and return to say that the Poles were a glum lot, one would be guilty of this fallacy. Before making a generalization, one must be careful that the generalization is well founded.

5. *Misuse of Statistics*

There are all sorts of fallacies that are involved in the use and the misuse of statistics. For example, one has to be very certain that the sample on which one is drawing the conclusion is suitably random. During the presidential campaign between Thomas Dewey and incumbent President Harry Truman, the Gallup pole conducted a survey by telephone and found that an overwhelming majority of voters said that they were going to vote for Dewey. But much to the surprise of the Gallup pollsters, Truman won the election. The error they made was almost too obvious to be noticed. By carrying out their survey by telephone, they only reached the people who could afford telephones. Their sample was not random.

One also has to be careful not to confuse the *mean* with the *average*. It's tempting upon learning that the average man in the Middle Ages in northern Europe died at around the age of thirty-five, to conclude that not many people lived beyond this age. But this would be a mistake. Most people died before the age of five, and this pulled the average down. Those who managed to live beyond five years usually lived for more than thirty-five years. Thomas Hobbes, for example, lived to be ninety-one.

Here is a final example. In 1965 it was discovered that alcohol was involved (as they say) in 85 percent of all car accidents that occurred in Britain on Christmas Eve. It was then concluded that alcohol was responsible (necessary condition) for a very high number of accidents. Although this might have been the case, the conclusion still doesn't follow. What also has to be known is what was the percentage of drivers who had been drinking. After all, if 85 percent of drivers had been drinking, then one would expect alcohol "to be involved" in 85 percent of the accidents!

There are all sorts of other ways that statistics can trick us, but the preceding examples should be sufficient to warn us to be on our guard.

Linguistic Fallacies

1. *Fallacy of Amphiboly*

We now turn to those fallacies that have their source more in the language used to present the argument than in the surrounding circumstances. Some find their source in the fact that one of the premises in an argument can be read in more than one way. For example, a famous Greek general once visited the Oracle at Delphi for advice on whether to go to war with the Persians. Upon being told that if he went to war the Persians would experience a great defeat, he lost no time in declaring war on them. As things turned out the Persians did experience a great defeat—but unfortunately for the Greek general, the defeat was his! The trouble with his line of thinking was that the premise 'If I wage war on the Persians they will experience a great defeat' is ambiguous. It can be read to say that the Persians will suffer a great defeat, and it can also be read to say that the Persians will witness a great defeat, without it being made clear whose defeat they will witness. To be misled by such ambiguous premises is to commit what is sometimes called the Fallacy of Amphiboly.

A second example of this fallacy is as follows: Suppose on a Sunday night a lecherous man, upon seeing the sign 'Clean and decent dancing every night except Sunday' posted outside a roadhouse, were to stop his car and rush for the door. If he were to do that then he would be guilty of this fallacy. A moment's reflection will show that the road sign is ambiguous. Newspaper headlines provide a rich source of amphibolous statements. Here are a few: "University Helping With Breeding Difficulties," "No Human Wastes in Slow Pitch Well" and "Psych Ward Closer to Reality."

2. Fallacy of Equivocation

In a deductive argument it's important that each word means the same in each statement in which it appears. For example, one cannot derive 'He keeps his gold in there' from 'He keeps his gold in the bank by the river' and 'That is the bank by the river' unless it is known that 'bank' means the same in each statement. If 'bank' refers to a riverbank in one premise and a money lending institution in the other, then nothing follows. The following argument is fallacious because the word "end" in the first premise means "the goal," and in the second premise it means "the limit." As a result nothing follows from the premises.

The end of a thing is its perfection.

Death is the end of life.

_____

Therefore, death is the perfection of life.

Such fallacies as these are often called Fallacies of Equivocation. Sometimes we have a botched up argument because one of the words has changed its meaning, but the change in meaning stems from the sentence structure rather than from the ambiguity of the word. Consider, for example, the following:

Nothing is better than steak.

Hamburger is better than nothing.

Therefore, hamburger is better than steak.

Here the ambiguity lies with the word 'nothing', but we cannot say what it means in the first premise as opposed to the second premise in the way that we could with 'bank'. In order to explain its meaning in each premise, we have to translate the whole of each premise into a more perspicuous statement. If we do this we get:

It's not the case that there is something that is better to eat than steak.

It's better to eat hamburger than not to eat at all.

And from these two statements nothing follows.

Before going on, it's worth noticing that 'nothing' is a word to be handled with the greatest care. For example, the following is one of the arguments used to show that everything has a cause:

If something could happen without a cause, then that thing would have nothing as a cause.

But nothing cannot be the cause of something.

Therefore, everything has a cause.

The argument is fallacious. The second premise looks to be a necessary truth that one can know on a priori grounds. But as David Hume pointed out, it cannot be known a priori. To say that nothing is the cause is not to say that there is some sort of emptiness that is the cause; it is only to say that it is not the case that there is a cause. As a result, to say that nothing cannot be the cause is not to say that an emptiness cannot operate as a cause; it is simply to deny that something can occur without any cause. And this is something that cannot be known a priori. Lewis Carroll (who was really Charles Dodgson, a nineteenth-century logician) exploits the slipperiness of 'nothing' in creating the following philosophical joke, which appears in *Through the Looking Glass*. Alice and the White King are looking down the road expecting to see some messengers. Alice says, "I see nobody on the road," and then the King remarks in a fretful tone, "I only wish I had such eyes. To be able to see Nobody! And at that distance too! Why, it's as much as I can do to see real people by this light!"

3. *Fallacies of Composition and Division*

There are things that can be said about wholes and groups that one cannot go on to say about a part of the whole or members of the group, and vice versa. The fallacies of composition and division ignore this fact. The fallacy of composition does so by making an illicit move from claims about the parts of a whole or members of a group, to claims about the whole or group. For example, to argue that a certain orchestra must be good because all the members were good, would be to make an illicit move from a claim about the members to a claim about the (whole) orchestra. The latter does not follow from the former, for even though the members may be good players, they may not play very well together. Similarly, if one were to argue that Volkswagens as a group do not use much gasoline, because Volkswagens individually don't, one would be arguing fallaciously. Volkswagens as a group may burn up lots of gasoline because there may be lots of them.

The fallacy of division is just the reverse of the fallacy of composition. Instead of involving an illicit move from the parts or members to the whole group, it involves an illicit move from the whole or group to the parts or members. For example, if we were to argue that since a car was poorly made, the parts were also poorly made, we would be arguing fallaciously. It doesn't follow from the fact that the car is poorly made that the parts are also poorly made. The car may be composed of well-made parts that have been poorly assembled. Similarly, it doesn't follow from the fact that buses as a group don't use much gasoline, that buses individually don't use much gasoline.

Moves from claims about a group to members of a group are apt to be much more deceptive than moves from a whole to parts of the whole. One of the reasons for this is that in some cases the same term can be used either *distributively* or *collectively,* and often it's not clear how it is being used. For instance, when someone says that buses burn a lot of fuel, it's not clear whether the speaker wishes to refer to each individual bus and say it burns a lot of fuel (in which case he is using 'burn' distributively), or whether he wants to say that when taken together buses burn a lot of fuel (in which case he is using 'burn' collectively). If 'burn' is used distributively in the first premise, then the argument

Buses burn a lot of fuel.

That is a bus.

Therefore, it burns a lot of fuel

is valid. But if 'burn' is used collectively, the argument is invalid. It doesn't follow from the claim that buses altogether (collectively) use a lot of fuel that those same buses individually use a lot of fuel. And so it doesn't follow that *that* bus uses a lot of fuel.

Failure to distinguish between using a term collectively and using it distributively can cause confusion in debates of the sort that take place between hunters and their opponents. Hunters will say to their antagonists that since hunting thins the deer population, it protects the deer against overgrazing and helps them to survive. As a result, if you go out and shoot some deer, you will be helping them to survive. No doubt you might be helping the deer as a collection to survive, but you certainly wouldn't be helping the survival of those deer that you shoot to survive! Consider the following argument:

> Hunting is good for the deer (for the reasons mentioned).
>
> That is a deer.
> _____
> Therefore, hunting is good for it.
> _____
> Therefore, it will be good for that deer to be hunted.

Here the same point can be made. It doesn't follow from the fact that it is good (collectively) for the deer to be hunted that any particular deer will be benefited by being hunted.

Not only does the failure to make this distinction precipitate disputes of the above type, it also muddies a very popular moral argument. Often when someone does something slightly anti-social—for example, throwing a paper wrapper on the sidewalk—someone else will say, "You shouldn't do that. Think what would happen if everyone were to do that!" What this person has in mind is something like: "If *everyone* were to throw their wrappers around, the place would be an unsightly mess. Therefore, it's wrong for *everyone* to throw wrappers around. And therefore, it's wrong for *you* to throw your wrappers around." The trouble with this argument is that 'everyone' is being used collectively, and so the final conclusion doesn't follow. It doesn't follow from the fact that it would be wrong for everyone collectively to throw their wrappers around that it would be wrong for you to throw your wrappers around. (This point is also discussed on page 291.)

Although arguments of this sort are liable to such confusion, we mustn't dismiss them out of hand. Knowing that it would be wrong for everyone (collectively) to do x might be a reason for me to refrain from doing x, because my doing x would set a bad example and lead to everyone doing x. Furthermore, if everyone would very much like to do *x*, then it might be said to be unfair for me to do *x*. Finally, as well as being wrong for everyone to do *x*, it might also be wrong for everyone individually to do *x*. If this were the case then it would be wrong for me to do *x*. I suspect that that is the substance of the wrapper example. Not only is it wrong for everyone collectively to litter the streets, it's also wrong for everyone distributively (or individually) to litter the streets. And so it would be wrong for me to litter the streets.

4. Bifurcation

This fallacy trades on a distinction that we have already marked out— the distinction between contraries and contradictories. It doesn't follow from the fact that *not all* the children are bright, that *none* of the children are bright. All that follows is that *some* are not bright. Similarly, it doesn't follow from the fact that the soup is not hot, that the soup must therefore be cold. The soup may be lukewarm.

Because it's so easy to confuse contraries, or opposites, with contradictories, we have to be very careful in our use of disjunctive statements. For example, it may be that in this world each person is either a winner or a loser, but it doesn't logically follow from the fact that someone is not a winner that he is definitely a loser. He may be just muddling along. Similarly, Christ may have been correct in claiming that people were either for him or against him, but it doesn't (logically) follow from the fact that someone is not for him that the person is therefore against him. The individual could be completely indifferent. It might have been a mistake for Christ to treat those who were not for him as being against him.

The failure to distinguish between contradictories and contraries (or opposites) is sometimes exploited in arguments of the constructive dilemma type (see page 114). Here is an example:

1. If a person is bright, he doesn't need a university education.
2. If a person is not bright (dim), it won't do him any good.
3. Either a person is bright or he is not bright.

---

4. Therefore, he doesn't need a university education or it won't do him any good.

The form of this argument is:

1. $(p \supset q)$ [2] $\cdot$ $(\sim p \supset r)$
3. $(p \lor \sim p)$
---
4. $\therefore q \lor r$

The trouble with this argument lies with the second and third premises. What do we mean by 'not bright'? If by 'not bright' we mean 'dim', then the second premise is true but the third premise is false. It is not the case that the world divides up into bright and dim people. Many people are average. On the other hand, if we interpret 'not bright' literally, then premise 3 expresses a true (analytic) proposition and premise 2 becomes false. It's simply not true that all those who are not bright enough to do without a university education will not benefit from one. One also has to bear in mind that even though the very bright may not *need* a college education, it doesn't follow from this that it would do them any harm. It is generally the very bright who benefit most from a university education.

5. Complex Question

Many of the things we say presuppose the truth of something else. For example, if I say "It looks like it's going to continue raining," my statement presupposes that it is already raining. If it's not raining at all, it's difficult to claim that what I say is either true or false. It's not just statements that can have presuppositions; questions can have them as well. In the question "Has Smith recovered from his operation?" it is presupposed that there is a Smith who had an operation. This feature is exploited by many wiley lawyers and politicians. For example, when the district attorney has the prisoner in the witness stand he might ask him questions like, "Did you return the money you stole?" Or a congressman might say in the House of Representatives, "Is the congressman from Ohio aware that the rate of unemployment is higher in Ohio than anywhere in America?" The best defense when asked questions of this sort is not to answer yes or no. Either answer will get you into hot water. The best defense is to accuse the questioner of asking a complex question and then ask him to divide the question. The first example divides into (a) "Did you steal some money?" and (b) "Did you return the money?" Notice though, that (b) cannot be asked unless (a) is answered in the affirmative.

This also explains why (as I mentioned at the beginning of this section) we have to be very careful in using the word "fallacy." If I say "Are you going to continue committing the ad hominem fallacy?" I first presuppose that you addressed the speaker and not his argument; second, I further presuppose that it is fallacious to do so. But as we have seen, even if it turns out that you addressed the man and not the argument, we cannot assume that you did something fallacious. There is nothing fallacious about the following ad hominem argument:

Smith is a born liar.

Smith has said that he will repay the debt.

Therefore, it's unlikely that Smith will repay the debt.

6. *The Fallacy of Arguing from Ignorance*

Although some statements are easily shown to be either true or false—for example, "There is a pencil in the cup in front of me"—statements like "All species of duck can swim" are very difficult to show to be true but easy to show to be false. To show that this statement is false all that we have to find is a species of duck that hates the water and doesn't know how to swim. To show that the statement is true, we would have to discover for every species of duck—past, present, and future—that it can swim. Even if we knew that every species of duck we were acquainted with could swim, we still couldn't be certain that the statement was true, for (a) unknown to us there may be other species around that can't swim, and (b) evolution may in the future throw up species that can't swim.

Some statements have just the opposite feature; they are easily shown to be true but difficult to show to be false. If someone says "Sasquatches exist," it's easy to see how this could be shown to be true. All we have to do is go out to the Rockies and capture a seven-foot fellow covered with thick hair. But to show that the statement is false is another matter. We would have to look everywhere all at once, and this is something that is very difficult to do.

Because of all this, it's tempting to argue that a given statement of the first sort is true because it has not been shown to be false. For example, if we have extensively tested the metal known as lead and found that it has always melted at 327°C., it seems quite reasonable to accept that all lead (past, present, and future) melts at 327°C. Similarly, it's tempting to argue with respect to a statement of the second type that if we have been unable to demonstrate its truth after trying very hard to do so, then we can assume it to be false.

Although both conclusions are tempting and perhaps reasonable, we must be careful not to reach these conclusions too quickly. To do so is to commit the fallacy of arguing from ignorance. That is to say, if I were to claim that all lead melts at 327°C. because I hadn't found any cases where it didn't (but had only found one case where it did), then I would be arguing from ignorance. It is generally accepted that arguments should be based on knowledge and not on ignorance. Similarly, if I were to argue that there were no Sasquatches, because I hadn't found one, but had only spent one day looking in the foothills of the Rockies, then I would again be arguing from ignorance.

Sometimes arguments of the latter sort, strange though it may seem, can go the other way. Some people will argue that the fact that we haven't found any Sasquatches supports, not the conclusion that there are none, but the conclusion that they do exist. These individuals will argue that not finding one is tantamount to being unable to show that there are none, and that it follows from this that Sasquatches exist. In other words, they will argue for the truth of 'Sasquataches exist' from the fact that it can't be proven that the statement is false.

However, to argue this way is to commit the same fallacy with a vengeance. Not being able to show 'Sasquatches exist' to be false could hardly count as a reason for claiming that it is true, for this is a statement that, as we have seen, is virtually impossible to show to be false. To show that it was false would require searching everywhere in the Rockies at virtually the same time and find no Sasquatches. The reason all such searches would have to be done at virtually the same time is that no one can know that after searching area A and then going on to search area B, a Sasquatch hasn't slipped back from B to A.

The same error is made by people who argue for the existence of UFOs, ghosts, gremlins, and the like, because we haven't shown that such phenomena in fact exist. But it proves nothing of the sort. The reason that we have been unable to show that there are no UFOs, etc. is that it is virtually impossible to do so.

Before going on, it might also be worth mentioning that in addition to statements that cannot be shown to be true and statements that cannot be shown to be false, there are some statements that share both of these features. They cannot be shown to be either true or false. Take for example, 'For every paint there is a solvent'. We can't show that this is true, because even if it looks as though every paint has a solvent, somebody might develop a paint that looks as if it had no solvent. On the other hand, we can't show that this statement is false, because if we did come up with a paint that appeared to have no solvent, we can't be absolutely certain that no solvent is possible. Perhaps a solvent will be developed next year.

It's worth noticing that the statement 'Everything that happens has a cause', which forms the basis of science, is a statement of this type. We can't show that it's true, because there are more happenings to come; and we can't show that it's false. Even if we did discover a happening that appears to have no cause, we can't be certain that it does not. Perhaps one will be discovered tomorrow. Someone may well wonder why we all believe that everything that happens has a cause. This is a puzzle that I shall leave for the reader to ponder.

7. *The Fallacy of Begging the Question*

This fallacy is committed by those who take for granted what they are setting out to prove, but do so in a way that is either not obvious to themselves or to their listeners. Consider this classic example:

> [To allow every man an unbounded freedom in speech must always be, on the whole, advantageous to the state.] You ask why? Well (it is highly conducive to the interests of the community that each individual should enjoy a liberty, perfectly unlimited, of expressing his sentiments).

Here it may be noted, on close examination, that the content of the conclusion (which is in the square brackets) is the same as the premise (which is in parentheses). At the same time, one can see how, in the midst of a rhetorical speech, this fact could slip by completely unnoticed.

Sometimes the circularity is hidden not so much because the conclusion is worded in a different way but because there is some distance between the premise and the conclusion. Consider the following:

> 1st Speaker: "Everything said in the Bible is true."
>
> 2nd Speaker: "How do you know?"
>
> 1st Speaker: "Because it's the word of God."
>
> 2nd Speaker: "How do you know it's the word of God?"
>
> 1st Speaker: "Because it says so in the Bible."

In this conversation the first speaker is presupposing that everything said in the Bible is true. But this is just the same as his ultimate conclusion; therefore, he is begging the question.

It's often been remarked that, in a sense, all deductive (but no inductive) arguments are circular because in every deductive argument the conclusion is contained in the premises. How then are we to distinguish the more disreputable sort, like the ones we just examined, from the normal respectable type of deductive argument? We notice in an argument like:

> All men are mortal.
>
> Socrates is a man.
> _____
> Therefore, Socrates is mortal.

that although the conclusion is contained in the premises, it is different from either of the premises. This is to be contrasted with the two more disreputable examples mentioned above. In each the conclusion was identical with one of the premises. Perhaps this could be taken as a way of distinguishing between the two. However, arguments like:

> It's raining and it's cold.
> _____
> Therefore, it's cold.

are thought by some to be respectable too, and here the conclusion is identical with one of the premises or at least with one of the conjuncts. Perhaps we shall have to say that this argument is not quite as respectable as some people have thought.

The main thing, however, that separates the disreputable cases, which are considered to be fallacious, from the others, is that in the fallacious cases either it's not clear that the conclusion is the same as one of the premises (as in our first example), or the premise, which is the same as the conclusion (as in our second example), is not stated. In arguing deductively it's important to be clear on what your premises—your assumptions—are. The first speaker in our second example was not.

Other Fallacies

I want to turn now to three fallacies that don't seem to fit neatly into any category.

1. The Red Herring Gambit

This is not so much a fallacy as a strategem used by those who are schooled in the black art of debate and rhetoric. One way it can be used is the following: Suppose someone wants to argue from A to B and his wiley opponent tricks him into arguing from A to C, where C is much more difficult to prove. The opponent, by showing the arguer that C does not follow, tricks him and perhaps his audience into thinking that B also does not follow. Suppose that Jones is attempting to prove that we would all be better off if we had a state-run medical system. Smith claims that state medicine will not create a utopia. Jones gets led astray by this "red herring" and attempts but fails to show that state medicine will create a utopia. As a result, it looks as though Smith has won the day. What Jones should have said is, "Look here, Smith, I'm not trying to show that state medicine will create a utopia; all I'm trying to show is that we shall be better off if we have it than if we do not."

Sometimes the gambit can be worked in just the opposite way. The speaker would like to prove C but he realizes that he hasn't a chance of making a case. He therefore attempts to prove B instead. And somehow it looks as though he has proven C. For example, a member of the Canadian government might set out to show that hunting seals is not cruel, but goes on to argue that the hunting of seals provides employment for Canadians and tax revenue for the government. Just listen to the politicians. Whenever a reporter requests that he be shown that one thing is the case, the politician invariably and almost automatically attempts to show that something else is the case.

2. *The Masked Man Fallacy*

This is a (virtually) long-lost medieval fallacy that has enjoyed a small revival in recent years. Here is an example that explains its name:

> He cannot recognize the man in the mask.
>
> The man in the mask is his father.
>
> ---
>
> Therefore, he cannot recognize his father.

Here is another example:

> I cannot recognize the man in the mask.
>
> I can recognize my father.
>
> ---
>
> Therefore, the man in the mask is not my father.

We are not apt to be led astray by the first example since we know on independent grounds that the conclusion is most likely false. But what is puzzling about this example is that even though the logic looks to be impeccable, it leads from premises that could be true to a conclusion that is most likely false. The second example is perhaps a bit more deceptive because the premises (given that they are true) lead to a conclusion that could be true. The man in the mask could turn out not to be my father. However, we know that the argument is invalid, for even if the premises are true we know that the conclusion might be false. The man in the mask could turn out to be my father.

In order to determine where the fallacy is located, let us look at the following example. Suppose that Smith, a fellow university student, goes to the beach and there he sees a man whose head is hidden by a large panama hat, looking out to sea with a pair of binoculars at all sorts of warships going by. Smith is suspicious and concludes that the man on the beach, who unbeknown to Smith is the president of his university, is a spy. With these ingredients we can concoct the following argument:

> Smith believes that the man on the beach is a spy.
>
> The man on the beach is the president of the University.
>
> ―――――――――――――――――――――――――――――――――――――
>
> Therefore, Smith believes that the president of the
> University is a spy.

If we read the conclusion as "Smith believes that the man, who unbeknown to him is president of the University, is a spy," then the conclusion quite happily follows from the premises. But if we read it as "Smith believes that there is a man who is both president of the University and a spy," then this conclusion clearly does not follow. The trouble with the conclusion, as it stands in the argument, is that it is ambiguous between these two readings. Because it follows under one reading, we are inclined to think that it follows under the other reading.

The same point can be made about our first example. If we take the conclusion to mean "He cannot recognize the man, who unbeknown to him, is his father," then it follows. But if we take it to mean "He cannot recognize the man who he knows to be his father," then the conclusion does not follow.

In chapter 2 (p. 61), I mentioned that there was more to be said about Thrasymachus. We are now in a position to do so. Thrasymachus' argument can be recast as follows:

> The citizens believe that actions x, y, and z are just.
>
> Actions x, y, and z are in the interest of the ruling class.
>
> ―――――――――――――――――――――――――――――――――――――
>
> Therefore, the citizens believe that these actions, which
> are in the interest of the ruling class, are just.

Again, the conclusion follows if it is read as "The citizens believe that actions x, y, and z, which unbeknown to them are in the interest of the ruling class, are just." But if it is read as "The citizens believe that actions x, y, and z have the property of being in the interest of the ruling class and also have the property of being just," then it does not follow.

We can on the basis of this see how it was possible for Plato (chapter 2, p. 61) to make the mistake of having Thrasymachus say both that (a) the tyrants act unjustly in laying down laws that are in their interest, and (b) acting justly means acting in accordance with those laws. There is nothing wrong with (a), but how was Plato ever tricked into putting (b) in the mouth of Thrasymachus? The explanation, I think, is that Plato thought that statement (c) " 'Justice' means what is in the interest of the rulers" follows from the highly plausible statement (d) "The citizens call those acts, and only those acts, which are in the interest of the ruling class 'just' " and that (b) follows from (c). But (c), and hence (b), as we can now see, would only follow from (d) if the citizens *knew* that those acts were in the interest of the ruling class. Since this is something that they did not know, neither (c) nor (b) follows.

If we look at the argument of Adeimantus (pp. 63-64), we see even more of the same mischief at work. Adeimantus would have us believe that people are interested in praising the appearance of justice, and not justice itself, because people often make the mistake of praising acts that they falsely believe to be just. But in praising these acts they are not praising them for appearing to be just; they praise them because they really believe that they are just.

3. The Democratic Fallacy

This fallacy is relatively simple. Once it has been exposed, we wonder how anyone could actually fall into it. And yet people do.

In a democracy it is often the case that each person's opinion, as far as political clout is concerned, is worth as much as anyone else's. From this it is tempting, at least to some, to conclude that each person's opinion is worth as much, with respect to its likelihood of being true, as anyone else's. For example, suppose that a referendum is to be held on whether public money is to be used to build a new sewage line to community A. In this political situation each voter's opinion, expressed as a vote, is worth as much as anyone else's. But in the sense of that opinion's likelihood of being correct, this is not true. The opinions of a city engineer and the public health inspector are worth much more than the opinions of those who do not know anything about the issues.

Or consider a different case. We say that in a democracy each citizen has the right to his own beliefs. But if one has a right to belief *b*, one cannot be doing wrong in believing *b*. And so one cannot be wrong in one's belief that *b*. The argument is fallacious. I may have the right to believe that the world is flat, and so perhaps I cannot be said to be *doing* wrong in believing that the world is flat. And yet my belief is wrong because it is mistaken.

Finally, it's often said that the state is right to do what the majority wants. From this it is tempting to conclude that whatever the majority wants is right. But as the following example shows, this view is mistaken. Suppose that an overwhelming majority of the citizens of state A have, out of spite, voted to invade and kill the citizens of state B. And let us assume that the citizens of B, though few in number, are kind and generous. It could hardly be said that it would be right for state A to invade state B. What has gone wrong? When it was said that it is right that the state does what the majority wants, all that was meant is that it would be wrong for an elected officer to act contrary to the wishes of the majority. It doesn't follow from this that it is in some broad sense right to act in accordance with the whims of the majority. What the elected chief executive could do in this case is resign.

More needs to be said about cases of this sort, but the discussion is best left until the chapter on morality (see chapter 7, pages 255-260).

Other Points

1. Sense and Nonsense

Not only can we be misled by arguments that appear valid but are not, we can also be misled by groups of words that appear to express sentences but do not. Groups of words that convey the appearance of expressing sentences but do not are generally called meaningless sentences. The same points that were made about invalid arguments can also be made about meaningless sentences. Just as an invalid argument is not a kind of argument but a group of statements that appear to express an argument, so a meaningless sentence is not a kind of sentence but only a group of words that appears to express a sentence. Every group of words that expresses a sentence must, by definition, express a meaningful sentence.

For any number of reasons, a group of words can fail to produce a sentence. It may be because one or more of the words in the sentence is without meaning. For example, if I tell you that the room next door is filled with ectoplasm, and neither you nor I nor anyone else has the foggiest idea of what ectoplasm is, then my sentence is without meaning.[14] Second, it may be because the sentence is in some way incomplete. If I say 'Smith is in the next', the group of words is incomplete and so fails to form a sentence. A much more interesting way that a group of words can fail to form a sentence is where the words, for some reason or other, do not go together. For example, 'The day Friday is under the bed' fails to express a sentence. The day Friday, unlike the man Friday, is simply not the sort of thing that can be or not be under the bed. Unfortunately, there are no hard and fast rules about what words go together and what words do not, though one can usually tell by examining the words themselves. For example, it makes perfectly good sense to ask how high the Empire State Building is because the Empire State Building is a physical object, and a physical object is the sort of thing that has height. But it makes no sense to ask how high is up. Up is a direction and not a physical object, and directions cannot (logically) have height. As a consequence, 'The Empire State Building is 1000 feet high' expresses a meaningful sentence but 'Up is very high' does not. Or consider the following example: Although we don't always realize it, when we talk about the constant motion of an object in a straight line, we are always talking about its speed relative to something else. When we say that the car is going at 100 mph we mean that the car is moving at 100 mph relative to the surface of the earth. When we say that Mr. Jones is walking 5 mph on the deck of a given ship, we mean that he is walking at 5 mph relative to the deck of the ship. Aviators are aware of this point, for they distinguish between air speed and ground speed—speed relative to the air and speed relative to the ground. It follows from this that 'The universe is moving through space at a high velocity' fails to express a meaningful sentence—that is to say, it fails to express a sentence, even though it looks at first glance to be doing just that. It fails, because the first part suggests that the universe is moving relative to something, but since the universe is, by definition, all that is, it follows that there is nothing for it to be moving relative to. Such groups of words look at first glance to express something profound, but owing to the fact that the words fail to go together, they do not do so. We think we have something meaningful here because we can form a mental picture of groups of stars whizzing through space, but the picture misleads us.

2. Verifiability

There is a fairly close connection between meaning and verifiability. When properly constructed sentences are used to express statements, they usually tell us what steps we must take in order to show that they are true or false—that is, in order to verify them. If I say to you that there is a nugget of gold in the left top drawer in the only desk in room 1006 of the Empire State Building, what I say tells you what you have to do to verify my claim. It tells you, in effect, to go to the only desk in room 1006 of the Empire State Building and look in the top left drawer. If a nugget of gold is found, then my claim is true; if not it, my claim is false.

If, however, it turns out that neither we nor anyone else has any idea of how to go about showing that a given claim is true or false, this suggests that the claim is meaningless. Let's return to our previous example: If someone were to tell us that the universe is moving through space at a high velocity, we would have no idea how to go about verifying his claim. In order to substantiate it we would have to compare the speed of the universe to some other object taken to be fixed. But since there are no objects left, the comparison cannot be made. Because of the close connection between meaning and verifiability, the latter is an excellent test for determining whether or not a group of words expresses something meaningful. If the group of words is not verifiable, then we have good reason to believe that it is not meaningful.

Some philosophers have wanted to argue that it is verifiability, or the lack thereof, that is responsible for the meaning of a group of words. This is to put matters the wrong way around. What makes a group of words meaningful is, as we have seen, dependent upon the words individually having meaning, and collectively hanging together. As a result, we cannot be certain that if a group of words is unverifiable, it is also meaningless. All that we can be certain of is that if a group of words is unverifiable, we have reason to believe that it is meaningless. If we look carefully at the structure of the sentence we will most likely find something defective.

3. Meaning and Truth

Strictly speaking, sentences are either meaningful or meaningless, and statements are either true or false. But there is obviously a connection since sentences are used to express statements. The connection is that only a meaningful sentence can be used to express a statement. Thus, if what is expressed turns out to be true or false, we know that the sentence used to express it is meaningful.

There was a flourishing philosophical movement in the 1930s and 1940s called Logical Positivism. According to A. J. Ayer, one of its leading exponents, the statement 'God exists' is meaningless.[15] The reason it is meaningless, according to Ayer, is that we have no idea of how to verify it. As a result of this claim, and many like it, Ayer was branded an atheist. However, the accusation was mistaken. An atheist is one who holds that the sentence 'God exists' is meaningful but expresses a false statement. It must be meaningful in order to be false.[16] Whereas the logical positivist held that 'God exists' was meaningless. Given that it was meaningless, it could not be used to express a statement that was either true or false. It might be thought that the logical positivist should have been classified as an agnostic, but even this is mistaken. An agnostic also presumes that 'God exists' is meaningful; his claim is that we don't know whether it expresses a true statement or a false one. If it is either true or false it must be expressed by a meaningful sentence.

We shall discuss the existence of God at some length in chapter 5, but perhaps it should be pointed out here that Ayer misused the verifiability test. The unverifiability of 'God exists' gives us some reason to suspect meaninglessness, but it does not give us proof. It simply does not follow from the fact that we are unable to verify 'God exists', that the sentence is logically ill-formed and so meaningless. It's perfectly possible that 'God exists' expresses a statement that is either true or false, but one that we are incapable of verifying.

NOTES

1. Strictly speaking it's indicative sentences and not statements that are analytic or synthetic. 'I am hot' is a synthetic sentence that expresses one statement when used by me, and a different one when used by you. The reasons that I have attributed analyticity and syntheticity (if there is such a word) to statements are as follows: (a) As a rule, each analytic sentence can express only one statement. There is only one statement that I can express by 'All husbands are married'. Therefore there is no need to distinguish between them. (b) If 'All water boils at 212°F' can be used to make two different sentences—an analytic one and synthetic one, what is the "it" that is used to express these two sentences? We can't say that it's just a group of words for it's more than that. Perhaps we should say that 'All water boils at 212°F', in the beginning, expresses a sub-sentence that can be used to make a synthetic sentence and to make an analytic sentence, and that the synthetic sentence can be used to express one statement and the analytic sentence is used to express a different statement. Perhaps we should say this but it's awkward to do so. We don't have the concept of a sub-sentence in everyday parlance. Thus, in order to keep matters under control, I shall say that its statements are either analytic or synthetic.

2. For example, 'Jones is a husband' entails 'Jones has a wife', since to assert the first and deny the second would involve a contradiction.

3. Notice, though, that '~ Jones is over 6 feet tall and ~ Jones is under 6 feet tall' is synthetic, for it is equivalent to 'Jones is just 6 feet tall.'

4. It won't work on all arguments. It won't work on

All men are mortal.

Socrates is a man.

_____

Therefore, Socrates is mortal.

but at least it will work on some.

5. We could join the premises together with "." because one is saying in effect—'Since if K then S *and* ~S, therefore ~K'. Notice '~~K' could be written as 'K'.

6. The complete truthtable is as follows:

	R	C	F·	H	(R⊃C) ·	(C⊃F·) ·	(~F· v $_w$H) ·	H	~~R
1	T	T	T	T	T	T	F	T	T
2	T	T	T	F	T	T	T	F	T
3	T	T	F	T	T	F	T	T	T
4	T	F	T	T	F	T	F	T	T
5	F	T	T	T	T	T	F	T	F
6	T	T	F	F	T	F	T	F	T
7	T	F	F	T	F	T	T	T	T
8	F	F	T	T	T	T	F	T	F
9	T	F	T	F	F	T	T	F	T
10	F	T	T	F	T	T	T	F	F

	R	C	F·	H	(R⊃ C)	· (C⊃ F·)·	(~F· v ᵥH)	· H	~~R
11	F	T	F	T	T	F	T	T	F
12	T	F	F	F	F	T	T	F	T
13	*F	F	F	T	T	T	T	T	F
14	F	F	T	F	T	T	T	F	F
15	F	T	F	F	T	F	T	F	F
16	F	F	F	F	T	T	T	F	F

*Row 13 is the row where all the premises are true.

7. It might be noted that Modus Tollens is really Modus Ponens in disguise. '~q ⊃~ p' (as is noted on page 115), is equivalent to 'p ⊃ q'. Now if we substitute 'q ⊃~ p' for 'p ⊃ q' in

$$p \supset q$$
$$\frac{\sim q}{\therefore \sim p}$$

we get

$$\sim q \supset \sim p$$
$$\frac{\sim q}{\therefore \sim p}$$

which is of the Modus Ponens form.

8. 'p · ~q' is equivalent to '~(p ⊃ q)', which is the denial of 'p ⊃ q'.

9. Kant actually used 'A straight line is the shortest line (distance) between two points'. The above rendition strikes me as being more manageable.

10. The reader might at this point find it interesting to revisit the discussion of the infinite divisibility of matter which appears in chapter 1, page 19.

11. The necessity referred to here is physical necessity.

12. Notice, though, the difference between saying that p is logically necessary and saying that p is logically necessary *for* q. To say that p is LN is to say that 'p' is analytic, while to say that p is LN for q is to say that 'If not p then not' is analytic. Notice also, although it makes sense to say that p is logically sufficient *for* q, it makes no sense to say that p is logically sufficient (period).

13. Irving Stone, *Clarence Darrow for the Defense* (Garden City Publishing, 1941).

14. I attempt to use the meaningless sentence 'The room next door is filled with ectoplasm' to express a statement, but since I fail to produce a sentence I fail to express a statement. Some authors like to talk about meaningful and meaningless statements, but it seems to me that, strictly speaking, it is the sentence and not the statement that is meaningless. Though it could, I guess, be said that when one attempts to use a meaningless sentence to express a statement, one expresses a meaningless statement.

15. See *Language Truth and Logic* (London: Collins, 1936, 2nd ed. 1946), ch. 1.

16. If 'p' is false, it's negation 'not p' must be true, and in order for a statement to be true it must be meaningful. Therefore if 'p' is false it must be meaningful.

4

René Descartes

Armed with a surfeit of logical distinctions and sensitive to all sorts of fallacies that might bewitch us, let us turn to the philosophy of René Descartes. First, a few words about his life.

Descartes was born in La Haye, France, in 1596 to a fairly well-to-do land-owning family. He was educated in La Flèche College, a new school, run by the Jesuits and considered by many at that time to be the best school in Europe. Descartes was a sickly boy, but the enlightened masters of the school allowed him to sleep until noon every day and not engage in any vigorous exercise. He kept to his daily routine for the rest of his life—staying in bed until noon and making a point of not doing more than three hours of work a day. Fortunately he inherited enough money to make this gentlemanly lifestyle possible.

Upon completion of his formal education, Descartes embarked, rather uncharacteristically, upon a life of adventure. He spent a number of years serving as an officer in various armies (he didn't see any action), traveling and leading the life of "the man about town" in Paris. Tiring of the dashing life of a youngblood, Descartes returned to his academic pursuits around 1625, and in 1628 he settled in Holland where he was to remain for most of the rest of his life. In 1637, his *Discourse on Method* was published; in 1641, *The Meditations,* his best work, appeared in print; and 1644 marked the publication of his *Principles.* (In what follows we shall only examine his *Meditations.*) On the basis of these publications Descartes's reputation was made as the most important philosopher in Europe. Pursued by "the madding crowd," he kept changing his address in order to keep them at bay. Descartes remained a bachelor, no doubt so that he could retain his life of tranquility, but he did have a daughter, who was born in 1635. Her death at the age of five was a source of great distress to Descartes.

By 1649 his fame had spread to Sweden, where Queen Christina invited him to visit her court and give her lessons on philosophy. Descartes accepted the invitation, but the queen insisted on having her lessons at five in the morning. This proved to be too much for Descartes's delicate constitution. He became ill and died on February 11, 1650.

There are a number of ways that Descartes can be classified philosphically. First, he is considered to be a "rationalist" as opposed to an "empiricist." An empiricist is one who believes that all knowledge is ultimately derived from experience, while a rationalist is one who believes that any knowledge worthy of the name is derived from reason. Plato and Parmenides are generally considered to be rationalists since they believed that experience could only give rise to what was at best true belief. As you will recall, according to Plato, one could only have knowledge of the Forms—entities apprehended by reason alone. Lucretius, on the other hand, could be classified as an empiricist since, although he was prepared to admit that the senses could sometimes deceive, they were the ultimate source of knowledge of the world around us. In modern philosophy—and that means from Descartes on—Gottlieb Leibniz and Benedict Spinoza are generally classified as rationalists, while John Locke, George Berkeley and David Hume are generally classified as empiricists. However, these terms ("empiricist" and "rationalist") must be thought of as nothing more than hooks to hang philosophical cloaks (in other words theories) on. Descartes had his empirical moments, for he was prepared to admit that some kinds of knowledge—for example, biological knowledge—would have to be based upon experience, while Locke, although he believed that all ideas were ultimately derived from experience, wanted to claim that the knowledge we come to have through those ideas is based upon reason. For example, according to Locke, experience provides the opportunity for us to have an idea of what whiteness is, and what blackness is, but our knowledge—e.g., the realization that if something is white, then it is not black (and vice versa)—is derived from reason.

The chief source of Descartes's rationalist predilection is perhaps his interest in mathematics. In his day, Descartes was one of the foremost mathematicians in Europe. His greatest achievements were in analytical geometry. Here he developed a system of coordinates that are still called (after him) Cartesian coordinates. As a result of his successes, Descartes felt he had discovered a technique with universal application. If confronted with a difficult intellectual problem, he would first break the problem into its simplest parts, and then, on the basis of intuitively obvious axioms, he moved deductively, step by step, until the conclusion, if any, was reached. Shortly, we will see that this technique is reflected in Descartes's approach in the *Meditations*.

Descartes can also be classified as a "dualist." That is to say, he believed that there were two ultimate substances, mental substance and physical substance (or matter). Plato, like Descartes, was also a dualist, for he believed that a person, at least until death, was composed of both a mind (or in other words, a soul) and a body. Descartes could be classified as a monist as well, since he held (a) that substance is what is not dependent for its existence on anything else and (b) that the only substance that does not depend for its existence on anything else is God. Mental substance and physical substance are, according to Descartes, created substances and so, according to his definition, not truly substances. Spinoza took this point seriously and claimed there is only one substance—God.

According to Descartes, each (created) substance had one essential attribute. For example, the essential attribute of mental substance was thought or, in other words, consciousness. What this meant was that an individual could not have a mind without consciousness or possess consciousness without also having a mind. This raised for Descartes the question of what happened to the mind when a person went to sleep and became unconscious. His answer was that the mind must continue to think to itself. He could have avoided this problem if he had said that the essential attribute of the mind was not thought per se but the ability to think.

The essential attribute of matter or, in other words, physical substance, was extension—that is, length, width, depth or, in other words, expansiveness. This raised a problem about empty space, for surely empty space can have length, width, and depth. Descartes's solution was to deny the existence of empty space. This in turn raised the problem of how motion was possible. How could the fish that Lucretius talked about move ahead if there is no space for it to move into? Descartes's solution was similar to that of some of the ancients. He claimed that all motion was ultimately circular.

Finally, the essential attribute of each substance cannot be ascribed to the other substance. It is impossible for matter to think, and equally impossible for mind to be extended.

Descartes can also be classified as a subjectivist, as opposed to a objectivist. Roughly speaking, an objectivist bases his philosophy on features that he observes in the physical world. On the basis of these, he goes on to speculate what the mind—the inner world—must be like. Lucretius could be classified as an objectivist. A subjectivist, on the other hand, begins with the inner world of thoughts, emotions, and feelings, and from these goes on to speculate about the nature of the external world.

One of the novel features of Descartes's *Meditations* is his technique of what might be called positive doubting. Take any belief, and if one has the least reason for doubting it, put it to one side. Carry on in this manner with the hope of finding at least one belief that cannot be doubted. If one such belief can be found, then use this as a corner stone and proceed to rebuild the whole edifice of human knowledge.

Descartes's singular attachment to this technique leads one to wonder why he found it so attractive. Part of the explanation is that he was born into a world where most of the accepted beliefs about the natural world were turning out to be false. Until the seventeenth century, cosmology was based on the writings of Plato and Aristotle. The Earth was considered to be stationary and at the center of the universe. Around it rotated the Sun, the moon, the planets, and all the stars, each moving in perfect circles. Ptolemy, the third-century (A.D.) astronomer, had plotted their orbits in the greatest of detail. Matter in the sub-lunary region—that is, the region between the moon and the center of the earth—was believed to operate according to one set of laws, while matter beyond the moon—that is, the matter that composed the stars and the planets—operated according to another set. Both ancient and medieval peoples believed there was something divine about the stars and the planets. If not, why were they called heavenly bodies? It was also believed that heavy bodies fell at a greater rate of speed than lighter bodies, and that a body set in motion in a vacuum (if such were possible) would continue until it tired; then it would slow down and stop. Many people also believed that the world was flat, although most serious thinkers down through the ages have believed that the earth was spherical. (However, I once had a student show me a high school textbook that his grandfather had studied in Poland before the First World War. There it was stated in all innocence that the world was flat.)

All of these beliefs, and many more, were shown to be false during the period in which Descartes lived. Copernicus (1473-1543) argued that the Sun and not the Earth was at the center. Kepler (1571-1630) proved that the planets moved in ellipses rather than in perfect circles about the Sun. Galileo (1564-1642) had shown (before the church imprisoned and threatened to torture him) that, in a vacuum, light objects fall at the same rate of acceleration as heavy objects. He also showed that an object in motion would continue in a straight line until acted upon by some other force.[1] And finally, Newton (1642-1727) showed that all physical objects, terrestrial and heavenly alike, are subject to the same forces. For example, the force that keeps water in the pail swung above one's head is just the same as the force that keeps the moon from crashing into Earth.

FIRST MEDITATION

In his search for something that is absolutely certain, Descartes decides to put to one side any belief that he can have the least reason for doubting. He realizes that he cannot go through his beliefs one by one, but he also realizes that if he has some reason to doubt a belief of some type this will give him reason to doubt all beliefs of that type.

He begins by noticing that sometimes the senses deceive him with regard to things that are far away. He doesn't give any examples of this in the first Meditation, but in the Sixth Meditation he mentions that sometimes square towers, when viewed from a distance, look round, and that huge statues on rooftops, when viewed from the ground, look quite small.[2] Some of the other examples that he might have used are: (a) straight oars when half immersed in water sometimes appear bent; (b) to someone suffering from jaundice everything appears yellow; and (c) on hot days in the desert it is possible, so we are told, to see mirages of distant oases. Since our senses sometimes deceive us about things of this sort, according to Descartes, we really shouldn't trust our senses concerning these things.

Although this gives us reason to doubt some of the things conveyed by the senses, it doesn't give us reason to doubt all the things. I may doubt that a distant tower is round but I still have no reason to doubt, for example, that I am sitting here and that I have arms and legs. For this a stronger argument is needed. This stronger argument is sometimes called the dream argument. "How do I know," Descartes asks himself, "that I am not asleep in bed and dreaming that I am here writing at this desk?" To further paraphrase this argument, how do I know that I have arms and legs and other bodily parts? Just as it's possible for a soldier (Descartes doesn't make use of this example) who has lost his legs to dream that he has legs, so it's possible that I don't have legs but am dreaming that I do.

But what about such claims as $2 + 3 = 5$ or a square has four sides? I cannot use the argument from the possibility of dreaming to doubt these. For whether I am awake or asleep, $2 + 3 = 5$ and a square appears to have four sides. But even here there is room for doubt. Couldn't there be a malicious deceiver, a kind of intellectual devil, who plays all sorts of tricks on me? If there were such a being, couldn't he lead me to believe that $2 + 3$ was 5 when really it was something else? Often I mislead myself in adding large numbers, so isn't it possible that there could be some powerful being who deceives me when I add small numbers?

The First Meditation ends on this note. Descartes has found reason to doubt all beliefs based on experience and the intellect, and has yet to find something he cannot doubt.

Before going on to the Second Meditation, there are a number of points that should be made. First of all, Descartes offers three arguments: the argument from illusion, the dream argument, and the argument from the possibility of a malicious deceiver. Each argument makes it possible to doubt not only what the previous argument made it possible to doubt, but something more besides. For example, the argument from illusion makes it possible to doubt the shape of far off objects but not the existence of one's arms and legs. The dream argument, however, makes it possible to doubt both.

Second, Descartes suggests in the first argument that just as we shouldn't ever again trust someone who has once deceived us, so, too, we shouldn't ever trust the senses since they have also deceived us. But there is a difference. If I find it necessary to rely on people, and Smith has proven untrustworthy, I can always find someone else who is not. But if the senses prove untrustworthy, to what can I turn? Someone might suggest reason. But if what has been said in the previous chapter is correct, it's only in the field of geometry that I might be able to rely on reason to give me knowledge of reality. Knowledge derived from reason will consist exclusively of synthetic a priori truths, and we know that the only truths that could be claimed to be synthetic a priori are the truths of geometry.

There is a further point. If Smith has proven untrustworthy, then how did I find out? It must have been either through someone else or through more direct evidence. If the senses prove to be untrustworthy, I could only find this out through the senses themselves. There is no other way. For example, I see an oar half immersed in water, and it looks bent. How do I find out that it is not? I find out by pulling the oar out of the water and taking a look at it. It's through the senses that I discover the deceptiveness of the senses. What this point shows is that it's difficult to see how I could argue from the fact that I am sometimes deceived by the senses to the conclusion that I should never trust the senses. It's only through not being deceived by the senses that I discover at times that I have been deceived. I must trust the senses some of the time.

What about the second argument? Is Descartes right in saying that I can't be certain that I am sitting here writing this chapter, that I could be asleep in bed and only dreaming that I am sitting here writing? Someone may argue that there are detectable differences between life in a dream and life while awake. The experiences of dreams lack the cohesion and coherence of life when awake. In a dream I am given a Ferrari car and it turns into a yacht. This latter event (let alone the former) never happens in real life. Therefore it is possible to distinguish between waking life and dreaming life. There is something in this objection, but not very much. Sometimes while I am dreaming I become aware of the improbability of what is going on; I realize that I am dreaming, and wake up. I may even find that I enjoy the dream so much that I keep it going. But now it's more of a daydream than a full-blooded dream. However, it's only for the length of time I am *not* aware of the incoherence of my experiences that I can be said to be truly dreaming. It's part of the logic of "dreaming" that to say that

I dreamt I was given a Ferrari car is to say, or at least to imply, that I falsely believed that I was given a Ferrari car. If I had some reason to suspect that I was really being given a Ferrari car, then I wasn't really dreaming. So Descartes's conclusion that I can't be certain I am sitting here writing, seems to be correct. There have been times when I mistakenly thought I was sitting here writing, and these were times when I was dreaming that I was sitting here writing.

Although Descartes is right about this, he wants to draw a much wider conclusion. He wants to conclude that it's possible that my whole life is a dream—that I literally live in a dream world. This seems to be mistaken. Consider the following: Any coin that I pick up may be counterfeit. But I cannot argue from this that perhaps all coins are counterfeit. The concept of a counterfeit coin only makes sense against the background of real coins. Of course it would be possible for some members of the Mafia to take all the U.S. coins out of circulation and replace them with their own coinage. But at least some of the coins at one time would have had to be real. Could the federal government take all the coins out of circulation and replace them with fakes? If it did, the coins that were used to make the replacement would become real coins! Or again, suppose I discover an island and decide to set up a state. However, instead of having real coins I decide to have counterfeit coins. This is impossible. Whatever coins I produced would have to be considered real coins.

The same point can be made about dreams. Just as some coins can turn out to be counterfeit (hence not real), so some experiences can turn out to be dreamt, and not real. But just as not all coins can be counterfeit, not all experiences can be dream experiences.

The logic of our language is apt to deceive us when we think about this. Suppose that we have been given a box containing six chocolates and suppose that we are told (truthfully) that one and only one is poisoned. Even though we have been told that only one is poisoned, it's tempting to argue that they may all be poisoned. Consider the following box of chocolates.

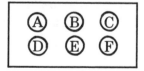

Concerning it, we might think in the following way: A may be poisoned, B may be poisoned, C may be poisoned, D may be poisoned, E may be poisoned, and F may be poisoned. Therefore, A, B, C, D, E, and F may be poisoned. Therefore, all may be poisoned. This conclusion cannot follow, since it's known that not all the chocolates are poisoned. Similarly, in the case of dreams, since it's already known that not all experiences are dream experiences, it's also known that it cannot be deduced from the claim that any experience may be a dream experience that all experiences may be dream experiences. The statement form 'All x may be y' is compatible with the statement form 'Any x may be y' but is not deducible from it.[3]

Before leaving the topic of dreams, there is one more question I would like to raise. I have said that any experience could turn out to be a dream experience. But there seems to be one experience of which this is not true. It seems impossible, at least to me, to dream that one is experiencing intense pain. In my case, when I begin to dream that I am experiencing intense pain, I become aware that I am not and wake up. So it seems to follow that every time we think we are experiencing intense pain we can be certain that we are experiencing intense pain and not dreaming that we are. We know that it cannot be a dream.

Let us move on to the specter of a malicious deceiver. Descartes introduces this possibility in order to make it plausible to doubt one's beliefs about mathematics and logic, and to increase the plausibility of doubting empirical beliefs. That is to say, beliefs derived from the senses. According to Descartes, as we have noted, 2 + 3 will continue to make 5, and a square will continue to have 4 sides, whether I am dreaming or awake. So the possibility that I may be dreaming gives me no reason to doubt this. Is Descartes right on this matter? Perhaps he is as far as 2 + 3 = 5 is concerned, but couldn't a geometrician dream that he had proved a new theorem only to wake to find that he was mistaken? However, Descartes feels that the deceiver is necessary, and perhaps where simple geometrical and mathematical claims are concerned he is right. Only if we accept that there could be a malicious deceiver will it be possible for us to doubt that 2 + 3 = 5.

In recent philosophy a possibility that covers both the dream argument and the malicious deceiver has been discussed. Suppose that someone is involved in an accident so serious that most of his body is in very poor shape. His brain however remains undamaged. In order to save the life of the person, his brain is hooked up to a number of life support systems and allowed to float in a nutrient-packed solution in a vat. Suppose further that the doctors hook up the brain to a number of communication channels so that the person will know what is going on. No doubt this sort of surgery cannot be performed today, but there is no reason to think that such surgical feats will not some day be possible. Now the skeptical question that we must consider is this: How do we know that we are not just brains floating in vats being fed false information? Perhaps we were abducted by a mad scientist (a modern-day malicious deceiver) in order to carry out strange and macabre experiments.

Someone might object that there is a difference between the mad scientist and Descartes's malicious deceiver, for although the mad scientist could feed false empirical information to the brain in the vat, he could not make that person think that 2 + 3 was other than 5. But why not? If the scientist is allowed to tinker with the circuits in the brain and he knows how the brain works, then surely he could get the person, who is nothing more than a brain in a vat, to believe that 2 + 3 was equal to 6.

There is, however, one big difference between Descartes's grounds for skepticism and the brain-in-the-vat argument. According to Descartes, both the dream argument and the deceiver argument give me reason to doubt that I have a body. Just as I can dream that I have arms and legs when I haven't, so I can dream that I have a body when I am nothing more than a disembodied soul or, in other words, a disembodied mind.[4] Similarly, the Cartesian deceiver could deceive a disembodied mind into thinking that it possessed a brain. But the mad scientist cannot do this. He has to have a brain to deceive. Perhaps he can deceive me into thinking that I have no brain, but if I think that I have a brain then it would seem that on this, at least, I cannot be mistaken. However, we must move carefully, because maybe I don't think with my brain but have been deceived by the mad scientist into thinking that I do. So I cannot be certain that my belief that I have a brain is true. Nevertheless, I must have some sort of a physical presence in order to be the object of the deception. So if I believe that I exist as some sort of a physical entity, I know that this belief must be true.

What this point raises is the question of whether, on the basis of the dream argument, I can doubt that I have some sort of a physical body (the brain is considered a part of the body). I can doubt whether I have legs because I might be dreaming that I have legs when I don't, and perhaps the same sort of argument can be made about my arms, torso, and so on. Is it possible that I don't have any body at all and am just dreaming that I do? Perhaps this doubt is possible. But somehow the idea that I might be a disembodied mind dreaming that I have a body doesn't seem to be quite as plausible as the idea that I am an embodied mind, dreaming that I have legs when in reality I don't.

The same point can be made about the malicious deceiver and the mad scientist. Perhaps either one could deceive me into believing that I have legs when I don't, but it seems less likely that either of them could deceive me into believing that I have some sort of a physical presence when I don't.

SECOND MEDITATION

The second of Decartes's meditations is perhaps the most important so it must be read with the greatest of care. Descartes begins by reviewing all the things that he can doubt, which seem to include practically everything, and then wonders if there is anything left that he cannot doubt. This brings him to the "cogito," the central thesis of the meditations. The argument runs something like this. One belief that I have is that I exist. Is it possible that I could have deceived myself on this? Obviously, if I did not exist I could not deceive myself into believing that I did exist. In order to deceive myself I must exist. Assuming that I do not exist, could a malicious deceiver deceive me into believing that I do exist? Again, the answer is no. I must exist in order to be deceived by the deceiver. So whether or not I postulate the existence of a deceiver, I can be absolutely certain that I exist. " 'I am,' 'I exist,' whenever I utter it or conceive it in my mind, it is necessarily true." (*Descartes*, p. 67)[5]

Now that I know that I exist, I must ask what sort of being this "I" is. I can doubt that I have a body but I cannot doubt that I am conscious, therefore I know that I exist (at least) as a conscious being.

This is Descartes's big point. He thought he knew himself better as a physical being than as a conscious being, but since he can doubt that he has a body yet not doubt that he is conscious, he therefore knows himself better as a conscious being. Furthermore, this application of positive doubting has given him a clearer grasp of what he is. He used to think of the mind, or soul, much like Lucretius did (see chapter 1, pp. 31–35) as some sort of rarefied vapor infused among the parts of his body. His thoughts on it were very obscure. But now he has a clear grasp of what it—the mind—is. It is pure consciousness: the part of him whose existence he cannot doubt. He knows what the mind, or soul, is and he knows that he is at least a mind.

The same argument is used by Descartes in his earlier work *The Discourse on Method*. In Part IV he writes:

> . . . I decided to feign that everything that had entered my mind hitherto was no more true than the illusions of dreams. But immediately upon this I noticed that while I was trying to think everything false, it must needs be that I, who was thinking this, was something. And observing that this truth "I am thinking, therefore I exist," [*cogito, ergo sum*], was so solid and secure that the most extravagant suppositions of the skeptics could not overthrow it, I . . . [decided] . . . to accept it as the first principle of philosophy that I was seeking. (*Descartes*, p. 31)[6]

Descartes's use of 'Cogito, ergo sum' to prove his existence was criticized by a number of people on the grounds that it had already been used for this purpose by Augustine. Descartes's reply to one of these critics was to point out that he was using "cogito" in an entirely new way. He had used it not just to prove that he existed, but to prove that he existed as a conscious being. He writes:

My own use of the argument, on the other hand, was to establish that this conscious I is an immaterial substance with no corporal element; these two uses are very different. To infer that one exists from the fact that one is doubting is in itself so simple and natural that it might have come from anyone's pen. (*Descartes,* p. 263)

It is difficult to overestimate the importance of Descartes's discovery. If we look at medieval paintings of people in the throes of death, often as not there is a cloud of smoke or vapor coming out of their mouths. Descartes put a stop to all that. Never again was "giving up the ghost" represented as giving up a cloud of smoke. In fact, one can go further and suggest that no philosopher before Descartes—not even Plato, who viewed the body as a vehicle for the mind—had any conception of what the mind was. Descartes's concept of the mind has come under vigorous attack in recent years, and many have felt the need to replace it. Still, in order for human thought to move on to a replacement, it was necessary to first move from the pre-Cartesian conception of the mind.

It would seem that if Descartes only knows that he is a conscious being, then he doesn't know very much. But his knowledge is richer than might first be thought. He knows that he is a being who doubts, understands, asserts, denies, wills, imagines, and perceives, for he doubts almost everything, understands one thing, asserts this one thing to be true, denies all others, wills to know more, imagines many things, and perceives many other things.

The reader might be puzzled about how Descartes can be certain that he perceives when there may be nothing to perceive and no eyes etc., to perceive with even if something did exist. No doubt Descartes cannot be certain that he perceives physical objects, but he does perceive *something*. There may not be a pen and paper in front of me, but at least I can be certain that there are colors and shapes in my visual field. I can doubt neither their existence nor that I perceive them.

Let me make this point a bit clearer. Suppose that you are given a drug that makes you "see" a green cube-shaped object on the empty desk in front of you. When asked what you see you say "I see a green cube." We say, "No you don't, it's just an hallucination, the effect of the drug." Here you would have every right to say, "Well, maybe I don't see a physical cube, but at least I perceive the image of a cube, and that image really is green." This is the sort of object that Descartes has in mind when he says that he can be certain that he perceives.

The Piece of Wax

Descartes, in order to show that he knows himself better through the mind as a thinking thing, goes on to argue that we know physical objects better through the intellect than through the senses. This argument comes as a surprise to many readers, for one may well wonder what Descartes is doing talking about how we know physical objects when he has yet to prove that there *are* physical objects. Actually, Descartes could have left this section to the Sixth Meditation. As it stands, we shall have to take it in a hypothetical way. What he is really attempting to do is to show that *if* there are physical objects, then they are known better through the mind than through the senses. There is also the further puzzle of how this conclusion could support the claim that he knows himself better through the mind, as a thinking thing, than through the senses, as a physical thing. Perhaps it does give some inductive support, but that support seems to be very weak.

Descartes invites us to consider a particular lump of wax. How do we know this lump of wax? It's tempting to say that we know it through the senses. But if we were to put it on the hearth by a fire so that all the sensible properties were to change as it melted, we would still say that it was the same piece of wax. If we are prepared to say that it's the same piece of wax after its color, taste, odor, shape and size had changed, we can hardly say it is through the senses that we know the wax. The reason for this is that color, taste, and so on are apprehended through the senses. Perhaps someone will say, according to Descartes, that it's through the imagination that we know the wax. However, our imagination cannot encompass the infinite number of changes the wax can undergo, so it cannot be through the imagination that we know the wax. If the piece of wax is not known through the senses or the imagination this only leaves the intellect. According to Descartes, we must come to know the wax by pure mental perception.

This argument may at first seem analogous to the following fallacious one. Suppose that someone were to wonder which leg is essential for supporting a horse. He lifts the right foreleg and the horse still stands. He concludes that the right foreleg is not essential. He puts it down and proceeds to the left foreleg. He lifts it and, as before, the horse still stands. So he concludes that this leg is not essential and moves on to the hind legs. Suppose now that after he tried all the legs and found that none is essential, he were to conclude that since something must be essential, there must be another but invisible leg that supports the horse! However, I don't think it fair to accuse Descartes of making such a simple error.

Let us start again. First of all, we should separate the question 'How do we know that the lump is composed of wax?' from the question 'How do we know that it's the same lump?' If we were scientifically minded, we would determine that the lump was composed of wax by subjecting it to a number of tests. Before we could say that it was wax we would have to know that it had the right specific gravity, the right melting point, and so on. It would be on the basis of empirical evidence—evidence derived from sense experience—that we would judge the lump to be wax. So Descartes is right in saying that the intellect is involved in coming to know that something is wax. He is mistaken, however, in thinking that if the senses are not sufficient they are not necessary either.

How, then, do we know that it's the same lump? (I'm reluctant to say "lump of wax," for if the molecular structure were to undergo a change, it would no longer be wax). If Descartes were to leave the room when the wax was solid and come back after it had melted he would have no way of knowing that it is the same lump. The way that he comes to know it as the same lump is by watching it and observing that no particles have left the lump and no particles from elsewhere have joined the lump. However, simply watching does not convey knowledge about the lump. Again, as Descartes would say, one must judge on the basis of what one has observed. So Descartes is right in saying that knowing it's the same lump is not just a matter of observing. His error is in thinking that since observation is not sufficient to know, it is not even necessary.

Matter

Lurking in the background of Descartes's discussion is a problem concerning matter, which must now be examined if we are to have a fuller understanding of his philosophy.

Sitting in front of me while I (now) write, is a black plastic paperweight. It's rectangular in shape and weighs about a pound. It's uncommon for physical objects to have proper names, but there is no reason to suppose they shouldn't. I shall call this paperweight "Fred." There are all sorts of things I can say of Fred. I can say that he was made in Japan, that he was given to me by a daughter, that his dimensions are $3'' \times 5'' \times 2''$. In fact, there is an almost inexhaustible number of things that can be said about Fred, and an almost inexhaustible number of properties that can be ascribed to him. Let's pretend, however, that being black, rectangular in shape, and weighing one pound are all the properties that can be attributed to Fred. Now consider the statement 'Fred is black, rectangular in shape, and weighs one pound'. We know the referents for the words "black," "rectangular," and "one pound" refer to. "Black" refers to the color black, "rectangular" refers to the particular shape of Fred. But what does "Fred" refer to? It can't refer to any of the properties of Fred, for they have all been listed in the right (predicate) side of the statement. But it must refer to something. After all, something has these properties. It's tempting to say that 'Fred' refers to a substance that supports these properties. It can't be perceived—since only properties can be perceived—but it must be there all the same.

It might be suggested that we can avoid this problem through noticing that Fred isn't an ultimate object but only a composite of smaller objects. However, we can't avoid the problem in this way. Suppose we find that Fred is composed of molecules $A, B, C \ldots$, then the same problem will arise with the molecule A or any other molecule. We can say "A has the following properties. . . ." If we have listed all the properties on the right, then what does "A" refer to? It looks like A must refer to that blob of substance that supports those properties.

One tempting but, I think, unacceptable solution is suggested by the following example. Suppose I have an old car called Beelzebub. Here, as in the case of Fred, I can make the same sorts of claims. I can say Beelzebub has a carburetor, a steering wheel, a fuel pump, and so on. Suppose further that I were to go on and list all of Beelzebub's parts. What then does the word "Beelzebub" refer to here? It would clearly be a mistake to think that "Beelzebub" refers to some mysterious substance that supports the parts. Suppose I take Beelzebub to a vacant lot and start removing its parts one by one until only the chassis and the right front wheel are left. I can remove the right front wheel from Beelzebub but can I remove the chassis from Beelzebub? Can I say that there would still be the invisible substance of Beelzebub left? Of course not. The mistake that is made here is to think that 'Beelzebub' refers to something different from the parts. But all that 'Beelzebub' refers to is the parts organized in a particular way. When I say "Beelzebub has a Holly carburetor" I use the word 'Beelzebub' to draw my listener's attention to the object that I want to say something about. I then use 'has a Holly carburetor' to say what I want about it. I refer twice to the same object, not to two different objects.

The solution suggested by this example is that just as 'Beelzebub' is nothing more than a number of parts organized in a particular way, so 'Fred' is nothing more than a bundle of properties organized in a particular way. And just as the grammatical structure of 'Beelzebub has the following parts. . .' can mislead one into thinking that Beelzebub is something different from the parts, so, too, can the grammatical structure of 'Fred has the following properties . . .' mislead the reader into thinking that Fred is a mysterious substance different from the properties.

As I mentioned before, I am inclined to think that this solution is mistaken. We can say that Beelzebub is nothing more than a number of parts organized in a particular way. But can we say that Fred is nothing more than a bundle of properties? A property, say the property of being black, has to be a property of something. Blackness cannot exist on its own. But the carburetor I remove from Beelzebub does not have to be a part of anything. It can exist on its own. Thus the relation between an object and its properties is very different from the relation between an object and its parts. A sand pile may be nothing more than a pile of grains of sand, but a grain of sand cannot be more than just a bundle of properties.

If we look at the history of philosophy, we find that philosophers fall out over this problem. Some, like John Locke and René Descartes, want to say that physical objects consist of material substance, or (in other words) matter and properties. Others like George Berkeley and David Hume want to say that physical objects are nothing more than bundles of sensible properties. In the early part of the twentieth century, this thesis that physical objects are bundles of sensible properties was refined into a theory called Phenomenalism, which contends that physical objects are logical constructions out of sense data. This theory is more sophisticated than the bundle theory, but its thrust is the same.

Returning to Descartes, one of the reasons he wanted to say that the piece of wax was known through the intellect and not through the senses was that the wax was really a blob of material substance and this, unlike its fleeting properties, which could be apprehended through the senses, could only be apprehended through the intellect. It is through the eyes that I know the color of wax, through the nose that I know the odor of wax, and through the mouth that I know the taste of the wax. But how do I know the physical substance of the wax? It can't be through any of the senses, I can't see the material substance. It can only be through the intellect. As Descartes puts it, "when I distinguish the wax from its outward form, and as it were unclothe it and consider it in its naked self, I get something which . . . I need a human mind to perceive." (*Descartes,* p. 74)

But Descartes is clearly mistaken on this. No doubt the intellect is required (i.e., necessary but not sufficient) to know what wax is, and to know that it is the same piece of wax in front of me. It may also be the case that there is something called matter that lurks behind the properties and supports them. But it certainly is not the case that this mysterious stuff is perceived through the intellect. If it were, then one could always know after leaving the room and returning that the same piece of wax was sitting there.

"Cogito, ergo sum"

This argument, which is perhaps the most celebrated feature of Descartes's philosophy, has been attacked on every conceivable ground. First, it has been claimed that 'sum' is not deducible from 'cogito'—which is true; second, it has been claimed that if the argument is put in the form 'I think therefore I am', the argument is circular—which is also true; and finally, it has been objected that if a malicious deceiver could lead us astray as we move from premise to conclusion in other arguments, he could do the same in this one. Descartes's reply to all this is that 'Cogito ergo sum' and 'I think therefore I am' are

not to be considered as arguments consisting of premises and conclusions but as statements that can intuitively be seen, all at once,
to be necessarily true. This fuss may explain why Descartes avoided
both forms in the *Meditations*. He does, however, deploy the first in
his later work, *The Principles of Philosophy*.

However, in order to avoid confusion, let us confine ourselves to
what Descartes says in the *Meditations*. Roughly put, he says that he
cannot doubt that he exists and he cannot doubt that he thinks, so
he can be certain both that he exists, and that he exists as a thinking
thing.

Some critics contend that Descartes has been duped by the deceptiveness of language. 'I exist' only gains its certainty because 'I' is an
indexical (pointing) word whose use presupposes the existence of what
it points to. In other words, 'I exist' only gains its certainty because 'I
don't exist' is logically and grammatically ill-formed. The same point
could also be made about 'He exists'. I can't assume on the grounds
that the sentence "He does not exist" is ill-formed that when I use "He
exists" there is necessarily someone to whom I am referring. It's always
possible that I am dreaming or hallucinating.

Although this objection focuses our attention on the fact that we
must use language with the greatest of caution, I don't think that it
affects Descartes's point. Although it's perfectly possible that I might
not have existed, I can be absolutely certain that I now exist as a conscious entity; this cannot be doubted. Just in case the reader thinks
that I am being misled by the 'I', let me put it this way: Although it's
perfectly possible that Patrick Mackenzie might not have existed—it's
a wonder that he ever did—I cannot doubt, and so I can be certain
that Patrick Mackenzie does exist. Of course I can doubt for "Cartesian reasons" that Patrick Mackenzie is called "Patrick Mackenzie," but
this is different from doubting whether Patrick Mackenzie exists. So
I think that in the end Descartes is right. There is one statement of
whose truth I can be absolutely certain, and that is that I exist, and
exist at least as a conscious entity.

THIRD MEDITATION

The Second Meditation may win the prize for being the most interesting, but when it comes to obscurity there is no doubt that the Third
Meditation wins hands down. The primary purpose of this latter meditation is to prove that there is a God, a task of strategic importance
for Descartes. Until he has proven that there is a God, he cannot ad-
vance beyond his own existence. A deceiver could be tricking him on
everything else. But once he has proven that there is a God—that is
to say, a being who is all powerful (omnipotent), all knowing (omni-

scient), and all good, he can be certain that a being such as the deceiver does not exist. God, being all good, would not permit the existence of a malicious being who was bent on deceiving others. However, once Descartes has shown that there is a God, (who would not deceive him) and no deceiver, he can rest assured that the external world (the world beyond his sense perceptions) exists in much the way that appearance suggests.

Descartes's skeptical doubts about the existence of an external world (notice that this would also include his body), and the necessity to prove that there is a God in order to remove them, loom much larger in Descartes's philosophy than the reader might suspect. Descartes held what might be called the representative theory of perception. (At least he thought that it was likely to be true.) According to this theory, one never sees physical objects directly; all one ever sees is a copy of the physical object, from which the existence of the object is inferred. Suppose, for example, that I am looking at a cube.

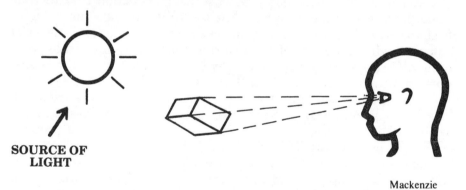

SOURCE OF
LIGHT

Mackenzie

Light waves or particles emanate from a source of light; some hit the cube, and some of these bounce off in the direction of the lens of my eye (let's assume that I have only one eye). This forms a physical image on the back of my eye, which in turn stimulates the optical nerve to carry a signal to my brain. In some miraculous way this physiological "signal" is transformed into a mental image of the cube, which is then presented to the mind—the real me. The image is what I see. It's all that I see and all that I ever can see. From it I spontaneously infer the existence and nature of the cube.

Although this is a natural way to account for visual perception[7] (other types of perception would be accounted for in much the same way), it is fraught with pitfalls. Imagine a man who lives in an underground, windowless bunker. Above the bunker is a T.V. camera that takes an on-going picture of the outside world. The picture is presented on a screen monitored by the bunkerman. All he sees is what appears on the screen and this is all he can see. He cannot step outside to take a look, make sure that what appears on the screen is similar to what he sees.

If our bunkerman is doomed to this sort of existence, then he has good reason to doubt that what appears on his screen is a faithful image of the outside world. Perhaps the picture is radically distorted. Perhaps there is nothing there at all. Now, if we are in the same predicament as the bunkerman, if all that we can even see of the outside world are images flashed upon our mental screens, then we also have good reason to be skeptical. What reason do we have to believe that the image we directly perceive bears any resemblance to the outside world? What reason do we have to believe that there is any world there at all? These are Descartes's real worries, and this is why he needed to prove there was a God. Until he has proved that there is a God who would not deceive him, he has no reason whatsoever to believe that there is anything beyond his immediate perceptions.

Even when Descartes has proven to his satisfaction that there is a God, he is not prepared to say that the world appears just as it is. He shares with the ancient atomists, Galileo and many others, the belief that although the objects of the external world have much the same shape and size as they appear to have, they do not have the colors, odors, and sounds they appear to have. In fact, they do not have any color, etc. at all. If the light waves that bounce off the cube are short, then the image of the cube I see is red, and if the light waves are long, then it is blue. But the cube itself is colorless. This raises a problem for Descartes: How can God, who is all good, allow me to believe that the cube is red when it is really colorless? The situation of the bunkerman would be comparable to this if he lived in a colorless world, but the images on his television screen of that colorless world were colored.

Clear and Distinct Ideas

Descartes begins the Third Meditation by reviewing all the things that he knows. He knows that he exists and he knows that he exists as a being who doubts, asserts, and so on. He then says that there could well be one more thing that he knows. He is certain that he is a conscious being.[8] Descartes' perception of his existence as a conscious being is clear and distinct. Therefore he can be certain that all perceptions are true which share the clarity and distinctness of my perception of myself.

There are lots of things that could be said about this argument. First, it's a bit reckless on the part of Descartes to argue that since one clear and distinct idea or perception is true, that all clear and distinct ideas are true. On the other hand, what other sort of criterion of truth could Descartes have? We would say that a statement like 'The cat is on the mat' is true if and only if it corresponds to the fact. But Descartes cannot have correspondence as a criterion. By his own admission, he can't even be certain that there is any external fact to which the statement corresponds. Anything that's going to count as a sign of veracity will have to be an internal sign. If one is going to be able to decide, on Descartes's account, whether an idea is true or false, one is going to have to do it on the basis of something about the idea. And what better internal evidence could there be than the clearness and distinctness of the idea? However, even though this may be the best evidence that there is, it's still not very good.

Second, strictly speaking, only statements, or (in other words) judgments can be true or false. If I hold up a cat and ask whether it's true or false, my question makes no sense. But if I ask whether the statement 'The cat is on the mat' is true or false, my statement does make sense. So the only ideas that can be said to be true or false are those that stand as real judgments. The same point can be made about images. If I have in mind an image that just happens to be the image of a cat, that image per se cannot be true or false. What can be true or false is the judgment that it's the image of a cat. It's because we are inclined to confuse judgments about the image with the image per se that we are misled into thinking that the image can be true or false.

The ideas that Descartes has in mind when he talks about ideas that are clear and distinct are the ideas or concepts to be found in geometry or mathematics. Descartes would say that the geometer's concept of a triangle is clear and distinct and therefore true. This, however, doesn't sit very well with our claim that only statements can be true or false. It can be fitted into our mold in the following way, however. The geometer will have a true (i.e., clear and distinct) concept of a triangle in the sense that he will be aware of a large number of analytic, if not synthetic, a priori statements that can be derived from it. For example, his concept of a triangle will allow him to derive such true statements as 'The sum of the interior angles of a triangle are equal to two right angles' and 'The square of the side opposite the right angle in the right-angled triangle is equal in size to the sum of the two other sides'. Strictly speaking, his concept of a triangle is not true, but it can be said to be true in the sense that it generates true statements.

Finally, it should be noted that 'clear' doesn't mean the same as 'distinct'. According to Descartes a concept can be clear without being distinct, but it cannot be distinct without being clear. For example, according to Descartes, the idea of pain is clear but not distinct. He can't distinguish it from other sensations or from the cause of the pain. On the other hand, his idea of a triangle is both clear and distinct. He can always distinguish a triangle from any other figure.

Proofs of God's Existence

Descrates realizes that he cannot be certain that clear and distinct ideas are true until he has proven that there is a God. That is to say, he cannot be certain that such statements as '2 + 3 = 5' or 'A square has four sides' or 'The sums of the angles of a triangle are equal to two right angles' are true until he has proven that there is a God. Not until he has proven that there is a God who would not deceive him and who would not allow others to deceive him on matters that strike him as manifestly clear and distinct, can Descartes be absolutely certain that such statements are true.

If we look at philosophers prior to Descartes who attempt to prove that there is a God, we find that they usually start out assuming that there is an external world, and then argue from the existence of the world to the existence of God. Descartes was the first philosopher to start with his own existence and build from there. He couldn't, of course, begin with the existence of the world, for he had no reason to believe that there is a world. The only thing that he had to begin with was his own existence.

His first proof goes roughly as follows. Every effect has a cause. The effect cannot have more reality than the cause, for then part of the effect would have come from nothing. I have an idea of God, that is to say the idea of an absolutely perfect and infinite being. This idea must have a cause. The immediate cause of this idea may be another idea, but the ultimate cause will have to contain all the reality that is represented in the idea. And that means the ultimate cause will have to be an infinite and absolutely perfect being, and that being is God.

Descartes offers two other proofs, but this first proof is his favorite, even though it convinced no one. What I shall now do is examine some of the criticisms made of it; maybe it can be put into a more convincing form.

First, the statement 'Every effect has a cause' is analytic, for an effect is by definition an event that has a cause. It says nothing more than 'Every event that has a cause has a cause', and from this nothing follows. That is to say, no synthetic statements can be derived from it. We can, however, patch up this difficulty by replacing 'Every effect has a cause' with 'Every event has a cause'. We now have a synthetic statement we can make use of, but can we be certain that it's true? Isn't it possible that something could happen without any cause at all? And don't think that if it had no cause, it was caused (*per impossible*) by nothing (see chapter 3, page 138). If it had no cause, it wasn't caused by anything, not even nothing.

This may not be too serious a difficulty, for we do live in a world where everything seems to have a cause. Let us move on to 'An event cannot have more reality than its cause'. This statement is obscure. In some interpretations it seems to be manifestly false. There is an apocry-phal story that goes something like this: A famous general was on the verge of a great victory. He saw that to obtain it, his left flank would have to attack in a certain way. He wrote out the necessary order and gave it to the dispatch rider, who rode out on his horse to deliver it to the commander of the left flank. However, for want of a nail in one of the horse's shoes, the shoe was lost, and for want of a shoe, the horse tripped. The rider was rendered unconscious, the message didn't get through, and the battle was lost. Here it is tempting to say that a very small cause—the loss of a nail—had a very large effect, namely, the loss of a battle. At the same time, it could be argued that the loss of a nail was only a necessary cause in the causal chain, and that when all the participating causes are added up, the total cause is equal to the effect. At the same time, it's still obscure how the measurement of causes and effects in a situation of this sort is to be carried out.

What Descartes has in mind when he says that the effect cannot be greater than the cause can be illustrated by this example: If you make a cake, it cannot weigh more than the ingredients that go into it. That is to say, Descartes is really invoking the venerable principle known as conservation of matter. However, he is not very clear about this.

What about Descartes's claim that when the effect is an idea, the cause, if not another idea, cannot contain less reality than what is represented in the idea? This is even more obscure, but it might be explained through the following analogy. If we consider an idea to be something like an image in a mirror, then just as there cannot be more represented in the image of the object than is found in the object, so the idea cannot represent more than what is found in the object it represents. Even if we assume that the mirror magnifies what is re-flected in it, if we know the rules of projection, we know that no more is represented in the image than is present in what it represents.[9] However, we mustn't think of the mind as a passive mirror. It would seem, at first blush, that a person is capable of expanding on the ideas he has received.

Descartes might agree with this, adding that what he had in mind is just that an imperfect and finite being cannot, from his own resources or from any other finite source, form the idea of a perfect and infinite being. That idea must have its source in an infinite and perfect being. But why can't a finite being form an idea of infinity? I can form, for example, the idea of an infinitely long piece of string. From time to time I come across pieces of string that come to an end. From this I can form the idea of a piece of string that does not come to an end. Descartes would claim that this is a negative idea of infinity, whereas his idea of God contains the idea of positive infinity. He seems to be mistaken here. My idea of an omniscient being is the idea of a being for whom there is *no* limit to his knowledge. *This* is a negative idea.

John Locke, the British empiricist (1632–1704), wanted to argue that all ideas are derived from experience. Thus, my idea of God must also be derived from experience. I experience myself as a being who has limited power, limited knowledge, and limited goodness. With these ingredients, I can put together a complex idea of a being with *no* limit to its power, no limit to its knowledge, and no limit to its goodness. And this is my idea of God. It seems to me that Locke is right about this.

However, Descartes has one more card to play. He argues that my idea of myself is an idea of a being with limited knowledge, power, and goodness. That is to say, it is the idea of a being who is *not* perfectly good, and so on. In other words, the idea of myself is the negative idea. But if it is a negative idea, how did I come to have it? I could only come to have it through having a prior positive idea of perfection. And this is my idea of God. Or to put it in a simpler way, I am aware of myself as a limited, imperfect being, but how could I be aware of myself as such a being unless I already had the idea of a perfect being? As Descartes puts it:

> I clearly understand that there is more reality in an infinite than a finite substance, and that therefore in a way my primary conception is rather of the infinite than of the finite—rather of God than of myself. How could I understand my doubting and desiring—that is, my lacking something and not being altogether perfect—if I had no idea of a more perfect being as a standard by which to recognize my defects. (*Descartes*, p. 85)

This is an intriguing argument. My idea of the infinity of God is prior to my idea of myself as a limited being. Therefore, that idea of God could not have come from me or any other source. It could only have come from God. Therefore God exists. Although this is an intriguing argument (and I think it's Descartes's basic argument), I don't think it's sound. I don't think it's necessary to have the idea of perfection or order to be aware that one is imperfect. Suppose that yesterday I knew (and only knew) *w, x,* and *y*. And let's suppose the thought that my knowledge was limited had not crossed my mind. If today I learn *z*, then I will be aware that yesterday my knowledge was limited, and imperfect. That is to say, one doesn't have to possess the idea of perfection to form the idea of imperfection. One can come to have it through realizing that today one is more perfect than one was yesterday.

For these reasons, then, I think we have to reject Descartes's first proof. Our idea of an infinite and perfect being can have its source in our own existence. The existence of such an idea does not imply that there is an infinite and perfect being. Descartes might want to argue that my very ability to see that today I am more perfect than I was yesterday presupposes that I have the idea of perfection, but it's difficult to see how the argument would go.

Let us move on to Descartes's second proof. This proof begins with his existence. He knows that he exists, and he knows that he must have had a cause. There are a number of possible causes here and they must be explored. First, isn't it possible that he is self-caused? Descartes's reply to this is that if he had the power to create himself he would have created himself perfectly. But he knows he didn't create himself perfectly, for he knows that he is an imperfect being. Therefore, he cannot be the cause of his own existence. Second, it's possible that some being less perfect than God created him. But what about that being? What created it? Sooner or later there must be a first cause, and that cause would have to be God. Finally, it's possible that he has always existed. However, Descartes rejects this possibility and finally concludes that the ultimate cause must have been God.

Descartes is not, however, altogether happy with this proof and so looks around for ways to prop it up. He is unhappy with it because he realizes in his heart of hearts that it's possible either that he always existed or that he is the last member in a series of finite beings stretching back to infinity. If either were the case, no God would be required. Thomas Aquinas had doubted the possibility of an infinite series, but I suspect that Descartes had sufficient mathematical sophistication to realize that either was possible.

Descartes's first prop is to point out that not only does he know that he exists, but he also knows that he exists with an idea of God. Now if he exists with an idea of God, then even if he is the last member of the infinite causal chain of finite beings, there would still have to be a God that would serve as the source of that idea of God. From this we can see that the second proof is not really an independent proof. It depends upon the first. And so, if the first proof is not sound (which it's not), then neither is the second.

The second prop is even more bizarre. Descartes claims that any period of time could be broken down into an indefinite number of parts. He also claims that from the fact that something exists at one time (t^1), it doesn't follow that it exists at another time (t^2). Thus, "from my having existed a little while ago it does not follow that I need exist now, unless some cause (God) creates me anew at this very moment, in other words, preserves me" (*Descartes*, p. 88).

We find in this world that there are some things that have to be created anew at each instant and others that (apparently) do not. For example, the patch of light that a desk lamp makes on a desk cannot exist without the existence of the lamp. Turn off the lamp and the patch ceases to exist. But the pen that I am writing with can, it would seem, continue to exist without the help of anything. It may be that, unbeknown to us, something is required to keep it in existence. But until we have evidence that supports this contention, we have no reason to believe it to be the case.

However, Descartes thinks that we do have reason. He believes that since it doesn't follow from the fact of something's existence at t^1 that it continues to exist at t^2, then if it exists at t^2 it must have been recreated. But what Descartes has done here is to confuse causal dependence with logical dependence. The existence of my pen at t^2 is not logically dependent on the existence of my pen at t^1. That is to say, the statement 'The pen existed at t^1' does not entail 'The pen existed at t^2'. But it doesn't follow from this that the existence of the pen at t^2 is not causally dependent upon its existence at t^1. Let me put the argument another way. What Descartes has done is to confuse causal implication with logical implication (or entailment). He is correct in pointing out that the pen existing at t^1 does not logically imply that it exists at t^2, but this is an altogether different matter from whether or not the existence of the pen at t^1 is causally or physically sufficient for the existence of the pen at t^2. It *may* be that the pen (and all other physical objects) requires the support of a divine being, but the fact that 'The pen exists at t^1' does not entail 'The pen exists at t^2' gives us no reason to believe that it does.

It might be argued, although Descartes does not do so, that human consciousness is different: that my existence as a conscious being is more like the existence of the patch of light than the existence of the pen, and that it does need constant support. Perhaps it does need constant support. After all, if the blood supply to a person's brain is shut off, that person ceases to be conscious. The consciousness ceases to be. However, I don't think this point will get us very far toward showing that there is a God, because what consciousness needs in the way of constant support is a living and properly functioning body. It would have to be shown that this was not sufficient. Furthermore, since Descartes was inclined to identify his existence with consciousness, he was also reluctant to say that a person was fully unconscious when asleep and not dreaming, or when the rest of the body failed to supply the brain with blood. According to Descartes, the mind continued to be conscious (to itself) on these occasions. Thus, consciousness was not dependent upon the body for its existence. Once again, if he wants to show that the continued existence of consciousness is dependent upon a God, he would have to give independent reasons.

It seems then that we have to reject Descartes's second proof along with the first. If he could give a reason for saying that his existence, as well as that of the world, requires some divine support that differs from that of establishing the existence of an object at one instant without entailing its existence at some other instant, then his argument might have some credibility. But without offering such a reason for the divine foundation, the argument fails.

The Natural Light and Teachings of Nature

From time to time Descartes distinguishes between what he calls the "teachings of nature" and what he terms the "natural light." What he has in mind when he talks about the teachings of nature are such lessons as: fire burns, odious smelling meat causes stomach cramps, and red spots on a person's face is the sign of measles. (These are not Descartes's examples). What he has in mind when he talks about truths revealed by the natural light are those clear and distinct truths that are apprehended directly through intuition or are deducible from intuitive truths. For example, we know by the natural light that if a = b and b = c, then a = c; and we also know that the sum of the angles of a triangle are equal to 180°. Now that God has been proven (to Descartes's satisfaction), we can be certain that those ideas revealed by the natural light are true, but we cannot be certain that the ideas taught to us by nature are true. We can take these latter ideas as true for the purpose of getting on in the world but not for the doing of science. For example, if the meat looks green, then this is a reason for not eating it. However, for the purposes of science this is inadequate. If the meat looks green, it doesn't follow that it is green. For as we have seen, it's highly likely, according to Descartes, that physical objects are colorless.

Innate Ideas

According to Descartes, there are three different sources of ideas. Some are acquired through experience—for example, the idea of redness and pain. Some are created through augmenting and compounding the ideas that we acquire through experience. We can form the idea of a centaur, even though there are none in existence, by taking the idea of the torso of a man, which we do gain through experience, and combining it with the idea of a horse. In this manner we form a new idea. Finally, there are innate ideas, and the most important of these is our idea of God. We simply couldn't have any idea of God unless we had been born with it.

Philosophers have always been very dubious about the existence of innate ideas. It's natural to think, as Locke did, that the mind at birth is like a blank slate and that all ideas, or at least all simple ideas, are derived from experience. The experience needn't be experience of an external world—it could be internal psychological experience—but the ideas would have to be derived from some sort of experience.

When Descartes was taken to task on the question of innate ideas, he was inclined to back down and say that he had "never written, nor been of the opinion, that the mind needs innate ideas in the sense of something different from its faculty of thinking" (*Descartes,* p. 302). For example, the *ability* to reason from '$(p \supset q) \cdot p$' to 'q', which is innate, can also be presented as the idea 'It follows from $(p \supset q) \cdot p$' that q'. So here we have an idea that is innate.

I don't think that anyone would want to question Descartes's claim that ideas of this sort are innate; after all, they are nothing more than reflections of intellectual abilities. But the idea of God, on Descartes's account, is quite different. It cannot be taken as a reflection of an ability to reason. Indeed, Descartes says at the end of this meditation that God implanted this idea in him in the same way an artist signs his work of art. So Descartes did want to say that at least one idea was innate in a strong and extraordinary sense.

FOURTH MEDITATION

Having proven to his satisfaction that there is an all-powerful, all-knowing, and all-good being, Descartes is in a position to put to one side the specter of an evil demon and most of the doubts he held previously. After all, since he knows that God exists, he also knows that such a being would not deceive him or allow the existence of a lesser being who could deceive him. However, it seems that Descartes has proved too much. He knows that sometimes he is deceived—the sun appears to be much smaller than it is, and physical objects appear to be colored—but if there is a supreme being, how can it be that Descartes was constructed in such a manner that he was capable of being deceived? Is this not the sign of shoddy workmanship?

Descartes's solution looks a bit quaint at first glance. But it is more than picturesque. Descartes is aware that he has at least two abilities: that of understanding and the ability to choose and act. He knows that he understands certain things and he knows that he can give his assent to certain ideas and refrain from believing others. There is, however, a difference between these two abilities or faculties. There is a limit to what he can understand, but there is no limit either to what he can choose to do or to that to which he can choose to give his assent. The faculty of understanding is perfect as far as it goes, but it is limited. Choice, on the other hand, is not only unlimited but perfect. There is nothing to which we cannot give our assent. It is also owing to choice that it can be said that we are made in the image of God. God's will is infinite, and so is ours.

Although we have nothing to complain about in these two faculties, the difference between them is the source of deception and error. It is because our will extends further than our understanding that we give our assent to judgments we do not really understand, thereby falling into error. Thus it is by our misuse of freedom that we fall into error as well as sin. God is not to blame, the fault is all ours. For example, we don't know whether the death penalty is a deterrent to murder, but we may disapprove of it and would like to believe that it is not a deterrent. I for one find myself believing that the death penalty is not a deterrent. Descartes would consider this to be a misuse of my freedom to believe. In this case I have gone beyond what is clear and distinct and have come to believe what I do not clearly understand. Descartes would recommend that we remain in a state of doubt on such matters.

There are two topics to be discussed here. First, is the intellect as passive as Descartes makes out? According to Descartes, it is possible to understand that the cat is on the mat without in any sense asserting that the cat is on the mat. This seems to me to be mistaken. Of course I don't have to assert publicly that the cat is on the mat after I have come to understand that it is so. What I notice is that the cat *is* on the mat. How can I notice that the cat *is* on the mat without at the same time asserting to myself that the cat is on the mat?

Second, are we as free as Descartes would have us believe? One must distinguish here between freedom of the body (physical) and freedom of the mind (mental). We shall deal with the general problem of human freedom later on, but it would be worthwhile at this point to deal with some of the facets of Descartes's philosophy that are relevant to it. We might agree with him that we are free to perform a great number of physical acts—we can scratch our ears, walk to the door, and turn on the radio. There are, of course, some things we are not free to do. We cannot walk on the ceiling, lift 300 pounds (at least most of us can't), or run at 30 mph, although we are free to try to do these things.

What then of mental freedom? I am, of course, free to perform such mental tasks as working out my income tax and doing my child's math homework. But if I am looking at the book in front of me, am I free to believe or refrain from believing that there is a book in front of me? Or, if I have been presented with '$p \supset q$' and 'p', am I free to believe or refrain from believing that 'q' follows? It would seem that in matters of belief I have little choice. I am free to *say* there is no book in front of me, but I am not free to believe that there is no book in front of me. My mind is, so to speak, made up for me.

One is tempted to say that the only time that we are free to believe or not believe is when we are ignorant or don't really understand. For example, suppose we are trying to decide whether there is a mouse in a dark room. We hear certain scratching sounds, but these could be caused by the wind blowing on the curtains. Here we have a choice, it would seem, between (a) believing there is a mouse, (b) believing there is not a mouse, and (c) refraining from believing. According to

Descartes, there is mental freedom of a sort here, but it is of the lowest kind.[10] The highest kind of mental freedom for Descartes, paradoxically enough, is when we are, so to speak, forced by the light of our intellect into reaching a conclusion. That is to say, even though we are compelled by our intellect into concluding 'q' after accepting 'p $\supset$ q' and 'p', the conclusion 'q' is a free choice of the highest sort. Logical determination and freedom go hand in hand.

What are we to say about this? Benedict de Spinoza, the great Jewish philosopher, also held that the highest form of freedom existed when thinking was determined by the rules of logic. So perhaps there is something here. Perhaps we made an error in thinking that when we think in accordance with the rules of logic, our thought is determined. Let me indicate to you why I think this might be so; why it might be claimed that to think freely is to think in accordance with the laws of logic. Suppose, for example, I expressed at t^1 my true belief that it is raining, then if I were to express my true belief on this matter at t^2, and I haven't had a change of heart, I would also say that it rained at t^1. Nothing forces me. But being a rational, consistent person, this is what I do. Similarly, if I express at t^1 my true belief that it is raining, and the streets are wet, then if I were to express my true belief on this matter at a later date, I could at least say that it rained at t^1. Again, nothing has forced me, even though 'p $\cdot$ q' entails 'p'. Finally, if I express my true belief at t^1 that if it rains then the streets will be wet, and it's now raining, then unless I have had a change of heart, if I were to express my true belief on this matter, one thing I will have to say at t^2 is that at t^1 the streets were wet. One thing I will not say is that the streets were not wet at t^1. Nothing forces me to refrain from saying this even though '(if p then q) and p' entails 'q'. But being a rational, consistent person, this is just the sort of thing that I shall do. In short, even though it looks as though the laws of logic were the sort of thing that determine thought, in reality they are the bare bones of rational, consistent free thought.

Although it looks as though Descartes is correct about this—that to think freely is to think in accordance with the laws of logic—I don't think he is altogether right in what he has to say about belief. Contrary to his claim, I don't think that people have the freedom to form their beliefs. I cannot but believe, for example, that there is now a book in front of me.

At the same time, his point about what is uncertain is well taken. Most people dislike being in a state of doubt. They want to have a settled set of beliefs. In this area people do extend their beliefs. In some roundabout way they come to believe what they really have no reason to believe.

Before going on, there are a couple of points of more general interest that should be mentioned. Some people have argued that Descartes is mistaken in claiming that one should refrain from belief where one doesn't understand. For example, suppose you have been told on the best authority that it's highly likely that the stock market will go up. Here it will be argued that you should make a leap of faith into a sea of uncertainty and believe that the market will go up. For if you do, you will invest and may make a lot of money. But if you just sit on the fence and say "I don't know," the opportunity will pass you by. The reply to this objection is that in this situation it would be proper to believe that it's highly likely that the stock market is going to go up, and then act on that belief. One can act on beliefs that involve uncertainties as well as beliefs that involve certainties. Or let us take a different example. Blaise Pascal (1623–1662), a French mathematician and theologian who was a contemporary of Descartes, presented the following argument. He puts it in the form of a wager.[11] Suppose you don't know whether there is a God, but you do know that if there is a God and you don't believe, you will be punished; but if you do believe, then the reward will be infinite. In that case the rational thing is to choose to believe. The wager can be illustrated by the following matrix:

	I believe there is a God.	I believe there is not a God.
There is a God.	+infinity	-1000
There is not a God.	-20	0

I can choose between the first column and the second. If I choose the first and there is a God, then my gain is infinite. If no God exists, there is a slight loss (-20 say), for I have gone in vain to masses, confessions, and the like. If I choose the second column and there is a God, then I will suffer some sort of punishment, let's say 1000 units of pain. If there is not a God, then there is no loss or gain. The obvious thing to do, even if it is improbable that there is a God, according to Pascal, is to choose the first column. It might not be likely that I am on the winning side, but if I am, the rewards will be infinite.

It might be objected on behalf of Descartes that the rational thing to do would be to choose a third column that might be headed "I neither believe there is a God nor that there is not a God, because I don't know one way or the other." Perhaps if I make this choice, then the penalty, if there is a God, will not be as great as if I had chosen the second, but it won't be the most rational choice. The most rational choice is still the first column, for here I have the chance of infinite reward.

A more serious objection is that, contrary to Descartes, one can't simply choose at will to believe or not to believe. It has been told that Benjamin Jowett, the famous nineteenth-century Platonic scholar and

Master of Balliol College, Oxford, once discovered that one of the undergraduates of the college did not believe in God. He had the student called on the carpet and told him that if he didn't believe by morning, he would be expelled. What was the poor fellow to do? It was in his power to decide to *profess* that there was a God, but how of his own free will could he come to believe that there was a God? Especially by morning! Pascal was aware of this but he thought that if one engaged in spiritual exercises—masses and confessions—in time, belief would come.

Finally, it might be objected that if there is God, and somebody were to come to believe on the basis of this sort of argument, God would most likely punish him. Pascal was also somewhat conscious of this objection. The wager was primarily for the consideration of the believers. Having understood it they would realize that they were on the right track and feel confirmed in their faith.

There is, I think, something distasteful about Pascal's wager. To be deceived by others is bad enough, but to launch oneself on a program that will engender self-deception seems, so to speak, to sin against oneself. Someone might object that if there is a God, there is no self-deception, but this is not so. If I believe there is a pot of gold in my garden because it makes me feel happier to do so and, unbeknown to me, there is a pot of gold, I am still guilty of self-deception. The only good reason for believing there is a pot of gold in the garden is that there is one.

FIFTH MEDITATION

This meditation opens with Descartes giving a rather Platonic account of geometrical figures. Perhaps there is no external world, and perhaps circles, squares, and so on do not exist anywhere but in my consciousness. But even so, since there are determinate statements that can be made about these figures, e.g., 'The sum of the angles of a triangle are equal to two right angles', these figures really exist as eternal and unchangeable objects.

I don't want to examine this argument in any detail but, in passing, two comments might be made: (a) Perhaps geometrical statements should be given a hypothetical rather than a categorical interpretation. When I say that the sum of the angles of a triangle are equal to two right angles, I am not saying that there is something called a triangle that may exist only in my mind, but simply that if there is an external world and something in it is triangular in shape, then its interior angles will be equal to two right angles. (b) A Platonist would argue that what exists in my mind is not a triangle but only the idea of a triangle. But if what is in my mind is only the idea of a triangle, then what it is an idea of must exist somewhere else; and that place is, of course, the Platonic world of Forms.

Although the Fifth Meditation opens with this topic, its goal is not to tell us more about the home of geometrical shapes, but to introduce a new argument for the existence of God. If it is true that any property that can be proven by pure thought to belong to a geometrical shape really does belong to it, then it will also be true that any property that can by pure thought be proven to belong to the concept of God will belong to it. Thus if I can prove, by pure thought, that necessary existence is a property of the concept of God, then it will follow that God necessarily exists. This brings us face to face with Descartes's version of a confusing and beguiling proof of God's existence—the Ontological Argument.

This proof was introduced by St. Anselm (1033–1109), resurrected by Descartes, and refuted by Immanuel Kant. As recently as fifteen years ago, it was considered to be a curio, a leftover from the past. But in recent years, primarily under the stewardship of the American philosopher Alvin Plantinga, it has undergone a revival.

The main tenet of the Ontological Argument is that existence is a perfection. As a result, an absolutely perfect being, which is not lacking in any perfection, must have existence. Some writers have argued that since necessary existence is even better, an absolutely perfect being must possess necessary existence. This argument will probably strike most readers as fallacious, and no doubt it is—you can't conjure something into existence, so to speak, out of thin air through thought alone. Although most people agree that the argument is fallacious there is little consensus about where the fallacy lies.

Descartes is aware of the problem that troubled Parmenides—the difficulty of thinking of anything without thinking of it as existing. Although Descartes is aware of this difficulty, he realized that his thought imposes no existence on things. Even though, for example, I cannot think of leprechauns without thinking of them as existing, it doesn't follow that leprechauns do in fact exist. He is aware that with most things, existence is separate from their properties. To say that the pen I hold in my hand exists is not to ascribe a property to it in the way that to say that the pen is black does ascribe a property. He feels, however, that the situation with God is different. Not only when I think of God must I think of him as existing, but I must also attribute to him every perfection; and one of these perfections is existence. Now what is the explanation here? Why is there one and only one object in the world to which I am obliged to ascribe existence? The only possible explanation of this phenomenon is that God necessarily exists. "It's not that my thought makes this so," rather it is "the necessity of the fact itself, that is, of God's existence, is what determines me to think this way" (*Descartes*, p. 104). In other words, since the only possible explanation of my inability to think of God as not existing is the necessary existence of God, it follows that God exists.

There are two weaknesses in this proof. Even if it is impossible for me to think of God as nonexistent, it doesn't follow from this that the *only* explanation of this phenomenon is the necessary existence of God. It is possible that there could be some other explanation. Unless Descartes can be certain that there is no other possibility, he can't be certain that there is a God. The second weakness is this. Descartes claims that when he thinks of God he must ascribe to Him every perfection. And since existence is perfection, we must ascribe existence to God. But is existence a perfection? When describing the most perfect car, I give it a powerful, reliable, fuel efficient engine; leather seats; and so on. But existence does not feature in the list of perfections. It is not one of the properties that a car can have. If I were a car designer and approached the car manufacturer with plans for two different types of car, and he were to ask me which one was the best, I would be laughed out of his office if I were to say that one car is better than the other because it has existence! Our language often fools us on matters of this sort. We say that giant panda bears exist and that giant panda bears growl. This makes it look as though existence is a property, something like the ability to growl. But, of course, this is a mistake. What we mean when we say that giant panda bears exist is nothing more than that there are giant panda bears. We do not use this statement to say something about giant panda bears. The point can be driven home by noticing that although it makes perfectly good sense to say that some giant panda bears do not growl, it makes no sense to say that some giant panda bears do not exist.

However, to be fair to Descartes, it should be noted that he says that existence is a property, or essence only in the case of God. Anselm, interestingly enough, also made the same claim. Yet neither thinker gives any reason for saying that existence is a property when ascribed to God, but not when ascribed to others. If either did have a reason, it's difficult to imagine what that reason could be, since, as we have just seen, to say that an object of a certain type has existence is just a misleading way of saying that there is an object of that type.

There is an added difficulty in talking about God. "God" is often used as a proper name, and whenever we use a proper name we presuppose the existence of the thing we are talking about. As a result, it is logically odd to say that the thing in question does not exist, and it is redundant to say that it does exist. For example, if I say "Pierre Trudeau is astute" or "Pierre Trudeau is not astute," it makes perfectly good sense for you to ask "Who did you say is astute?" But if I say "Pierre Trudeau exists" or "Pierre Trudeau does not exist" it sounds very odd for you to ask "Who did you say exists?" or "Who did you say did not exist?" In the case of God, we can remove this difficulty by replacing "God" with a description. If we do this we can go on and replace "God exists" and "God does not exist" with "There is a being who is omniscient, omnipotent, all good and the creator of the universe" and "It is not the case that there is a being who is omniscient, omnipotent, all good and creator of the universe." In this manner, we avoid the awkward existential presupposition of proper names. Although there is something logically odd about saying God does not exist, there is nothing logically odd about saying it's not the case that there is a being who is all powerful, all knowing, and all good, and creator of the universe. Furthermore we can replace the logically awkward question "Does God exist?" with the question "Is there a being who is omniscient, omnipotent, all good, and the creator of the universe?" If the reader feels that this description is too exacting, he can replace it with a weaker one and inquire whether there is a being who satisfies that description.

SIXTH MEDITATION

In this Meditation Descartes attempts to do a number of things: (a) to prove the existence of the external world, (b) to explain how it is possible that even when one is engaged in the lowly practice of attempting to get on in this world, one can be deceived by the teachings of nature; (c) to bring the distinction and relation between mind and body into clearer focus; and (d) to show that mind is not only distinct from the body but could exist without it. Since the last of these is perhaps the most interesting effort he puts forth, we shall spend more time on it.

(a) The proof that there is an external world does not proceed quite as quickly as one might expect. Descartes begins with an attempt to see if he can derive the existence of the world from the existence of the imagination. The imagination, he contends, is quite distinct from the understanding. I can imagine (form a mental picture of) a triangle, and I can also form a concept of a triangle. Although I am inclined to confuse the imagination with the understanding, if I go on to consider a chiliagon (a thousand sided figure) I realize that they are quite distinct. I can with ease conceive a chiliagon but it is beyond my powers to imagine one. Pentagons form an interesting intermediate case. I can with ease conceive one, but it is only with great difficulty that I can form a mental picture of one. It can be seen from this not only that the imagination is distinct from the understanding, but it's highly likely, according to Descartes, that I could exist without the imagination.

Given, then, that the faculty of the imagination is distinct from the understanding, and given that it is superfluous, we must ask why we have an imagination. Descartes suggests that it has something to do with the body. That is to say, it's because I have a body that I have an imagination. His thinking here seems to be that since only physical things can be imagined, the fact that I have an imagination makes it likely that I have a body. However, this argument doesn't give the certainty that Descartes requires. "I can as yet see no way of arguing conclusively from the fact that there is in my imagination a distinct idea of a corporeal nature to the existence of any body." As a result he turns to sensation to see if the existence of an external world can be derived from it. He knows that he is bombarded with sensations that cause him to believe in the existence of external physical objects. He knows that these sensations do not come from himself since they are often produced against his will. They must either come from God or from corporeal substance. Since God is not a deceiver they could not come from Him; they must come from corporeal substance. Therefore, the external world exists.

An objection that immediately comes to mind (at least to my mind) is this: sensations that come in dreams are produced against the will, so how can Descartes be certain that he is not dreaming? I suppose Descartes's reply would be (i) that the ideas of sensation that come in dreams and lead us to believe that we are owners of Ferrari cars, yachts, and the like, must ultimately have their source in corporeal substance. Ultimately, I must have got my idea of length, width, and depth from real physical objects. (ii) Even if it were conceivable that I could be the source of those ideas, God being all good, etc., would not allow me to be deceived on such a massive scale.

(b) In the Fourth Meditation Descartes gave us his explanation of how it is possible that we fall into error. It is now necessary for him to fill in a few more of the details. We fall into error because our will extends farther than our intellect, and we find ourselves, when prompted by the teachings of nature, giving our assent (act of will) to what we don't really understand. Such teachings are adequate for getting on in this life but not for doing science. Thus, for example, if we are aware of greenness when presented with an apple, this will give us reason, on pain of stomach cramps, to refrain from eating it. But it will not give us knowledge of the apple, for the apple most likely is colorless, and so not green.

We may accept Descartes's point that when we are in our scientific lab doing science we should not take the apple as colored green, and yet feel that when involved in such enterprises as a trip to the green grocer or supermarket we may take the apple to be green. Descartes, surprisingly enough, will not have any of this. He declares that such conclusions are the result of "inconsiderate judgment" and are not a part of the teachings of nature. They are to be ranked alongside such beliefs as that the tea cup that has been emptied of tea has absolutely nothing inside it, and that a star is not larger than a candle.

One can't help but feel that Descartes has made a mistake here. We can, through simple procedures, discover that the empty cup is full of air and that the star is quite large but very far away. But no such procedures are available in the case of the apple. No matter how carefully we scrutinize the apple, it still looks green. Thus I think that Descartes doesn't recognize the problem on his hands: How could God allow us to be deceived into believing that the apple is green (or for that matter that anything else is colored) when really it is colorless?

There is another problem, however, that Descartes does recognize and attempts to resolve: Suppose that someone is suffering from dropsy. As a result he has a great desire to drink water, but to drink water is the worst thing that a dropsy sufferer can do. The problem here is that, in the task of getting on in the world, nature instructs him to drink, and yet drinking would be very bad for him. It's not enough to reply to this problem by pointing out that the man is sick, for, as Descartes quaintly puts it, a sick man is no less God's creature than a healthy man.

Descartes's solution, though presented in rather a complex way, is really quite simple. In order, for example, for a man to feel pain in his left big toe there must be nerves running from his toe to his brain. If a neural "message" similar to the one that causes the mind to experience the pain in the big toe, is introduced, say, at the thigh, then the percipient will experience pain as if it were in his toe. Thus the system that makes it possible for a person to experience sensations in various parts of the body is, by its very nature, going to be vulnerable to intrusions of this sort. But it's better that we have some neural system than no system at all. The situation is the same in the case of the man suffering from dropsy. He desires to drink because his brain has been stimulated, owing to the disease, in just the way that the brain of a normal person is stimulated when he is in need of drink. Again, it's always better to have a system that by its very nature is susceptible to these disorders than to have no system at all. We can't blame God for giving us a vulnerable neural system when any neural system is bound to be vulnerable.

(c) Descartes is ambivalent about what he thinks he is. At one point he wants to say that he is not present in his body as a pilot is present in a ship but, rather, he is so tightly bound with it that he and it form a unit. At another point he wants to identify himself with that unit. That is, he wants to say that he is that combination of mind and body. Finally, at yet another point, he wants to identify himself with just his mind. What, then, are we to take as Descartes's real view? I suggest that he believes himself to be essentially a mind, but a mind united with one particular body for the duration of his sojourn on earth. While he is on earth he is a union of mind and body, but after his death, if he continues to exist, he will be just a mind.

The sharp division Descartes makes between the mind—indivisible, unextended, and whose essential attribute is consciousness—and the body—extended, divisible, and incapable of consciousness—raises the problem of how there can be any interaction between the two. How can changes in my consciousness bring about changes in my body? How can I, through desiring and willing to raise my arm, bring it about that my arm goes up? According to Descartes, the interaction between the mind and the body takes place in the pineal gland. The reason he picked the pineal gland is that it was the only known organ in the head that did not exist in duplicate, and since the mind had to have a *common* seat, only the pineal gland would do.

Descartes's description of how the interaction takes place is a sheer flight of fancy, but interesting all the same. The pineal gland hangs from the ceiling of the cavity in the center of the brain, swinging to and fro like a punching bag in a prize-fighters' gymnasium. Suppose a tiger enters my field of vision and my eye is not closed. (I shall assume that I have only one eye.) The tiger gives off particles (or waves) of light. Some pass through the lens of the eye, and a physical image of the tiger is formed on the surface of the back of the eye. This causes a sequence of impulses to be carried along the optic nerve and into the brain. This sequence of impulses causes the suspended gland to move in a certain way, and the movement of the gland results in the mind being presented with a mental image of the tiger. If I am the perceiver then this is what I see. I don't see the tiger; I only see the mental image of the tiger.

Now suppose that I am frightened of tigers and want to keep away from them. Suppose further that as a result of being presented with a mental image of the tiger, I will to run away from it. This willing will cause the pineal gland to swing in a certain way, and this in turn will affect some of the nerve endings in such a way that the muscular contraction and expansion required for running away will occur.

This, then, is how Descartes attempted to explain the interaction between the mind and the body. When the nerve impulses caused the pineal gland to swing in certain ways, the person (the mind) saw certain things, and when the mind caused the pineal gland to swing in certain ways, the body moved in certain ways. The main problem with this explanation is that we still need an account of how the swinging of the gland causes the appearance of a mental image—how can the physiological change have a purely mental effect?—and of how the willing to move in a certain way causes the gland to move in a certain way—how can a purely mental act like a willing be translated into the swinging of a hunk of flesh?

Descartes thought that he had part of the solution to the problem. He accepted, along with many others of his era, that there was in nature a conservation of motion. That is to say, the total amount of motion in the physical world was always constant. Presumably by total motion he means the sum of the mass of each physical object multiplied by its speed. Now according to Descartes, when the mind acts on the punching bag-like pineal gland there is no change in the total amount of motion. All the mind does is to *change* the direction (and not the velocity) of the swinging. However, even if Descartes is correct in claiming that it is the total amount of motion that remains constant, it's still not clear how desiring or willing a swinging object to change its direction can cause it to do so. For example, if a ball attached to the ceiling is swinging to and fro in front of me, no matter how hard I will, I can't get it to change its direction. Furthermore, Descartes's principle of the conservation of motion is not correct. It was realized during his lifetime that it's not the total amount of motion but the total amount of energy that remains constant. If the mind, per impossible, were to change the direction of the swinging pineal gland, there would have to be an increase in the total amount of energy. (Unless of course there was a magical [proportional] decrease in energy somewhere else in the physical system.) But there cannot be an increase in the total amount of energy; therefore, Descartes's theory has to be rejected. Fifty years after Descartes's death, his theory of how the mind and body interact had been relegated to the dustbin of obsolete theories.

A number of the philosophers who followed in Descartes's footsteps made various attempts to provide an acceptable account of the interaction between mind and body. Arnold Geulincx (1624–1669), a Dutch philosopher, proposed that any mental occurrence can be the *occasion* for a physical occurrence, and vice versa. For example, after I see a tiger and experience the desire to run away, this is the occasion for God to set my limbs in motion. When the tiger appears in my visual field, this is the occasion for God to see to it that I am presented with a mental image of the tiger. Thus, although there is no causal interaction between the mental and the physical, there appears to be one. Not many people seriously countenanced this theory, which is usually called *occasionalism*. They realized, and we should also realize, that when we have, so to speak, philosophically painted ourselves into a corner to such an extent that we have to invoke the existence of God to save the day, it's time to scrap the theory and begin again.

A second attempt to bridge the gap between the mental and the physical was provided by the German philosopher and mathematician Gottfried Leibniz (1646–1716). According to Leibniz, there is a pre-established harmony between mental events and physical events. It has been determined for all time that there would now be a black pen in my hand. It has also been determined for all time that there would now be the image of a black pen in my mind. I think that the pen is the cause of the image, but in thinking so I am mistaken. In order to make this theory more attractive, Leibniz invites us to consider the following analogy. Imagine two clocks, the first has hands but no bell, while the second has a bell but the hands have been removed. Both clocks have been wound up and synchronized with one another. (We assume that the synchronization took place before the hands were removed.) As a result, when the first clock points to 3:00, the second clock rings three times, and when the first points to 4:00, the second clock rings four times, and so on. Now if we didn't know that there was a pre-established harmony between the two clocks, we would think that the first clock pointing to 3:00, say, was the cause of the second clock ringing three times.

We may accept Leibniz's point that there *could* be a pre-established harmony between events in the physical world and events in the mental world, but we have no reason to accept that there *is* a pre-established harmony until independent reasons are found that support this conclusion. In fairness to Leibniz, I should point out that the bit about pre-established harmony appears as a part of a more general theory. That theory could be thought of as the reason for accepting pre-established harmony. Nonetheless, Leibniz's general theory has difficulties of its own and, for that reason, it finds few supporters today.

(d) Finally we come to Descartes's attempt to show that the mind is truly distinct from the body and could exist without it. There are in the Meditations two things that Descartes set his heart on proving. The first is that there is a God, and the second is that man is immortal. We have already seen that his proof of God is a flop. Let us now examine his second goal and see how well it fares. In an earlier book, *The Discourse on Method*, Descartes made the following attempt to prove that man was immortal. He says:

> And then, examining attentively that which I was, I saw that I could conceive that I had no body, . . . but yet that I could not . . . conceive that I was not. On the contrary, I saw from the very fact that I thought of doubting the truth of other things, it very evidently and certainly followed that I was; . . . . From that I knew that I was a substance the whole essence or nature of which is to think, and that for its existence there is no need of any place, nor does it depend on any material thing; so that this, "me," that is to say, the soul by which I am what I am, is entirely distinct from the body, . . . and even if body were not, the soul would not cease to be what is.[12]

In the Preface to the *Meditations* Descartes admits that this argument is not very strong and that it doesn't follow from the fact that he can conceive of himself existing without a body, that he could actually exist without a body. He goes on to say that he will prove, presumably in the Sixth Meditation, that it really does follow from the fact that he knows of no other thing besides consciousness belonging to himself, that nothing else does belong to himself. And so, he could exist without a body. In the Sixth Meditation he says:

> Now I know that I exist, and at the same time I observe absolutely nothing else as belonging to my nature or essence except the mere fact that I am a conscious being; and just from this I can validly infer that my essence consists simply in the fact that I am a conscious being. (*Descartes*, p. 114)

We have noticed that the word "nothing" has to be handled with the greatest of care. Descartes, it would seem, has fallen into one of the many traps that surround the word. Compare two people, *A* and *B*, looking into separate rooms. The room that *A* looks into is so dark that he can see nothing inside it. The room that *B* looks into is fully illuminated but there is nothing inside it—that is to say, no chairs, beds, or that sort of thing. Now both are in a position to say "I see nothing in this room." But each means something different. What *A* means when he says "I see nothing in this room" is "I don't see anything in this room," while what *B* means is "I see that there is nothing in this room." It would be a great mistake for *A* to infer from the fact that he sees nothing in the room that there is nothing in the room. There could be something in the room but he hasn't seen it, because it is too dark. This, I think, is precisely the error that Descartes makes. Descartes can't conclude from the fact that he observes nothing other than consciousness as belonging to his nature, that nothing else does belong. Something else could belong but he just doesn't know it. Descartes continues:

> It is indeed possible (or rather, as I shall say later on, it is certain) that I have a body closely bound up with myself; but at the same time I have, on the one hand, a clear and distinct idea of myself taken simply as a conscious, not an extended, being; and, on the other hand, a distinct idea of body, taken simply as an extended, not a conscious, being; so it is certain that I am really distinct from my body, and could exist without it. (*Descartes*, p. 114)

Descartes's error here is, I think, to confuse what is logically possible with what is actually possible. From the fact that I can doubt that I have a body and can conceive of myself existing without a body, it follows that it is logically possible that I could exist without a body. But it doesn't follow from the fact that it is logically possible for me to exist without a body that it is actually possible for me to exist without a body. Consider this example: I cannot conceive of a pedestrian without legs. Thus I know that it's logically impossible for a being to be a pedestrian and not have legs. But I can conceive of a pedestrian who does not breathe. Thus it's logically possible for a being to be a pedestrian and not breath. But even though it's logically possible, it's not actually possible, as we know all too well on smoggy days.

However, we mustn't be too quick with Descartes, for he may have the following argument in mind. I have a clear and distinct idea of consciousness, and a clear and distinct idea of extension. Furthermore, my idea of consciousness is an idea of something distinct from extension, and my idea of extension is an idea of something distinct from consciousness. But neither extension nor consciousness can exist on its own. Each must inhere in a substance. But since each is distinct, each must inhere in a separate substance. Now substance is what can exist independently of anything else. Finally, since I know and cannot deny that I am conscious, it follows that I am a conscious substance. If I am a conscious substance, then I, as a conscious substance, exist independently of anything else.

We have already seen that our concept of substance, either physical or mental, is incredibly obscure. But even if we put that worry to one side and accept Descartes's claim that I exist primarily as a conscious substance, it still doesn't follow that I shall exist without my body—that I will survive my death. All that follows is that it's conceivable that I *could* survive my death. Granted that a substance, and so mental substance, is something that could, in the sense of being logically possible, exist on its own, it still doesn't follow that it will exist on its own. It may be that physical substance is a necessary though not sufficient prerequisite for the existence of mental substance. Mental substance may be as tenuous as the morning dew.

Descartes concludes this paragraph with "so it is certain that I am really distinct from my body, and could exist without it." The "could exist without it" has to be handled with the greatest of care. If he only means to say, as has been pointed out, that it's logically possible to exist without body, then we have no dispute; but if he wants the meaning to go beyond this to suggest that he could exist without it in the same way as he could exist without his left arm, then we have no reason whatever to accept this conclusion. All that we can say is that Descartes's argument points to the logical possibility of life after death, but not the likelihood.

DESCARTES IN A NUTSHELL

This brings us to the end of the *Meditations*, but before we move on into other, and I hope less murky, waters, it might be useful to provide an overview of Descartes's argument. This will also make it easier to reach a general appraisal of Descartes's position.

Descartes, in his search for something certain, decides to put to one side everything that it is possible to doubt. He can doubt that distant towers are round because his senses have deceived him on matters of this sort in the past. He can doubt that he is sitting at his desk writing because he could be in bed asleep and dreaming that he is sitting at his desk. He can even doubt that he has a body, for he could be a disembodied mind dreaming that he has a body. Furthermore, he can doubt that 2 + 3 is really equal to 5 and that a square has four sides, because it is conceivable that there is an evil demon, a malicious deceiver, who leads him astray on these matters. The one thing he cannot doubt is his own existence and that he exists as a conscious being.

In order to show that there couldn't be a malicious deceiver and that he couldn't be a disembodied mind dreaming that he has a body and is surrounded by physical objects, Descartes sets out to prove that there is a God, that is to say, a being who is all powerful, all knowing and all good. Such a being would not permit the existence of a malicious deceiver; nor would He allow Descartes to be deceived on such a massive scale. Descartes offers three proofs. The first is based on his idea of God, the second on his (Descartes's) existence, and the third is based on the assumption that existence is a perfection-making property. None of the proofs are successful.

Having proved, at least to his satisfaction, that there is, in addition, himself, a Being who is all good, all powerful, and all knowing, Descartes is now in a position to show that most of his previous worries can be laid to rest. He knows that there is no deceiver, for God would not permit the existence of such a being; he knows that clear and distinct judgments such as 2 + 3 = 5 and a square has four sides are true, for God would not deceive him on judgments such as these, where the negation involves a manifest contradiction. Finally, Descartes knows that he has a body and that there is a wider external world of which his body is a part. God simply would not let him be deceived by the overwhelmingly persuasive evidence presented by his senses. He cannot assume that the physical objects of the external world are as they appear to be. However, as long as he confines himself to clear and distinct judgments, he has, so to speak, God's guarantee that he will not go wrong.

The reader may think that Descartes has wound up back where he started from, but this would be a mistake. Before he embarked on his meditations, Descartes thought that he existed primarily as a body, and that mind was something very obscure, something like a wisp of smoke. Furthermore, he thought that physical objects existed in much the way that they appeared to exist. But having completed his odyssey, he realizes that he is primarily a mental thing and not a physical thing. He also knows what the mind (his self) is, or in other words, what a mental thing is. It is not a wisp of smoke; it is consciousness, or rather consciousness inhering in a substance. Finally, he knows that for the purpose of doing science, the only properties that are worth attributing to a physical object are those having to do with the shape, size, and position of the object.

We are now in a position to examine a famous objection to Descartes's general theory. The objection is as follows: In order for Descartes to be certain that clear and distinct judgments like 2 + 3 = 5 are true, he must show that there is no malicious deceiver, and to show that there is no malicious deceiver, and he must prove that there is a God. However, the very best proof that can be provided will be one that uses clear and distinct judgments—such as "Every event has a cause" and "Something cannot come out of nothing"—as its premises. In short, in order to show that clear and distinct judgments are true, Descartes has to *assume* that they are true. His argument is therefore circular and should be rejected.

I don't think that this objection is as serious as it appears to be. We have utterly no reason to believe that there is an evil demon lurking in the philosophical bushes, and so we have utterly no reason to doubt that 2 + 3 = 5 or that a square has four sides. We know that 2 + 3 = 5 because 2 is analyzable as 1 + 1, 3 is analyzable as 1 + 1 + 1, 5 is analyzable as 1 + 1 + 1 + 1 + 1, and because (1 + 1) + (1 + 1 + 1) is equal to 1 + 1 + 1 + 1 + 1. We know that a square has four sides because a square is defined as an enclosed, right-angled, four-sided plane figure in which all sides are of equal length. The statement is analytic. Of course, it is always possible to make mistakes in doing arithmetic; any time one is carrying out an arithmetical calculation may be the time that a mistake is made. But any calculation is checkable, either by someone else or by a calculator. Furthermore, even though any calculation may be mistaken, it doesn't follow that every calculation may be mistaken. Just as it's logically impossible that all coins are counterfeit, so it's logically impossible that all calculations are mistaken.

A much more serious problem is as follows: Descartes needs to prove that there is a God not only so, as he says, he can be certain that clear and distinct ideas are true, but also to guarantee that the external world is something like what it appears to be. Given that we can only perceive our sense impressions, we have no reason whatsoever, without some sort of divine guarantee, to believe that there is an external world, and if there is, that it is anything like the sense impressions that we directly perceive. But Descartes, as we have seen, utterly fails to prove there is a God. Thus, it looks like we are caught in a highly skeptical position. We can know nothing about the external world until we know that there is a God, yet we are incapable of proving that there is a God.

In the next chapter, I shall take a look at some of the other attempts to prove God's existence, but in the end we will see that all such attempts are doomed to failure. After that, I shall endeavor to show that we are not locked in the skeptical cave mentioned above, and that it is possible to know without a divine guarantee that there is an external world and what it is like. In the course of doing so I shall attempt to show that free action is possible, and I shall also say something about the mind-body problem.

NOTES

1. There is reason to think the ancient atomists accepted both of these principles. For example, Lucretius assumed that atoms, heavy and light, all fell at a constant rate of speed. In order to explain how physical objects came to be formed he had to postulate the random waverings of the atoms. He also said that empty space offers no resistance to the movement of an object, and this suggests that it will continue to move in a straight line at a constant rate until it is acted upon.

2. Lucretius, interestingly enough, also makes use of the example about square towers (*The Nature of the Universe*, p. 376). This suggests a singular lack of imagination on the part of philosophers.

3. But "All x may be y" is not compatible with the conjunction of "Any x may be y" and "Only one x is y."

4. Descartes uses the words "soul" and "mind" interchangeably.

5. Descartes doesn't mean to say that "I exist" is a necessary truth for I might not have existed. In fact it's a wonder that I ever did exist. What he means to say is that when I conceive it it is necessary that it is true. (All quotations, unless otherwise noted, are from *Descartes, Philosophical Writings*, [trans. Anscombe and Geach], Nelson 1954).

6. The words in the square brackets are mine.

7. Lucretius' account of perception, it might be remembered, was fairly close to this. The main difference is that for him there is no mental perceiver at the end of the process.

8. I shall switch from the third person to the first person when doing so helps the argument along.

9. If we take the analogy between the idea and the image seriously then it seems that the idea must have an ultimate source. No doubt mirror A can obtain its image from B, B from C and so on, but ultimately the image must be obtained from a non-image source—even if the series of images is infinite. Suppose for example that you arrange two mirrors like this and look into one of them. If you adjust the mirrors correctly you

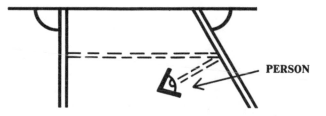

PERSON

will see a series of images of your face that approaches infinity. But even if there is an infinite series of images of your face, there must be a source of

the series. And this must be something which is not an image but your face!"
(The man in the diagram is viewed from above.)

10. But even here I would find it very difficult to believe either that there
was a mouse or that there was not a mouse. I don't think I could do other
than refrain from believing.

11. B. Pascal Pensées Sec. III, No. 233.

12. *The Philosophical Works of Descartes,* Vol. I., trans. by Haldane & Ross,
(Cambridge University Press, 1981), p. 101. I have used this translation because
it brings into clearer focus the point I want to discuss.

5

The Existence of God

Although traditional philosophers believed that it was possible to give a demonstrative proof that a god exists, this hope is considered by most modern philosophers to be highly unrealistic. If by a demonstrative proof we mean one in which the statement 'God exists' is deduced from a set of self-evident premises, and if only analytic statements are self-evident, then a proof of God's existence is impossible. From analytic statements only further analytic statements can be deduced, and the statement 'God exists' is not analytic (see chapter 3, pp. 106–107). There are two reasons for saying that it is not analytic: (a) its negation is not self-contradictory and (b) an analytic statement is true by virtue of the way its words are defined, but 'God exists', if true, is true by virtue of there being a god.

However, we mustn't give up all hope, for it may be possible to deduce the statement 'God exists' from a set of synthetic a priori statements. These would also be classified as self-evident. At the same time, it seems, at least to me, highly improbable that there could be such a proof. The only statements we have come across that might be classified as synthetic a priori are geometrical, and these are hardly the sort of statements from which the existence of God could be derived.

Even if we are unable to give a proof of the sort mentioned above, this doesn't mean that we would have no reason to *believe* that there is a god. Perhaps there are features about the world, or about ourselves, that make it highly likely that there is a god. It might turn out that the existence of God is deducible from a number of highly certain though synthetic a posteriori statements, and it might turn out that it can be inductively inferred from a number of facts about the world. This last approach is probably the most promising. It's highly unlikely that there could be any facts about the world or the people who inhabit it from which the existence of God could be deduced. As we have already seen, in any deductive argument the conclusion is in some sense contained in the premises, and it's difficult to see how the statement 'God exists' could be contained in premises having only to do with the physical world and human beings. So it looks as though any acceptable 'proof' of the existence of God is going to have to be inductive.

PROOFS

Aquinas's *Five Ways*

Let us put our reservations to one side for the moment and take a look at some of the various proofs. I shall begin with Thomas Aquinas's *Five Ways*. Here I shall only discuss the second, third, and fifth ways. The first is much the same as the second, and the fourth doesn't really warrant discussion.

The Second Way is as follows:

> The second approach starts from the nature of efficient causality. Among phenomena we discover an order of efficient causes. But we never come across, nor ever shall, anything that is an efficient cause of itself; such a thing would be prior to itself, which is impossible. It is also impossible to go on to infinity with efficient causes, for in an ordered series the first is the cause of the intermediate and the intermediate is the cause of the last. Whether or not the intermediate causes be one or many is irrelevant. Take away the cause and the effect also goes. Therefore if there were not a first among efficient causes—which would be the case in an infinite series—there would be no intermediate causes nor an ultimate effect. This plainly is not the case. A first cause, generally termed God, must therefore be inferred. (*Summa Theologica,* Ia. ii.3)

> An infinite series of efficient causes in essential subordination is impossible. Causes essentially required for the production of a determinate effect cannot consequently be infinitely multiplied, as if a block could be shifted by a crowbar, which in turn is levered by a hand, and so on to infinity. (*Summa Theologica,* Ia. xvi.2, ad 7)[1]

This looks like a standard first-cause argument, i.e., everything has a prior cause, but there cannot be an infinite series, therefore there must be a first cause that is self-caused and that is God. Although it looks like a standard first-cause argument, it is not, for Aquinas says later on, as he also suggests here, that an infinite series (though not an infinite series of causes) is possible. Thus it is not on the basis of the (mistaken) assumption that an infinite series is impossible that Aquinas wants to claim that there is a god. The point Aquinas wants to make in this argument can, I think, be explained by the following illustration. Suppose we have a person, Smith, playing pool. Smith hits ball

A, which in turn hits ball *B,* which in turn hits *C,* and *C* rolls into a pocket. What is the cause of the movement of *C?* We might say that the cause is the movement of *B.* But *B* is nothing more than a passive intermediary. *B* simply passes on what it received from *A.* The real cause of *C*'s movement is Smith, the one who hit *A* with his cue. In order for the movement of *C* to be a real effect, it has to be brought about by a real cause, and this can only be the action of an agent. If we have an infinite series of billiard balls each passing on what it received from the previous ball, then we don't have a cause. No ball can be said to be the cause. But if we don't have a cause, we don't have an effect. Since we do have an effect, an infinite series of causes is impossible.

Let us now apply this illustration to the natural world. Suppose that as a result of ice melting from a mountainside, a rock is dislodged and rolls down into the valley below. Since this is an effect, it must have had a cause. But if it is the last member of an infinite series, then it doesn't have a cause. Therefore, it can't be the last member of an infinite series. Hence, there must have been a first cause that is self caused (a divine pool player) who got the series going.

If this is Aquinas's argument, and I can't see what else his argument could be, it's not very convincing. We may, if we want, restrict the word 'effect' to those events that are ultimately the result of an action on the part of an agent. But if we do this we shall not change the way the world is. The falling rock may be the result of an infinite series. Our refusal to call it an effect won't change that. But is there any reason to restrict the word 'effect' in this way? Suppose that the windows in my greenhouse have been broken by hail. Here I say that the breaking of windows was the effect, and the falling of the hail was the cause, without in any way thinking of the hail as a possible "go between" for the effect and the workings of an agent. Thus we see that there is no reason for restricting the use of the word 'effect' (and also the word 'cause') in the way suggested by Aquinas. Since an infinite series of causes is possible, Aquinas has, as yet, no reason to say that there is a god.

Aquinas's Third Way is as follows:

> We observe in our environment how things are born and die away; they may or may not exist; to be or not to be—they are open to either alternative. All things cannot be so contingent, for what is able not to be may be reckoned as once a non-being, and were everything like that, once there would have been nothing at all. Now were this true, nothing would ever have begun, for what is does not begin to be except because of something which is, and so there would be nothing even now. This is clearly hollow. Therefore all things cannot be might-not-have-beens; among them must be a being whose existence is necessary. (*Summa Theologica,* Ia. ii. 3)

This argument is based upon the distinction between contingent existence and necessary existence. According to Aquinas, a thing exists contingently if it might not have been, and it exists necessarily if it's not the case that it might not have been. Now it's not the case, according to Aquinas, that everything exists contingently. Take any object, if it exists contingently, that is, if it might not have been, then given an infinite amount of time, there must have been a time when it did not exist. Now if everything is contingent then there must have been a time when nothing existed, but if there had been a time when nothing existed, there would, contrary to evidence, be nothing in existence now, for something cannot come from nothing. Therefore, there must be in existence a being whose existence is necessary, and that being is God.[2]

It might be thought that it doesn't follow from 'For each thing there was a time when it was not' that 'There was a time when there was nothing'. Perhaps it doesn't follow deductively, given that each thing is independent, but it is highly likely. Imagine that I have ten true pennies.[3] Each can be flipped and each can come up heads or tails: for our purposes here, heads will represent existence and tails will represent nonexistence. Now the argument runs as follows: If I flip any coin enough times, sooner or later it will come up tails. Therefore, if I take the set of ten coins and flip them as a group, sooner or later they will all come up tails; that is to say, they will *all* represent nonexistence. Although the conclusion does not follow deductively, the premises do render it highly likely.

The main thing that is wrong with Aquinas's argument is that it doesn't distinguish between logical necessity and physical necessity. The atoms postulated by Lucretius, and presumably some of the subatomic particles postulated by modern-day physicists, have physically necessary existence but not logically necessary existence. We would not be contradicting ourselves if we were to say of a given (Lucretian) atom that someday it will cease to exist, though we would be saying something false. Thus it doesn't follow from the fact that atoms have (logically) contingent existence that there was (or will be) a time for each atom when it did (will) not exist. And so it doesn't follow that it is likely that there was a time when there was nothing.

Finally, Aquinas's argument assumes that the existence and nonexistence of each object is independent of every other object. But this is not so. Even if there are no eternal atoms or subatomic particles, it may be that the stuff out of which objects are made never ceases to exist. If that were so, then even if there was a time when each object did not exist, there would not and could not be a time when nothing existed. Consider a child who has a large hunk of clay out of which he shapes objects. Even though for each object he creates there was a time when it did not exist, there wasn't a time when no object existed.

The objects are interdependent. The creation of each object involves the destruction of others.

Let's continue with Aquinas's arguments by considering his Fifth Way to establish the existence of God. We can consider it an argument from apparent design:

> Contrary and discordant elements . . . cannot always, or nearly always, work harmoniously together unless they be directed by something providing each and all with their tendencies to a definite end. Now in the universe we see things of diverse natures conspiring together in one scheme, not rarely or haphazardly, but approximately always or for the most part. There must be something, therefore, whose providence directs the universe. (*Summa Contra Gentiles*, I, 13)

> We observe that things without consciousness, such as physical bodies, operate with a purpose, as appears from their co-operating invariably, or almost so, in the same way in order to obtain the best result. Clearly then they reach this end by intention and not by chance. Things lacking knowledge move towards an end only when directed by someone who knows and understands, as an arrow by an archer. There is consequently an intelligent being who directs all natural things to their ends; and this being we call God. (*Summa Theologica*, Ia. ii. 3)

If we look at the world around us we notice not only that there is an apparent plan (or at least an apparent set of plans), but also that a great number of things appear to work toward the realization of that plan. Consider, for example, a seed developing into a flower. Every part of the seed seems to be working in harmony with every other part of the seed towards becoming a part of that flower. Now Aquinas's point is that since each part is without knowledge and without intelligence, there must be some being who has worked out the final plan and guides each part towards the actualization of that plan. And that being is, of course, God.

Lucretius attempted to account for the apparent order and apparent goal-directed behavior on the part of objects lacking intelligence and knowledge by claiming that given an infinite amount of time a world was bound to be thrown up which looked that way. The parts of the seed are not being directed toward the creation of a flower; we just happen to live in a world where the parts of the seed appear to act in that way. We don't have eyes in order to see—we see because we happen by chance to have eyes. Lucretius' account has always been considered too preposterous for words, and has for this reason been largely ignored. Give a large number of monkeys a large number of typewriters and a large amount of paper, and they do not write Shakespeare's sonnets. In fact, they don't write anything.

However, as a result of the impact of Darwin's theory of evolution, and more recently the rise of molecular biology, the situation has radically changed. Many people are now beginning to think that our world and everything in it could have come about by chance. As a result of a small number of key happenings (possibly by chance), living matter could have come about and divided itself up into a number of species, that could (by chance) have reproduced themselves. Once we have this much, we are well on our way to our world, or one that is something like it. The species with the members that happen to live long enough to reproduce themselves, survive; and if they reproduce themselves in great numbers they multiply.

Random changes in the genetic structure of a member of one of the species can lead to the development of a new species. Some of the new species will have great difficulty in surviving, but others (by chance) will have an easier time of it. The emergence and prosperity of new species will make life difficult for some of the species that had prospered in the past. Some of these will become extinct, while others will all but disappear. The process could go on like this until the creation of beings like ourselves takes place. Perhaps things didn't happen this way, but they could have happened this way. If they could have happened this way, then we cannot be certain that there is a divine planner behind the manifold. Though, on the other hand, we cannot be certain that there is not.

One interesting point is that if living matter could be brought into existence by a small number of key happenings, why do we not find that the universe abounds with all sorts of living organisms? However, not only have no other intelligent beings been found, we haven't found organisms of any sort on other celestial bodies—so far. This suggests that Earth was especially picked out to be the home of all that lives. On the other hand, though, the uniqueness of life on this planet suggests that it could have been just by chance. Given the immense improbability of the right elements coming together in just the right way to form life, it's hardly surprising to find that it happened, as far as we kncw, in only one place.

We mustn't be too hasty in writing off the argument from design. Perhaps given certain initial conditions, we can, by means of the theory of evolution and molecular biology, account for the apparent design in our part of the universe. But things couldn't have evolved in the way that they did unless those initial conditions had obtained. Had things not been set up in a certain way, creation of life and the evolution of the species simply would not have occurred. So perhaps a deity set up the initial conditions in just the right way so that things could evolve in the way that they have evolved. This would suggest a greater sophistication on the part of the deity than might otherwise be suggested.

It might be objected that the initial conditions are really very simple ones and that it wouldn't require very much in intelligence to set them up. This objection misses the point, however. To set up a number of very simple initial conditions that will result in the evolution of a very complex and apparently designed world, requires a high degree of sophistication. If there were a designer, we can be certain that that designer, though not necessarily omniscient, was highly sophisticated— though we cannot be at all certain that any such designer ever existed. The very simple initial conditions that made the evolution of our world possible could have come about just by chance. The upshot is this: If there was a designer he was more sophisticated than might otherwise be supposed, but there is no really strong reason to accept that there ever was a designer.

The very acute Scottish philosopher David Hume (1711-1776) was impressed with the argument from design. (Though it is doubtful if he would have been so impressed if he had had access to recent information on genetics and related fields.) Even though he was impressed, he was at pains to point out[4] that if there is a designer, one has no reason to attribute more to the designer than is to be found in what has been designed. We cannot, first of all, infer that the designer created the universe out of nothing; all that we can infer is that he imposed his design on what might have already existed. Second, if we notice any faults in what has been designed, we cannot assume that the designer is omniscient. If what is designed is not perfect, we cannot assume that the designer is perfect. Even though some species—e.g., porpoises and killer whales—seem to be very well designed, others—e.g., sloths and the like—don't seem to be at all well designed. Furthermore, often a member of a species is born deformed or defective. We have no reason to believe that the designer who is responsible for this is either omniscient or omnipotent.

It might be objected that we are in no position to say, for example, that sloths are poorly designed, because we don't know the ultimate reason for their existence. But if we are in no position to say that they are poorly designed, we are also in no position to say that porpoises are well designed. Here, as in the case of the sloths, we are ignorant of the ultimate reason for their existence. As a result, we are in no position to even say that the designer is a competent designer. If we rely on the evidence available, this leads to the conclusion that although the designer is competent and at times very impressive, he is not omniscient. If we do not rely on the evidence available, then we cannot draw any conclusions.

Finally, Hume, with philosophical tongue in cheek, points out that we have no reason to assume that the designer of our universe is not a second-rate member of a guild of universe builders.

This world, for aught he knows, is very faulty and imperfect, compared to a superior standard; and was only the first rude essay of some infant Deity, who afterwards abandoned it, ashamed of his lame performance; it is the work only of some dependent, inferior Deity; and is the object of derision to his superiors; it is the production of old age and dotage of some superannuated Deity; and ever since his death, has run on at adventures, from its first impulse and active force, which it received from him.[5]

The Ontological Argument

We have already looked at Descartes's version of this argument, but it will profit us to examine St. Anselm's version, primarily because it contains a number of seductive errors. Some are so seductive that a couple of present-day philosophers have been hoodwinked into thinking that the argument is valid and sound.

Here is what Anselm has to say:

I do not seek to understand that I may believe, but I believe in order to understand. For this also I believe,—that unless I believed, I should not understand.

And so, Lord, do thou, who dost give understanding to faith, give me, so far as thou knowest it to be profitable, to understand that thou are as we believe; and that thou art that which we believe. And, indeed, we believe that thou art a being than which nothing greater can be conceived. Or is there no such nature, since the fool hath said in his heart, there is no God? (Psalms xiv. 1). But, at any rate, this very fool, when he hears of this being of which I speak—a being than which nothing greater can be conceived—understands what he hears, and what he understands is in his understanding; although he does not understand it to exist.

For, it is one thing for an object to be in the understanding, and another to understand that the objects exists. When a painter first conceives of what he will afterwards perform, he has it in his understanding, but he does not yet understand it to be, because he has not yet performed it. But after he has made the painting, he both has it in his understanding, and he understands that it exists, because he made it.

Hence, even the fool is convinced that something exists in the understanding, at least, than which nothing greater can be conceived. For, when he hears of this, he understands it. And whatever is understood, exists in the understanding. And assuredly that, than which nothing greater can be conceived, cannot exist in the understanding alone. For, suppose it exists in the understanding alone: then it can be conceived to exist in reality; which is greater.

Therefore, if that, than which nothing greater can be conceived, exists in the understanding alone, the very being, than which nothing greater can be conceived, is one, than which a greater can be conceived. But obviously this is impossible. Hence, there is no doubt that there exists a being, than which nothing greater can be conceived, and it exists both in the understanding and in reality.

And it assuredly exists so truly, that it cannot be conceived not to exist. For, it is possible to conceive of a being which cannot be conceived not to exist; and this is greater than one which can be conceived not to exist. Hence, if that, than which nothing greater can be conceived, can be conceived not to exist, it is not that, than which nothing greater can be conceived. But this is an irreconcilable contradiction. There is, then, so truly a being than which nothing greater can be conceived to exist, that it cannot even be conceived not to exist; and this being thou art, O Lord, our God.

So truly, therefore, dost thou exist, O Lord, my God, that thou canst not be conceived not to exist; and rightly. For, if a mind could conceive of a being better than thee, the creature would rise above the Creator; and this is most absurd. And, indeed, whatever else there is, except thee alone, can be conceived not to exist. To thee alone, therefore, it belongs to exist more truly than all other beings, and hence in a higher degree than all others. For, whatever else exists does not exist so truly, and hence in a less degree it belongs to it to exist. Why, then, has the fool said in his heart, there is no God, since it is so evident, to a rational mind, that thou dost exist in the highest degree of all? Why, except that he is dull and a fool?

Anselm's argument is really two arguments. The first begins by defining God as a being than which none greater can be thought of or conceived. This appears to fit in fairly well with our description of God. It would be hard to conceive of a being who was greater than a being who was all good, omniscient, omnipotent, creator of the universe, and so on. Suppose now that someone were to deny that there is a god. Well, at least the idea of a being than which none greater can be conceived would exist in his understanding. For he understands this definition and "what he understands is in his understanding." But according to Anselm, that than which none greater can be conceived cannot exist in the understanding alone. If it existed in the understanding alone it can be conceived to exist in reality as well, and this is greater. Therefore, if that than which none greater can be conceived exists in the understanding alone, then it is one than which a greater can be conceived (one who also exists in reality). Thus, that than which none greater can be conceived must also exist in reality.

There are two things wrong with this argument. First, it takes existence to be a perfection. It assumes that a being who exists in reality is greater, that is to say, more perfect, than one who does not exist. We have already discussed this error (chapter 4, page 185), so there is really no need to say any more about it. The second thing wrong with this argument is that it trades on a confusion between the "idea of a thing" and the "thing the idea is an idea of." A being than which none greater can be conceived does not exist in the mind of the atheist (let alone in anyone else's mind); all that exists in his mind is the idea of such a being plus the judgment that there is no such being.

It might be objected, as Anselm points out, that just as a painting can exist in the mind of a painter as well as on canvas, so there is a sense in which God can exist in the mind of the fool as well as in reality. But even if we allow that God can, in this extended sense, exist in the mind, this gives no support to Anselm's argument. In the case of the painting, its existence in the mind of the artist is no more perfect if there is also the painting in reality. Whether there is a painting or not has nothing to do with the perfection of the painting in the artist's mind. Similarly, in the case of the fool, the God that is in his mind is no more perfect if there is a God in reality. Once again, whether there is a God or not has nothing to do with the perfection of the idea that is in the mind of the fool.

Even if we allow that there is a sense in which the painting can exist in the mind of the artist, it's not at all clear that there is a sense in which God can exist in the mind of the fool. What exists in the mind of the fool is the idea of a being than which none greater can be conceived, and this is clearly different from a *being* than which none greater can be conceived. When Anselm says "For, suppose it exists in the understanding alone then it can be conceived to exist in reality, which is greater," the second "it" is ambiguous. If it is the idea that exists is in the fool's mind, then it is not something that can be conceived to exist in reality. What would it be like for the idea of something than which none greater can be conceived to exist in reality?

It follows from this that the previous line—"Hence even the fool is convinced that something exists in the understanding, at least, than which nothing greater can be conceived"—is also mistaken. What exists in the understanding is the *idea* of something than which none greater can be conceived, not something than which none greater can be conceived.

We can make all this clearer by setting out the form of Anselm's argument in the following way. First of all, we have the following definition of God:

"God" = "A being than which none greater can be thought."

Such a being can exist in (a) the understanding and (b) outside the understanding. Now to prove that there is a god, that is to say, that He exists in (b) as well as in (a). Let us assume that He exists just in (a). Then He is not a god, for if He exists just in (a) then he is limited. Therefore, He must exist in (a) and (b). And therefore God exists.

The crucial error in the argument is, as we have seen, that it's not a *god* that exists in (a) but *an idea of a god*.

It might also be objected that what Anselm really wanted to say is that in order to think of a being than which none greater can be conceived, it is not sufficient just to *think* of a being than which none greater can be conceived, we must also think that there is such a being. In other words, we cannot think of the greatest being without thinking that there is such a being. But even if this is true, even if we couldn't think of the greatest being without thinking of that being as existing, it doesn't follow that there is such a being. Nothing follows about the nature of reality from the way that people are obliged to think about it.

But let us move on to the second argument. Here Anselm begins with the reference "And it assuredly exists so truly that it cannot be conceived not to exist." The argument runs something like this. Not only is it possible to conceive of a being which exists, it is also possible to conceive of a being which necessarily exists, that is to say, a being which could not *not* exist. Now if we are forming the idea of a being than which none greater can be conceived, this idea will include not just the claim that this being exists, but also the idea that this being *necessarily* exists. Again, the same point can be made. Even if it were impossible to think of the greatest possible being without thinking of that being as necessarily existing, it still wouldn't follow that there was such a being. As was mentioned before, nothing follows about the nature of the world from the way that we are obliged to think about it. Anselm may be right when he says of God "Thou canst not be conceived not to exist," but nothing follows from this about the existence of God.

Although I said before that Anselm's definition of God as a being than which none greater can be conceived appears to fit in fairly well with our description of God as a being who is omniscient, omnipotent, all good, and so on, the fit is not quite as good as it appears to be. If I conceive of a car than which none greater can be conceived, I am not thinking of such a car if I just think "a car than which none greater can be conceived." I am not thinking of such a car until I give my thought some content. I must think of it as, say, having a top speed of 160 mph, giving a comfortable and silent ride, providing 40 miles to the gallon, looking like a Jaguar, and so on. Similarly, I am not thinking of God when I think "a being than which none greater can be conceived." I have to think "a being who is omniscient, etc." The attempt at thinking of this being as not existing doesn't offer any difficulties. All I have to think is "there might not be a being who is omniscient, etc.," and there is nothing difficult about this. My point is just this: There might be some difficulty in thinking "There might not be a being that which none greater can be conceived"; but there is, as far as I can see, no difficulty in thinking "There might not be a being who is omniscient, etc." This is the thought that one must have if one is going to be thinking of God.

We must not be too hasty in dismissing Anselm's second argument, for it can be given an interpretation that is more difficult to handle. This interpretation is, I think, at the heart of many of the recent attempts to show that the argument is valid and sound.[7] Even though existence, it may be pointed out, is not a property, necessary existence is. Indeed, if any being is going to be considered a god, that being would have to have necessary existence. We can see from this that it's possible that there is a being who is all powerful, all knowing, all good, and necessarily exists. Or, to shorten our description, it's possible that there is a being that necessarily exists. Now if there were such a being, it would be impossible for it not to exist. After all, if it were possible for it not to exist, it could hardly be a being that possessed necessary existence! But this means that it's impossible for this possible being not to exist. Therefore, this being does exist. And since this being is God, God exists.

This argument, like many of the others we have examined, stumbles over a failure to distinguish between what is logically possible, necessary, etc., and what is possible, necessary, etc. in some other sense. First of all, it's logically impossible that something can exist by logical necessity. There may be something contradictory about saying that God does not exist. But it cannot be deduced from this that there is a God. One cannot move from statements about the logic of words to the way the world is. Suppose, for example, that a group of horse lovers used the word 'horse' in such a way that it was self-contradictory to say that there were no horses. In other words, for them 'existence' was part of the meaning of 'horse'. No doubt these people could use the word 'horse' in this sense. But if they did, all that would follow would be that in their sense of 'horse' there wouldn't be any horses! The reason for this is that any being that we recognized as a horse might not have existed.

Given, then, that it's logically impossible for something to exist by logical necessity, it must be the case that the sort of necessity that is being talked about here is some other sort of necessity. It can't be physical necessity; let us call it *divine necessity,* and let us accept that it's logically possible for there to be a being that possesses (divine) necessary existence. Let us also accept that if there were such a being, it would be eternal; it could not have begun to exist at some time, and could not cease to exist. So if there were such a being, it would be logically impossible for this being not to exist in the sense of ceasing to exist. It still does not follow that there is such a being. Although it is (logically) impossible for a divinely necessarily existing being to cease to exist, it is still, and this is the important point, (logically) possible for there not to be one in the first place. To conclude, we cannot argue from 'If there were a necessarily existing being, it would be impossible for such a being not to exist' to 'There is a God'. We could only make the inference if the necessity in question were logical necessity. But as we have seen, it's logically impossible for there to be a being that exists by logical necessity.

THE PROBLEM OF EVIL

We can see from our examination of Aquinas's second and third ways, and our examination of the ontological argument, that demonstrative arguments offer us little hope. The only arguments that give us any reason to believe that there is a god are inductive ones like Aquinas's fifth way—the argument from design. We notice certain features about the world and argue from them to the likelihood of there being a god.

Unfortunately, even though there are some features about the world that lead us to believe that there is a god, there are other features that lead us to believe that there is not a god. One would expect that a being who was omnipotent, omniscient, and all good would create a world that was free of evil, but the existence of earthquakes, famines, tidal waves, and wars testify to there being a tremendous amount of evil in the world, and so to the nonexistence of a god. If God were described as a being who lacked at least one of the features that we have attributed to him, then the evil in the world would not rule out the existence of God. If God were not all powerful, then we could say that even though God knows that there is evil (because he is omniscient) and wants to get rid of it (because he is all good), he is incapable (because he is not omnipotent) of doing so. Or, if God were not all knowing then we could say God wants to get rid of the evil (because he is all good), has the power to get rid of it (because he is omnipotent), but fails to do so because he doesn't know how. But as long as all three features are ascribed to God, it's difficult to see how his existence is compatible with the existence of evil.

The favorite way to attempt to escape this problem is to argue that the responsibility for evil falls on human beings, not God. However, this gambit, which is sometimes called the free will defense, will not work. Perhaps God is not responsible for the evil that is the result of humankind's handiwork—e.g., murders, wars, and the like—but human beings could hardly be said to be responsible for such natural evils as exploding volcanos, earthquakes, and tidal waves. It might be argued that God gave humans enough intelligence to know not to live in earthquake zones and at the bottom of volcanic mountains. But this argument is rather flimsy. Perhaps we shall someday know enough about our habitat to know where all the earthquake zones are, but lots and lots of people in the past, who had no way of knowing anything about earthquake zones, have died and suffered immeasurably as a result of earthquakes.

Again, it is argued that evils such as pain and suffering are necessary; necessary for human existence. The child learns not to put his finger in a burning candle when he experiences pain upon first putting his finger in the flame. As a result, the child grows up with unburnt fingers. Children who are incapable of experiencing pain usually do not survive adolescence. Pain, as it is sometimes said, is one of the great rudders of life. However, if the world were a Garden of Eden where there was nothing that could do us any harm, pain would not be required to teach us to avoid certain things. There would be nothing that needed to be avoided. Even if for some other reason it was impossible to create a world free of things that could harm us, not all the pain that we experience is instrumental in keeping us out of harm's way. As well as experiencing what might be called instrumental pain, we also experience gratuitous pain, such as the pain of a migraine headache or that of terminal cancer, neither of which is in any way needed to direct our actions. It's difficult to see how a being who satisfies our description of God could be responsible for gratuitous pain.

A much better defense of the existence of natural evil can be made along the following lines. God, being all good, wanted us to develop into highly moral persons. If he had created a lotusland for our habitat, this would not have been possible. Just as one can only become a courageous person by doing courageous acts, and it is only possible to do courageous acts in a world where danger lurks, so one can only become an honest person who has respect for the welfare of others in a world where there is a shortage of the wherewithal for human existence. The normal function of statements is to tell the truth. In a lotusland it simply wouldn't occur to people to tell lies. Why would they? It's only when there is a shortage of the goods required to stave off pain and misery that people are tempted to lie. Now the truly moral person, so it might be argued, is not one who unwittingly always tells the truth. The truly moral person is the one who is tempted from time to time to tell lies but, owing to his respect for other people, refrains from doing so. The point is this: God can't just create a highly moral person. A person can only become a highly moral person through being tempted to do, but refraining from doing, immoral acts. In order to be tempted, the person must live in an imperfect world. Thus the reason that God created an imperfect world was to make the development of highly moral people possible. Of course, along with the development of moral people will come the development of immoral people, but that is only to be expected if temptations exist.

There are two difficulties with this argument. First of all, some people, at least in the past, did live in an almost perfect world—for example, the Tahitians until the arrival of Captain Cook. If God had felt an imperfect world was necessary, he would have made *all* of the world imperfect. Second, even if we grant that an imperfect world is necessary, was it necessary for God to make the world so imperfect? The dreadful drought that is so often experienced across the southern fringe of the Sahara Desert could hardly be said to be character building. Perhaps a bit of imperfection is necessary, but not nearly as much as we find in the world today.

Finally, it will be argued, in much the same way that white is difficult to distinguish in an all white world, so too, if we lived in a world that was all good, we would not be aware that it was good. It is necessary that there be some evil in the world so that we will become aware of the goodness that is to be found. Again the reply is, perhaps a bit of evil is necessary, but why so much? If we lived in a world that was all white, with the exception of one or two objects, then we could be aware that the world was mostly white. Similarly if we lived in a world that was almost all good, then we could be aware of the goodness in the world.

Let us turn now to the moral evil for which humankind, and not God, is directly responsible—murder, rape, torture, pillage, war, and the like. Here it is argued that in order for human beings to be moral, as opposed to nonmoral, it is necessary for them to have a free will—to be able to choose between doing and not doing a particular act, and then carry out that choice. If we had no freedom we would be no more moral agents than lobster would be. But if humans are to have the freedom required to be moral, as opposed to nonmoral, it's always going to be possible for them to do what is wrong. And this is why moral evil exists.

This is perhaps the strongest argument that the theist can present, but it's to be noticed, first of all, that it only covers moral evil. It does not cover natural evil. Second, it must be asked, was it necessary for God to create so many people with such unpleasant dispositions? We read about tribes of people who were kind, generous, and who lived entirely at peace with one another. Also, we meet from time to time people who have the most kindly of dispositions. Why couldn't God have populated the world with people like that? Perhaps it was necessary to create *some* people who would be responsible for a bit of moral evil, so that moral goodness would shine in contrast, but it was not necessary to create the vast numbers of misanthropes we find around us. From all this we may conclude, I think, that the facts about the nature of the world and the nature of human beings suggest that it is more likely that there is not a god than that there is.

At this point, however, the theist, in a last ditch stand, might be tempted to argue either that what we call 'evil' is not really evil, or that if we were aware of the master plan we would see that what we take to be evil is really not evil after all. Sooner or later it will result in the best of all possible worlds. Let me deal with the second move first. The main thing that is wrong with this move is that it puts a limitation on God's power. If this is the best of all possible worlds that

God is capable of creating, then one would have to conclude that God's powers are limited. As Candide put it in Voltaire's novel by that name, if this is the best of all possible worlds, then what are the others like? Furthermore, if God is all powerful, it's not necessary for him to create a world that will evolve toward perfection. He can, straight off, create a perfect world.

Let us move on, then, to the claim that what we call 'evil' isn't really evil; that, contrary to all appearances, there really isn't any evil in the world. First of all, our words mean what we want them to mean. If we use 'evil' to refer to pain, suffering, torture, and willful deceit, then that is its meaning. If God used the word in some other way, this would only show that the word was ambiguous, not that our use was mistaken. Second, if it had already been shown on other grounds that there was a god, then we might think that perhaps we were mistaken in calling pain, suffering, and the like evil (though I can't see why); but if we are trying to build an argument for the existence of God on the evidence available, then it has to be built on that evidence alone. That evidence, in part, consists of great pain, suffering, misery in the world, and that these are evils.

Closely connected with this point is the following. It is sometimes said that God will make up for the pain and suffering in this world when we enter another world after death. But such claims only become relevant once it has been shown that there is a god. If we already know that there is a god, then we could offer the hypothesis of another world in order to square the existence of evil with the existence of an all-good, all-powerful, all-knowing being. But if we are at the stage of trying to show that there is a god, such speculations are irrelevant. We can say that if there is a god then there must be an afterlife. But we cannot say that there is a god *because* if there is a god, there must be an afterlife.

The same point can be made about claims that this world is a testing ground (a place where we must prove our mettle) for the next world. If we already know that there is a god, then we can say that this world must be a place where we prove our worthiness for the next world. If we are at the stage of trying to show that there is a god, such speculations are irrelevant. We cannot argue that there must be a god *because* if there is a god, this world exists as a testing ground for another world.[8]

FAITH WITHOUT EVIDENCE

It looks like we have no demonstrative proof of the existence of God: no deductive proof of the existence of God from facts about the world, and little inductive evidence for his existence. In fact, what inductive evidence we do have appears to point more toward there not being a god than toward there being one. However, we mustn't give up all hope. Many people have argued—among them Blaise Pascal, Søren Kierkegaard, and William James—that it is inappropriate for faith to be based on reason, that the basis of faith must be found somewhere else.

I once had a colleague who, in the course of a series of lectures on the philosophy of religion, announced to his class that the next day he was going to give them an empirical proof for the existence of God. The next day he arrived with a mysterious black box. He opened the box and announced that here was the proof. Inside the box was a shrunken human head. The members of the class were bewildered, and rightly so. Empirical evidence, at least of this sort, doesn't and couldn't have anything to do with whether or not there is a god. In fact it is hard to think of any direct empirical evidence that could support the claim that there is a god.

Søren Kierkegaard (1813–1855), a Danish philosopher, argued in the following way. Consider an object in front of you, a pencil, say. After you have picked it up, written with it, and crossed out some words, you can be certain that it is a pencil—you can say that you know there is a pencil in front of you. But can you say that you *believe* there is a pencil in front of you? It seems not. In order to *believe* something, there has to be reason to doubt. You can believe, and very strongly, that your girlfriend is being faithful to you because you cannot be absolutely certain. If you came to know absolutely that she was faithful to you, then you could no longer believe it. In fact, according to Kierkegaard, the weaker the evidence, the stronger can be the belief. When we reach something absurd like Christianity, this calls for a blind and passionate leap of faith. Why is Christianity called absurd? Well, for one thing, according to some authorities the doctrine of the Holy Trinity, which is one of the keystones of Christianity, is absurd. How can God be the Father, the Son, and the Holy Ghost and still be one? If God is the Father, He cannot be the Son; if He is the Son, He cannot be the Father. Kierkegaard writes:

> Anything that is almost probable, or probable, or extremely and emphatically probable, is something that he can almost know, or as good as know, or extremely and emphatically almost know—but it is impossible to believe. For the absurd is the object of faith, and the only object that can be believed.[9]

Although Kierkegaard has been very influential in recent years, there are two points that his argument brings to our attention, and when they have been brought to our attention his argument loses its significance. The first point was remarked on in chapter 2 when we discussed Plato's distinction between knowledge and belief. The logic of 'believe' is different from the logic of 'know'. In order to be in a position to say that we believe that something is the case—for example, that it is not snowing—we cannot be completely certain. If we are completely certain, we can only say that we know; we cannot say that we believe. The second point is that we must distinguish between (a) believing *that* something is the case and (b) believing *in* someone or something, and between (c) knowing *that* something is the case and (d) knowing something or someone. Let us start with the distinction between (c) and (d). When I say that I know *that* water boils at 212°F., for example, the object of my knowledge, to express myself in a misleading way, is the fact, but when I say that I know Joe Clark, the object of knowledge is the person. I can come to know that water boils at 212°F. a number of different ways, but in order to know Joe Clark I must be acquainted with him. I must have met him from time to time. To be acquainted, though, is not the same as knowing. I could be slightly acquainted with Joe Clark, but not really know him or know him well. There is some dispute as to whether knowledge of the second kind reduces to knowledge of the first kind. In other words, when I say that I know Joe Clark it is just a shorthand way of saying I know this and that about him. Although it's tempting to analyze knowledge of the second kind into knowledge of the first kind, I don't think that a complete reduction can be carried out. I could come to know a great deal of "thats" about Joe Clark without coming to know him. It seems that in order to know him, I have to *also* be acquainted with him.

Somewhat the same sort of distinction can be made between 'believe that' and 'believe in'. The object of 'believe that' is, again, a statement—'I believe that it is going to rain'—while the object of 'believe in' is a person or a thing—'I believe in Christ'. Although the term 'believe' in the phrase 'believe that' operates in much the same way as the word 'know' in the phrase 'know that', 'believe' in 'believe in' operates in a somewhat different way from 'know' in 'I know Joe Clark'. To believe in a person, thing, or idea is to have faith in that person, thing, or idea. When I say that I believe in Joe Clark, what I mean is that I have faith that he will make a great leader—that he will not let us down. When I say I believe in Keynesian economics, I mean that I have faith that if the theory is properly applied, the present economic woes will go away.

Now, to return to Kierkegaard. The sort of belief that he has in mind when he says that one can only believe the absurd is 'belief in', but 'belief in' presupposes the existence of the object that is believed in. I can believe in a being that is difficult to understand. I can have faith that this being will not let me down. But I cannot, in this sense of 'believe', believe that such a being exists. I must believe *that* the object exists. Where the question is a matter of existence, as opposed to the question of having faith in a presupposed being, the more absurd the being the less reason I have to accept or believe that there is such a being. To put it briefly, a leap of faith presupposes the existence of the being we intend to trust. Our beliefs concerning existence cannot be based on a leap of faith. In other words, we find in Kierkegaard no basis for a belief that there is a god. The point that Kierkegaard brings to our attention in fact seems to point the other way. If, in order for there to be a Christian God, there must be a being who satisfies an inconsistent set of descriptive words, this gives us reason to doubt that there is such a being.

Let us turn now to William James (1842-1910) to see whether he offers us a better basis for faith. James was a leading exponent of the American school of philosophy called Pragmatism. Other members of the movement were Charles Sanders Peirce and John Dewey. James's most celebrated attempt to give a nonevidential basis to religious belief is found in his essay *The Will to Believe*. It was first published in 1896. What William James offers us in this essay is really a more sophisticiated form of Pascal's Wager.[10] There is, however, a difference in that James's argument is based largely on his pragmatic theory of truth. According to this theory, a synthetic statement is true if it pays to believe it. This theory makes a certain amount of sense if it is confined to hypotheses in science. We have seen that general scientific hypotheses cannot be conclusively shown to be true. Future experience can always show them to be false. We cannot be absolutely certain that the law of gravity is true. Future experience having to do with far away objects or microscopic particles might force us to replace this hypothesis with a more embracing one. However, we find that in and around our world the law of gravity works. We find that we can make predictions on the basis of it, and these predictions turn out to be true (in the ordinary sense of 'true'). So we can say that this hypothesis is true in the sense that it works—it pays to use it in our dealings with the environment.

Although it is useful to use the word 'true' in this sense when talking about hypotheses in science, it would be a mistake to think that this is the central meaning of the word 'true'. When we say that the law of gravity is true in the sense that it works, and it works in the sense that the predictions based upon it turn out to be true, we don't mean that the predictions are true in the sense that they work. We mean that predictions are true in the ordinary sense. For example, suppose that a lead ball is dropped in a vacuum from a height of 100 feet at time t^1. If we know the mass of the ball and the mass of the earth then we can predict at what time the ball will hit the ground. Suppose we predict that the ball will land at t^1 plus x seconds, and the ball does land at that time. Thus we can say that the prediction is true. But in saying that the prediction is true, we don't mean that it works.[11]

William James was tempted to extend the scope of 'works'. At one point he found himself saying that a religious belief was true if it worked. But here by 'worked' he meant that it made the believer happier. But this is clearly a travesty of the original pragmatic position. I may be happier believing that I have a million dollars in the bank. But the truth of 'Mackenzie has a million dollars in the bank' has nothing whatever to do with what makes him happy!

I should hasten to add, however, that this last version of the pragmatic theory of truth is not involved in James's argument in the *Will to Believe;* still, one has the feeling that it is lurking in the background.

The Will to Believe is really addressed to those who want very much to believe that there is a god but, because of their scientific upbringing and scruples, feel guilty about doing so. What James says, in effect, is that one can freely go ahead and indulge in religious belief with a clear scientific conscience.

He begins by pointing out that some of the options we are faced with in life are living, forced, and momentous. Such options James calls genuine options. By "living" he means that they come out of the fabric and surroundings of one's everyday life. For example, the option to become a Christian or an atheist would be a living option for many a student at Harvard around 1890, but not the option to become a Theosophist or a Moslem. By "forced" he means there is no third alternative. The choice of whether to see a play or go to the cinema is not forced, while the option offered by a gunman who says "your money or your life," is. Finally, an option is momentous if it makes a great deal of difference to our lives. For example, the choice of whether to accept the offer of a place on a mountain climbing team setting out to climb Mt. Everest would be momentous.

James then claims that when we are faced with a choice having all three features, and the choice cannot be settled on rational grounds, then it is proper to choose according to our desires. For example, suppose that I am faced with the decision of whether to propose marriage to a girl by the name of Jane. And suppose (a) I want to marry her; (b) I am not certain that she will make a good wife and there is really no way of finding out; and (c) if I don't hurry up and propose, she will go off and marry Charlie. In this case, I am faced with a choice that is living, forced, momentous, one cannot be settled on rational grounds—I have no way of finding out whether or not she will make a good wife. In this case, James would say, and I'm sure we would all agree, that the sensible thing to do is to take the risk and marry the girl (if she will). Furthermore, even if I am not absolutely certain that she will make a good wife, if I act as if she will make a good wife, the chances are that she will. As James puts it, "The desire for a certain kind of truth here brings about that special truth's existence."

No doubt James has a point here; that (a) sometimes we have to act on the basis of insufficient evidence and (b) that we can sometimes help a future state to be so by believing it to be so. We treat a person as a person who can be trusted and he becomes a person who can be trusted. But the question we must ask ourselves is whether any of this makes it (in some sense) rational to believe that there is a god. If I already know that there is a god, then acting as if this were so, showing respect and reverence toward that being, will make it possible for me to enter into a special relationship with that being. But if the question is whether there is a god, and not a question of whether to enter into a special relationship with that being, how can it be rational for me to believe that there is a god? Believing that a particular person is to be trusted may bring about that trust, but believing that there is a god will not bring it about that there is such a god. Even if the option to believe that there is a god is momentous, living, cannot be settled on evidential grounds, and in some sense forced, I still have no reason to believe that there is a god. What I should do is accept what in fact is the case; that I simply don't know.

James would say that even if I don't know that there is a god, it is still in some sense rational for me to believe that there is, for if there is a god then that god may—but only under the circumstances that I believe there is a god—make himself known to me. It may be the case that, as James puts it, "the evidence will be forever withheld from us unless we meet the hypothesis half way." Imagine, for example, that I have some reason to believe that a hermit lives on Mt. Eisenhower, and that I also have some reason to believe that this hermit, if there is one, will not let himself be known to me unless I believe that he exists. Let's imagine further that a legend has grown up that the hermit will give an ounce of gold to each of those who believe that he exists. In this case I might, in order to discover that there is a hermit, act as if there is a hermit—even try to believe that there is a hermit—so that the hermit, if there is one, will make himself known to me.

There are two questions to be asked here. First, can we have reason to believe what is not known to be the case? Of course, we can have reason to *act* on the basis of what is not known to be the case. If I have reason to believe that the price of shares in Occidental Petroleum is likely to go up, but don't know that it is going to go up, then I have reason to buy lots of shares; but do I have reason to believe that it's going up? Or, if you tell me that you will give me a hundred dollars if I believe that there is a cat in the next room, then I have reason to pretend to believe that there is a cat in the next room. But do I have reason to believe that there *is* a cat in the next room?

There is a sense of 'reason' in which I do have reason to believe. I have reason to believe in the sense that it would be prudential to believe. But in the more ordinary sense of 'reason', I have no reason to believe. In this sense, just as the only reason I can have for accepting that there is a cat in the next room is the existence of evidence of a cat, so the only reason I can have for believing (in this sense) that there is a cat in the next room is the existence of evidence of a cat.

The second question to be asked is this: We can imagine the sort of evidence the hermit could give for his existence—he could jump out from behind a large rock—but what sort of direct evidence could God give? Suppose the skies darken and a loud voice saying "I am God, I exist!" thunders down from the clouds. Does this give us any reason to believe that there is a god? We would probably think that a large-scale prank had been perpetrated and look around for natural causes. If we hear voices in the dark, well, this is most likely just our imaginations working overtime. If it's as if He came in a dream, well, this may be just a dream. So, we cannot accept James's argument that would-be believers should believe that there is a god because God, if He exists, will reveal Himself to those who do. Nothing would ever count as evidence that He had revealed Himself.

The main thing that goes wrong with James's argument is, as we mentioned before, it muddies the distinction between believing *that* there is a god and believing *in* an already-known-to-exist god. James's argument gives us reason to believe in God, in the sense of having faith in God, if we already know that there is a god. But his argument gives us no reason to believe (in the sense of accept) that there is a god. Believing in a god may bring about a state of grace if a god exists, but believing that there is a god cannot bring it about that God exists.

RELIGION AND THE MEANING OF LIFE

It is sometimes said that there must be a God because life would be without meaning and purpose if He did not exist. Although it is recognized by most people that this is a fallacious argument, it is assumed that the premise upon which it is based—if there were no God, human life would be without meaning and purpose—is true. In what follows I shall argue that this assumption is mistaken—that there is just as much (or as little) purpose in a godless world as there is in a theistic one.[12]

Why is it believed that there is more purpose in a theistic world? The answer usually given is that if there is a God, then we can assume that He created Earth as a home for us, and that He created us, ultimately, to serve and worship Him. Thus, if there is a God, then we have a purpose—which is ultimately to serve God—and if there is no God, then we have no purpose. But is it true that our lives lack purpose if there is no God? Can one not find a purpose in serving humankind by working for Oxfam, Amnesty International, or even by teaching philosophy? However, it will be replied to this that if *human* beings have no purpose, if they simply exist, then it follows that doing things that serve humankind, such as working for Oxfam, can have no ultimate purpose. But can't the same point be made about serving God? How can serving God have a purpose if God, as an end in Himself, has no purpose? There is then no difference between serving Oxfam in a godless world and serving God in a theistic world. Both serve a purposeless end.

The fact that, ultimately, we shall reach a purposeless end should not surprise or upset anyone. It is part of the logic of the situation. To explain something is always to explain it in terms of something else. As a result, it is logically impossible to have an explanation of everything. If there is no God, and we ask why is there a universe, we just have to say that there is. If there is a God, then we can explain why there is a universe. We can say that the universe exists because of God. But if there is a God, and, instead of asking why is there a universe, we ask why is there a universe *and* a God, again no explanation can be given; all that we can (logically) say is that there is. To give an explanation, we would have to give it in terms of something else, but there is nothing left.

It is sometimes thought that if *A* is explained in terms of *B*, and *B* is explained in terms of *C*, but *C*, being an ultimate (logically), has no explanation, then *A* has no explanation. But this can be seen to be a mistake. Sooner or later we are bound to reach an explanation that has no explanation, so unless we are prepared to make the absurd claim that it is logically impossible for anything to be explained, we have to accept that *C* can be the explanation of *B*, and *B* the explanation of *A*, while *C* itself has no explanation.

Similarly, just as the fact that *C* is the explanation of *B* but has itself no explanation does not preclude *C* from being an explanation, so, too, the fact that *B* finds its purpose in terms of *C* but *C* itself has no purpose does not preclude *B* from having a purpose. If there is a God, humankind's purpose could be to serve Him; but we can also say that if there is no God, the purpose of humanity could be to serve fellow human beings. So we must reject the claim that if there is no God, then human life has no purpose. One can find purpose in life under the assumption that there is not a God as well as under the assumption that there is.

CONCLUSION

The fact that no argument can be found to give us any reason to believe that there is or is not a god, and the fact that no direct evidence counts one way or the other, suggests that perhaps we have approached religion in the wrong way.

Ludwig Wittgenstein (1889–1951), a very influential Austrian philosopher who taught at the University of Cambridge in England, offers the following example.[13] Suppose someone were to say with great passion "I believe in the Last Judgment," and someone else were to remark "Well, I'm not so sure, possibly." We would feel that there was something out of place about what the second person had said, that somehow what he says doesn't connect with what the first person had said. If the first person had said something like "I think it will rain this afternoon," and the second person had said "Well, I'm not so sure, possibly," that would connect. This suggests that religious claims are not to be taken in a literal way, that what they do is express one's attitude toward life. The person who says "I believe in the Last Judgment" is saying he feels as though he is being watched—that it's as though he is being held responsible for everything that he does; or perhaps he is just expressing that he feels very, very responsible for what he does.

Suppose there was someone who possessed a high-tech video screen on which he could "see" into the future. Let's assume that in the past this person had been very successful in making predictions. Now, if this person were to "see" on his video screen the occurrence of the sorts of events that usually feature in descriptions of the Judgment Day, and then announced that the Judgment Day will be in two hundred years, we would feel, I think, that he isn't expressing a religious belief. He isn't saying the same sort of thing as the man who says that he believes in the Judgment Day.

What this suggests is that the man who says that he believes in God, or even that Christ was sent to save us, is not making a factual claim about the world. What he is doing is expressing the feeling that the world is a rational, friendly place, or that the life of the son of a certain Joseph and a certain Mary should be seen in a certain light. Both he and the atheist can be acquainted with all the available information on the life of Christ, and yet each can come away with a different attitude toward that life. The atheist sees him as a truly impressive moralist, while the Christian sees him as the Son of God who represents the hope of all humankind.

No doubt many religious people will feel that there must be more to religious proclamations than just this. They must be taken as saying something about the way things are. But if they are, then they are open to the sort of investigation that scientists engage in. And somehow, we feel that they are not.

So, returning to our original question of whether there is a god, the upshot seems to be this. If we take the statement "God exists" in a literal way, we have no more reason to believe that it's true than that it's false, and so we should be agnostic. But if we take it as an expression of the feeling that the world is a rational place filled with beauty

and goodness, then we can be theists. But we must realize that, in saying that God exists, we are not making a factual claim based on reason, we are only expressing our deepest feelings toward the world at
large.

It was once said to me that the best proof that there is a god is
Bach's *The Art of Fugue*. At first, I didn't see why this should be
thought of as a proof, but the reason it can, I think, is this. What
that divinely inspired work does is let us experience the world as a
place illuminated with beauty—the beauty that is felt by the person
who expresses himself by saying that there is a god.

NOTES

1. From St. Thomas Aquinas *Philosophical Texts*, trans. by Thomas Gilly,
(London: Oxford University Press, 1951).

2. Note that if Aquinas is right on all this, he has only proven that there
is a being which is a first cause and exists necessarily. Though, presumably,
Aquinas would argue that any being which had of these features must have
all of the others of God.

3. By a true penny I mean one that has its center of gravity at the center
of the penny.

4. Hume's *Dialogues Concerning Natural Religion*, edited by N. Kemp
Smith, (London: Oxford University Press, 1935).

5. Ibid., p. 209.

6. Saint Anselm of Canturbury, *Basic Writings*, trans. by Sidney Norton
Deane, (LaSalle, Ill.: Open Court Publishing Co., 1903), chapters I and II.

7. See Norman Malcolm's "Anselm's Ontological Arguments" *Philosophical Review* 69 (1960): 41–62.

8. This point is well made by Hume in his *Dialogues Concerning Natural
Religion*, op. cit., p. 245.

9. *Concluding an Unscientific Postscript*, trans by D. F. Swenson and W.
Lowrie, (Princeton University Press, 1941), Book I, Part II, Ar. 2.

10. Previously discussed in chapter 4, pp. 183–184.

11. What do we mean? It's tempting to say that what we mean is that
the prediction is true in the sense that it corresponds to the fact. The fact is
what the statement says it is. Although this is perhaps the best answer, it can
lead into all sorts of philosophical labyrinths—What is a fact? What is meant
by "correspond"? and so on.

12. By a theistic world I mean a world like the one that Descartes had
in mind.

13. *Lectures and Conversations on Aesthetics, Psychology and Religious
Belief*, edited by Barrett, (Oxford: Basil Blackwell, 1966), p. 53.

6

Problems of Philosophy

INTRODUCTION

It was mentioned at the end of chapter 4 that if we were unable to show that God exists, it would look as though we had no reason to believe that there is an external world beyond our immediate sensations. What I now want to do is to argue that this belief is unfounded and that even without a divine guarantee, we have no reason to doubt that there is an external world.

However, the path that I shall follow toward this goal is circuitous. I shall begin with a discussion of the free will problem and the mind-body problem, and only then shall I go on to discuss skepticism concerning the existence and nature of the external world. My reasons for following this roundabout route are as follows: (a) I think that the mind-body problem and the free will problem are best discussed together, and (b) we will not be in a position to deal with our skeptical doubts about the external world until we are clear on what the relationship is between the mind and the body.

HUMAN FREEDOM AND THE MIND-BODY PROBLEM

The primary problem concerning human freedom is that, on the one hand, we feel we are free to act in alternative ways—there is a pencil sitting in front of me and I am free to go ahead and pick it up or not pick it up. On the other hand, we live in a physical world where everything that happens is causally determined by what went before. Furthermore, the human body, including the brain, belongs to the physical world, and so it is reasonable to assume that everything that happens in the body and the brain has been causally determined by what has gone before.[1] The problem of determinism can also be raised on other levels. For example, it might be said that we are not free, because we are psychologically determined in everything that we do, or that we are sociologically determined in everything that we do. However, neither of these forms of determinism seems to be as threatening to human freedom as physical determinism. I may be sociologically determined not to walk around in the nude, and I may be psychologically determined to make certain types of errors, but it could hardly be said that either brings into doubt my present freedom to pick up the pencil that is lying in front of me. Furthermore, if I am psychologically determined in everything that I do, this kind of determinism is most likely reducible to neurological determinism, which, of course, is really physical determinism.

There are two ways that people have dealt with the problem of physical determinism, i.e., the problem that everything that happens in the physical world appears to be causally determined by what went before. The first way is to postulate the existence of a Cartesian type of mind. The mind is internally free, independent of the body, and capable of interacting with it. My picking up of the pencil (let's assume that I went ahead and picked it up) is a free act because it was brought about by a free act on the part of the mind. The second way is to assume that the mind is not independent of the body, that everything that goes on in the mind is determined by what goes on in the body. Even so, free action is possible, for it's possible for an act to be both free and determined at the same time. In other words freedom and determinism are compatible.

PHYSICAL DETERMINISM AND THE CARTESIAN MIND

We have seen that *Cartesian dualism* is a difficult position to hold. The chief difficulty is that it seems inconceivable that something mental, say a thought or a desire, could causally bring about a physical happening like the lifting of a pencil. At the same time, people have been attracted to it because it seems to offer a neat solution to the free will problem. However, let us put these difficulties concerning interaction to one side and ascertain the extent to which we can say we are free if Cartesian dualism is postulated. What this investigation will show, I think, is that the concept of human freedom, even in the most favored theoretical situation, is not as clear as we might at first think it is.

Let us begin with the very simple action of choosing what we desire the most. Suppose I am at a cocktail party and I have to choose between a scotch and soda and a gin and tonic. The waiter has brought around a tray with both types of drinks and has asked me to take one. Now even though I desire the scotch and soda much more than the other, I would, at first glance, say that if I take the scotch and soda, I freely take it because I believe that I *could have done otherwise*. I could have taken the gin and tonic or nothing at all for that matter. Some people will say that one must always act on the basis of the strongest desire, but unless the strongest desire is defined as the one that one always acts on, there seems little reason to believe that this is so.

But even if we assume that it is possible to not act on the strongest desire, there are still puzzles. Suppose that even though I prefer a scotch and soda, I decide to have a gin and tonic, and therefore take one. Since my act of taking a gin and tonic is a result of my *deciding* to take a gin and tonic, it can only be a free act if my deciding to take a gin and tonic is a free act. Or, so it would seem. But was my decision a free act? It would seem that in order for it to be a free act I must have freely decided to decide to have a gin and tonic. But nothing of this sort happened, nor do we have any idea what it would be like for it to happen. All that happened is that I found myself deciding to have a gin and tonic.

But this isn't the only area where we find puzzles. When I remember something, it seems inconceivable that I could have freely remembered it. I can't freely remember that the meter has expired on my parking place. In order to do this I would have to choose to remember this rather than something else. But in order to choose, I have to have already remembered! Memories simply occur to us. Of course we can freely concentrate on certain areas—I'm trying to remember the kings and queens of England—but what I remember simply occurs.

Or suppose I am working out the puzzle of how the farmer can get the fox, the goose, and the bag of grain across the river in a rowboat that will only hold the farmer and one of the other three.[2] I think and think about this and suddenly I say "I know," and then give the solution. We want to say that I freely chose that answer, but at the same time there is a sense in which I didn't choose the answer. The solution simply came to me, almost as though someone had whispered it in my ear.

I shan't attempt to deal with these problems now. My reason for mentioning them is only to point out that the concept of human freedom, even in its purest form, is very, very obscure. Even if we assume that the mind is free and does control the body, we are still faced with puzzles when we try to spell out what this freedom is.

However, not many people nowadays subscribe to the theory of Cartesian dualism. The idea of a little ghost in a physiological machine strikes modern thinkers as too silly for words. Perhaps it can be represented in a different form—and I shall attempt to do so. But the idea that there is a place in the brain where the mind and the brain interact has to be rejected.

If we reject this account of the relation between mind and matter, what have we got left?[3] First of all, there is materialism of the kind espoused by Lucretius.[4] But this theory also seems to require rejection. If the world consists of nothing more than space and atoms, it's difficult to see how consciousness is possible. It seems that no matter how complex the arrangement of atoms, no consciousness will result.

Second, there is *epiphenomenalism*, which was popular with such nineteenth-century thinkers as T. H. Huxley. This theory claimed that mental phenomena, through a brute fact about the world, are the spin-off of underlying neurological processes in the brain. Epiphenomenalists did talk at times about the emergence of consciousness. The idea behind this is that through evolution the brain of a species becomes sufficiently complex to provide for the emergence of consciousness. That is to say, members of the species become capable of experiencing the world around them. Now if our point about materialism of the kind offered by Lucretius is correct, then we would have to accept that no amount of neurological complexity could ever lead to the emergence of consciousness. Mental phenomena would have to be accepted as brute fact.[5] In any case, according to epiphenomenalism, just as the sparks created by the blacksmith are caused by, but play no role in, the forging of a horseshoe, so mental phenomena are caused by what goes on in the brain, but have no effect upon the brain. They are only the sparks of the higher regions of the natural world. For example, I see a mosquito land on my arm. I decide to swat it and do so. I think it was my seeing that resulted in my deciding, and my deciding that resulted in my swatting. But this is not so. The physiological process of the light waves from the mosquito entering my eyes and so on, somehow resulted in my having a mental image of the mosquito, but my having the mental image was not the cause of my deciding, nor was my deciding the cause of my swatting. The physiological process of the light waves entering my eyes, and so on, resulted also in a neurological change, which was the cause of my "deciding" to swat, and that neurological process in turn was the cause of my hand moving in the way required to swat the mosquito. If P_1 etc., stand for physiological *cum* neurological events, and M_1 etc., stand for mental events, we think that what happened might look like this:

A

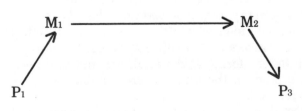

where P_1 is the physiological process of lightwaves entering the eyes from the mosquito,

M_1 is the seeing of the mosquito,

M_2 is the deciding to swat, and

P_3 is the swatting.

But really it looks something like this:

B

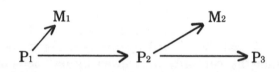

We think that the mental event of deciding (M_2) was a result of the mental event of seeing (M_1) and the cause of the physiological event of swatting (P_3), but we are mistaken. We think that both events are a part of the causal nexus, but both events are merely epiphenomena.[6]

There are two difficulties with this theory. The first is that (again) it's difficult to see how a physical-neurological event can result in a mental event—how the physiological process of the lightwave entering the eye, etc., can result in being presented with a mental image of the mosquito. The second difficulty: It seems internally certain that the deciding to swat results in the swatting of the mosquito. How can we be mistaken over something as obvious as this?

Third, we have the *identity theory*. This offers, I think, a much more promising account of the relation between mind and matter. According to this theory, mental events are neither caused by, nor are they the cause of, neurological events—they are identical with neurological events that cause and are caused by other neurological events. Not all neurological events are identical with mental events, but all mental events are identical with neurological events. It might be objected that neurological events can't be identical with mental events, because if they were, then most people would know that they were. For example, a crèche is identical with a nursery even though there are many people who do not know that the words "crèche" and "nursery" mean the same, but—and this is the point—once they knew, they would not doubt that a crèche is a nursery. The situation, so it is argued, is altogether different with mental events. Not only do we not know that some neurological events are identical with mental events, but this is something that is doubted by many.

The standard reply to this objection is to point out that even though many identities, as in the crèche case, are a consequence of the ways that words have been defined, not all are. Some identities are non-definitional; they are facts about the world. For example, suppose I visit the home of a famous but humble author. I ask the housekeeper where the author's desk is, and she replies that his desk is that old packing case. Here the identity between the desk and the packing case is clearly a contingent matter. It might have turned out to be something else. Here is another example: recently it was discovered that a gene is a molecule of DNA. Again, even though each gene is identical with a molecule of DNA, the identity between the two is a contingent matter.

The main trouble with identity theory is that although one has no difficulty in seeing how a desk could be a packing case or a gene a molecule, one does have difficulty in seeing how a thought could be a neurological event. They seem to belong to such different logical categories. Notice, for example, that the neurological event, like the packing case and the desk, can be viewed by many different people, but the thought, qua thought, can only be viewed by one person—given that it makes sense to talk about a thought being viewed. Notice also that although it is logically possible for a caveman who lived long, long ago to have the same thing going on in his brain as I have when I think that John Turner was a Prime Minister of Canada in 1984, it is logically impossible for him to have that thought. To have this thought he would have to know who Turner is, what Canada is, and so on. Therefore the thought, or at least *that* thought, cannot be identical with a neurological process.

If we accept either epiphenomenalism or the identity theory, we must accept universal determinism. If I have the thought that I would like a gin and tonic, and that thought is identical with or caused by a neurological event in my brain, then since that neurological event was caused, the thought that I would like a gin and tonic was also caused. However, we mustn't let pessimism gain the upper hand. Many authors have argued that human freedom and determinism are compatible, in the sense that the same event can be both free and caused at the same time. Trying to show that determinism and freedom are compatible may strike the reader as difficult, like trying to show that an object can be spherical and cubical in shape at the same time; and so should be ignored as a waste of time. However, 'freedom' and 'determinism', as will shortly be pointed out, are not quite as contradictory as they might appear to be at first glance. This brings us to the second of the two ways (mentioned on page 226) that the problem of physical determinism can be dealt with—i.e., the attempt to show that freedom and determinism are compatible.

COMPATIBILISM

There are two approaches that people have used in their attempt to show that freedom and determinism are compatible. The first approach comes from David Hume via twentieth-century Viennese philosopher Moritz Schlick.[7] The second comes from the recent Cambridge philosopher G. E. Moore.[8] According to Schlick, freedom is compatible with determinism because the opposite of freedom is not determinism but coercion, while the opposite of determinism is not freedom but indeterminism. When we say, for example, that falling bodies are determined to fall at 32 ft. per sec.[2], we are not saying that they are forced or coerced to fall at this rate. All we are saying is that we have discovered that they do, and are predicting that they will. Of course falling bodies will act in accordance with the law of gravity, but that law does not force objects to fall at a rate. It is not a prescriptive law. All it does is describe, in a general way, how objects do fall, and predict how they will fall. In short, the reason that determinism is claimed to be compatible with freedom is that when we say an event is determined, all we mean is that it is covered by or can be predicted by a general (true) statement. But this needn't deter us from saying that the event is free, for the same event can be both free and predictable. If I were to throw handfuls of twenty-dollar bills around in a shopping plaza, I can predict that many people will freely run about trying to pick them up. The predictability of their actions does not detract from the freedom of their actions. Picking up twenty-dollar bills is just what we would expect free and rational people to do.

Indeed, Schlick goes on to say, not only can an event be both free and determined at the same time, it can't really be free unless it is determined. A free act is one that is brought about by the wishes and wants of the agent. If the act was not determined it would be indeterminate. It would be cut loose from the wishes and wants of the agent. If I were suddenly to start throwing my arms about in a wild way for no reason, my act might be a random, indeterminate act, but it could hardly be said to be a free act.

Furthermore, our whole social system of punishments and rewards assumes that human acts are determined, at least by the agent. We do not punish a person for the acts he performs while he is in a hypnotic trance. We do not do so, because he is not the source of his actions. There would be no point in doing so, because the punishment would not modify his future behavior; it would have no effect upon his future behavior. We only punish a person for the acts that are a consequence of his thoughts and feelings. We hope that by changing his thoughts and feelings through punishment, we will change the way that he behaves in the future.

There are a number of things wrong with this attempt to show that freedom and determinism are compatible. First of all, the sort of freedom we are talking about is quite compatible with coercion. If I am kept in a room and told that if I try to escape I will be beaten, then we would say that I can, of my own free will, walk out, if the door is open, and be beaten. Of course, if the armed guards are in the pay of a ruthless dictator, then I would most likely have no political freedom. But political freedom is not the sort of freedom that we are talking about here. The only sort of situation where coercion would jeopardize my (human) freedom would be where, for example, I was so afraid of being beaten that I could not move my legs.

Second, is physical determinism just a matter of predictability? Surely when one billiard ball comes in contact with another, it forces the other to move. Of course it's always logically possible that the second might not move. It's conceivable that it might disappear, or the first ball might move through it. But this only means that there is no internal contradiction in the description of the envisioned situation. The fact that the first ball doesn't logically determine or, in other words, *logically* force the second ball to move in no way implies that it doesn't *physically* force the second ball to move. We can conclude, then, that to say one event physically determined the occurrence of another is to say more than just that from the occurrence of the first event the occurrence of the second event can be predicted.

But even if we accept that determinism means no more than predictability, we still have a problem on our hands. Suppose we have two apartment blocks; in one block we have a conscientious and reliable janitor who has been instructed to turn the furnace on when the temperature drops to 20°C, and off when it reaches 22°C. In the other block we have a thermostat that has been set to turn the furnace (in that block) on at 20°C and off at 22°C. Now if by 'determinism' we just mean 'predictability', then we can say of the janitor that his actions are both free and determined, for we can predict his actions with the greatest of accuracy. But why can't we also say that the thermostat is free? If showing that 'determinism' means 'predictability' makes it possible to say that the janitor is free, then there is nothing to preclude us from saying that the thermostat is also free. This is not only something that we don't want to say, it's something that is absurd to say. It is absurd to say that the thermostat is free. A thermostat is simply not the sort of thing that can or cannot be free. Therefore, we must conclude that 'physical determinism' means more than 'predictability'.

Given that 'physical determinism' does not mean 'predictability', and given that every mental event is physically determined by what went before in the same way that everything that the thermostat does is determined by what went before, then just as we are reluctant to attribute freedom to a thermostat, so we should also be reluctant to attribute freedom to a person. In short, we are faced with the following dilemma: either we just mean 'predictability' by 'determinism' or we do not. If we do, then there is no reason for not saying that the thermostat is free. If we do not, then we have no reason for saying that the janitor is free.

Even though we are for these reasons obliged to give up Schlick's attempt to show that physical determinism and human freedom are compatible, there is still one point that can be drawn from it that is worth noting. If we accept that mental events are determined by physical (neurological) events, then whether we accept that these physical events are completely determined, partly determined, or completely indeterminate, we have a problem. We saw that Lucretius thought that partial indeterminancy would save the day for freedom. But if my thoughts and actions are the result of the partial indeterminate behavior of the molecules in my brain, my thoughts and actions are no more free than if the behavior of those molecules were completely determined. This is why the Heisenberg *principle of indeterminancy* cannot be invoked to save the day for freedom. Schlick saw that if we postulate physical indeterminism, it is difficult to account for human freedom, but he failed to see that if we postulate physical determinism, it's also difficult to account for human freedom. This is one reason human freedom is such a profoundly paradoxical topic.

Let's now move on to the second approach. This approach was used by Moore and his followers.[9] According to Moore, to say that someone, say Smith, freely did *x*—or, in other words, did *x*, of his own free will— is to say that Smith could have done otherwise. And to say of a man, say James, who did *y*, that he did not do *y* of his own free will, perhaps because he was hypnotized, is to say that James could not have done otherwise. So far so good. But now the fun begins. Next it is claimed that what we mean when we say 'Smith could have done otherwise' is 'Smith would have done otherwise if he had chosen'. This is claimed to be compatible with determinism because, so it is argued, he could have been determined to choose to do *x*. Therefore, freedom and determinism are compatible.

Sometimes the argument takes a different form. 'Smith could have done otherwise' is taken to mean 'Smith would have done otherwise if he had desired to do otherwise'. This, again, is claimed to be compatible with determinism. Smith was determined to have the desires he had, and he was determined to act upon those desires.[10]

Let us examine the second version first. When it is said that someone could have done otherwise, much more is being suggested than that he would have done otherwise if he had desired otherwise. It is also being suggested that even if he had not desired otherwise, he still could have done otherwise. Here, it should also be noted, 'could' is not reflecting our limited knowledge. Sometimes when a china plate falls on the floor and does not break, we say something like "You must be more careful, that plate *could* have broken." In this case, all we are suggesting is that from the limited information we have about the height from which the plate was dropped, the composition of the floor, etc., we cannot draw the conclusion that the plate would not break. Or, in other words, we are suggesting that we could not be certain that the plate will not break. We are not suggesting that the plate had a will of its own and might have done otherwise. In the case of Smith, the situation is entirely different. Here we *are* suggesting that Smith has a will of his own and could, regardless of his desires, have acted differently.

In the first version, these points are even more obvious. We may take 'Smith could have done otherwise' to mean 'Smith would have done otherwise if he had chosen', but this is not compatible with determinism, for Smith's choice (logically) could not have been determined. If what we take to be a choice is determined, then it is no choice at all. If Smith said "Now I shall do *x*" and then went ahead and did *x* because he had been hypnotized to say this and hypnotized to do it, then we would say that he didn't really choose to do *x*. Or take a different case. Suppose that a small programmed computer is implanted in Smith's brain. The computer is programmed so that at t_1 Smith will say "I now choose to do *x*," and at t_2 (which is immediately afterwards) Smith will do *x*. Again, it's clear that if these events come to pass, Smith didn't choose. He said "Now I choose . . ." but these words do not express a choice.

It also seems fairly clear that Smith didn't really do *x*. Of course *x* was done, but nobody did it. If the wind blows and, as a consequence, a tree falls on a man who is walking along the road, something happened, but the tree didn't do anything. The tree fell on the man, but this is not something that the tree did. To suggest that the tree did something is to speak anthropomorphically—it is to suggest that the tree is a person.

We can conclude, then, that neither attempt at showing freedom and determinism to be compatible will work. The first approach gives us no good reason for not also attributing freedom to thermostats and to similar machines, and this is not only something we do not want to do, it is something we think it would be absurd to do. The second is no more than a piece of linguistic sleight of hand. It fails to realize that 'Smith could have done otherwise' cannot be analyzed as 'Smith would have done otherwise if he had chosen', if what is taken as a choice is determined by what went before. For if it was determined, then it wasn't really a choice.

Furthermore, the 'could' in 'Smith could have done otherwise' is very different from the 'could' in 'The dice could have fallen otherwise'. The first reflects our belief in Smith's freedom, while the second reflects our lack of information about the height from which the dice were dropped, the way they were held, and that sort of thing. If we think that what we take to be Smith's choice was determined, then we must retract the claim that he could have done otherwise.

We may conclude, then, that whether we accept epiphenomenalism or identity theory, it is impossible to show that freedom and determinism are compatible. If we have accepted that our thoughts are rigidly determined by, or identical with, what goes on in our brains, then human freedom is utterly inexplicable. What all this suggests is that if we are going to explain how human freedom is possible, we must give a new account of the relation of the mental to the physical. Unless we can come up with something new we shall have to accept defeat and admit not only that human freedom does not exist, but that it could not exist.

A DIFFERENT APPROACH

The Mind and the Body

I now want to offer an example that may point toward a new account of the relation between the mental and the physical. I think it will be possible on the basis of this account to solve our nagging problem concerning human freedom.

Imagine the following situation: a boy named George is sitting in a classroom looking at the teacher, and the teacher asks him to go to the blackboard and add 2 and 3. Let's assume that the boy does as he is asked and gets the correct answer. There are two radically different ways that we could describe what happens. First we could say that the boy hears the teacher's request and decides to obey. He rises from his seat and walks toward the board. Upon arriving at the board, he picks up a piece of chalk, and with the chalk he adds 2 and 3 and obtains 5. The second way would be a physiological account that begins with a complete description of the sound waves (in terms of length, intensity, and so on) that left the teacher's mouth when she asked George to go to the board and add 2 and 3. No doubt it would be difficult to give a complete description, but perhaps with the help of graphs the task could be carried out. This account would continue with a description of how the sound waves affected the eardrum, how these in turn affected the inner ear, and finally how this in turn resulted in certain changes in George's brain. At present, we are not in a position to give a description of this sort, for we have little idea of how the brain works; though we expect that some day, when the brain has been more fully mapped, such a description will be possible. Our second account would continue with a description of how the goings on in the brain ultimately resulted in the movements of the legs, which caused George's body to rise from the chair and be propelled forward toward the board. Finally, it would conclude with an account of the neurological process that resulted in George picking up the piece of chalk, making a mark that looks like this—"2," a second that looks like this—"+," a third that looks like this—"3," a fourth that looks like this—"=," and finally one that looks like this—"5." Again, today we couldn't begin to offer such a description, but still, we do have some idea of how it would go.

Now, the thing to notice here is that each account is complete in itself, nothing more needs to be added. It might be thought that the physiological account is more basic and so more complete, but there are all sorts of things that this account leaves out—things that are inexpressible within it. In the physiological account there couldn't be any mention of the teacher *asking* the boy to go to the board and add 2 and 3, nor could there be any talk of the boy *deciding* to obey the request, and *walking* to the board; and finally, there couldn't be any mention of the boy *adding* 2 and 3.

According to the Cartesians, our physiological account would be incomplete until we showed how the proper impulses were transferred from the brain to the mind and how the mind in turn brought about certain changes in the brain. But as we have already seen, the interaction between the mind and the brain, which this account presupposes, is inexplicable. Furthermore, what the boy experiences is the teacher asking him to go to the board and add 2 and 3. He doesn't experience neurological impulses being passed on to him (the mind) for interpretation. He doesn't experience effecting certain changes in his brain, which result in his body rising from his chair. What he experiences is deciding to rise from his chair and getting up. For these reasons, as well as for those already mentioned, the Cartesian picture of how the mind interacts with the brain must be laid to rest.

The difference between the two ways that we can talk about George is much greater than might be thought. In fact, the difference is so great that we might almost say that we have two different languages. When we talk about George as a person, it makes perfectly good sense to say that he heard, he decided, he looked, he walked, he added, and so on. But when we talk about George as a physiological organism, it makes no sense to say any of these things. Here we say such things as light waves entered the eyes, impulses were sent along the optic nerves, certain synapses opened and others closed, and so on.

We must now ask the dark question, why are there these two languages that can be used to talk about human beings? Why do we have these two radically different ways of talking about George? The only answer that can be offered here is that we really have two radically different entities. We have George the person, who hears, looks, thinks, walks, adds, and so on, and we have George the physiological organism, that has sound wave receptors, light receptors, a brain that manipulates impulses, and the like. But doesn't this get us back to the puzzles of Cartesian dualism? No, not at all. George is not a physiological organism with a mind behind it. When George looks at something, it's not the case that light waves ultimately cause a mental image to be presented to the mind; rather, it's that in having light waves affect his brain in a certain way, George looks at something. This view does not recognize a mind per se; there is only the person and the organism. No doubt George could not look at the teacher if he didn't have eyes and a brain set up in the proper way, but he doesn't look at the teacher as a *consequence* of having eyes and a brain that are stimulated in a certain way. Rather, in having eyes and a properly set up brain that is stimulated in a certain way, George looks at the teacher. The act of looking at the teacher is not to be identified with the physiological process. The two can't be identical since the description of each belongs to a language that cannot be translated into the other. Nor is the physiological process the cause of the looking. Again, this cannot be the case. Events that can be described in physiological language can only be the cause of events that can also be described in that language. It does not even make sense to say that events of the one type are the cause of events of the other type. All we can say is that a certain physiological process takes place when George looks at the teacher. It might be thought that this claim has exceptions. For example, it might be said that someone saw the image of a pink elephant because he was taking an hallucinogenic drug. The drug, it will be claimed, is the cause of the experience of seeming to see a pink elephant. But this way of talking is, I suggest, mistaken. The taking of the drug causes certain changes to take place in the brain. When these changes take place in the brain, the person seems to see a pink elephant. But strictly speaking, his seeming to see a pink elephant is not caused by the changes that take place in the brain. It's rather that, in having the changes take place in the brain, the person seems to see the pink elephant. Similarly, the pain I experience when I sit on a pin is not caused by the pin. It causes certain neurological changes and, in undergoing these changes, I experience pain. But strictly speaking, the pain and other sensations that I experience are not caused by the neurological changes. This point, however, should not deter us from saying in everyday discourse that pins can cause pain.

It might also be objected that the fact that we have two radically different ways of talking about George, or anybody else, doesn't imply that we have two entities—the person and the organism—for we can talk in these two radically different ways about a computer or even a hand-held calculator, and we wouldn't want to say that the computer or calculator consists of two entities. For example, suppose you press the "2" button, then the "plus" button, and then the "3" button on a calculator. It could be said that during the time between when the "3" was pressed and the "5" appeared, the calculator was adding 2 and 3. But one could also say that during that time certain changes were occurring in the circuit of the calculator. This wouldn't lead one to say that in addition to the mechanical entity there was also a mental entity. There is, however, a difference between the calculator and George. George can be considered both an organism and a person (though not at the same time), but the calculator can only be considered a mechanism. Of course, the calculator can be thought of *as if* it were a person, but it cannot be thought of *as* a person. Let me attempt to make this point clearer. Suppose that, instead of a modern solid state calculator, we have an old fashioned mechanical calculator, one that is filled with wheels, gears, and levers that are big enough to watch as they go around. The mechanism is designed in such a way that when I press the lever with the mark "2" on it, the lever with the mark "+" on it, and the lever with the mark "3" on it, the last wheel with the mark "5" on it moves around so that that mark faced the viewer. The calculator doesn't *do* any adding; in fact, it doesn't do anything. As a result of the operator initiating certain mechanical changes, other mechanical changes take place. Of course, what happened can be understood *as if* the calculator is adding. Indeed, the calculator is designed so that will happen. But it cannot be said of the calculator, as it can be said of George, that it really adds.

Let me attempt to present the whole argument once again. We find in this world that we have two radically different ways that we can talk about human beings. We can talk about them as physiological organisms to which things happen, and we can talk about them as persons who do things. These two ways are so different that they are almost like different languages—one cannot be translated into the other. When George looked at his teacher a physiological change took place within him, but to say that George looked at his teacher is not to say that a physiological process took place. We cannot translate the statement 'George looked at his teacher' into one or more statements about physiological processes. Why then do we have these two different ways of talking about persons? The only possible answer must be that there are two entities—the person and the organism—not in tandem, as the Cartesians suggest, but together. When we say that George watched the teacher, we are talking about the person, and when we say that light waves from the teacher caused the brain to be affected in a certain way, we are talking about the organism.

Someone might object that if George is identical with the organism called "George" and also identical with the person called "George," it must follow that the person called "George" is identical with the organism called "George." (If *A* is identical with *B* and also with *C*, it follows that *B* is identical with *C*.) This would be a mistake. When we say "George looked at the teacher," 'George' is not being used in the same manner as when we say "George was affected by lightwaves in such and such a way." In the first sentence, it is used as a part of the "person" language and refers to the person; and in the second sentence, it is used as a part of the "physical" language and refers to the physiological organism.[11] In certain contexts this difference can be felt. Compare the use of "George" in "After carefully examining the situation, George decided that decisive action was required," with the use of "George" in "The famous surgeon said to his students 'If the orderly will hurry up and bring George in on the operating trolley, I'll demonstrate to you how the gall bladder is to be removed.' "

Finally, the following objection might be raised. If "physiological organisms" and "person" belong to different languages, and if neither is translatable into the other, then claims such as "The organism George is not the person George" simply cannot be made. In order to make such claims, it would have to be possible to translate each language into the other, and this, *ex hypothesi*, is impossible. This objection is well taken. Strictly speaking, such statements as "The physiological entity is not identical with the person" cannot be made. Or, even more strictly speaking, sentences of this sort are ill-formed and do not express statements.

Even though what these sentences attempt to express cannot be expressed, it can be shown. The fact that we have these two radically different and untranslatable ways of talking, *shows* that we have two radically different entities. It also explains why we are misled and stumble when we attempt to talk about the relation between the two entities. How, it might be asked, can there be the person George and the physiological organism in the same place at the same time? If they are there at the same time, is the person George like a ghost that interpenetrates the organism? And if he is, then what is the relationship between this ghost and the organism? All these misleading questions are a result of assuming that the organism and the person can be talked about in the same breath.

Even though the sentence "The person George is not the organism George" does not express a statement, the sentence "We have two radically different languages and 'George,' when it is used in one refers to a different entity than when it is used in the other," does express a statement. There is nothing ill-formed about this. As long as it is possible to make statements of this latter sort, it is possible to state our case. Or, to adopt a distinction once made fashionable by Rudolf Carnap, what cannot be expressed in the material mode can be expressed in the formal mode.

Descartes said that the mind and the body were different substances. What he meant by a substance is something that is not dependent upon something else and did not need to be explained in terms of something else. Descartes's concepts of mental substance and of physical substance were obscure, as we saw in chapter 4, but at least it can be gleaned from them that he recognized the mental to be very different from the material and could not be thought of as a strange sort of matter. Descartes claimed, and rightly so, that he was not, as he put it, "something subtle like air or fire or ether mingled amongst the grosser parts of his body." But Descartes did not conceptually distance his idea of a mind far enough from that of an organism, and this is why he was led to think that there was an entity called the mind that lurked mysteriously behind the brain. We begin to see matters clearly when we realize that there are not two entities, one behind the other, that can be talked about in the same breath, but rather there are two radically different ways that we can talk about our fellow human beings. When we talk about the George, who sees, hears, thinks, loves, and laughs, 'George' picks out the person who sees, hears, and so on; but when we talk about the George whose brain is not receiving sharp impulses from his eyes, because of the presence of a tumor on his optic nerve, 'George' picks out the physiological organism whose optic nerve has been affected in the aforementioned way. We can use 'George' to pick out the person, and we can use 'George' to pick out the physiological organism, but we cannot use 'George' for both at the same time.

Human Freedom

We are now in a position to deal once again with the problem of human freedom. Let us return to George. We can say that George, upon hearing the request from the teacher, decided of his own free will to obey. George could have done otherwise. He could have stayed in his seat and glowered at the teacher. Of course, George might have been compelled. He might have been so frightened of the teacher that, when she cast her evil eye upon him, he literally found himself rising from his chair and moving toward the blackboard. But unless we can point to a reason for saying that George acted under a compulsion of this sort, we would have to say that George acted freely. Indeed the normal action is the free action. Many of the verbs in our "person" language assume that the agent could have done otherwise. In saying that a person rose, walked, added, and so on, we presuppose that the agent could have done otherwise. Doing presupposes freedom. There are exceptions: for example, hearing, seeing, and understanding. But these are not, strictly speaking, "doing" verbs. "Hearing," "seeing," and "understanding" may not presuppose freedom, but "listening," "watching" and "reflecting" do.

When we talk about George the organism, the opposite is the case. Here it is assumed that every physiological/neurological happening is a causal result of what went before. We cannot make the connection now but it is assumed that someday we will be able to establish a causal link between the sound waves that entered George's ears with the contraction of the muscles that caused his body to rise from the seat. Not only is determinism assumed, but it doesn't make any sense to talk here about freedom. Could an impulse freely move down a nerve? Is a synapse at liberty to open and close? The questions do not begin to make sense.

So what we find is that of the two radically different ways we have of talking, one way presupposes that what is before us (the person George) is free, while the other way presupposes that what is before us (the organism George) is determined, in the sense that everything that happens to the organism is determined by what went before. The determinism is as strong as, but no stronger than, the determinism we find in the case of the thermostat.

We found difficulty in attributing freedom to the person George because we did not distinguish clearly enough between the person and the organism. Since George, as organism, is subject to determinism, we thought that George, as person, is also subject to determinism. But once we distinguish between the two entities that can only be talked about in two different languages, we are no longer tempted to consider George the person subject to determinism. Indeed, in speaking about George the person, we presuppose that George is free. The person-language pre-supposes freedom.

But now it will be objected that if the movement of George's right arm was determined when he added 2 and 3 on the black board, he didn't freely move his arm—he could not have done otherwise. What George the person does cannot be out of step with what happens to George the organism. And since everything that happens to the organism is determined, everything that George the person does is also determined. This is probably the most serious objection that can be brought against this solution. Let's begin to answer it by recalling what was said in the chapter on Descartes about the compatibility of logical determinism and thinking freely (pp. 181–182). There it was pointed out that to think freely was to think consistently, and that means to think in accordance with the laws of logic. If I believe that if it's raining then the streets are wet, and I also believe that it's raining, then there is one belief that I will not find myself having, and that is that the streets are not wet. In fact, I shall most likely find myself believing that the streets are wet. Free and rational thinking will prevent me from believing that the streets are not wet. The thing to be noted here is that I cannot think correctly and freely unless my brain is functioning properly. In order for me to arrive freely at the right conclusion through deduction, my brain must function properly. It is not the case that what is going on in my brain causes me to have certain thoughts. We have already seen that we cannot in the same breath talk about the person who thinks and the processes that go on in the organism. Rather, in order for me, the person, to think freely and correctly, the brain of the organism Patrick Mackenzie must be functioning in the proper way. And, as we have seen, we have good reason to believe that everything that happens in the brain is determined by what went before.

Let's return to George. Suppose that George has already written "2 + 3 =" on the board and is deciding what to do next. First of all, if George is a rational agent and accepts that "1 = 1," and that "2 = 1 + 1," and so on, then having asked himself what 2 + 3 equals, he will arrive at 5 as the correct answer. Suppose that he arrives at 5. True, in order for George to arrive at 5, his brain would have to be working in a rigidly determined way; but George doesn't arrive at 5 on the basis of what is going on in his brain, but on the basis of adding 2 and 3. Assume that George has yet to write anything on the board. He could write "5," he could write another number, or he could glower at the teacher and write nothing. Suppose that George decided to write "5." Again, in order for George to decide to write "5," his brain would have to be functioning properly. Unless his brain was functioning properly he would be incapable of reaching any decision, but his decision would not be caused by what went on in the brain. No claim of this sort makes any sense at all. If the alleged decision was caused, then it wasn't a decision after all. In order to count as a decision it would have to be based on beliefs, perhaps about what he thought was the best thing to do. Next, suppose that George, upon deciding to write 5, goes ahead and writes "5." Again, in order for him to do so, his brain would have to be working properly, and the goings on in his brain would have to cause his right hand to move in a certain way. But it doesn't follow from this that George's *act of writing* 5 was not a free act. This was the result of the decision to write 5; it was not the result of the goings on in the brain, even though the movements that his hand made when the act was performed were (causally) the result of what was going on in the brain.

So, to return to the original objection, it was claimed that when George wrote 5 on the board, he couldn't have done otherwise, because the movement of his arm was fully determined by what had happened before. We can see that this claim is mistaken. The movement of his arm was fully determined, yet his writing on the board was a free act because he could have arrived at a different decision. Granted, he would not have arrived at a different decision unless something different had been going on in his brain; still, the decision was not a result of what was going on in the brain. The decision was the result of the beliefs he happened to hold at that time. Again, there is no doubt that in order to have those beliefs something particular had to be going on in his brain. But those beliefs would have been derived from evidence that could only have been derived if his brain was functioning properly. Suppose that his decision was based on the belief that the teacher would keep him after school if he didn't answer this question correctly. Now if this belief of George's is correct, then given that it wasn't a lucky guess, he would only have arrived at this belief if the organism George was functioning in a proper but fully determined way.

Some people will not be happy with this answer. They will feel that if this is the best that can be done, assuming that the distinction between mind and body is only a reflection of the fact that there are two radically different ways of viewing a human being, then Descartes must have been right after all. There must be a mind that can reach decisions independently of the body. However, as we have noticed, even under Cartesian assumptions the concept of human freedom remains obscure. Although it makes sense to talk about free actions, the idea of a free decision upon which those actions are based remains in a fog of obscurity. When I say that I freely took the gin and tonic, I mean that I could have done otherwise. What I mean when I say that I could have done othewise is that I would have done otherwise if I had decided otherwise.[12] If this is right, then it must follow that when I say that I freely decided to have a gin and tonic, what I mean is that I could have decided otherwise. What this means, so it might be argued, is that I would have decided otherwise if I had decided to decide otherwise. But what can *this* mean? It makes no sense to talk about deciding to decide.[13] If this is so, it can make no sense to talk about a free decision. Thus we can see that no matter what hypothesis we accept, we have puzzles about freedom.

At this point, some people might be tempted to raise the following objection to my thesis: If the boy's decision is not free, then the act that is based on it is also not free. But since we have no reason to believe that the decision is free—indeed, it makes no sense to say that it is free—it follows that the act is not free. The idea behind this objection is that if *a* causes *b*, then if *a* is not free neither is *b*.

The main error in such an objection is simply this: just because a decision cannot be said to be free, it does not follow that the act that issues from the decision is also not free. A free act simply is an act that is based on a decision.[14] If decisions were the sorts of things that (logically) could be free or not free, then the fact that a given decision was not free would count as a reason for saying that the action following from it is not free. But since it doesn't make sense to say that either a decision is or is not free, nothing follows about a given act from the fact that the decision upon which it is based cannot be said to be free.

To conclude, the solution to the free will problem seems to be this. We have in the world, along with other things, persons and human organisms. We think about persons in and through the person language, and we think of human organisms in and through the physiological-neurological language. When we think of persons, it is presupposed that they are free. We only doubt this in cases where special reasons can be presented: for example, when the person in question is hypnotized, drugged, or demented. When we think of physiological organisms, it is presupposed that they are determined. Even if it could be shown that some of the processes internal to an organism were partly indeterminate, this would give us no reason to say that the organism was free. In fact we have no idea of what it would be like for an organism to be free. The idea makes no sense to us.

It might be suggested that the "person language" with its free will presupposition is an old-fashioned vehicle for thinking about human beings—that it ought to be scraped for the more modern, streamlined language of physiology. This move has been suggested by a number of people but it seems impossible to give it up. Can we doubt that we think, believe, doubt, desire, walk, write things on blackboards, and so on? Furthermore, we have no reason to doubt it in the case of others. To return to George, can we really doubt that he heard the teacher's request, decided to obey, walked to the board, and really added two and three?

FATALISM

There is, however, one form of determinism that our clarification fails to evade. In fact, no theory, not even Cartesian dualism, evades it. It is referred to as fatalism, or predeterminism, as it is sometimes called. Fortunately, fatalism is based upon a philosophical blunder, and once that blunder has been exposed, it collapses.

I shall now offer an example of the standard sort of argument used to support fatalism, and then go on to show what is wrong with the argument. At 12:06 P.M., G.M.T., June 24th, 1988, I plan to break a piece of chalk in half. I go ahead and do so. Thus the statement 'At 12:06 P.M., G.M.T., June 24th, 1988, P. T. Mackenzie breaks a piece of chalk' is true. Let's call this statement 'B'. Now we saw in chapter 3 that, strictly speaking, statements do not become true or cease to be true. Each statement simply is true or not true. Thus, if someone (Smith) had asserted B ten years ago, he would have asserted a true statement. But a statement that is true cannot cease to be true. Having asserted B, it could not cease to be true. Therefore, I had to break the chalk at 12:06 P.M., G.M.T., on the 24th of June, 1988. Whatever happened was to be.

This puzzle is not just a philosopher's curiosity; it finds its expression in such songs as, "Qué Sera Sera" ("Whatever will be, will be") and such poetic lines as Omar Khayyam's

And the first morning of creation wrote
What the last dawn of reckoning shall read[15]

And yet, it is based on a philosophical blunder. The first thing to notice is that the statement 'Whatever will be, will be' is analytic. Ask yourself what it would be like for what is going to happen not to happen. If it's going to happen that I am going to rise from this chair in the next five minutes, then it's not the case that I am not going to rise from this chair. 'Whatever will be, will be' is one of those wiley statements. It looks as though it makes a profound claim about the world, but it is utterly vacuous. 'Whatever will be, will be' says no more than 'If it's going to rain, it will rain'. And there is nothing earthshaking about that.

The second thing to notice is that truth is timeless. Statements do not *become* true or *cease* to be true; they also fail to be eternally true. What is eternally the case could, logically, be otherwise. Suppose, for example, we have a Lucretian atom—call it atom A—which is eternally cubical. It has always had a cubical shape and always will. It makes sense in cases like this to say that something has a property eternally because we can imagine it ceasing to be cubical. But this is not the case with truth. We cannot imagine a statement *becoming* true or *ceasing* to be true. Therefore, we cannot say of any statement that it is eternally true. All that we can say of a statement is that it *is* true.

Now if we cannot apply temporal words to truth, this means that we cannot make such claims as 'B was true', 'B will remain true', and so on. All we can say is that B (in the nontemporal sense of 'is') is true. What this means is that if Smith had asserted B ten years ago, and if I had of my own free will broken the piece of chalk at 12:06, he would have asserted a true statement. If I did not, then he would have asserted a false statement.

Some will object that this can't be right, because if it were, then I could change the past. I could in the present change the truth value of Smith's statement in the past. As we know, one thing we cannot do is change the past. What is done is done and cannot be undone. No doubt this is true; if yesterday I tied a knot, today I cannot erase the tying of that knot, though I can untie it! But the tying of the knot is an event that can be dated—it's something, to which temporal words can be applied. But the statement 'At 12:06 . . .' is not such an event. It doesn't even make sense to apply temporal words to it. It doesn't make sense to talk about making it true or false in the past, or changing its truth value in the past. All that can be said is that if I break the piece of chalk, then the statement that Smith asserted sometime before *is* true (not "would have become true"), and if I did not, then the statement that Smith asserted sometime before *is* false (not "would have become false"). In other words, all that can be said is, whether or not the statement Smith asserted *is* true depends upon whether I break the piece of chalk. And there is nothing paradoxical about this.

Fatalism or predeterminism is a sham. A soldier may stand up in the trenches because he believes there could be a bullet about with his name on it, and if there is, there is nothing he can do about it. Another may believe that there is no point in looking after his health because it is already written in the book of destiny what is going to happen to him. But both the soldier and the man who ignores his health have been beguiled. No doubt whatever happens was to be, but this only means that whatever happens, the statement expressing what happens is nontemporally true.

THE EXTERNAL WORLD

We are now in a position to deal with Descartes's skeptical doubts about the existence and/or nature of the external world. His real reason for thinking that things might not be as they appear is that he believed our perception of the world to be indirect, that we only see an image of the world projected upon the screen of the mind and can never see anything else. Thus we never could be in a position to know that the external world (if there is one) is anything like what was projected upon the mental screen. Now, if we can show that Descartes's beliefs on perception are mistaken—that we do not see an image of the world upon a screen of the mind, but see the world directly—then we shall have no reason to share his doubts about the external world. Of course, we can't in this way get rid of the specter of the malicious deceiver; but since we have no reason to believe that there is one, this worry is very remote. Perhaps only a proof of God would get rid of it, but even without such a proof it can be ignored.

According to Descartes's theory, when I look at the cup in front of me, light waves bounce off of it, entering the eye and forming an image on the back of the eyeball. This image is translated into a series of impulses, which are carried back along the optic nerve for further processing. In some mysterious way, the series of impulses are decoded and a (mental) image is presented to the mind. The mind (the real me) looks at an image of the cup and not the cup itself. If the view I championed is correct, this account of what happens is correct, except for the last bit. At no point is the impulse changed into a (mental) image to be presented to the mind that lurks within. But is this all that happens? If there is no mind at the other end of the physiological process, then how can there be any seeing? The answer is similar to the one offered before.

Suppose that George, after adding 2 and 3 and returning to his seat, is asked to give the name of the following figure □, which the teacher draws on the blackboard. Here, as before, we can say that George the person hears the request, decides to obey, takes a close look, recognizes it as a square, and says "It is a square." Or, we can say that sound waves in a certain sequence enter the ears of the organism that may be called "George" with the result that the head of George turns so that the eyes are able to receive light waves from the figure on the blackboard. Light waves in a certain sequence enter the eyes of the organism. The light waves work certain effects upon the brain with the ultimate result that sound waves in a certain order issue from the mouth of George. Talking in this language, we can give a complete account of everything that can be said to have happened to George at this level. But note that there is no, nor can there be any, mention of the hearing, seeing, recognizing, and speaking that goes on. These can only be talked about and thought about in the other language—the language of persons. The Cartesian is mistaken in thinking that George undergoes a physiological process and then, as a consequence, sees; rather in the organism undergoing the physiological process, the person sees.

Yet the old Cartesian account of how perception works tends to die hard, partly because there are all sorts of arguments that can be paraded in its support. Let's look at a couple of them. First, it might be argued that what I see when I look at the penny lying on the desk in front of me is not the penny itself, for the penny is round and what I see is elliptical. Therefore, what I see must be an elliptical image of the penny. (I am assuming here that I am looking at the penny at an angle.) Furthermore, since what is true in this case must be true in every case, it follows that I never directly see physical objects. All I ever see are the mental images of them. The first thing to notice about this objection is that the word 'round' is ambiguous. Sometimes it is used to refer to the three-dimensional shape of a spherical object, and sometimes it is used to refer to the shape of a two-dimensional circle. If we are talking about the three-dimensional object that is seen when looking at the penny, what is seen is not a round (spherical) object but a rather squat, cylindrical object. If we talk about the coin as a cylindrical object, we have no reason to distinguish between what is directly seen and what is indirectly seen. The coin looks cylindrical no matter from which angle we look at it. However, clearing up this point doesn't really get rid of the objection, for it can still be claimed that when I look at the top surface of the coin, what I directly see cannot be the top surface, because the surface is circular and what I see is elliptical. Even this argument is faulty. What I see when I look at the coin, at an angle, certainly looks ellipticial, but what we mean when we say that the surface looks elliptical is that it looks the way an elliptical surface looks when viewed straight on.[16] That is to say, at a 90° angle, to the viewer. Thus when I say that the top surface of the coin in front of me looks elliptical, what I mean is that it looks the way the top surface of an elliptical coin would look when viewed straight on. Now it doesn't in any way follow from this that what I directly see is not the coin but something else. I don't see a *look* of the coin. What I directly see is a cylindrical coin whose top surface *looks* the way an elliptical top surface would look when viewed straight on.

Second, it might be argued that when I have too much to drink, or press and eyeball and then look at a physical object, it seems as though I am seeing two objects and not one. But since there is only one object, what I directly see must be two images of the object and not the object itself. Or, for example, I look at this dot—•—on the page in front of me and press my left eye. As a result it seems as though I am seeing two dots. But since there is only one dot, it must be the case that I am seeing two images of that dot. Now what goes on in this case must go on in every case. Therefore, I only see the images of objects and not the objects themselves. This example is more difficult to deal with since it's quite tempting to think that I must have seen two somethings. However, I think it can be dealt with in the following way. I see the dot with my left eye and with my right eye. There is only one dot but there are, we might say, two "seeings" of that dot.[17] When I press against my left eye, these two seeings are out of phase. I simply don't see the dot in the same place with each eye. Therefore, I don't see two images of one dot; what I do is see the dot in one place with one eye and in a different place with the other eye. No doubt if I had three eyes I could see the dot in three different places. There would be three "seeings," but only one dot.

Third, it might be argued—as Lucretius, Descartes, Locke, and many other have argued—that we see the images of physical objects and not the objects themselves, for what we see has color, and objects, as we know from science, are colorless. But do we know from science that physical objects are colorless? I know from science that the apparently red pencil in front of me gives off only short wavelength light waves and that these light waves have a certain effect on the brain of this physiological organism, but it doesn't follow from this that the pencil that I (the person) see is not red. Could it not be that red pencils are the sort of objects that give off light waves of this length?

From the fact that the pencil, which appears red, gives off light waves of a certain length, nothing follows about whether or not the pencil is red as opposed to being colorless. Furthermore, the fact that the pencil, when carefully examined, looks red gives us ample reason to believe that the pencil is red. The belief that objects are really colorless finds its source in the mistaken belief that seeing is something that happens after the physiological process has taken place. But as we have seen, the pencil isn't seen as a consequence of the physiological process; it's rather that in the body undergoing the physiological process, the person sees the pencil.

But still, it has to be admitted that there is something ephemeral about secondary properties such as color, sound, odor, and the like as opposed to primary properties such as mass, velocity, shape, and size.

I look at the sea one minute and it is bright blue, but then the sun goes in behind a cloud and suddenly it's a dull grey. However, this everyday fact and hundreds like it need not lead us to say that the sea is colorless. We can say, if we like, that a shining sun makes the sea blue and that clouds make it grey. Most physical objects do not change their colors very quickly, but there is no reason that there should not be objects that do.

The much more interesting problem is sometimes called the reversed spectrum problem. Isn't it possible that I could wake up tomorrow and discover that everything had changed color in an apparently systematic way? I happen by chance to look at a spectrum and notice, much to my amazement, that all the colors are reversed. At the end where there used to be dark red there is now deep purple, and at the end where there used to be deep purple there is now dark red. All the colors in between, with the exception of the middle color, have systematically changed places. Since this is possible, it must be the case, so it is argued that objects really aren't colored and that the Cartesian account, or something like it, is right after all. Nothing in the objects has changed, and yet the colors I experience when I view them have systematically changed. Short waves instead of long waves now cause me to experience deep purple, and long waves instead of short waves now cause me to experience dark red.

The fact that something of the sort is possible does not, however, support the conclusion that objects are colorless. What I would most likely say if this were to happen is that something has gone wrong with my sight, the result of which is that I now mistakenly experience red pencils as blue and so on. It would not (logically) force me to to say that the pencil is colorless. We have no reason to assume that our ability to perceive is perfect and that we always see things as they are.

CONCLUSION

We began this chapter by pointing out that since we are unable to show that there is a god, it looks as though we have no reason to believe that there is an external world, and that if there is an external world, we have no reason to believe that it is similar to how it appears. We have seen in this chapter that these assumptions are mistaken. If there is a mind, and if what goes on in the mind went on largely as a consequence of what went on in the body, then our beliefs about the external world do indeed need a divine guarantee. But the belief that there is a mind, and that what goes on in the mind goes on largely as a result of what goes on in the body, is mistaken. We come to think that there is a mind because we are misled by the fact that we can think about human beings in two radically different ways. Because we can say that sound waves entered George's ears (to return to our previous example) and also say that George heard the teacher's request, we think that the hearing of a request must be a consequence of the sound waves entering the ears. Since all we can see is George, and all we could see if we looked very closely are the sound waves entering George's ears, we assume that the hearing must be going on somewhere else, somewhere behind the scenes in a mysterious place called the mind. But once we realize that George does not hear as a consequence of having sound waves enter his ears and affect his brain but, rather, that what can be described one way as a physiological organism being affected in a certain way can also be described as the person George hearing the teacher's request, we can give up all temptation to think of the mental goings on as a consequence of the physical goings on.

Given that we have no reason to think that what we hear and see constitute a copy of what goes on in the external world, we have no reason to think that the world is very different from the way it appears. Of course, the apparently solid wooden desk upon which I am writing is composed of cells, and these are composed of various compounds, which in turn are composed of molecules, which in turn are composed of atoms, which are partly composed of swirling electrons with large spaces between them; but the *wood* out off which the desk is made is much as it looks to me. What I mean by solid wood is the sort of wood out of which the desk is made. The desk looks to be made of wood that is solid, and so it is.

Finally, as we noticed when we were discussing Descartes, sometimes we dream, and when we are dreaming in a full-blooded way, we do not believe that we are dreaming but believe that we are experiencing the world as it really is. But even this fact gives us no serious cause for alarm. We know that there will be times when we shall be deceived, but we also know that we (logically) cannot be deceived all the time (see chapter 4, p. 161). There will be many times (most times in fact) when we are not being deceived.

Our clarification of the mind-body problem—our coming to realize that our belief that there is a mind behind the brain is simply a result of our failure to appreciate the distinction between the two radically different ways that George, or anyone else, can be talked about—also makes it possible to take care of the free will problem. When we view a human being as a person, we (logically) must, unless special reasons are offered, assume that he is free. When we view a human being as an organism, we (logically) cannot assume that he is free, for it makes no sense to say that he is free. It makes no more sense to say that an organism is free than it does to say that a thermostat is free.

NOTES

1. In what follows, it should be kept in mind that the brain is a part of the body.

2. The main worry is that the fox will eat the goose if left alone, and the goose will eat the grain if left alone.

3. See Chapter 4, pages 190-191, for two more speculations on the relation between the mind and the body.

4. There is also the more radical form of materialism that denies the existence of consciousness altogether. Very few people have actually subscribed to this theory, though many have said that they did. Hobbes, I think, can be said to fall into this category. Some materialists of a more sophisticated variety have wanted to argue that, strictly speaking, there is only space and matter. We think there are also mental phenomena, but since statements about mental phenomena are reducible to statements about matter, there is really only the latter. No one, however, has managed to carry out this reduction.

5. This is not to say there couldn't have been a time when no consciousness existed but, if there were such a time, how it ever came into existence would be a complete mystery.

6. It might be noted that there are two ways that diagram A can be interpreted. On one way, there is an input on the part of the agent at M_2. M_2 is causally independent of M_1. I could have decided not to swat the mosquito. This is essentially the Cartesian view. On the other interpretation of diagram A, M_2 is caused by M_1, which in turn is caused by P_1. On this view, as on the Epiphenomenalist's view, there is no room for human freedom. Most people would, I think, interpret diagram A the first way.

7. See M. Schlick's *Problems of Ethics,* trans. D. Rynin, (Prentice-Hall, 1939), ch. 7.

8. See G. E. Moore's *Ethics* (London, Home University Library, 1912), ch. 6.

9. Ibid.

10. 'He was determined to act upon those desires' is to be taken here to mean something like 'His acts were causally determined by those desires'. 'Determined' is *not* being used as it is in 'The detective was determined to discover who the murderer was'. In this latter case, 'determined' is being used to mention the resolve or determination on the part of the detective. This has nothing to do with causality or determinism.

11. What, then, are we to make of such statements as 'George stubbed his toe while watching the teacher'? Are we to say that 'George' refers to two different entities, the physiological and the person? No. In this context 'George' refers to the person, as it does in 'George stubbed his toe and experienced great pain'. Only in statements that refer solely to physiological changes does 'George' refer to the physiological organism—statements such as 'A needle was inserted in George's big toe and as a result the following neurological changes took place'. On the view I am presenting, it would be a mistake to say 'George had a needle inserted into his toe and this caused him to experience pain'. What one should say is that in having a needle inserted in his toe, he experienced great pain.

12. The same points can be made about choice as well as about decision.

13. One can talk about deciding to decide in the sense that I can now decide

that next week I am going to reach a decision on who to hire for a certain job. But one cannot decide to decide in the sense of deciding to decide right now to hire James.

14. This isn't quite right. When I drive a car it's not the case that every move I make with my arms is based on a decision. And yet, when I drive, provided that I am not under the influence of drugs or hypnotized, I move my arms freely.

15. Omar Khayyam *The Rubaiyat,* trans. by E. FitzGerald, (Pocket Books, 1941).

16. It's not even certain that we should say that the surface of the coin looks elliptical. I'm more tempted to say that the surface in front of me looks circular. That is to say, it looks the way a circular surface looks when viewed from an angle. And that is circular and not elliptical. In other words, it looks the way it is. Now, I am prepared to admit that if there were a screen between me and the coin at right angles to my line of vision, then the image of the coin that I would see if it were projected upon that screen would be elliptical. But since what I see is the surface of a three-dimensional coin and not a two-dimentional image of the coin, what I see is and looks circular and not elliptical.

16. Notice that I don't see the seeing. Indeed, it would make no sense to say that I see the seeing.

7

Moral Philosophy

THE CENTRAL PROBLEM

I want to introduce you to moral philosophy by presenting what I take to be its central problem. However, in order to do so, it will be necessary first to introduce a number of distinctions.

Fact and Value

Examine the following lists of statements[1] and ask yourself if there are any differences between those on the left and those on the right:

A	B
1. James is six feet tall.	1. James is a good man.
2. It would be imprudent for him not to return Smith's lawn mower.	2. It would be wrong for him not to return Smith's lawn mower.
3. Those people believe that eating people is wrong.	3. Eating people is wrong.
4. If you don't keep your promises, no one will trust you.	4. You ought to keep you promises.
5. James's revolver weighs two pounds.	5. James has a good revolver.

The main difference between the statements on the left and those on the right is that those on the left are used to describe, and those on the right are used to evaluate. When I say that James is six feet tall, I describe him. I say something factual about him; but when I say that James is a good man, I evaluate him or I appraise him. As a rule, those on the left, and others like them, are called factual statements, while those on the right are called value statements. We shall, for the most part, be concerned only with moral statements, which form a subclass of value statements. 'James has a good revolver' can be classified as a value statement, but it could hardly be classified as a moral statement. We could hardly be said to be evaluating or appraising the gun from a moral point of view. The statement labeled 4B fits a bit awkwardly in its column. It could be argued, however, that in it promises are being appraised as things that ought to be kept. We might also puzzle over the distinction between 3A and 3B. The difference is that in 3B we are actually evaluating the eating of people, while in 3A we are making a factual claim about the moral judgments of other people. Statement 3B is the sort of claim a moralist might make, while 3A is the claim an anthropologist might set forth.

Not all statements fit nicely into one category or the other. Some sentences are ambiguous and can be used to express either moral statements or factual statements. For example, 'All men are equal' may be used to say 'All men are of equal ability' or 'All men ought to be treated equally'. If used in the first way, it expresses a factual statement; if used in the second way, it expresses a moral statement. The sentence 'We believe that eating people is wrong' is also ambiguous. It can be used to make an anthropological claim about the morals of the tribe to which the speaker belongs or, more likely, it can be used to make a moral claim—that is, it can be used to say that eating people is wrong.

There are other statements that are hard to categorize, not because they are ambiguous in the way just mentioned, but because they hover halfway between the two. For example, 'He drove the car negligently' sounds factual and moral at the same time. In making this claim, the speaker is describing how the driver drove the car, but what he says has moral implications. We shall notice later on that most statements about persons belong in this zone.

Analytic and Synthetic

The distinction between the analytic and the synthetic cuts across the distinction between the factual and the evaluative. For example, 'James is a good man' is synthetic but 'You ought to do your duty' is analytic. The latter is analytic because a duty is by definition something that ought to be done. Although all the statements that appear in column A are synthetic, there is no reason that an analytic statement could not be included: for example, 'Either James is six feet tall or he is not'. I realize it is a bit awkward to classify this statement as factual, since if it is analytic, it cannot assert a fact. But it's factual in the sense that it is composed essentially of factual words.

Moral^I and Moral^{II}

Sometimes when we call something a moral judgment we mean to contrast it with a nonmoral judgment, and sometimes we mean to contrast it with an immoral judgment. This, of course, can lead to confusion. Let's use "moral^I" when we want to say that a judgment is moral as opposed to factual, and "moral^{II}," when we want to say that a judgment moral as opposed to immoral. Thus, for example, we might say that 'Incest is good' is a moral^I judgment but not a moral^{II} judgment. By this we would mean that it is a moral judgment as opposed to a nonmoral judgment, but not that it is a moral as opposed to an immoral judgment. The context should usually make clear which way 'moral' is being used, but when there is room for doubt I shall inscribe 'moral' according to how it is being used.

Moral Knowledge

The central problem of moral philosophy is this: We all know how we go about showing that the statements in column A are true or false. We can determine whether James is six feet tall by measuring him. We can determine whether James has blonde hair simply by taking a look. But how do we determine whether James is a good man? Where do we look and how do we measure?

The natural response is to say that although we cannot directly ascertain the truth of statements like 'James is a good man', we can do so indirectly. That is to say, although we cannot discover whether James is a good man by taking a close look at him—there are no moral properties in the way that there are factual properties like colors—we can discover whether James is a good man by examining the facts that surround him. We can look at the record of what sort of life James has been living for the past fifteen years and infer from this whether he is a good man. Or, if we have to decide what we ought to do when faced with a difficult situation, we can look at the facts and decide on the basis of them. If a child is drowning in a deep pond in front of me and I can't swim, then if there is a long pole but no one around, I hold out the pole, while if there is no pole but there are others about, I call for help.

Although this is the natural response, it has the following difficulty. We know from our examination of deductive arguments that the conclusion of a deductive argument is contained in the premises. What this means is that if the statements that form the premises of our argument are purely factual, the conclusion must be purely factual as well. This means that no moral statement can be deduced from a set of factual statements. Or, to put it another way, we can never decide on the basis of the facts alone what we ought to do, what is right or wrong, what is good or bad, and so on.

Logicians have long been aware that nothing new can be deduced from a set of premises, but David Hume was the first to realize the significance of this fact for morality. In Hume's justly famous *Treatise*, which was first published in 1739, he writes:

> I cannot forbear adding to these reasonings an observation, which may, perhaps, be found of some importance. In every system of morality, which I have hitherto met with, I have always remarked, that the author proceeds for some time in the ordinary way of reasoning and establishes the being of a God, or makes observations concerning human affairs; when of a sudden I am surprised to find, that instead of the usual copulations of propositions, *is*, and *is not*, I meet with no proposition that is not connected with an *ought*, or an *ought not*. This change is imperceptible; but is, however, of the last consequence. For as this *ought*, or *ought not*, expresses some new relation or affirmation, 'tis necessary that it should be observed and explained; and at the same time a reason should be given, for what seems utterly inconceivable, how this new relation can be a deduction from others, which are entirely different from it.[2]

What Hume is saying is that from purely factual statements about the nature of God or the nature of man, one cannot deduce statements about what ought to be done.

The natural response to Hume is to point out that, although there is a gap between fact and value, one can bridge the gap with the help of a moral principle. That is to say that although from

1. The house is on fire,

one cannot deduce

3. One ought to phone the fire department,

one can from

1. The house is on fire,

and

2. Whenever a house is on fire one ought to call the fire department,

deduce

3. One ought to phone the fire department.

The trouble with this response is that it only postpones the problem. The moral principle (2) is a moral statement and it, like (3), cannot be deduced from a set of factual statements. Statement (2) can, of course, be derived either from a higher-order moral principle or a higher-order moral principle in conjunction with a number of factual statements: for example, from

4. One ought to do whatever will help to reduce human misery,

and

5. Calling fire departments whenever a house is on fire will help to reduce human misery,

one can deduce

2. Whenever a house is on fire one ought to call the fire department.

But this, again, only postpones the problem. What about (4)? No doubt it could be derived from a higher moral principle, but then we will be faced with the same problem once again. The upshot of all this is that we have problems either if regress of principles goes on forever, or if it stops. If it goes on (forever), we can never be certain that we ought to phone the fire department, and if it stops then our conclusion will be supported by an unsupported principle; so, again, we cannot be certain that we ought to phone the fire department. Since the regress must either go on or stop, with no third alternative, we never can be certain that we ought to phone the fire department, even though it looks so certain that we ought to phone. Of course, not only can we never be certain about this, we can never be certain about any other moral judgment. If one were to see a child being tortured, it's not even certain, on this view, that one ought to do something about it.

Perhaps the most natural reply to this problem is to argue that there are some principles that can be known to be true on the basis of reason alone. That is to say, there are some principles that, because they are self-evident, do not need to be deduced from any higher principle. I think this is going to be the right answer in the end. But at present it doesn't look very promising. We have already seen that, with perhaps a few exceptions, the only statements known to be true on the basis of reason alone are analytic. We have also seen that from analytic statements only analytic statements can be deduced. The same point holds in moral thinking; from an analytic moral principle only analytic moral statements can be derived, and this means that from an analytic moral principle we can never arrive at a substantive synthetic judgment about what we ought to do.

Religion and Morality

In his book *The Brothers Karamazov*, Dostoyevski has one brother say to the other that if God did not exist, all would be permitted. What this suggests is the popular view that morality must be in some way grounded in religion, and that if there is no God, there is no right or wrong. In what follows I shall argue that this view, according to most interpretations of what religion is, is entirely mistaken.

The main source of this view is the assumption that moral rules are like the rules of a state, and that just as a terrestrial sovereign can make something law by saying it is law, so God, if He exists, can make something right by saying it is right. For example, at one time, if the Prince of Liechtenstein wanted to say that the speed limit in his principality was to be 50 kph, all he had to do was to proclaim "The speed limit is now 50 kph" and so it was! In the same way, so it was thought, if God wanted to make it wrong to commit adultery, all He had to say was "It is wrong to commit adultry," and, as a consequence, it was wrong to commit adultery.

Now, there is no doubt that along with statutory law, there could be divine law, and it would be possible for God, through saying "Thou shalt not commit adultery," to make it a divine offense to commit adultery. There is also no doubt that there could be divine sanctions attached to the divine law: those who committed adultery could expect to be confronted with hell-fire and brimstone at some later date. All this is possible. But the question that we must ask is: Could God make it wrong to commit adultery simply by saying that it is wrong?[3] No doubt, if we know that God has said that it is wrong to commit adultery, we know, since God is omniscient, that it is wrong to commit adultery. But the saying that it is wrong cannot make it wrong. It must be the case that if God says it is wrong, he says it is wrong because it is wrong and not the other way around. This means that if there is a God who says that adultery is wrong, adultery would still be wrong if there wasn't a God. In other words, the ultimate source of the wrongness of adultery is quite independent of God. Thus adultery would be wrong whether God existed or not.

This point, surprisingly enough, was first made by Plato in a Socratic dialogue called the *Euthyphro*. The dialogue proceeds in a roundabout way and finally settles on the question of what is the nature of piety. Socrates asks Euthyphro what piety is, and the young man replies that it is what all the gods love. Socrates then asks, is it pious because it is loved by the gods, or is it loved by the gods because it is pious? Euthyphro, realizing that loving something (even when it's the gods doing the loving) cannot make that thing pious, replies "The gods love the pious thing because it is pious; it is not pious merely because they love it." Socrates then points out that if it's not their loving it that makes a thing pious, then it must be something else. In other words, the source of piety, and so any other moral quality, must be quite independent of any god.

We mustn't conclude from this, however, that morality must be completely independent of religion. First of all, as we have already noted, if we know that God says (to choose a different example) that we ought to do unto others as we would have them do unto us, and we know that God is omniscient, we know that this is what we ought to do. The problem here, though, is this: How could we ever be in a position to know that God says that we ought to do unto others as we would have them do unto us—let alone know that there is a god? Second, although religion cannot be the ground of morality, it can be the source of moral sanctions. If adultery is wrong and God exists, then it's highly likely that He will punish those who commit adultery. This gives us a prudential reason for refraining from adultery. This may have been what Dostoyevski had in mind when he had Ivan Karamazov say that if there is no god, all is permitted. In other words, if there is no god, then no one will receive divine punishment.[4] Third, if we know that God does not want us to do x (whatever x may be), or if we know that God has willed that we are not to do x, then this gives us a slim moral reason for not doing x. Just as one ought to respect the wishes of an aged patriarch, so one ought to respect the wishes of God, whatever they may be. So if God has requested that we not do x, this fact alone, though it does not make x in itself wrong, does give us a (moral) reason for refraining from doing x.

Finally, as will be recalled from the *Republic*, Plato considered the ultimate Form, the Good, to be responsible for the existence, as well as for the illumination, of the other Forms. In fact, at one point, Plato goes so far as to say that the Good was beyond Being. This has led some philosophers, for example Plotinus (who lived in Alexandria, Egypt, from 205-270 A.D.) to identify God with the Good. Now, if God is goodness itself, then morality must be dependent on God. An act is right to the extent that it participates in the ultimate form of the Good, and wrong to the extent that if fails to participate.

The main trouble with this doctrine, apart from its obscurity, is that, in addition to saying that God is good, we want to say that God is omniscient and omnipotent. But it's difficult to see how He can have these features if He is identified with goodness. Furthermore, as a rule, when we say that God is good, we don't want to identify God with goodness; all that we want to do is ascribe goodness to him. In saying that God is good, we no more identify God with goodness than if we were to identify the pen with blackness when we say that the pen is black.

The fact that we cannot ground morality in religion is really an outcome of Hume's point that we cannot derive statements of value from statements of fact. Just as we cannot deduce statements of morality from factual statements about the world, so we cannot, as Hume pointed out, deduce statements of morality from statements about the nature of God.[5] However, let's put this worry to one side and have a look at some of the other attempts that have been made to show how we discover what is right and wrong and how we decide what we ought to do.

Egoism

Egoism comes in two forms, moral egoism and nonmoral egoism. A nonmoral egoist will say, yes, Hume is right, we can't arrive at moral principles, not because there are some principles and we don't know what they are, but because there just aren't any.[6] Thrasymachus was right after all. Morality is just a put-up job.[7] Members of the ruling class pass laws in their own interest and call them just and right in order to get the simpleminded citizens to act in accordance with them. Since morality really doesn't exist, the only rational way for a person to act is in his own interest. If I feel like going to the beach, I go to the beach. If I feel like going for a drive in my car, then I go for a drive. I don't say that we *ought* to do what we like. I don't know what that would mean. All I say is that it is rational to do as we like and that I make a point of doing what I like. If others want to act differently, well, that's no business of mine.

This, then, is roughly the position taken by the nonmoral egoist. We must admit, it is a position that is very difficult to refute; however, we shall try. No doubt the egoist wants to continue to be able to use his car and to go to the beach. He can, of course, obtain a large gun and threaten anyone who comes near, and scare away those who might prevent him from sitting on the beach. But it is much more in his interest to make a deal with the other members of the community to abstain from taking their possessions if they will abstain from taking his. He will therefore abstain from preventing others from using the beach if they will abstain from preventing him. But now the question we must ask is this: Is it possible for him to make such a deal without entering the moral arena? Isn't it the case that the parties to the deal or contract each place themselves under a moral obligation to abstain from taking the possessions of others? Our friend might reply that entering a contract really amounts to no more than expressing an intention. All he is doing is *saying* that he will in fact abstain from taking the possessions of others as long as they abstain from taking his. But if they are also rational egoists, then they will only abstain from taking his possessions as long as it's to their advantage to do so. As soon as our friend's back is turned, these rational egoists will grab his car and drive away. Furthermore, if our friend has any foresight, he will see that this is likely to occur and will feel that he has to stand guard over his possessions day and night.

However, if our friend belongs to a community of people who, with the exception of himself, think that morality is not a put-up job, that moral terms mean roughly what we think they mean, then our friend will, like the Thrasymachian rulers, be able to make deals with the other members of the community knowing that they will keep their side of the bargain. He can pretend to enter contracts without believing that he is actually doing so. He can rest assured that others will believe that he and they really have entered contracts. He can also be assured that the others will not take his possessions, while he feels under no obligation to refrain from taking theirs. The reason he feels under no obligation is that he believes moral words—"obligation" being one of them—are devoid of meaning. Furthermore, he will tell others that stealing and doing harm are wrong in order to trick them into refraining from stealing his property and doing harm to him, knowing all the while (according to him) that such claims are meaningless.

Later on we shall talk about the question of whether moral terms are meaningless, but for now there are two ways that we might attempt to deal with our friend the nonmoral egoist who holds this view. First we can point out to him that if, for example, an unscrupulous court of law were to find him guilty and sentence him to five years hard labor for something he and the members of the court know he did not do, he could not claim, at least to himself, that the court had been unjust. The reason he could not honestly claim that the court had been unjust is that, according to him, the word 'just' is devoid of meaning, and used by rulers to keep the masses in their place. But to claim that the court has really behaved in an unjust way is something that we will most likely want to do.

Second, we can attempt to show him that his position is incoherent by asking him how he wants other people to behave. On the one hand, believing that it is rational for him to act only in his own interest, he will want others to act in his interest. But, on the other hand, believing it is rational for a person to act in his own interest, he will want others to act in their interests. But since their interests are not always his interest, he will sometimes want others, contrary to what has already been said, not to act in his interest.

Let me put this point in a different way. Our friend believes that he is rational and, as a rational being, he is to act in his own interest. It follows from this that he will believe that others, given that they are rational, are to act in their interest. So, where there is a conflict of interest, he will believe that the others are to act (only) in his (our friend's) interest and (only) in their interest. But how can he believe both? How can he believe that in situations where there is a conflict, the others are to act solely in his (our friend's) interest and also (solely) in their interest?

In this way, it can be argued that nonmoral egoism is incoherent. It leads, logically, to the holding of two inconsistent beliefs. I cannot consistently believe that in a particular situation Smith is to act (only) in my interest and (only) in his interest.

Moral Egoism

Not many people are prepared to accept a position as radical as non-moral egoism. It requires accepting that moral terms are bereft of meaning, and this is something that is very difficult to do—partly because it would mean that we could never envisage a situation where we could justly claim that we had been wronged, and partly because we have no reason, as we shall see later on, to believe that moral terms are without meaning.

Although not many people are prepared to accept nonmoral egoism, many are prepared to accept moral egoism—the theory that one *ought* to do what is in one's own interest because it is rational to do so. We must be careful not to confuse this theory with *psychological egoism*—the theory that each person acts in what he takes to be his own interest. Psychological egoism is not a moral theory, not a theory about how human beings ought to act, but about how they do act. If true, it belongs to the province of science and not to the province of morality.[8]

Psychological egoism comes in both strong and weak forms. The strong form states that each person acts in what he takes to be his own interest and is incapable of acting in any other way. This theory presumes that human beings have no freedom, that they are incapable of acting in other than their own interest. We have already seen that people are free and capable of not acting in their own interest. Therefore, this theory can be rejected without further ado. In its weaker form it states that although each person is capable of not acting in his own interest, he rarely if ever does so, and that if we look at the history of humankind, even though we will often find people claiming that they are not acting in their own interest, we generally find that they are.

If the weak form of psychological egoism is true, it does give some support to moral egoism, since morality has to deal in the realm of what people can be expected to do. It might be argued that if people are virtually incapable of acting in the interest of others, it is idle to tell them that they ought to do so. A viable moral theory, it must be remembered, has to work within the realm of what can be expected in human behavior.

Psychological egoism, in the strong form, even if it were true, could give no support to moral egoism. There are two reasons for this. First of all, it makes no sense to tell a person that he *ought* to do something if he is in fact *incapable of doing otherwise*. Assuming that someone can be put in a trance and programmed, say, to pick up a cup, what would be the point in telling him that he ought to pick it up? To tell him that he ought to pick up the cup is to presuppose that he could choose not to. Many have pointed out that it is unfair and out of place to tell a person that he ought to do something he is incapable of doing; but it's not often noticed, as we have just made clear, that it's also out of place to tell a person that he ought to do something if he is incapable of doing otherwise.

The second reason for claiming that psychological egoism in its strong form cannot give support to moral egoism is more profound. Morality, and the language that goes with it, can only belong to beings who are free. Only such beings can be said to be responsible for their actions. Only such beings can perform acts that have moral worth. Think of it this way, suppose we have a beehive where it is the job of the worker bees to go out, collect the nectar from the flowers, and bring it back to feed the baby bees. We can say they go out and collect nectar. But we can't say that their actions have moral worth or that they are responsible for their actions. In the same way, if people are like bees, if they are incapable of acting in a way that is different from the way they do act, then we cannot say that they are responsible for what they do or that their acts have moral worth. This is the point that Immanuel Kant had in mind when he said that 'ought' implies 'can'. In order for an agent's action to have moral worth, it has to be one that he can do; and in order for it to be an action that he can perform, it has to be an action that he can refrain from doing. Strictly speaking, feeding the baby bees is not something the workers *can* do, it's only something that they *just* do. Better still, it's only something that happens. From this it follows that if psychological egoism in the strong form were true, no moral[1] theory would be relevant to human beings, which in turn would make moral egoism irrelevant to human beings as well. It is for this reason that the strong form of psychological egoism gives no support to moral egoism.

We can see the importance that freedom plays in morality. If people are determined in everything that they do by what went before, then they are incapable of doing right or wrong. Their actions have no moral worth. Morality may apply to angels but it does not apply to people.

Although it's fairly obvious that psychological egoism in its strong form can give no support to moral egoism, it's surprising the number of people who have thought that it does. It's very tempting to argue that people ought to act in their own interest because they always act in their own interest and are incapable of doing otherwise. But as we have seen, if we always act in our own interest and are incapable of doing otherwise, then it makes no sense to say of us that acting in our own interest is what we ought to do. It is probably through confusing the strong sense with the weak sense that people have been led to think that psychological egoism in its strong sense supports moral egoism.

Justification for and Criticism of Moral Egoism

The reader might be tempted to ask how it could be possible to give any sort of justification for moral egoism, given (1) the nonverifiability of moral claims and (2) Hume's point about the logical gap between factual claims and moral claims. The moral egoist is aware of Hume's point (at least some are) but feels that it is still possible to give a justification for moral egoism. He says that because of Hume's point, the only reason that could be given for saying that we ought to behave in a certain way is that is rational to do so. Now since it is only rational to act in one's own interest, it follows that this is the way that one ought (morally) to act. To put it a different way, given that Hume's point is valid, the only moral theory that we can go any distance toward justifying is moral egoism. It is rational to me to act in my own interest—to act so as to maximize my pleasure and happiness in the long run—so if anything is going to count as a valid moral theory, it is going to be moral egoism.

The main criticism of moral egoism is that, like nonmoral egoism, it contains a logical aberration; both moral egoism and nonmoral egoism lead to inconsistent conclusions. The problem arises when the moral egoist thinks about what others ought to do. On the one hand, the egoist will think that since everyone ought to act in accordance with their own interest, he, too, ought to act in his own interest. And this means, if possible, getting others to act in accordance with his interest. In other words, the egoist will think that others ought to act to further his interest. On the other hand, our egoist will think that since each person ought to act to enhance self interest, Smith, say, ought to act in Smith's interest and not in the interest of the egoist, especially if there is a conflict of interest.

The point of this argument has nothing to do with what, for example, I will *say* to Smith concerning what he ought to do, but what I *think* he ought to do. For example, suppose that I am a moral egoist and I employ Smith as my gardener. On the one hand, I will think that since we ought to act in our own interest, I ought to trick Smith into working the longest of hours at the lowest of wages. I will tell him that work, like virtue, is its own reward, that my flower garden will stand as a living monument to his achievements, that my income has been substantially reduced, that the cost of living hasn't really gone up, and so on. But on the other hand, I will think that since we ought to act in our own interest, Smith ought to act in *his* interest and not mine, that he should spend more time with his wife and family, that when he works for me he should be paid higher wages, and so on. Thus we have an inconsistency: on the one hand, I think that Smith ought not to be paid more and, on the other hand, that he ought to be paid more. From this we can conclude that moral egoism is logically defective. The view must be so if it is capable of generating two or more mutually inconsistent conclusions.

Enlightened Moral Egoism

It might be objected that such inconsistencies arise only if it is assumed that there is a conflict of interests. But we have to take the world as we find it, and we do we find that in the long run there is no conflict. It is in everyone's interest to act for the general good, because only by acting for the general good can our own well-being be maximized.

This theory is really an echo of the theory discussed by Glaucon in the *Republic*. Each person realized that since every other person is a threat to him, the best thing to do is to enter into a contract with the others not to do harm to them on the condition that they in turn do no harm to him. Owing to it being an echo, it is open to the same objection. It may be in my interest to work for the general good, or at least to enter into a contract not to harm others, as long as others pose a threat to me. But if others do not pose a threat, if I possessed the Ring of Gyges, then it would not be in my interest to work for the general good. If it was not in my interest, the logical aberration common to all forms of egoism would arise once again. On the one hand, I would think that others ought to act in my interest and, on the other hand, I would think that they ought to act in their interest.

Second, moral egoism, whether enlightened or not, can be criticized on the ground that it considers rational only those acts that are believed to be in our own interest. But this claim is never defended by the moral egoist. It is simply taken for granted. Later I shall argue that its not rational to act on our own interest (see page 288).

Third, moral egoism can be criticized on the grounds that even if we start there, we cannot stay there. What I mean when I say that I ought only to act in my interest is that I ought only to act so as to maximize my long-term pleasure or happiness. Of course, acting in my interest means ensuring that I am paid enough to take a summer vacation and provide a pension for my old age. But these are only means to an end, and that end is happiness. Now, if I ought only to act so as to maximize happiness, how am I to distinguish between my happiness and the happiness of others? If it's happiness that wants maximization, then I should be acting so as to maximize the general happiness and not my own. It might be objected that surely we can distinguish between our own happiness and the happiness of others. No doubt we can in terms of location. But if it's happiness that makes an act worth doing, how can I claim that it's only my happiness that makes an act worth doing? If it's happiness, it must be anyone's happiness. In this way, then, if we start with moral egoism, we can be lead to a position that is usually called Utilitarianism. Most utilitarians hold that we ought to act so as to maximize the general happiness. If asked why we ought to act in this way, they will respond that we ought to act so as to maximize happiness because happiness is the ultimate good. I shall leave the discussion of why they believe that happiness is the ultimate good until the section on Utilitarianism.

Moral Relativism

Before we plow any deeper into moral thinking, there is one moral theory that must be put to one side, and that is *moral relativism*. When I was in high school we used to have enormously long arguments about whether or not morals were relative, and the arguments went on all day long—primarily because we didn't have the foggiest idea of what we were talking about. I think that once we clarify what we're talking about, this question, or at least a part of it, can be settled fairly quickly. First of all, we have to distinguish between *anthropological relativism,* sometimes called *cultural relativism,* and the version referred to as *moral relativism.* In its simplest form, anthropological relativism is the theory that moral codes vary from place to place. This is something that very few will deny. Few will deny that what is *believed* to be right or wrong varies from place to another.

When discussing cultural relativism, we have to be careful as well to distinguish between the claim that *derivative* principles vary from place to place, and the claim that *ultimate* principles vary from place to place. For example, in one society it is considered wrong to go around without clothes, while in another society it is considered quite proper to do so. Pigmies, for instance, have no aversion to nudity. But we may find that the reason the people of society *A* believe that nudity is wrong while those of society *B* do not is because both the people of *A* and *B* believe that we ought to do what is conducive to human health. But the people of *B* have found, owing to the tropical rain forests they inhabit, that nudity is conducive (perhaps clothes cause rashes) to good health, while the people of society *A* have found, owing to an abundance of snow and ice in the land they inhabit, that it is not. In this situation, we don't have a difference of principle. Both believe that we ought to do whatever is conducive to human health. Society *B* merely believes that we ought to go around in the nude because it views nudity as conducive. Society *A* believes that we ought not to go around in the nude, because it views nudity as not conducive.

The cultural relativist states that *ultimate* principles and not derivative principles vary from place to place. For, as we have seeen, derivative principles are not really principles. If I hold that we ought to do whatever is conducive to human health, I may also hold that the people of society *B* ought to go around without their clothes, while it would be wrong for the people of society A to do so. But in holding the latter, I could hardly be said to be holding a different principle.

Some anthropologists have wanted to say that ultimate principles do not vary from place to place—that all people hold the same ultimate principles—but his view seems to be mistaken. According to the philosopher Peter Singer in an interesting book called the *Expanding Circle,* the Greek historian Herodotus chronicled different practices in many lands. He tells a story of how Darius, King of Persia, brought some Greeks before him and asked them how much he would have to pay them to eat their fathers' dead bodies. They refused to do it at any price. Then Darius brought in some Indians whose practice it was to eat the bodies of their fathers, and asked them what would make them willing to burn their fathers' bodies. The Indians cried out that he should not mention such a terrible act. So here we have, I think, two ultimate but inconsistent moral principles. The Greeks believe that we ought not to eat our fathers' bodies, and the Indians believe that we should.

Now, and this is the important point, even if the accepted ultimate moral^l principles do vary from place to place, showing that cultural relativism is correct, this does nothing toward showing moral relativism is correct. I could be the most "dyed in the wool" absolutist and yet be prepared to admit the facts of cultural relativism. I could say "Yes, of course, what are taken to be ultimate moral^l principles vary from place to place, but this only shows that most people are mistaken. What most people take to be ultimate moral^l principles may be so called because of their importance in governing their lives, but they are not ultimate principles in the sense of being *true* ultimate principles." Moral relativism is, in part, the theory that what is ultimately right and ultimately wrong does vary from place to place. This theory is not in any direct way supported by the claim that what is *believed* to be ultimately right varies from place to place. This may only show that some people are mistaken.

Actually, when we come to think of it, it's not at all clear how moral relativism could be correct. How could it possibly be ultimately right in one society for people to eat their fathers' bodies yet wrong in another? What is usually said by moral relativists is that it is ultimately right *for* these people to eat their fathers but wrong *for* those. But what does the 'for' mean here? If 'It is wrong for these people to . . .' simply means 'These people believe it is wrong to . . .', then we are back again to cultural relativism. While if it doesn't mean this, then what role does the 'for' serve? Moral relativism, like moral egoism, also seems to be an incoherent theory.

We mustn't dismiss moral relativism too quickly. If we look at the discoveries that social anthropologists such as Émile Durkheim made, we can guess what they had in mind. What people like Durkheim noticed was that the moral code of any society is always directed toward the survival and prosperity of that society. Farming societies located in the valleys considered industry and prudence to be the highest of virtues, while societies whose members were located in the mountains and who survived through raiding the valley societies, valued such things as courage and honor. Each had a moral code that fostered the ends of that society. As a result, some anthropologists began to feel that the principles that made up the codes were determined by the cultural backgrounds of the societies, that moral principles were really nothing more than the expressions of the society's feelings.

Now if moral relativism is taken as asserting that moral principles are nothing more than an expression of deeply held group moral[I] feelings, and that what people feel is culturally determined and varies from society to society, then moral relativism is at least a coherent theory. If it is taken as asserting that what is really right or wrong varies from place to place, then we have an incoherent theory. But if it is taken, as we have seen, as the claim that moral[I] principles are nothing more than the expressions of group moral[I] feelings, and these do vary from place to place, then we do have a theory that could be true. There is just one question left to be asked. Is it true?

The way that some of our moral[I] principles have changed, as our technology and social conditions have changed, certainly does suggest that moral relativism, taken in this way, is correct. In the nineteenth century, when the infant mortality rate was very high, birth control was frowned on by virtually everyone. Even the British philosopher John Stuart Mill spent a night in jail for distributing pamphlets on birth control. But nowadays, when the infant mortality rate is very low and the world is coping with population problems, almost everyone feels that it is one's moral duty to practice birth control. Facts such as these are inclined to change us into moral skeptics and turn us toward moral relativism.

Even though such facts may give some credence to moral relativism, they do not entail it. Even though some people may consider such principles as 'One ought not practice birth control' to be ultimate, it may be argued that they are not. It could be argued that one of our ultimate principles (that is to say, a principle that is not only ultimate but true) is that we ought to do what is required for human survival. When this requires that we should not practice birth control, then we should not, and when it requires that we should, then we should. Principles about birth control and the like are merely derivative.

A more serious objection to moral relativism has to do with its claim that ultimate moral principles are nothing more than expressions of group feeling. It was a moral[I] principle of the German Nazis that Jewish people should be exterminated. No doubt many Nazis had strong moral[I] feelings of antipathy toward the Jews, and no doubt this feeling was expressed in the principle. But at the same time, most people would claim that there is more to the principle than that: it said something about the Jewish people, and what it did say was outrageously mistaken. On the other hand, the opposing principle, 'It's wrong to take the life of another person', strikes us as more than just an expression of emotion. It also strikes us as a statement—not just a statement, but one that is true.

Summary

Cultural relativism must be distinguished from moral relativism. Cultural relativism is in part the factual theory that what are *believed* to be ultimate moral[II] principles vary from society to society. Moral relativism is the theory that an ultimate moral[II] principle can be rationally supported in one society and not in another. Cultural relativism gives no direct support to moral relativism. It doesn't follow from the fact that what is *believed* to be ultimately rational varies from culture to culture, that what *is* ultimately rational varies from culture to culture as well. It is possible that most people, if not all people, are mistaken.

Although cultural relativism gives no direct support to moral relativism, it does give indirect support by suggesting to us that moral[I] principles are not really statements that can be true or false, but rather that they are nothing more than culturally determined expressions of group feelings. Later we will examine the theory that moral[I] principles are nothing more than expressions of feelings; however, reflection on some of the facts of moral life suggests that this view is mistaken.

UTILITARIANISM AND KANT

As was mentioned before, utilitarianism is the natural outgrowth of moral egoism. If we start with the theory that we ought to act so as to maximize our happiness, and we also accept that the happiness of one person cannot, except for location, be distinguished from the happiness of another, we wind up with the conclusion that we ought to act so as to maximize the general happiness. This commitment to enhance general happiness is the utilitarian principle.

The great traditional utilitarians were Jeremy Bentham and John Stuart Mill. With the help of some carefully selected quotations, I will discuss what they had to say about utilitarianism. Having done so, I will go on to discuss what some more recent theorists have had to say about this moral position.

Jeremy Bentham (1748-1932)

Bentham was the son of a London lawyer, who was sent to Oxford at the age of twelve to study law. People are impressed by this but it was not altogether unusual for boys at that time to enter universities at such a tender age. He soon realized that he strongly disagreed with the lectures of the famous right-wing professor of law, W. Blackstone. Bentham decided to forego the practice of law in order to work out his own system of law. Fortunately, his father was a wealthy man who left him a great deal of money, which gave Bentham the wherewithal to pursue his goal. His first work, *Fragment on Government,* a virulent attack on Blackstone's *Commentaries,* was published in 1776; his main work, *Introduction to the Principles of Morals and Legislation,* was published in 1782.[9] The latter work was published some twelve years after it had been written: Bentham was prompted to publish it because it was claimed to contain certain theories that it in fact did not. The *Principles* is written in a blunt and matter-of-fact way, a style that might almost be called utilitarian.

> Nature has placed mankind under the governance of two sovereign masters, pain and pleasure. It is for them alone to oint out what we ought to do, as well as to determine what we shall do.

Notice that if Bentham is saying that man is incapable of doing anything but pursue his own pleasure, then, as we have seen (pp. 262–263), he can hardly go on to say that each man *ought* to pursue his own pleasure. However, let us be charitable and interpret him as saying merely that each man, as a rule, acts so as to maximize his own pleasure, but he is capable of doing otherwise. This would be tantamount to categorizing Bentham as a psychological egoist in the weak sense.

This quotation also misleadingly suggests that Bentham could be classified as a moral egoist. However, he considered the ultimate good to be not the pleasure of the individual but the pleasure of the community in general. As a result, according to Bentham, one ought to act in accordance with the principle of utility. About this principle he says:

> By the principle of utility is meant that principle which approves or disapproves of every action whatsoever, according to the tendency which it appears to have to augment or diminish the happiness of the party whose interest is in question: or what is the same thing in other words, to promote or to oppose that happiness. I say of every action whatsover; and therefore not only every action of a private individual, but of every measure of government.

At another place he interprets this principle (which may also be called the *greatest happiness principle*) to mean that the only right and justifiable end of government is the greatest happiness of the greatest number.

Having stated his principle so baldly, we feel that Bentham should offer us a proof. By way of presenting such a proof, he first points out that, being an ultimate principle, utility is incapable of proof. He says:

Is it susceptible to any direct proof? it should seem not; for that which is used to prove everything else, cannot itself be proved: a chain of proofs must have their commencement somewhere. To give such a proof is as impossible as it is needless.

But this raises the question of why utilitarianism should be accepted as an ultimate principle. If it is the ultimate principle, it is incapable of proof, but how then can we show it to be the ultimate principle? Bentham's reply is more ingenious than it appears to be at first glance. What he says, in effect, is that the utilitarian principle wins by default. First of all because, as a rule, when it is criticized it is usually unwittingly criticized on utilitarian grounds. For example, as Bentham points out in the notes that come at the end of the *Principles,* "The principle of utility (I have heard it said) is a dangerous principle: it is dangerous on certain occasions to consult it." But as Bentham also notes, to say that there are times when it is dangerous to consult the principle is tantamount to saying that there are times when, for utilitarian reasons, it should not be consulted. As he puts it, in his own inimitable way, "This is as much as to say, what? That it is not consonant to utility, to consult utility; that it is not consulting it, to consult it."

Second, the principle of utility wins by default because to accept a principle like 'Let your conscience be your guide' is just the same as letting actions be guided by feelings, or to act on no principle at all. For example, if we accept 'Let your conscience be your guide' as our ultimate principle, and our conscience tells us that abortion is wrong, while others of equally sincere conscience claim that it is right, then what this really comes down to is that we are letting our feelings be our guide. Some feel abortion is wrong and so act in accordance with their feelings, while we feel abortion is right and so act in accordance with ours.

Finally, any other principle that really is a principle will usually turn out to be nothing more than a misapplication of the utilitarian principle. For example, suppose that someone argued that the highest kind of life was the life of work and the lowest kind of life was that of pleasure. Chances are that the person originally approved of work because of the pleasurable fruits it brought in its wake, and he originally disapproved of pleasure because of the pain that it often brought in its wake. The pleasure of drink is often followed by the greater pain of a hangover. But in his enthusiasm he forgot his original reason for approving of work and disapproving of some pleasures, and found himself approving of work in itself and disapproving of pleasure in itself.

In short, according to Bentham, we must accept that the utilitarian principle is the ultimate (valid) principle because if criticized, it usually, though unwittingly, is criticized on utilitarian grounds and because any other suggestion usually turns out to be either (a) no principle at all, or (b) nothing more than a misapplication of the utilitarian principle. So, if any principle is going to count as an ultimate principle, it is going to have to be utilitarianism. In this way, then, utilitarianism (according to Bentham) wins by default.

John Stuart Mill (1806-1873)

Mill was the eldest son of James Mill, a disciple and close friend of Jeremy Bentham. It could almost be said that John Stuart Mill was raised to proselytize utilitarianism. He was educated by his father at home with this goal in mind. No one in the history of philosophy had such a formidable education. He was introduced to Greek at the age of three, Latin at four, and by the age of twelve he was deep into logic and economics. Unfortunately, all this proved to be too much for him, and around the age of twenty-one he suffered a nervous breakdown. He felt that this was the result of an overconcentration on the intellectual aspects of life. He tried to counteract this by turning to poetry and music.

When he was twenty-five, Mill fell in love with Mrs. Harriot Taylor, whom he married some years later, after her husband's death. She was the inspiration, if not the co-author, of a large number of his works. A scandal was caused when Mill dedicated his *Principles of Political Economy* to her at the time of poor Mr. Taylor's death.

Mill's clearest thoughts on utilitarianism are presented in a work of his by that name. The work is largely a defense of the utilitarianism of Bentham, though Mill does make a couple of changes. In his enthusiasm to defend utilitarianism against its detractors, Mill makes a number of blunders. It will be well worth our time to examine some of these in order to ensure that we don't make similar ones.

Mill begins by taking up Bentham's points that (a) it's logically impossible to justify an ultimate principle, and (b) most people unwittingly accept the utilitarian principle as their ultimate principle. Mill's presentation of the principle is as follows: "The creed which accepts as the foundation of morals *utility,* or the *greatest happiness principle,* holds that actions are right in proportion as they tend to promote happiness, wrong as they tend to produce the reverse of happiness." Mill continues by agreeing with Bentham that by "happiness" he means pleasure and the absence of pain; and by "unhappiness," pain and privation of pleasure. Finally, he says that pleasure and freedom from pain are the only things desirable as a means.

Although Mill has said that no proof is possible of the utilitarian principle, he does attempt a proof in chapter 4. The proof is presented in two parts: the first part is designed to show that happiness (in other words, pleasure) is a good, and the second part is to show that pleasure (in other words, happiness) is the only good. For this it would follow that happiness must be the ultimate good. The first part begins as follows:

> The only proof capable of being given that an object is visible, is that people actually see it. The only proof that a sound is audible, is that people hear it. . . . In like manner, I apprehend, the sole evidence it is possible to produce that anything is desirable, is that people do actually desire it.

This argument, at least on one reading, is obviously fallacious. To say that a sound is audible is to say that it is capable of being heard, but to say that something is desirable is not to say that it is capable of being desired, but that it is worthy of being pursued or, in other words, that it is good. It follows logically from the fact that a sound is heard that it is audible. The statement '*x* is heard' entails '*x* is audible'. But as we have learned from Hume, it doesn't follow from the fact that something is desired that it is therefore desirable or, in other words, good. The statement '*x* is desired' does not entail '*x* is good'. In fact, in many cases the opposite seems true. A life of leachery and sloth may be desired, but it could hardly be said to be desirable.

We may wonder how Mill, who no doubt read Hume, could have made such a blunder. Perhaps we have misinterpreted him. Perhaps all that he wanted to say was that since no compelling proof of utilitarianism is possible, the only evidence that can be produced to show that something (and here Mill has pleasure in mind) is a human good is to demonstrate that people desire it. If, ultimately, pleasure is desired and the only thing desired, then if anything is going to count as the ultimate good, it is going to have to be pleasure. But if this is all that Mill wanted to say, why all the talk about what is visible and what is audible? With respect to this interpretation, the connection between desire and desirable is not the same as that between being seen and being visible, so why mention the latter? It still looks as though Mill was trying to pull the wool over the readers' eyes, if not over his own.

The first part of the proof continues as follows:

> If the end which the utilitarian doctrine proposes to itself were not, in theory and in practice, acknowledged to be an end, nothing could ever convince any person that it was so. No reason can be given why the general happiness is desirable except that each person, so far as he believes it to be attainable, desires his own happiness.

Again we have a fallacious argument, but on another level we don't. Mill could be interpreted to be arguing as follows:

1. Everybody desires his own happiness.

2. Therefore, everybody desires the general happiness.

3. What everybody desires is desirable.

6. Therefore, the general happiness is desirable.

Expressed in this way, it contains not only the illicit move from desired to desirable; it also commits the fallacy of composition. It simply doesn't follow from the fact that everybody desires his own happiness, that everybody desires the general happiness. In fact, if everybody desires his own happiness, this suggests that the opposite is the case.

Fortunately, we can give this last quotation a much happier interpretation. It is as follows:

1. Each person desires his own happiness.

4. Therefore, each person's happiness is desirable.

5. But if each person's happiness is desirable, the general happiness is desirable.

6. Therefore, the general happiness is desirable.

We still have the dubious move from desire to desirable, but if this is interpreted in the way suggested on page 273, we can accept it. But at least the fallacy of composition has been avoided. There is nothing fallacious about the move on line 5 from the claim that if each person's happiness is desirable, the general happiness is desirable.

Let us, however, move on to the second part of the proof, which is concerned to show that happiness is the *only* thing desirable. Having shown that happiness is desirable, if Mill can now show that happiness is the only thing desirable, then he has, in effect, shown that happiness is the ultimate good. If happiness is desirable, and only happiness is desirable, then it is a good and the only good. Therefore, it is the ultimate good.

Mill's approach is the same as before. That happiness is desired gave him reason to say that happiness is desirable. Now if he can show that happiness is the only thing desired, then this will give him reason to say that happiness is the only thing desirable.

Mill begins with an empirical approach. He realizes that we desire lots of things, but argues that we either desire them as a means to happiness or as a part of happiness. For example, an elderly man might desire money as an end, as well as happiness as an end; but in the beginning, he only desired the money as a means to happiness. As the years rolled by, he would have come to associate the happiness that money brought with the money itself; and as a result, he would have desired the money as an end instead of as a means to an end. Thus he would come to desire money as a part of happiness. He would, in his miserly way, find happiness in the amassing of wealth.

We may suspect that Mill felt that this argument was not good enough, for he goes on to offer a second argument, which he claims is also empirical (based upon fact), but, as we shall shortly see, it is nothing of the sort. Mill says:

> We have evidently arrived at a question of fact and experience, dependent, like all similar questions, upon evidence. It can only be determined by practiced self consciousness and observation . . . I believe that these sources of evidence, impartially consulted, will declare that desiring a thing and finding it pleasant, aversion to it and thinking of it as painful, are phenomena entirely inseparable, or rather two parts of the same phenomena; in strictness of language, two different modes of naming the same psychological fact.

Mill is here out to show that 'Man only desires pleasure', when taken as a synthetic statement, is true. But of what does this proof consist? It consists of nothing more than defining 'pleasure' in terms of desire. No doubt he can do so, but if he does, all he has shown is that people desire only what they desire. This could hardly support the claim that people desire only pleasure, where 'pleasure' is defined independently of desire. Furthermore, if 'pleasure' is defined as what is desired, our resulting analytical statement 'Man only desires pleasure' could hardly give any support to the moral claim that pleasure is the ultimate good. For 'Pleasure is the only good' is supposed to express a synthetic statement; and an analytic statement, as we have seen (chapter 3, p. 106), can give no support to a synthetic statement.

We may conclude, then, that Mill has not proven pleasure to be the ultimate good, or that people ought to act with the general happiness as their supreme goal. At the same time, however, the fact that people desire to be happy and that ultimately they do not desire much else, suggests that if anything is going to count as the ultimate good, it is going to have to be pleasure.

So far we have been discussing some of the ways that Mill attempts to defend the Bentham's utilitarianism. Now let's look at one of the ways in which Mill's presentation differs from his predecessor. According to Bentham, since pleasure is the measure of value, the endeavor that affords the most pleasure is therefore the best.[10] Thus, for example, if we are trying to determine what is the best course of action to take (the action with the highest value), where we have a choice between playing Pushpin (a popular pastime in the brothels of London at that time) and reading Shakespeare's sonnets, and it turns out that Pushpin affords more pleasure, then that is what we ought to do. We ought to forego Shakespeare and play Pushpin instead.

Mill would have none of this. Even if Pushpin affords more pleasure, Mill maintains that it is still the case that reading Shakespeare is of higher value. He writes, "It is quite compatible with the principle of utility to recognize the fact that some kinds of pleasure are more desirable and more valuable than others. It would be absurd that while, in estimating all other things, quality is considered as well as quantity, the estimation of pleasure should be supposed to depend on quantity alone."

Few would deny that some pleasures are more valuable than others, and that pleasure should be judged on quality as well as quantity. But the question we must address is whether a utilitarian can hold such a view. If we hold that pleasure is the only good, then pleasure becomes the yardstick by which all human activities and possessions are to be valued. To decide whether x is better than y, we merely have to ask whether x affords more pleasure than y. If it does, then it is the better of the two. But if pleasure is the yardstick, then there is one thing that cannot be measured by it, and that is pleasure itself. We cannot say that the total pleasure that x gives rise to is better than the total pleasure that y gives rise to, because that could only mean that the total pleasure that x gives rise to, gives rise to more pleasure than the total pleasure that y gives rise to. And it's not clear what that means.

Mill, then, falls between two stools. On the one hand, he wants to stand by Bentham's belief that pleasure is the only good; and on the other hand, he wants to be fair to his own intuition that some pleasures are higher than others. But he cannot have it both ways.

The Influence of Utilitarianism

In order to appreciate the importance of utilitarianism in nineteenth-century thought, we must take note of its influence in other areas. I shall mention two: economic thought and legal reform.

Economic Thought

According to utilitarianism, the function of government is to maximize the happiness of its citizens. Since there is a fairly close correlation between income and happiness, this means that it is the function of government to arrange the economic institutions in such a way that the income of the citizenry will be maximized. As a rule, real income will rise to the highest level when there is free entry into the marketplace (anyone can manufacture, buy, or sell), reasonably complete but universal knowledge (no one has any inside information), and a fairly large number of buyers and sellers. When manufacturers are allowed to compete freely and openly in the marketplace, the quality of goods will rise, prices will fall, and the consumer will benefit. Thus, it becomes the responsibility of the government to set up the playing field, act as a referee, and let the players (the entrepreneurs) get on with the job of maximizing their incomes. This position is often called laissez-faire capitalism.

However, this policy was not advocated by all utilitarian economists. It was realized by some (sometimes called welfare economists) that there is no one-to-one correlation between income and happiness. If Brown earns $5,000 per year and Jones earns $95,000 per year, there will not be as much happiness as there would be if each earned $50,000 per year. Although we are made happier by every added increment of income, we are usually not made as happy as we were by the last increment. If a man's income moves from $10,000 to $15,000 he will be made happier, but his happiness will not increase by as much as when it moved from $5,000 to $10,000. It follows from this that if Brown makes $5,000 and Jones makes $95,000, their combined happiness will not be as much as it would be if each made $50,000. The happiness that Jones loses when his income moves from $95,000 to $90,000 will be more than offset by the happiness that Brown gains when his income moves from $5,000 to $10,000. Indeed, happiness can only be maximized where incomes are equal. This can be demonstrated in the following manner. Suppose that Brown makes $45,000 and Jones makes $55,000, then Brown will gain more happiness when his incomes moves to $50,000 than Jones will lose when his income falls back to $50,000. Therefore, the total happiness will only be maximized when their incomes are equal.

If we apply this argument to the state as a whole, we have a strong reason for saying that people ought to earn roughly the same. Of course, there are all sorts of other factors that have to be taken into account. Jones may be used to a style of life that requires $95,000, while Brown may be perfectly happy with $5,000. If we take $5,000 away from Jones he may bitterly resent it, while Brown may spend the added $5,000 on alcohol. But even if we take all these other factors into account, a fairly good argument can be presented for moving incomes slowly and gently toward an equal footing.

The main utilitarian objection to this argument is that if incomes are moved toward an equal position, incentive will decrease, people will not produce as much, and so total real income will decline. If total real income declines too much, the total happiness might not be as great as it was before the move toward equality of income began. If Brown and Jones each earn $4,000, they will not, when considered together, be as happy as when Brown earned $5,000 and Jones earned $95,000. The real trick is to determine the policy that will maximize happiness, not income.

In these ways, then, utilitarianism had an influence on economic thought.

Legal Reform

The moving force behind Bentham's *Principles of Morals and Legislation* was a desire to bring the law more in line with the principle of utility—and in this endeavor Bentham was highly successful. The main problem was that during the eighteenth century, when Bentham wrote, the punishment attached to many types of crime was greater than what was required to deter most people from committing a crime of the given type. Bentham writes:

> The general object which all laws . . . ought to have in common, is to augment the total happiness of the community; and therefore, in the first place, to exclude, as far as may be, everything that tends to subtract from that happiness.

> But punishment is an evil . . . . Upon the principle of utility, if it ought at all to be admitted, it ought only be admitted in so far as it promises to exclude some greater evil.

Part of what Bentham is saying here is that, as utilitarians, we must try to maximize happiness. But the pain a person suffers through punishment reduces the total. Therefore, we must make sure that the pain involved in the punishment is no higher than what is required to deter the normal person from committing the crime in question.

But this was not the only problem. The other problem was that many actions were classified as crimes, which, according to utilitarian principles, were not crimes at all. The only acts that should be classified as crimes are those that reduce the total happiness. For example, suppose I desire a wristwatch that I see in a shop window. There are two ways I might obtain it. I could get a job and earn the money required to purchase it, or I could steal it. In order to maximize happiness, the legal system should be set up to steer me toward the first alternative and away from the second. If I earn the money to buy the watch through clipping people's hedges, then I make those people, plus the jeweler from whom I purchase the watch, happy. But if I steal the watch, I make no one except myself happy. Indeed, I make the jeweler very unhappy. Therefore, the legal system will permit me to perform acts of the first sort, but will attach penalties to acts of the second sort.

However, the legal system, according to Bentham, should not attach penalties to those acts that may strike the more prudish as offensive, but do not reduce the general happiness. On this view, neither private homosexual acts between consenting adults nor sexual acts between farm boys and barnyard animals will be classified as crimes. Nor will pornography be banned, provided that it does not fall into the hands of those who would be upset by it or incited to the performance of antisocial acts.

Criticism of Utilitarianism

The development of utilitarianism over the years has been accompanied by a the growing number of criticisms. We will now pause to examine a number of them. Some are, as you might expect, more serious than others. I shall deal with the less serious first.

(a) It is claimed that Mill is mistaken in identifying pleasure with happiness and in saying that pain is nothing more than the opposite of pleasure. No doubt this is true, since pleasure cannot be identified with happiness. It's perfectly possible for a hungry but unhappy man to find great pleasure in eating a steak. However, this difficulty can be circumvented by taking the utilitarian principle as merely saying that one ought to act so as to maximize happiness and minimize unhappiness. It is also true that pain is not the opposite of pleasure; it is not negative pleasure. If I put on a new pair of shoes and go for a walk, I can tell roughly when the pain caused by the new shoes began and when it ended. But if I found pleasure in going to the theater last night, I cannot say—indeed, it doesn't make sense to say—when the pleasure began and when it ended. Again, this difficulty needn't worry the utilitarian, provided he is simply concerned with the maximization of happiness.

(b) Perhaps pain can be measured, but neither pleasure nor happiness can be measured. As a result, we cannot add up the various "scores" and know what is the best course of action. Though it's true that neither pleasure nor happiness can be measured, this needn't worry the utilitarian too much. We know that people are happier under some conditions than they are under others. The job of the utilitarian is to bring about, as best he can, those social conditions where people will be happiest.

(c) We never know what the total consequences of our actions are going to be, so we never know what we ought to do. This is also an unimportant criticism. We know that if we persist in driving through town at 60 mph, we will cause more unhappiness than if we drive at 30 mph. Therefore, we have good utilitarian reasons to drive at the slower speed.

(d) People cannot be expected to act so as to maximize the general happiness; therefore, it's impossible for anyone to act continuously in an altruistic way. This is true, but the utilitarian does not expect that people will ever do so. All that he hopes is that each person will recognize that both his happiness and the happiness of others, is important.[11] Furthermore, because the classical utilitarian is also a psychological egoist, he has difficulty in explaining how anyone could ever be expected to act in the public interest, and so he has difficulty in explaining how anyone could be expected to construct a legal system that was in the interest of the public and not himself. Bentham felt that this problem would be solved if there was at least one person who mainly found (his) happiness in creating a legal system that would be in the public interest. There is good reason to believe that Bentham and Mill were such persons.

Let us turn now to some more serious objections:

(e) Bentham says that one should act to bring about the greatest amount of happiness for the greatest number of people. But this injunction can lead to one of two inconsistent policies. If I am the ruler of a country, am I to bring about the *greatest distribution of happiness*, or am I to bring about the *greatest amount of happiness?* For example, suppose that there are five people in my country; am I to follow policy *A*, as illustrated below, which will give 5 units of happiness to each person—making a total of 25 units of happiness,

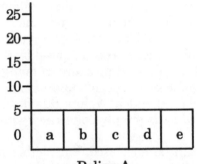

Policy A

or am I to follow policy *B*, which will give 22 units to one person and 1 unit to each of the other persons—making a total of 26 units of happiness?

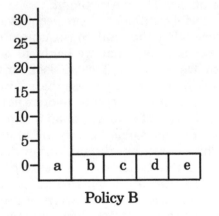

Policy B

It would appear that Bentham must settle for the latter; for given that happiness is the ultimate good, what counts is the total *amount* and not its *distribution*. Many people will feel that policy *B* is manifestly unfair, and so it is. However, this fact won't upset the staunch utilitarian. He will simply say that distribution does not count.

The reader may be surprised at this outcome since it has already been claimed that utilitarianism points toward an equal distribution of income. But utilitarianism only points in this direction because, given that everything else remains the same, this is the only way that happiness can be maximized. To think that utilitarianism points to an equal distribution of happiness is to confuse income with happiness. The utilitarian is only concerned with maximizing the latter. It's only because of the diminishing marginal utility of income that utilitarians concern themselves with the equal distribution of income.

(f) The utilitarian principle cannot be the ultimate principle, because it tells us nothing about the parameters of life. For example, suppose that there are now five people in our state and each enjoys five units of happiness, giving us a total of twenty-five units of happiness. Now suppose that we can increase the total amount of happiness by increasing the total number of people to ten, where this will involve a reduction in the amount of happiness per person to 3 units. This will give us thirty units of happiness instead of twenty-five units. However, some people will feel that the first alternative is the best: it is better to have fewer happy people than more people who are less happy—better a Canada than an India. But, according to the utilitarian maxim, one should always work toward increasing happiness, even if that can only be achieved by reducing the average happiness and increasing the number of people.

Some will claim, for the reason just given, that utilitarianism doesn't maximize the total amount of happiness, but instead maximizes the average amount of happiness. If this is what utilitarianism recommends, then it leads to more serious, if not more sinister, conclusions. Suppose our society already has ten members, each enjoying three units of pleasure. This results in an average of three units per person. Then suppose that the average happiness can be increased by *reducing* the number of people to five. Let us assume that reducing the number to five will give five units per person. How is the population to be reduced? Are we to wait until nature takes its course, or shall we take steps to hurry the process along? Utilitarianism seems to suggest the latter, and this means that some people are going to have to be liquidated—not a very happy prospect!

(g) This last objection leads naturally into the following criticism. The way that we test a new hypothesis in science is to see what observation statements it entails, when viewed in conjunction with other accepted hypotheses of science. If these observation statements turn out to be false, then we know (by modus tollens) that the hypothesis in question must be rejected.[12] We have a similar way of testing a moral principle. If the moral principle entails the doing of what we intuitively know to be morally outrageous, then the principle has to be rejected. On this test, it is argued that utilitarianism fails miserably. Not only does it seem in certain curcumstances to accept, if not condone, murder, it also points toward doing other unsavory acts. Suppose, for example, that in a simmering southern town in the United States, a white girl has been raped and that it is impossible for the local authorities to discover who did it. The local white population has gathered outside the court-cum-jailhouse and is howling for blood. The local authorities fear that if the mob is not appeased there is no telling what it will do. Just at this moment the police bring in an unknown, drunken black hobo who has fallen off a freight train, and put him in the jailhouse to sober up. Now if the sheriff and judge are good utilitarians they might argue as follows: Why not pin the rape on the hobo? After all, he doesn't remember anything. In this way the mob will be appeased and a possible race riot averted.

By the use of examples like this one, it is often argued that since utilitarianism leads to the doing of what one intuitively knows to be wrong—in this case punishing an innocent man by execution—it follows that the utilitarian principle cannot be an ultimate principle.

Alternative Forms of Utilitarianism

The fact that these and many more objections can be brought against the classical form of utilitarianism has lead some thinkers to wonder if the view can be presented in a different form—one that will take care of at least some of these objections.

In 1903, G. E. Moore, in a book called *Principia Ethica,* suggested that what we ought to try to promote is not happiness or pleasure but goodness. Moore claimed that goodness was a non-natural property that could be apprehended by the intellect. It almost sounds like a tautology to say that one ought to maximize goodness; but even this theory, which is usually called *ideal utilitarianism* (IU), has its difficulties. First of all, it's not clear how we are supposed to discover whether something is good or not. We have seen that statements of the form '*x* is good' are value statements and are not verified in the ordinary way. Moore said that 'good' is an indefinable property that can be apprehended through the intellect. But how we are to carry out this act of cognition is never made clear. Second, we still have the problem of distribution. Are we to maximize goodness or are we to maximize the amount of goodness that can be equally distributed? It might be objected that equal distribution is also good, but if so, it would no longer make sense to talk about maximizing goodness. We would no longer know what we are to do. Finally, we still have the difficulty raised in (g) above. We can imagine cases where, surprisingly enough, acting on the IU principle will lead to the performance of acts that we intuitively know to be wrong. Suppose I have promised to do *x,* but very slightly more goodness can be brought into the world by doing *y,* and the doing of *y* precludes the doing of *x.* In this case, according to the IU principle, I ought to do *y;* but my intuitions tell me, according to Sir David Ross in an interesting book titled the *Right and the Good,* that I ought to keep the promise through doing *x.*

Since the Second World War, a new brand of utilitarianism has flourished. This brand is usually called *ruled utilitarianism* (RU). There are about as many subtypes of RU as there are rule utilitarians, but generally speaking, its main claim is that one ought to act, not directly to maximize happiness, but indirectly on the basis of rules that, if followed by most people, would maximize happiness.[13] It is felt that if utilitarianism is taken in this form it will pass the test mentioned in (g). It will no longer point to the doing of outrageously immoral acts. For example, if the sheriff and the judge, mentioned above, are rule utilitarians, then they will not hang the poor hobo, for the rule "Always hang an innocent person when a lynch mob is on the move and you can get away with it" would not, if generally applied, be a happiness-maximizing rule. They would find, as we do, that for the most part, happiness-maximizing rules are the everyday run-of-the-mill maxims of morality. Here I have in mind such maxims as "Always keep promises," "Always tell the truth," and "Always pay your debts."

Although rule utilitarianism has experienced great popularity in recent years, it still faces many difficulties, the main one being that if we subscribe to RU because we want to maximize happiness, and we think that happiness can best be served by acting on the basis of rules, then if we have a case where happiness can only be maximized by not acting on a rule, it would follow that we should not act on the basis of rules but directly on the basis of the utilitarian principle. If the sheriff and the judge are only concerned about the maximization of happiness, and this can only be achieved by hanging the hobo, then why should they worry about rules—why not hang him?

There is also the residual problem that faces all utilitarian theories. Why should we accept the utilitarian principle as an ultimate if not *the* ultimate principle? Bentham and Mill both said that since it is an ultimate principle it cannot be proven, but this claim assumes that it is an ultimate principle and this needs to be proven. As we saw, neither thinker was very successful in this endeavor. Furthermore, in acting morally, there are other matters to consider. For example, if someone has done a lot for us in the past, then surely this counts as a reason for giving him special consideration in the future, even if this involves not acting in a happiness-maximizing way.

Immanuel Kant (1724-1804)

Kant was one person who took Hume's dictum seriously. He realized that Hume was right, and that we could not derive what we ought to do from facts about the world. However, Kant thought that all was not lost, for he believed that on the basis of reason alone we could determine what we ought to do. This endeavor does not look very promising, for, as we have seen, from moral analytic statements (statements known to be true through reason) only further moral analytic statements follow, and these, it would seem, are incapable of telling us what to do. However, let us put our preconceptions to one side and see what Kant has to say.

We have talked about Kant before (chapter 3) but now something should be said about his life because his upbringing bears significantly on his later work. He was born in 1724 in a Prussian town by the name of Koenigsberg. His parents were not well off. His father was a poor saddler with a large family. Kant's family belonged to a religious sect called the Pietists who were, as we can conclude from the name, a very pious lot. This morally severe background is reflected in his work and gives his writings a certain flavor, although it is not a necessary feature. His theory can be presented without it.

Kant remained a single man and may never have ventured more than twenty miles from Koenigsberg. It has been said that the only "moral" problem he ever had to face was how much jam to have on his tart at tea time. This may be true, but it did not prevent him from being aware of what was going on in the world around him. He was very concerned with the revolutionary happenings in France, and was greatly moved by the writings of Jean-Jacques Rousseau.

It is also said that when Kant grew old he became very set in his ways. Every afternoon he would go for a walk, and he always passed certain landmarks at certain times. Many of his neighbors found this useful when it came to setting their clocks.

Kant was a late developer. Most philosophers do their best work in their twenties, but he didn't begin his writing career in any earnest way until he was in his fifties. His first philosophical work (his best in my opinion) was the *Critique of Pure Reason,* published in 1781. His best work in ethics, *The Foundation for a Metaphysics of Morals* was published in 1785, after which there followed the *Critique of Practical Reason* (1788), the *Critique of Judgement* (1790), and the *Metaphysics of Morals* (1803). In what follows we shall only concern ourselves with what Kant had to say in the *Foundation for a Metaphysics of Morals.*

The Good Will

Although Mill thought that happiness was the ultimate good, not everyone agreed with him. Suppose that we have a herd of happy cows. We might say that we have bovine bliss, but we could hardly say that here moral goodness is to be found. Or, take a different case. Suppose we have a society of people who have been brainwashed into slavishly following their leader. Such a society might be supremely happy but it could hardly be said to exemplify moral goodness, especially if the leader was putting their money into his Swiss bank account!

It seems, then, that in order for a society to exemplify moral goodness, it is necessary, though not sufficient, that the members of the society are free agents who are largely responsible for their actions. A society of completely brainwashed people could never exemplify moral worth or moral goodness even though such a group could be very, very happy. But if only free agents of a society can have moral worth, what is it that gives them that status? Obviously they cannot gain moral worth through doing nothing. Thus human action seems to be the source of moral goodness.

We can, if we want, divide human acts into those of inclination and those of will. Acts of inclination are of two kinds: those in which the agent *could not* do otherwise, and those in which the agent *could* do otherwise. Neither kind of act of inclination could have moral worth. The opium addict who fills and lights his opium pipe because he could not do otherwise could hardly be said to exemplify moral worth, even though his action prevents a nonaddicted juvenile from smoking the opium. Similarly, acts of inclination in which the agent could do otherwise do not manifest moral worth either. If I order a large T-bone steak at a restaurant and eat it because that is what I desire to do, my act, even though I could have ordered a filet mignon instead, could hardly be said to have moral worth.

Suppose now that a rich philanthropist gives a great deal of money to build a hospital for crippled children, not because he feels he ought to but, being a good-hearted soul, it's just the sort of thing he enjoys doing. Does his act have moral worth? The utilitarian will say yes, but Kant would say no. According to Kant, and I'm inclined to agree with him, in order for his act to have moral worth it must be done *out of a sense of duty,* and not in order to satisfy some desire. If it is done in order to satisfy some desire, even though it brings about a great deal of nonmoral goodness—it makes the crippled children happy—it has no more moral worth than the eating of the steak. We may be fortunate to have people around who possess a desire to build hospitals, as well as people with a desire to eat steak, but since each act is in itself nothing more than the satisfaction of a desire, there is no intrinsic worth in either act. We may conclude, then, that no act of inclination can have moral worth.

If any act is to have moral worth, it's going to have to be an act of will.[14] What then is an act of will? Suppose that you accepted a nonpaying job with a charitable organization and you have promised that you will be at work at eight o'clock. You set your alarm for six o'clock, and it goes off at the proper time. You lie in bed where it's warm and cozy. The last thing on earth you want to do is climb out into the cold, dark dawn. However, you tell yourself that you ought to get up because you promised that you would be at the worksite at eight o'clock, and so you grit your teeth and climb painfully out of bed. This would, at least at first glance, count as an act of will. You didn't get up because you desired to get up. You only got up because you felt you ought to.

It therefore looks as though the source of moral worth is going to be acts of will. However, according to Kant (and here I think he is mistaken), this is not quite so. According to Kant, what is really going to have moral worth is not the act, but the will with which the act is done. Suppose, for example, that you had tried to get out of bed in order to go to work, but found that you couldn't because, during the night, your little brother had tied you down. Here one might say that your intention—your will to get out of bed—has as much moral worth as the action would have had if you had gotten out of bed. Now suppose, on the other hand, that you got out of bed but only did so because you felt restless and because you falsely believed that you would receive a great sum of money when you turned up at the job site. In this second case, what you do is just the same as what you do in the very first case, but what you do has no moral worth since you did it in order to satisfy a desire. It was, after all, only an act of inclination. Now, if what you did in this situation has no moral worth, and if it is identical with what you did in the first situation, then what you did in the first situation has no moral worth. But something in the first situation has moral worth. It cannot be the act, so it must have been the will with which the act was done. It's on the basis of this sort of thinking that Kant arrives at the conclusion that the only thing that can be good in itself is a will or, as he puts it, a good will.

Categorical and Hypothetical Imperatives

In order to grasp the rest of Kant's argument it is necessary to understand his distinction between categorical and hypothetical imperatives. According to Kant, a truly rational being—e.g., an angel (if there were one)—would always act freely and rationally on the basis of universal laws. These laws would appear to such a being in the indicative form. This being would derive from these laws such conclusions as 'Now I shall do this and now I shall do that'. Human beings, however, are not purely rational. Being of the flesh, although capable of acting on the basis of reason, people usually act on the basis of desire. Reason may suggest that x be done, but often as not the passions urge us to do y in the place of x. Because people find themselves in these situations—one foot in the material world and one foot in the nonmaterial world of reason—the laws of reason present themselves not in the indicative mood, but in the imperative mood.

This point can be made clearer by returning to our previous example.

If we were purely rational beings, we would say to ourselves when the alarm went off, "I said I would turn up at the job site at eight o'clock, so now I will get up." But because we are partly controlled by desires, we say to ourselves, "Oh, I really want to stay in bed, but I said I would be at the job site at eight o'clock, therefore I *ought* to get up." The law of reason presents itself to us in the imperative form, rather than in the indicative form.

This explains how imperatives are in general possible.[15] It is now necessary for Kant to distinguish between hypothetical and categorical imperatives, and to explain how each is possible. By a hypothetical imperative he means the consequent of any statement of the form 'If you want *x*, you ought to do *y*'; for example, 'If you want to be rich, you ought to study medicine and become a doctor'. Kant's explanation of how this imperative—'You ought to study medicine and become a doctor'—is possible is that since (according to Kant) one who wills or at least desires the end wills the means, and since one is always apt to be led astray by temptation, the consequent of the hypothetical appears in an imperative form. Presumably, for a fully rational, nonmaterial being, the hypothetical would have the following indicative form: 'If you are to do *x*, then you will do *y*'.[16]

In the case of a categorical imperative, Kant has in mind an ought statement that has nothing hypothetical about it. It might be thought that such statements as 'You ought to keep your promises' or 'You ought to tell the truth' are categorical imperatives, but, according to Kant, we cannot be certain. Even if we believe that we only tell the truth because we believe that we ought to do so, we cannot be absolutely certain. We may be telling the truth partly because we do not want to be caught telling a lie and have our reputations ruined. In other words, we may be subscribing to a hypothetical and not a categorical imperative. Since the same point can be made about any other candidate—for example, 'You ought to keep promises' or 'You ought not to steal'—it looks as though the possibility of discovering a genuine categorical imperative is exceedingly slim.

In order to discover whether or not there is a genuine categorical imperative, and if there is, what it looks like, let us return to what we said about acts. There it was pointed out that acts of inclination have no moral worth, and that if any act is going to have moral worth it's going to be an act of will. But what is an act of will? It cannot be an act that is based upon a hypothetical imperative like 'If you want to be rich you ought to study medicine', because this will ultimately only be an act of inclination. Nor can it be an act that is based upon an imperative like 'You ought to tell the truth', because this will most likely turn out to be a hypothetical imperative, which would render the act ultimately an act of inclination.

Now, we have seen that humans are partly like animals, who are determined by their desires, and partly like purely rational beings, who act freely on the basis of reason. Thus it looks as though a genuine act of will is going to be a free act that is based solely on reason. But what sort of an act can this be? Again, it cannot be based on a hypothetical imperative, for then it is not truly an act of will. Kant's solution to this problem is ingenious. He says, and I think he is right, that an act can only be an act of will—that is, based upon reason—if it rests upon a maxim[17] that the person can will to be a universal law. This provides us with the categorical imperative we've been looking for. According to Kant, there is only one categorical imperative: "[You ought to] act only on that maxim through which you can at the same time will that it should become a universal law."[18]

We must now see (a) why it is that if we act on this principle we will be acting solely on the basis of reason, and (b) why it is that we will also be acting morally. It's not difficult to see why we will be acting on the basis of reason. If I say that the color of my pen is black, then reason demands that I say of any other object of the same color that it, too, is black. If I say that the object in front of me is made out of gold, given its various properties plus an atomic weight of 79, again reason demands that I say of any other object exhibiting the same properties, that it is also made of gold. I can, of course, refuse to speak, but at least I cannot consistently say that the other object is not made of gold. Similarly, if upon witnessing a young thug beating and robbing an old lady, I say that the act is vicious and cruel, reason demands that I judge any other similar act vicious and cruel.

Suppose, now, that one of my maxims is 'Always hit the other man when he is down'. Again, reason demands that if I am prepared to say that it is right for me to take advantage of others when they are down, then it is right for anybody to take advantage of someone else when that other person is in a weakened position. And that means it would be right for others to take advantage of *me* if I were in a weakened position. But this is something that I cannot will, for I do not want others to hit me when I am down. As a result, I am, through an act of pure reason, obliged to give up my insidious maxim.

We must now move on to the second question: Why am I acting morally if I act on those maxims that I can will to be universal laws? Part of the reason is simply that application of the categorical imperative leads to the acceptance of rules that we consider to be moral and to the rejection of rules that we consider to be immoral. To take one of Kant's examples, I cannot will the following maxim to be a universal law: 'Whenever I believe myself short of money, I will borrow the money and promise to pay it back, though I know this will never be done'; (a) I cannot will that others make lying promises to me, and (b) if everyone were to accept this principle, promising would become impossible. If everyone were to adopt this principle, no one would bother to make a promise, because no one would accept the promise. In this way, then, the categorical imperative leads to the rejection of a maxim that most people would consider to be immoral.

This line of reasoning might be thought to be peculiar, but it does square with normal practice in moral theory. Just as a scientist will test a hypothesis by seeing if it entails true observation statements, so a moral theorist will test his hypothesis by seeing that it entails rules we all accept as moral. This doesn't *prove* that his theory is valid, but it does give us *some reason to believe* that it is valid.

The other reason for claiming that one acts morally when acting in accordance with a universal maxim is that if we agree that people are capable of moral action, and if all acts on the basis of inclination are ruled out, it follows that if any act is going to be a moral act it's going to be a pure act of will. But since there is only one type of act that is a pure act of will—acting on the categorical imperative—it follows that only acts of this type are going to be moral acts.

It should be noted that in order for the act to have moral worth it must be done on the basis of (out of reverence for, as Kant would put it), and not just in accordance with, the categorical imperative. If a merchant does not cheat the children who come to shop at his store, he may be acting *in accordance* with the categorical imperative, but he will not be acting *on* the categorical imperative if his reason for not cheating his junior customers is that he is afraid of what will happen if their parents find out.

We are now in a position to express Kant's argument in a tighter form. Human beings are capable of moral action. They can act on the basis of inclination or on the basis of will. No act on the basis of inclination can be a moral act. Therefore, only an act of will can be a moral act. But what can a pure act of will be? It can only be a pure act of will if it is performed on the basis of a maxim that one can will to be a universal law. People will be drawn by their rationality to act on such maxims. Just as they will not want to call a lump of matter a lump of gold if its properties are different from what has been called gold, so too they will not want to act on any maxim that cannot be willed to be a universal law. Therefore, rational people will accept the principle 'One ought to act only on that maxim that one can at the same time will that it should become a universal law'. And only through acting on the basis of this principle will humans be acting morally.

Criticism and Appraisal

It should be noted that Kant presents his categorical imperative as a necessary and not a sufficient condition. He does not say that we ought to act on a maxim if it can be universalized, but that we ought to act on a maxim only if it can be universalized. As a result, Kant wants his imperative to tell us what we should not do, but not what we should do.[19] If the maxim cannot be universalized, then, according to Kant, we know we ought not to act upon it. But if it can be universalized, then all we know is that it is not the case that we ought not to act upon it; we do not know that we ought to act on it. We can see why Kant presents his categorical imperative as a necessary and not as a sufficient condition if we notice that such maxims as 'Always whistle in the dark' can be universalized; but no one would want to say that we are under an obligation to act upon it.

We might be tempted to beef up Kant's categorical imperative in the following way: (a) If we can will a maxim to be a universal law and also will that its negation be a universal law, then the act in question is to be classified as right. For example, both 'Always whistle in the dark' and 'Don't always whistle in the dark' can be willed to be universal laws, so it's all right to whistle in the dark. (b) If a maxim can be willed to be a universal law but its negation cannot, then the act in question is obligatory. For example, 'Always tell the truth' can be willed to be a universal law, but its negation, 'Don't always tell the truth', cannot. Therefore, telling the truth is obligatory. (c) Finally, if the maxim cannot be willed to be a universal law but its negation can, then the act is wrong. For instance, 'Steal when it is to your advantage to do so" is not universalizable, but its negation, 'Do not steal when it is to your advantage to do so'[20] can be universalized. Therefore, stealing is wrong— something that we are obliged not to do.

Although we might be tempted to beef up Kant's categorical imperative in this way, there are all sorts of difficulties that would have to be overcome. It might be argued that there are certain situations where we ought to lie, therefore 'Always tell the truth' cannot be willed to be a universal law, but its negation can. (It should be noted here that the negation is 'Do not always tell the truth', and not 'Always lie'.) It's not always clear how we can use Kant's technique here to determine what we ought to do.

This brings us to another point about Kant's categorical imperative. There are, according to Kant, two independent reasons why I might be able to will a maxim to be a universal law. First, there are cases where even though I can envisage a society in which a maxim was a universal law, I cannot will that it be a universal law. For example, although I cannot will that the maxim 'Never help those in distress' be a universal law, I can envisage a misanthropic society in which it is a universal law. There are also cases where not only can I not will a maxim to be a universal law, I cannot even envisage a society in which it is a universal law. I cannot envisage a society in which everyone acts on the principle that we are to make a lying promise when it is to our advantage to do so, because in such a society it would be impossible to make a lying promise. The reason it would be impossible to make a lying promise is that it would be impossible to promise. No one would believe anyone who attempted to make a promise, and so no one would attempt to make a promise. We have, then, two independent reasons for rejecting a maxim: (a) on grounds that it cannot be willed, and (b) on grounds that a society in which it was a universal law cannot be envisaged.

It might be objected that even though I (Patrick Mackenzie) cannot will 'Never help those in distress' to be a universal law, there are plenty of people who can. Those "fat cats" of our society who advocate free enterprise and believe that in the marketplace we should "let dog eat dog," have no difficulty in willing that the maxim 'Never help those in distress' be a universal law. But if this maxim can be willed to be a universal law, then Kant, at least in this case, gives us no reason to say that it is wrong not to help those in distress. However, it's not clear that the fat cats of this world can will their maxim to be a universal law. One of the reasons they think they can is that they lack the imagination to realize what it would really be like to be down and out. I'm certain that if we could trick one of these people into believing that he was down and out, he would soon change his tune. He would soon find it very difficult to will that we should never help those in distress.[21]

It might well be objected that there are a few hard core fanatics who believe in free enterprise so strongly that even if they were down and out, they would still believe that it was wrong to help them. R. M. Hare discusses this problem in a very interesting book titled *Freedom and Reason,* and reaches the conclusion that such people are beyond the pale of reason. If Hare is right about this, and I think he is, then pointing out that there are fanatics does nothing to show that the categorical imperative fails to work. However, the objection does bring to our attention that only beings, in so far as they are capable of reason, will be drawn, through their reason, to the categorical imperative.[22]

There is one final point that must be made about Kant's categorical imperative. Many people have been guilty, through committing the fallacy of composition (see chapter 3, pp. 139–140), of misapplying the categorical imperative. If I cannot will that each person, independent of other persons, do a certain act, then that act is wrong; but if I cannot will that everyone, as a group, do a certain act, it doesn't follow that that act is wrong. If, for example, I were to argue that since I cannot will that everyone have a picnic in that particular spot in the local public park, then no one ought to picnic in that particular spot, I would be arguing fallaciously. To argue in this way is just as fallacious as arguing that since I cannot will that everyone, as a group, drink from a particular public water fountain, no one ought to drink from the water fountain. I can will that each person drinks from the fountain (when no one else is) and so there is no reason to say that no one ought to drink from the water fountain. Similarly, I can will that each person picnic on the select beauty spot (when not many others are picnicking in the same spot), and so there is no reason to say that one ought not to picnic in that particular place.

We may conclude by saying that Kant did an immense service to moral theory through pointing out the universality of moral thought. If I am wondering whether it would be right for me to do *x*, and I find that I cannot will that it is right for others to do *x*, then I cannot consistently say that it is right for me to do *x*. This means that I must admit that it would be wrong for me to do *x*. Furthermore, if I am wondering whether it would be right for me to do *x*, and I know it would be wrong for others to do *x*, then I also know that it would be wrong for me to do *x*.

NEW APPROACHES

We have seen that although Kant gives us the shape of morality, he does not give us much in the way of content. That is to say, although he gives us a necessary condition that a maxim must satisfy in order to count as a moral rule, he does not, as a rule, give us the sufficient conditions. Furthermore, even in those cases in which Kant does manage to identify valid moral rules, we still don't know why they are valid. For example, from the fact that I cannot will 'Don't keep promises when it is not to your advantage to keep them' to be a universal law, it follows that I must accept 'One ought to keep promises'; but so far the only reason we have for saying that I must accept it is that I just must, in effect, will it. In finding myself unable to will 'Don't keep promises when it is not to your advantage to do so', I find myself willing 'One ought to keep promises'. But we still don't know why promises ought to be kept or, in other words, we still don't know why 'One ought to keep promises' is a valid moral rule. All we know is that, as rational creatures, we have to will it. I now want to patch up this deficiency in Kant by offering a new approach.

In a game such as chess, it is possible to distinguish between what might be called *constitutive rules* and what might be called *regulative rules*. The latter regulate what could exist independently of the rules, while the former, surprising thought it may seem, create certain events: that is to say, they make certain events logically possible. For example, the rule that I must move my next chesspiece in less than one minute is a regulative rule, since what it regulates exists independently of the rule: it is logically possible that I could take longer than a minute in making my next move. But the rule that the piece called Bishop only moves diagonally actually *creates* the Bishop piece and makes the Bishop move possible. A Bishop, although it is recognized by its shape, could have a different shape. But a Bishop could not be a Bishop in chess if it were allowed to move directly up and down the board. The Bishop is defined as that piece which can only move diagonally.

Not only is it possible, as a result of the Bishop-constitutive-rule, to have Bishop moves, there are also other events that are made possible by that rule in conjunction with other constitutive chess rules. Take away the chess rules and moves like checkmating and castling become impossible. Of course, we could physically move the lumps of wood about in the same way, but that would be neither checkmating nor castling.

Now the language that we use in thinking about the world shares certain features with games. In our language we have rules that are analogous to the constitutive rules of chess, and additional rules that are analogous to the regulative rules of chess. For example, the rule that states 'If I am going to give you permission to have one of my chocolates, I should say that you *may* have a chocolate, rather than that you *can* have a chocolate' is a regulative rule, while the rule 'Physical objects have three dimensions' is more akin to a constitutive rule. I cannot think of something as being a physical object unless I think of it having three dimensions.

We have already seen that in order to think about the world, our thoughts must be couched in language. Perhaps we can think very simple thoughts without language. But try thinking 'It is likely to rain the day after tomorrow' without putting it into words. The language we have, and that means the constitutive rules that we have, is largely determined by the sort of creatures we are and the sort of world we live in. If I lived alone as a center of consciousness in a gaseous world, my language, if I had one, would lack the concept of a three-dimensional physical object. In my world of swirling gases I would be incapable of thinking that the universe could contain discrete, countable three-dimensional objects. I can only think what is expressible in language, and this thought would not be expressible in my language. Furthermore, if the world were just as it is now, but we were all colorblind, then we would have no language in which to think about colors. One simply could not think that red was a color or that scarlet was brighter than brown.

Although some of the constitutive rules of our language are a result of the sort of world we live in and some are the result of the sort of beings we are, others are the result of the sort of beings we are vis-à-vis the sort of world we live in. And some of these latter rules, so I am going to argue, are our moral rules. Take, for instance, the rule that it is wrong to steal property. If we lived in a world where there was an unlimited amount of wealth to satisfy our needs, or if we were beings with no needs—suppose we lived on air and had no need of clothing or shelter—then it is more than likely that we would have no idea of property. The concept wouldn't be a part of our language. I simply wouldn't and couldn't view the land that you were sitting on as be-longing to you, to me, or to anyone. I would just see it as being there. Now what do we mean when we say that it is wrong to steal prop-erty? First of all, when I say that you own the pen in your hand— that is, when I recognize it as being your property—I am not merely saying that is in your possession, though this could be a part of what I am saying. After all, it could be *in* your possession but not *yours!* What I am saying is that you have a right to deal with the pen as you see fit, provided, of course, that you do not use it to harm others. I am implying that I and others have a correlative obligation not to take the pen away from you. After all, you could hardly be said to have a right to keep the pen in your possession if others did not have a correlative obligation not to take it away. Now, since it is wrong to do what we have an obligation not to do, and since to recognize some-thing as the property of another is partly to recognize it as something that we are under an obligation not to take away, it follows that it is wrong to take away the property of other people. Finally, since steal-ing is the taking of other peoples' property, it follows that it is wrong to steal. Once we know what 'property' means, and once we know what 'stealing' means, we find that we must think of stealing as wrong. Or to put it a different way, once we have grasped the concept of property and the parasitic concept of stealing, we immediately grasp that steal-ing is wrong. 'Stealing is wrong' is a constitutive rule of our moral language.

The same point can be said about the moral rule 'Promises ought to be kept'. If we had no wants or needs, and if we were rather antiso-cial, then it would not be necessary for us to fix our future activities in such a way that others could rely upon us. It's because Farmer Brown must get his crop in today and cannot do it alone, and Farmer McDon-ald must get his crop in tomorrow and cannot do it alone, that it is important that it be possible for McDonald to say to Brown, "I'll help you get your crop in today if you *promise* to help me get my crop in tomorrow." What Brown does, if he promises, is to place himself under an obligation to help McDonald tomorrow. In placing himself under an obligation to help McDonald tomorrow, he (Brown) fixes his future activities so that McDonald can rely on them and act in the light of them. Thus, we see that it's because of our wants and needs that we have this instrument through which we can place ourselves under an obligation to do something in the future. We can also see that the re-sulting rule 'Promises ought to be kept' is a constitutive rule of our moral language. If we hear someone say to someone else "I promise to do *x*," we cannot take what the first person said to the second person as a promise without seeing him (the first person) as having placed him-self under an obligation to do *x*.

It's more difficult to show that such rules as 'We ought not to inflict pain and suffering on other people' are analogous to the constitutive rules of games, but the following points in that direction. If we had no wants and needs, and if we were rather antisocial beings, it seems, at least to me, that it would never occur to us to inflict pain on one another. Just as I never want to inflict pain upon myself, so, seeing pain as pain, I would never want to inflict it on anyone else. But because we do have wants and needs and we do live in a world where there is a shortage of the wherewithal to satisfy those needs, we are sometimes tempted to inflict pain on others. That is to say, we are sometimes tempted to do what we have no natural desire to do.

If you and I are bedouins, for example, who share a well that provides just enough water to take care of our needs, and the well begins to dry up, then I might be tempted (as you might be if you were me) to inflict suffering on you, either by reducing your share of the water or, more directly, by attacking you, so that you will be frightened into running away. Now it is, I think, because I naturally do not want to inflict pain and suffering on you—simply because I see it as pain and suffering, and because this is something that I am tempted to do—that I come to see this as something I ought not to do. Thus it is the human condition—the sort of beings we are vis-à-vis the world we live in—that makes possible such constitutive moral rules as 'One ought not to inflict suffering on others'. If we were without wants and needs, then such rules would simply not form a part of our language. The concept "ought" would not form a part of our conceptual apparatus, because there would be nothing we naturally wanted to do but were tempted not to do.

MORAL SKEPTICISM

If what I have been saying is to some extent true—if moral rules are at least somewhat analogous to the constitutive rules of games—then we are in a position not only to take care of the central problem raised by Hume, but to see why it is that we ought to keep promises, why should not inflict suffering on others, and so on.

Let us begin with the problem raised by Hume. According to Hume, as we have seen, we can never know that a moral statement is true because (a) it cannot be directly verified and (b) it cannot be deduced from a set of factual statements. It can, of course, be deduced from a set of factual statements in conjunction with another moral statement, but this only raises the question of how we determine the truth value of that other moral statement. Just a few pages ago (see p. 257), I suggested that one possible solution to this problem is that some moral principles can be known to be true on the basis of reason alone; but then I rejected this solution, at least for the time being, on the grounds that only analytic statements could be known to be true on the basis of reason, and that from analytic statements only further analytic statements can be derived.

What I now want to do is to argue that since moral rules such as 'One is under an obligation not to steal', etc., are constitutive rules, they are fairly close to being analytic, and can, for that reason, be known to be true. Furthermore, I want to argue that this analyticity does not, surprisingly enough, render them altogether useless.

We have already seen, in effect, that moral rules are close to being analytic. The important sign of an analytic statement is that its denial involves a contradiction. This is the case with the other constitutive rules that we have examined. Since a Bishop is defined as that piece which can only move diagonally, the rule 'Bishops can only move diagonally' is analytic. To deny it would be tantamount to saying 'It is not the case that the piece that can only be moved diagonally can only be moved diagonally'. It is also the case with 'One is under an obligation not to steal'. Since stealing is the taking of that which we are under an obligation not to take, it follows that 'It is not the case that we are under and obligation not to steal' can be rendered as 'It is not the case that we are under an obligation not to take that which we are under an obligation not to take', and this is clearly self-contradictory. So 'We are under an obligation not to steal' is analytic, or at least pretty close to it.

Let us move on then to the puzzle of how a moral rule can be analytic and still be somewhat useful. First, allow me spell out in more detail one reason it is thought that if moral rules are analytic, they are therefore useless. In what follows I shall take 'MS' to mean 'moral synthetic statement', 'MA' to mean 'moral analytic statement', 'FS' to mean 'factual synthetic statement', and 'FA' to mean 'factual analytic statement', (see page 255). Now, given the truth of Hume's point that we can't deduce a moral statement from a set of purely factual statements, and given what we already know about logic, it follows that of the arguments below, (I) must be rejected,

> I. The house is on fire. (FS)
> ———————————————————————————
> Therefore, we ought to call the fire department. (MS)

but II is permitted:

> II. We ought to call the fire department when the house is on
>   fire. (MS)
>   The house is on fire. (FS)
> ———————————————————————————
> Therefore, we ought to call the fire department. (MS)

Though here we have the problem of how we came to know the truth of the first premise (see p. 255),

the following is also permitted:

III. All brothers are siblings. (FA)
    James is a brother. (FS)
    Therefore, James is a sibling. (FS)

Here, the first premise, being analytic, is superfluous. We could move directly and deductively from the second premise to the conclusion.
    Furthermore, IV is also permitted.

IV. You ought to do your duty. (MA)
    Fighting the enemy is your duty. (MS)
    Therefore, you ought to fight the enemy. (MS)

Here, again, the first premise is superfluous. We could, as before, move directly from the second premise to the conclusion. But notice that here we can't be certain of the truth of the second premise.
    In addition, V would also be permitted.

V. Pleasure is good. (MS)
    Playing chess affords pleasure. (FS)
    Therefore, playing chess is good. (MS)

In this argument, as in II and IV, we have the problem concerning the truth of the first premise. However—and this is one of the points that I have been leading up to—it is accepted on all sides, and I would agree, that VI must be rejected.

VI. 1. Pleasure is good. (MA)
    2. Playing chess affords pleasure. (FS)
    3. Therefore, playing chess is good. (MS)

'Pleasure is good' may be used to express a synthetic statement, in which case we are using the word 'pleasure' in a purely factual way. 'Pleasure is good' may also be used to express an analytic statement, but in this latter case we have defined 'pleasure' as 'good', and so 'pleasure' ceases to be a purely factual word.[23] If it ceases to be a purely factual word, then the second premise, 'Playing chess affords pleasure', cannot be purely factual. But if it's not purely factual, then how do we know that it is true? The sting of Hume's point is that if (1) is synthetic, then we cannot know that the conclusion is true, because we cannot know that (1) is true; but if (1) is analytic, then even though we can know that it is true, we still cannot know that the conclusion is true, because (2) is now a moral statement, and we cannot know that it is true. We could only know that (3) is true if (1) were MA and (2) were FS, but this combination is, as we have seen, impossible.

Now let us look at the following argument:

VII 1. We are under an obligation not to steal.
     2. Taking that pen would be stealing.
     _____
     3. Therefore, we are under an obligation not to take that pen.

Here it will be objected that if (1) is analytic, (3) could not be derived since (2) is factual. That is to say, as in the case of VI, we cannot have an argument of the form

           1. MA
           2. FS
           _____
           3. Therefore, MS

No doubt this is true, but why should we assume that the second premise is purely factual? To recognize something as belonging to someone is to evaluate, since it is in effect to recognize that someone has the right to keep the object in question in his possession, and that others are under an obligation not to take it away. Since stealing is taking away something that belongs to someone, to say 'Taking that pen would be stealing' is tantamount to saying 'Taking that pen would be taking something that one is under an obligation not to take', and this is not a purely factual claim.

However, it will be argued that if argument VII is cast in this unobjectionable form, it looks like this:

           1. MA
           2. MS
           _____
           3. Therefore, MS

The first premise is unnecessary, since we can go directly from (2) to (3). That is to say, just as in III, which is

    1. All brothers are siblings.   (FA)
    2. James is a brother.   (FS)
    _____
    3. Therefore, James is a sibling.   (FS)

we can go directly from (2) to (3), so too with VII; or we can go directly from 'Taking that pen would be stealing' to 'We are under an obligation not to take that pen'. Furthermore, it will be objected that if 'Taking that pen would be stealing' is MS, then Hume's point comes back to haunt us once again. Although we can know that VII (1) is true, we can't be certain that the conclusion is true, for since (2) is not purely factual, we can't be certain that it (2) is true.

Let me deal with the first objection. In a way I am inclined to accept it. If we listen to the conversations of people involved in moral debates, we rarely hear them enunciate moral principles. What we hear are such things as 'You ought to return that lawn mower; after all, you only borrowed it', 'You ought to tell that student as soon as possible that he passed; it's cruel to keep him in suspense', or 'Because Jones was innocent, it was wrong to hang him for the murder of Smith'. This seems to suggest that most people consider moral rules to be superfluous. It's only when the going gets heavy—when people need to be reminded of conceptual points—that moral rules get an airing, e.g., 'You ought not to have an abortion; after all, abortion is killing a person, and killing a person is wrong'. In this case, 'Killing a person is wrong', which I take to be a constitutive rule, can feature in the argument; but it serves more as a conceptual reminder rather than as a part of the argument.

The same thing happens in nonmoral discussions: *X* might say to *y*, "A point cannot be a physical object, since a physical object has three dimensions, and a point has none." Here the constitutive rule 'A physical object has three dimensions' operates more like a conceptual reminder than as a premise.

There is one more curious but seldom noticed reason to suggest that moral rules are not quite as unnecessary or useless as might be thought. As a result of 'Spheres are round' being analytic, a sphere cannot but be round. There is no way, so to speak, that a sphere can deviate from roundness. But even though 'We are under an obligation to keep promises' is analytic, we can deviate from it by refusing to keep promises. I cannot deviate in the sense of accepting 'We are not under an obligation to keep promises' as a moral maxim, for this involves a contradiction; but I can deviate in the sense of deciding that even though I am under an obligation to keep promises, I shall not do so. I cannot build a sphere that is not round, but I can refuse to keep a promise. Now if I can refuse to keep promises, then I can, in a sense, be guided by 'We are under an obligation to keep promises', by taking it as a reminder to always keep promises. In this curious way, a moral rule can be analytic without being useless.

Let us move on to the second objection, namely that if the second premise, 'Taking that pen would be stealing', is a moral synthetic statement, then we can't be certain that it is true and so we can't be certain that the conclusion is true. The answer to this objection is a long one but I'll attempt to given an outline of how it would go.

We are inhabitants not only of a physical world but a social world as well. A social anthropologist from Mars could observe a wedding just as well as we can. He could see the long, pastel colored dresses being worn by some people, the dark suits being worn by others, and he could see the fizzy liquid being poured into glasses and down various throats. But he could not see what was going on until he could see that it was a social event where two people were getting married, and that champagne was being poured into glasses for the purpose of making toasts. Similarly, when we visit a marketplace, we can see different people in possession of different objects, and we can see objects being passed back and forth, but we cannot see what is going on until we can see that objects owned by some people are being bought and sold and sometimes stolen. In other words, seeing what is going on isn't always a matter of viewing what is going on at the physical, purely factual level. It is also a matter of interpreting at the social level, and this involves evaluation. If we see someone grab a clock and run out of a store, with the proprietor in hot pursuit, we can say "He took something from the store," but we haven't grasped what is going on at the social level until we say, at least to ourselves, that he stole something. In saying that he stole something, we are in effect evaluating. In other words, in order to understand what is going on at the social level, we must recognize the act as stealing, but in saying that he stole, we are evaluating the act.

THE EMOTIVE THEORY OF ETHICS

There is in the history of philosophy a long tradition of thought whose adherents maintain that moral statements are without meaning, that they are nothing more than expressions of emotion. The Sophist Thrasymachus in Plato's *Republic* argues that this can be taken as his view (chapter 2, p. 59). It is also the view of the nonmoral egoist (see this chapter pp. 260–261). Furthermore, it is only through taking moral statements as expressions of emotion that moral relativism can be presented in a coherent form (see this chapter, pp. 266–267).

Even though the belief that moral claims are nothing more than expressions of emotion has been very durable, we now have, I think, enough conceptual artillery at our command to show that it is mistaken—at least enough artillery to show that the view that moral *rules* are nothing more than expressions of emotion is mistaken. The chief source of emotivism, at least in its present form, is the *verification principle.* This principle was the backbone of a philosophical movement known as *logical positivism,* which flourished in the 1930s and 1940s (see chapter 3, p. 150). According to logical positivism, a statement, if not analytic, is meaningful if and only if it is in principle empirically verifiable. If a statement is not in principle empirically verifiable, then it is not meaningful. In other words, the statement is meaningless. The thinking behind this principle is that a properly constituted statement will, by its very nature, tell us the steps we would have to take to show whether it is true or false. For example, the statement that all Koreans have black or red hair gives us some ideas of the steps we would have to take to show that it was true or false. There would, of course, be difficulties: there would be problems about who should be classified as Korean, and problems about what counts as red hair and black hair. Furthermore, even if these problems were surmounted, there would still be the problem of whether we had examined every Korean. In order to know that we had examined every Korean, we would have to know that there were no Koreans other than the ones we had examined. How could anyone ever be in a position to know this (see chapter 3, p. 141)? But in spite of all these difficulties, we would at least have some idea of how to go about discovering whether this statement was true or false.

However, in a case like 'The universe is as a whole moving through space at 2000 mph', the situation is entirely different. For although this gives us a picture of a cluster of bodies whizzing through space, we have utterly no idea of how we would go about determining its truth value. The reason this is so is that in order to talk about the constant speed of something, we have to consider the constant speed of that thing *relative to something else*. But if we are talking about the relative speed of the universe as a whole, there is by definition nothing (not even ourselves) left with which to compare it (chapter 3, p. 150). Statements like this would therefore have to be rejected. They look meaningful, but since we have no idea of how we could begin to verify them, they are quite meaningless.

Armed with the verification principle, the logical positivists embarked on a campaign to show that a large number of philosophical claims were meaningless. For example, the claim of the nineteenth-century British metaphysician F. H. Bradley that "the Absolute enters into but is itself incapable of evolution and progress" was declared to be devoid of meaning. In the same vein, the declaration of the German existential philosopher Martin Heidegger that "Annihilation is neither an annihilation of what-is, nor does it spring from negation . . . Nothing annihilates of itself" was also rejected. The reason these statements, along with many others, were rejected was that they couldn't pass the verification test. In neither case do we have any idea how to go about determining, on empirical grounds, the truth value of the statement.

But the logical positivists were not content with expunging from philosophy statements that could not pass the test; they also trained their sights on moral utterances. The problem here was, as we have already noticed, that since we have no way of verifying such statements as 'James is a good man' or 'Eating people is wrong', and since such statements are not deducible from purely factual statements, which are meaningful, they must therefore be meaningless. Statements such as 'These people believe that eating people is wrong' would pass muster, but then, of course, such statements as these are not purely moral. They are statements about the moral beliefs of others rather than expressions of those beliefs.

However, the logical positivists were a bit embarrassed about claiming that moral statements were utterly devoid of meaning. Since people spend a large amount of time engaged in moral disputes, this would mean that people spend a large amount of their time, unbeknown to themselves, uttering meaningless statements! What the logical positivists said is that although moral claims were devoid of cognitive meaning, they had emotive meaning. For example, according to A. J. Ayer in *Language Truth and Logic*,[24] if upon apprehending a boy who had run out of a candy store with some pieces of candy, we were to say to him 'Stealing is wrong', what we said would be tantamount to 'Stealing!' said with a tone of horror. In other words, 'Stealing is wrong' is equivalent to 'Stealing!' but since the latter is not a statement but an expression of emotion, it follows that the former is nothing more than an expression of emotion.

Because of its indicative form, 'Stealing is wrong' looks like a proper statement that is either true or false; but since it is equivalent to an expression of emotion, it is nothing more than an expression of emotion. There is no doubt that the logical positivists were on to something here. Moral disputes are over topics that are emotionally charged. There is no doubt that moral statements are sometimes used just to express emotion, but it would be a mistake to think that this is their basic use. Notice, first of all, that emotion does not preclude factual content. For example, if you drop and break my favorite Ming vase, my claim 'You broke my Ming vase!' may be charged with anguish but that does not prevent it from being factual. Furthermore, moral claims could hardly be said to be nothing more than vehicles for expressing emotion, for they are often devoid of emotion. For example, I might say to you that you ought to return Smith's hedge clippers since you have had them for a month, and say it without feeling any emotion. There is no doubt that to appraise or evaluate is to do something different from factually describing, but it is not to evince emotion.[25]

I mentioned earlier that we were in a position to refute the claim that moral rules are only expressions of emotion. The refutation is surprisingly simple. According to the verification principle, upon which emotive theory rests, a statement, unless analytic, is meaningless if it is not empirically verifiable. The reason analytic statements are put to one side is that it doesn't make sense to talk about the verification of an analytic statement. Imagine carrying out a survey to determine whether or not all husbands are married! But the fact that analytic statements have been put to one side is what makes the refutation possible. Moral rules, as we have seen, are analytic, or at least close to it. Emotivists make the mistake of thinking that moral rules are synthetic. If they were synthetic and unverifiable they would have to be classified as (cognitively) meaningless. But since they are analytic they can be classified as meaningful, even though they do not pass the verification test.[26]

However, we are not yet quite out of the woods. It might be objected that even though the first premise in the following argument can be classified as meaningful because it is analytic, the second premise cannot.

1. We are under an obligation not to steal. (MA)
2. Taking that pen would be stealing. (MS)
3. Therefore, we are under an obligation not to take that pen. (MS)

And since the conclusion follows, it also must be classified as meaningless. This objection has, in effect, already been dealt with (on page 298). There it was pointed out that, if we want, we can restrict our statements to the physical realm; but if we want to be cognizant of what is going on at the social level, we must be prepared to make such statements as 'Taking a pen would be stealing', and in making that statement, we are, in a way, making a moral claim. Though perhaps this statement cannot be empirically verified at a basic level, there are situations where only statements of this type can tell us what is going on. In these situations, they can be considered meaningful, and sometimes true.

MORAL CONFLICT

One of the facts of life that any moral theory has to face is moral conflict. Suppose, for example, I have promised to meet you at the local cinema at 9 P.M., but on my way there I come across a car accident and I am asked to take a seriously injured man to the hospital. Now it seems clear that, although I am under an obligation to meet you at the cinema, because I promised, I am under a much greater obligation to take the injured man to the hospital.

Kant's theory, at least as he presented it, was unable to handle conflicts of this sort. If we apply the categorical imperative, we find that we can neither will that the promise not be kept nor that the man not be taken to the hospital. The categorical imperative does not tell us what we are to do in this situation, and in the others like it where we cannot comply with all obligations simultaneously. Kant was inclined, for the most part, to think that such conflicts would not occur. However, in his essay "On a Supposed Right to Tell Lies from Benevolent Motives," he considers the case in which person A pursues person B with the intention of murdering him. B takes refuge in the house of C, and then A comes along and asks C whether B is in his house. Now, according to Kant, it is the duty of C to tell the truth. We can detect that Kant felt there was something wrong with this answer, for he hastened to add that it's likely that when C tells A that B is in $C's$ house, B will make his escape, so telling the truth was the best course of action after all! But something has gone wrong. For clearly C should do whatever he can to put A off the scent, and if telling A that B is not in the house will do the trick, then this is what he should do. Sir David Ross, a twentieth-century disciple of Kant, has an interesting solution to this problem. According to Ross, we do not have an *actual* duty to tell the truth, keep promises, and so on. All we have is a *prima facie* duty, or what appears at first glance to be a duty.[27] In a given situation, in order to determine what is our actual duty, we would examine all the competing *prima facie* duties and then, through intuition, we might come to know what our actual duty is.

One difficulty with Ross's thesis is that the expression 'prima facie' suggests that our duties to keep promises and the like are not really duties, whereas it looks like they really are. I really do have an obligation to meet you at the cinema and I really do have an obligation to take the injured man to the hospital. However, this difficulty is only a terminological one that can be overcome in the following way. I can say that I am under a real obligation to keep the promise and that I am under a real obligation to take the man to the hospital. But since my obligation to take the man to the hospital is much greater than my obligation to keep my promise, this is what I *ought* to do. My obligation to keep my promise really exists, but it is overridden by my obligation to take the man to the hospital. It is through determining the overriding obligation that I determine what I ought to do.

But how am I to determine which obligation overrides? Unfortunately, there is no settled way in which this can be done. Some writers have said that when there is a conflict between moral rules, we should settle the matter on utilitarian grounds, through choosing the course of action that will bring about the least amount of suffering. Thus, for example, if I promised to give my wife a diamond ring on her birthday but found I can only keep my promise through stealing one, then I would choose the proper action by noting which action in the long run would cause the least suffering. Presumably, the best course of action would be to refrain from stealing even though I break the promise.

But sometimes, as in our first example, the conflict is between the utilitarian rule and some other rule, and this cannot be settled on utilitarian grounds. It might be suggested, where there is a conflict between the utilitarian rule and some other, that we should always side with the utilitarian rule. But this seems to be a mistake. For example, suppose that a child has started to cry because he wants a chocolate bar, and the chocolate bar can only be obtained by stealing it. Here, it seems to me, it would be wrong to steal the bar even if I can be certain of escaping detection and I know that the owner of the candy store will never miss it. When there is a conflict between moral rules, we can only look at the particular case and decide as best we can. Sometimes the choice is obvious—as it was in our first example—but sometimes the conflicting obligations are so evenly balanced that we can only hope that we have made the right decision.

SUMMARY

We have reached the end of our investigation into moral philosophy, and have arrived at the following conclusions: Although a rule must satisfy the Kantian criterion of universalizability if it is to count as a moral rule, the immediate source of the validity of the rule is not to be found in its universal application but in the logic of language. We must accept that we are under an obligation to keep promises, because to deny it will involve us in a contradiction. The reason the denial of this rule, and others like it, will involve a contradiction can be found in the fact that moral rules form a part of the conceptual lattice work of the language we use in deciding what we ought to do. However, moral rules are for this reason of little use. Because I promised to do *x*, I know that I am under an obligation to do *x*. I don't need 'We are under an obligation to keep promises' to get me from the premise to the conclusion. Nevertheless, the fact that moral rules are of little use doesn't mean that they are of no use. Sometimes they act as conceptual reminders. Just as it is sometimes necessary to remind ourselves that points have no dimension, so it is sometimes necessary to remind ourselves that we are under an obligation to keep promises.

Finally, even though we know, on the basis of the law of contradiction, which putative moral principles are valid, more is required in order to decide what to do in cases where there is a moral conflict. Here we must look at all sides of the particular case. Sometimes the right decision will be obvious, but sometimes we can only hope that we have made the right one. If I am caught, so to speak, between my obligation to aid a seriously injured person and my obligation to keep a promise to meet you at the cinema, then I know which is the overriding, and so I know what I ought to do. But if I am caught between my obligation to look after my family and my obligation to go and defend my country, then, although I must choose, I can only hope that I have made the right choice.

EPILOGUE

It would be remiss to me to spend so much time talking about the philosophical aspects of morality while saying nothing about the moral problems that confront people every day. Let's take a look at a moral problem in the light of what has already been said and see if any conclusion can be reached. Take the problem of abortion, if for no other reason than that this seems to stir up a great deal of controversy. However, before I begin, I must caution the reader. As I mentioned at the end of the last section, although we know what our obligations are—that is, we know what our prima facie obligations are—we don't always know what we ought to do in particular cases. When our obligations conflict, all we can do is act in accordance with what we take to be the weightiest obligation and hope that we have made the right choice.

Since, as we have seen, the moral egoist, the relativist, and the utilitarian approaches to morality have all been found wanting, let us try the Kantian approach. Let's make the extraordinary supposition that on the very threshhold of a brilliant competitive skiing season, I find, much to my horror, that I am pregnant. I ask the potential father what he thinks should be done, only to find that he doesn't care one way or the other, since he is about to marry another girl. I ask myself whether I can will that the maxim 'In circumstances such as these, have an abortion' become universal law. Right away I see that I cannot, for in willing it I would be willing that if my mother had been in a similar situation, she would have had me aborted, and this is something that I cannot will. Therefore I must conclude that, *prima facie,* it would be wrong for me to have the abortion.

There are a number of objections that can be made to this argument, and they must be examined. First of all, it will be argued that since I am a person and what would have been aborted is a fetus, what would have been aborted if my mother had an abortion would not have been me but something entirely different. And so, even though I cannot will that my mother abort me, I can will that she abort a particular fetus.

But this objection will not stand up, for even if that fetus is not me, it became me, and so the question I must ask is, can I will that if my mother had been in similiar circumstances that she have the fetus—which became me—aborted. And this, presumably, is something I cannot will.

Perhaps the point can be put in a simpler form. What I want to do is to determine whether it is right to have the abortion that I am planning. Now if that abortion is right, then any abortion in similar circumstances is right. And that means that it would have been right for my mother, if she had been caught up in similar circumstances, to have the fetus—which became me—aborted. But this is something I cannot accept. Therefore, I must reject the claim that it would be right to go ahead and have an abortion.

It might be thought that if the fetus—which, in fact, became me—had been destroyed, another fetus might have become me. But this thought is mistaken. Suppose there are identical twin sisters, Mary and Jane, and let us also suppose that the doctors discovered that Mary developed from one particular fetus, let us call it *A*, and Jane developed from another particular fetus, let us call it *B*. Now could Mary have developed from *B*, and Jane from *A*? No doubt the doctors might have discovered that Mary developed from *B*—it might have turned out that Mary developed from *B*. But given that Mary did develop from *this* fetus—i.e., *A*—is it physically possible that Mary could have developed from *B*? Suppose that fetus *A* died; could fetus *B* have developed into Mary? Of course *B* could have developed into the girl called "Mary," for we could have called Jane "Mary," but fetus *B* could not (physically could not) have developed into Mary. From this it can be concluded that although it is not known which fetus I developed from, there is a particular fetus that could have been identified, and if that fetus had been killed, it is physically impossible that I would have been here today.

Although the Kantian-universality test shows us that we cannot accept a maxim that permits the abortion, it does not show us in any concrete way why abortion is wrong. We must now turn to this task. Although, as was mentioned before, a fetus cannot be said to be a person or even a human being, a fetus is that which becomes a person. (It also becomes a human being.) Now if it's true that it is prima facie wrong to kill a person, it follows that it is prima facie wrong to kill a fetus. If it's wrong to rob a bank then it is also wrong to rob money-lending companies that are about to become banks. So the task at hand is to show that it is wrong to kill a person.

I mentioned in the last chapter that if we were without wants and needs, it would never occur to us to inflict suffering upon others, just as it would never occur to us to inflict suffering upon ourselves. But because we live in a world where we do have wants and needs, we are sometimes tempted to do what we naturally do not want to do, and that is to inflict suffering on others. It is through being tempted to do things that we naturally do not want to do that we come to see them as things we ought not to do. If we were without wants and needs, we might have a language but the concepts of "ought," "ought not," "right," "wrong," and so on would not be a part of it. The human condition makes it possible to apprehend inflicting pain and suffering on another as something that ought not to be done. I cannot see it as something that is right to do. Although there is no formal contradiction in 'It is right to inflict pain and suffering on others', I must reject it, for I cannot conceive of a world in which it would be true.

The same sorts of points can be made about killing. Just as I naturally do not want to kill myself, I also do not want to kill others. But others, owing to the shortage of wherewithal to satisfy wants and needs, sometimes pose a threat to me. As a result, I am sometimes tempted to do what I naturally do not want to do, and in this manner I become aware of my obligation not to kill others. Thus, because I cannot conceive of a world in which it would be (prima facie) right to kill others, I must accept that I am under a prima facie obligation not to kill others. And from this it follows, since fetuses develop into persons, that it is wrong to kill fetuses.

It might be objected that there are lots of people who want to kill themselves and some who do, and that therefore the analysis I have offered cannot get off the ground. My reply to this objection is that people do not naturally want to kill themselves, but either owing directly to the lack of wherewithal to satisfy their wants and needs, or indirectly to something they did as a result of their inability to satisfy their wants and needs, they are tempted to kill themselves and sometimes do. In other words, the human condition that makes it possible to be tempted to kill another, makes it possible to be tempted to kill oneself. But again, killing oneself is something one naturally does not want to do.

Although we are under a prima facie obligation not to kill others and so under a prima facie obligation not to have abortions, there are some situations where this is what we (actually) ought to do. For example, if someone has his finger on "the button" and will blow up the world if he is not killed, then he ought to be killed. Similarly, if it is quite certain that a pregnant single woman will die, along with her five small children, if she does not have an abortion, then she ought to have an abortion. Although there are some situations where it is clear that a person ought to be killed, and cases where it is also clear that a fetus ought to be destroyed, there are many situations where we do not know what to do. Here we can only act because we have to act, and hope that we have made the right choice.

NOTES

1. Strictly speaking, what one has here are indicative *sentences*, since they are not being put to any use. But if we think of them as being put to use (if 'James is a good man' is used to refer to a particular man and to say something about him) we then can think of them as being statements.

2. David Hume, *A Treatise of Human Nature,* edited by L. A. Selby-Bigg (Oxford: Oxford University Press, 1960), p. 469.

3. Is there any other way that he might make it wrong to commit adultery? We can conceive of God creating a world in which adultery is possible, but we cannot, at least I cannot, conceive of God creating the wrongness in adultery. What else would he do?

4. It might be noted that if God is defined as the divine permitter, this means that if there is no God, then it's not the case that everything is permitted; rather, it's not the case that anything is permitted or not permitted.

5. See the quotation from Hume on p. 256.

6. I assume here that a moral principle is a *true* universal moral statement.

7. See chapter 2.

8. Nonmoral egoism is also to be distinguished from psychological egoism. Nonmoral egoism is a theory about how humans are to act. It says, in effect, always act in your own interest, for it is rational to do so. It presupposes that human beings can act otherwise. Psychological egoism, on the other hand, is supposed to be a scientific theory about how humans do act. It presupposes, at least in the stronger form, that we cannot act in any way that is different from the way we do in fact act.

9. Both Bentham's *Introduction to the Principles of Morals and Legislation* and Mill's *Utilitarianism* appear in *The Utilitarians* (New York: Anchor Books, 1973). All references to Bentham and Mill in the text are from this work.

10. In chapter 4 of *The Principles of Morals and Legislation,* Bentham worked out a calculus to determine the value of an activity. All you had to do was to multiply the (average) intensity of the pleasure by the duration and then consider whether it will bring pleasure or pain in its wake. For example, suppose that an evening's skating and an evening's drinking will afford the same amount of pleasure but the drinking will leave you feeling wretched the next day, while the skating will leave you feeling better. In that case, an evening's skating has for you a higher value.

11. There are other problems concerning happiness. For example, in the turn-of-the-century Russian play *The Three Sisters* by Chekhov, the philosophically-minded army officer Vershinin remarks, "The other day I was reading the diary of a French minister written in prison—he'd been sentenced over the Panama swindle. He gets quite carried away with enthusiasm writing about the birds he sees from his cell window, the birds he'd never even noticed when he was minister. Now he's been let out and of course he takes no more notice of the birds than he did before. Just as you won't notice Moscow when you live there. We have no happiness. There's no such thing. It's only something we long for."

12. An observation statement is something like, 'The indicator on the meter will at t^n point to numeral n'.

13. Rule utilitarianism can also be couched in terms of goodness. In this case we have Ideal Rule Utilitarianism. I have decided to stay away from Ideal Rule Utilitarianism for the reasons mentioned above.

14. J. S. Mill also entertained the thought that the will was the source of morality and that only acts of will can have moral worth. However, he rejected this thought for the following reason. According to Mill, the will is the child of desire and that "we may will from habit what we no longer desire for it-

self." In other words, an act of will is really an act based on habit. But the habit finds its source in desire, that is to say, in inclination.

15. Kant was inclined to think that all imperatives either implicitly or explicitly contained an "ought."

16. I assume here that 'You will do y' is in the indicative mood and 'You shall do y' is in the imperative mood. This contrasts with the first person, where 'I will do x' is in the imperative mood and 'I shall do x' is in the indicative mood.

17. By a maxim Kant means a rule of thumb such as 'Let bygones be bygones' or 'Always help those in need'.

18. The words in square brackets are mine.

19. Although this is what Kant wants to say, it's not what he actually does say. What follows from the claim that we ought to act only on that maxim through which we can at the same time will that it should become a universal law, is not that if we cannot will that it be a universal law we ought not to act on it; but that if we cannot will that it be a universal law, it's not the case that we ought to act on it. The reason for this is that morality is a three-valued affair. We can say of an act either that it is (a) one that ought to be done or (b) one that ought not to be done or (c) one that is all right to do. Thus, although it follows from 'He will come to the party only if there will be champagne' that 'If there will not be any champagne, he will not come to the party', it does not follow from 'One ought to act on a maxim only if it is universalizable' that if the maxim is not universalizable, one ought not to act on it, but only that if the maxim is not universalizable, it's not the case that one ought to act on it. In other words, all that follows is either that one ought not to act on it or it is all right for one to act on it. If Kant had expressed his categorical imperative as 'You ought to act or it is all right for you to act on a maxim only if you can at the same time will that the maxim be a universal law', then the desired consequences would have followed. Do you see why?

20. This is not to be read as 'Steal when it is not to your advantage to do so'.

21. It might, in the same vein, be thought that if the maxim is suitably restricted, then we will have no difficulty in willing it to be a universal law. For example, it might be thought that although I cannot will that 'Make a lying promise when it is to one's advantage to do so' be a universal law, I can will the following to be a universal law: 'Those who were born in Toronto on September 21, 1932, are 5 feet 11 inches tall and now reside in Saskatoon are to make lying promises when it is to their advantage to do so', because chances are that there is no one other than myself who fits that description! However, this objection will not work, for even if there is no one else who satisfies that description, I can imagine that there is a person who satisfies it and I cannot will that he (or she) makes lying promises to me when it is to his (or her) advantage to do so. In other words, I cannot will that if there was someone else who satisfied the above description, that he (or she) makes lying promises to me when it is to his (or her) advantage to do so, and so I cannot will the maxim to be a universal law, no matter to what extent it is restricted.

22. Although I said that categorical imperatives only tell us what we should not do and not what we should do, it can be seen from the above example that this is not always the case. It follows from the fact that I cannot will

'Never help those in distress' to be a universal law that I ought to help those in distress. This point will hold for any maxim that comes to us in a negative form. Another example would be 'Do not keep promises when it is to your advantage not to do so'.

23. One could instead define 'good' as 'pleasure', in which case 'good' becomes a factual word. But if 'good' becomes a factual word, then the conclusion becomes a factual claim and not the moral claim we are looking for.

24. (Dover, 1946), p. 107.

25. See also the objection on page 268 of this chapter.

26. There is a terminological difficulty here. It might be objected that even if moral rules were synthetic and unverifiable, we would still have no reason for dismissing them as meaningless, for rules, as we have seen (chapter 3, pp. 95–96), are by their very nature unverifiable. We can verify the claim that 'Lights are to be out at 10 P.M.' is a rule of an army camp, but the rule itself cannot be verified. The reply to this objection is that moral rules such as 'Promises ought to be kept' are in the indicative mood, and so if they are synthetic and unverifiable, there would be some reason for suspecting them as being meaningless.

27. See W. D. Ross, *The Right and the Good* (Oxford University Press, 1930), p. 19.

Appendix

At the beginning of this work I evaded the question "What is philosophy?" by pointing out that just as we couldn't tell a person what mathematics is until he had done some mathematics, so we couldn't tell a beginner in philosophy what philosophy is until he had done some philosophy. Now that we have done some philosophy, it is time to tackle this question.

In a way we already know what philosophy is. It is what we have noticed Plato, Descartes, Kant, and others doing, and it is also what we have been doing to some extent. But this answer seems unsatisfactory, so let us try again.

In order to think about the world, if we are to move beyond our simplest thoughts, we must make use of language. To recognize a bowl of sugar as consumer surplus, we need a language; and to realize that if Jim is the uncle of Mary, then one of the parents of Mary is a brother or sister of Jim, we also need a language.

The language we use to think about the world contains many aberrations, and these aberrations lead to confusion. This holds true for any language. For example, until the time of David Hume it was assumed that everything that happened had to have a cause, because if something happened without a cause it would have had to have come out of nothing, and this is impossible. But as we have seen (p. 138), we only arrive at this conclusion because our language is faulty. We are deceived by language into thinking that "nothing" is a peculiar sort of "something." Now it is my belief that many of the problems and confusions that philosophers investigate are the result of these linguistic aberrations. As a result, philosophy becomes, or should become, the endeavor to remove these aberrations, and in so doing remove the problems and confusions.

Unfortunately, this is no easy task. Imagine the difficulty an astronomer would have in detecting the defects in the lenses of his telescope if the only way he could do so was by looking through the telescope.

Well, we are in much the same position. There are defects in our language, but we can only think about them in the language that contains them. We cannot step outside of our language. We might ask, if there are aberrations in English, why not think about them in French? Unfortunately, this won't work, for they are present in every spoken language. But, we might also ask, why not develop a new defect-free language to think about our present language? Unfortunately, this also will not work, because in developing the new language we would have to think about it in the old language. So any undetected or poorly understood aberration that was present in the old language would reappear in the new.

It must not be thought that this battle against the bewitchment of the intellect by language is a trivial task. These defects are present in the language used by natural scientists, political thinkers, moralists, and virtually everyone. As a result, scientists, political thinkers, and many others are led astray in their thinking about the physical and social world. If philosophers can do something toward removing these problems through the clarification of the language we use in developing and presenting our thoughts, the world will be a better place, or so we hope.